International Organization Initiatives

International Organization Initiatives

How and Why Organizations Adapt and Change

Edited by
GABRIELLE MARCEAU
HENNER GÖTT

OXFORD
UNIVERSITY PRESS

OXFORD
UNIVERSITY PRESS

Oxford University Press is a department of the University of Oxford. It furthers the University's objective of excellence in research, scholarship, and education by publishing worldwide. Oxford is a registered trade mark of Oxford University Press in the UK and in certain other countries.

Published in the United States of America by Oxford University Press
198 Madison Avenue, New York, NY 10016, United States of America.

Library of Congress Cataloging-in-Publication Data
Names: Marceau, Gabrielle, editor. | Gött, Henner, editor.
Title: International organization initiatives : how and why organizations adapt and change / [edited by] Gabrielle Marceau, Henner Gött.
Description: New York : Oxford University Press, 2025. |
Includes bibliographical references and index.
Identifiers: LCCN 2025002397 (print) | LCCN 2025002398 (ebook) |
ISBN 9780197803295 (hardback) | ISBN 9780197803318 (updf)|
ISBN 9780197803301 (epub) | ISBN 9780197803325 (online)
Subjects: LCSH: International organizations. | International agencies.
Classification: LCC KZ4850 .I583 2025 (print) | LCC KZ4850 (ebook) |
DDC 341.2—dc23/eng/20250118
LC record available at https://lccn.loc.gov/2025002397
LC ebook record available at https://lccn.loc.gov/2025002398

DOI: 10.1093/9780197803325.001.0001

Note to Readers

This publication is designed to provide accurate and authoritative information in regard to the subject matter covered. It is based upon sources believed to be accurate and reliable and is intended to be current as of the time it was written. It is sold with the understanding that the publisher is not engaged in rendering legal, accounting, or other professional services. If legal advice or other expert assistance is required, the services of a competent professional person should be sought. Also, to confirm that the information has not been affected or changed by recent developments, traditional legal research techniques should be used, including checking primary sources where appropriate.

(Based on the Declaration of Principles jointly adopted by a Committee of the American Bar Association and a Committee of Publishers and Associations.)

The manufacturer's authorised representative in the EU for product safety is Oxford University Press España S.A. of El Parque Empresarial San Fernando de Henares, Avenida de Castilla, 2 – 28830 Madrid (www.oup.es/en or product.safety@oup.com). OUP España S.A. also acts as importer into Spain of products made by the manufacturer.

Contents

Preface

Actions of international organizations (IOs) in times of crises have always fascinated us. In general terms, IOs are created by states to enhance their cooperation and coordination in predefined areas. But on multiple occasions, faced with novel needs from their members or the outside world, IOs have been able to adapt in a remarkable manner in order to efficiently assist their members and, as a result, have recalibrated the ways in which they deliver their mandate. In doing so, IOs continue to evolve and change. This volume focuses on adaptations and changes within IOs and those who initiate them. It is born out of the experience(s) of IOs responding efficiently—and very often creatively—to new needs through novel action(s) beyond their respective previous scope of activities.

By 'IOs', we understand intergovernmental organizations, including those with 'mixed' or 'hybrid' state and non-state membership, but excluding entirely non-governmental organizations (NGOs). The term 'IO change' denotes the process through which an IO's governance model—that is, its constitution, tasks, means, activities, practices, and leadership—evolves, partly or wholly, beyond its pre-existing setting into an 'updated', recalibrated setting, based on which the IO operates from then onwards. Importantly, the comparison between the 'prior' and the 'updated' settings focuses on whether the IO's activities evolved rather than, for instance, on whether the 'new' activity was already somehow implied in the black-letter law of its constituent instrument (which often can hardly be determined with certainty to begin with). The collection of case studies included in this volume, first and foremost, provides a compilation of historical examples of exceptional responses given by IOs.

IO change often takes place when a need arises that cannot sufficiently be addressed through the IO's pre-existing setting. The notion of a 'need' is understood here in a wide sense: it can be an external impulse, for example, an economic crisis, a war, a pandemic, or a change in third states' behaviour. But a need can also arise because the IOs' constituents voice new demands. Finally, a need can originate within the IO's international bureaucracy itself, for example, when heads of secretariat and staff bring in new priorities, convictions, political agendas, or efforts to assist their members. A need can be, but does not necessarily have to be, unforeseen.

While IO change as a process is often complex and unpredictable in many ways, it is decisively shaped by human action, interaction, and sometimes inaction. The research underlying this volume shows that when it comes to taking action that initializes change, IOs' secretariats and their heads have often been key actors. Consequently, they are this volume's main protagonists. Secretariat action necessarily takes place within the respective IO's organizational frameworks, institutional logics, and functional rationalities, and every secretariat initiative will (eventually) need to be accepted by the IO's members. Yet the mounting empirical evidence of secretariat activities, along with several structural features of secretariats, justify a closer look at their role. These include their relative autonomy as an international bureaucracy, their uniquely international perspective, their role as custodians of the IO as a whole, their capacity to sometimes act more expediently than members, and their ability to draw on incrementally amassed institutional knowledge, an administrative apparatus, and the status, visibility, and charisma of their head—all of which are important prerequisites for launching initiatives successfully. Finally, there is academic interest to zoom in on secretariats, because their role is still not well researched and analysed, and further studies in this area could yield significant insights on IOs.

We conceptualize the way IO secretariats initialize change as 'initiatives', by which we understand the action of IO secretariats, their heads, or both, which

1) aims to meet a need of the IO, its membership, its secretariat, or other internal or external stakeholders,
2) is novel, or previously unfamiliar to the IO in question, and
3) pushes the boundaries of the IO beyond its founding or prior operational activities, thus resulting in IO change.

This volume focuses on initiatives stemming from an IO's secretariat, its executive head, or from a request by the IO's members, subsequently implemented in an innovative manner by the secretariat's international civil servants. It includes both instances in which the secretariat is reacting and situations in which it is proactive in initiating change.

***

This volume is the latest iteration in a larger research project on IO initiatives. During the 2008 financial crisis, Professor Gabrielle Marceau was in the WTO DG Pascal Lamy's cabinet when WTO called on international banks to join forces to ensure more liquidity for small economies. During the same period, faced with the SARS pandemic, the WHO DG took the initiative to involve private actors and NGOs to map out infection localizations while WHO members hesitated to do so. This increased her interest for the role of IGOs during international crisis, reflected inter alia in the *International Organizations Law Review's* editorial entitled 'IGOs in Crisis? Or New Opportunities to Demonstrate

Responsibility?'. In 2020, she initiated a mix of open-source research on IO initiatives and interviews with current and former civil servants. This initial investigation lasted a year and led to the identification of about 70 initiatives in 15 IOs.

This research looked deeper into about 30 of these initiatives, resulting in a publication entitled '"IGOs" Initiatives as a Response to Crises and Unforeseen Needs' in the *International Organizations Law Review* in 2022, authored by Nicola Bonucci, Gabrielle Marceau, André-Philippe Ouellet, and Rebecca Walker.

The article—which became the overture to this volume—was a landmark in the project, yet the gathered information on initiatives was only the tip of the iceberg. To dig deeper and uncover more initiatives, as well as to contextualize them, there was a need to bring together civil servants, both current and retired, with academics, in order to understand them through IO-related theoretical approaches. With the kind help of several colleagues, Gabrielle Marceau organized a symposium entitled 'Evolution of IGOs: Initiatives and Enhanced Responsibilities' at the University of Geneva on 28–29 July 2022. This event was generously supported by the University of Geneva, the Swiss National Science Foundation, the Société genevoise de droit et législation, and the Centre d'études juridiques européennes of the University of Geneva. The symposium brought together over 30 specialists on IOs, including international civil servants, legal practitioners, law professors, and researchers. Among them was Henner Gött, who later became co-editor of this volume. The outcomes of the symposium paved the way for this volume, in which many of the symposium's participants joined forces with additional renowned international experts, practitioners, and academics.

This book features IO practitioners who—taking the role of what anthropologists might call 'participant observers'—describe specific initiatives, while academics and theorists discuss the responses of IOs and their capacity to adapt their initial mandates to meet new needs. The book, which delves deeper into the initiatives of IOs, is intended to inspire and guide future studies in this area, furthering our collective understanding of the role and impact of IO initiatives.

* * *

This volume would not have been possible without the contributions, assistance, advice, kind help, and generous support of many esteemed colleagues and friends, who we gratefully acknowledge. André-Philippe Ouellet, Ana Balcazar-Moreno, Rebecca Walker, Ioana Motoc, Puloma Mukherjee, and Akshaya Venkataraman assisted us either with the initial or subsequent research, or with the organization of the symposium or the subsequent work. Charles Di Leva,

Jacob Katz Cogan, and Christiane Ahlborn engaged as editors at different stages of the volume's genesis. Niels Blokker, Laurence Boisson de Chazournes, and José Enrique Alvarez accompanied the project with interest and kind advice.

Gabrielle Marceau, Prof
Department of Public International Law and
International Organization
Faculty of Law, University of Geneva, Switzerland

Henner Gött
Legal and Policy Advisor, Federal
Chancellery, Berlin, Germany
Professor of Law honoris causa,
Leuphana University, Lüneburg, Germany
Geneva and Berlin
March 2025

Contributors Biographies

Jean Abboud is the Principal Legal Counsel at the Global Fund, a US and Canadian Qualified Lawyer, an Accredited Mediator, and a Board Member of the Forum on Institutional Law in International Organisations (FILIO). Abboud has co-authored multiple book chapters on international organizations.

Jane Aeberhard-Hodges was the former Director of ILO's Gender Equality Bureau and served as the Gender Equality Director for Investing in Women, an Australian Government initiative for women's economic empowerment in South East Asia (2016–2019). Now, an International Gender Equality Consultant, Aeberhard-Hodges also edits the *International Labour Law Reports*.

Christiane Ahlborn is an Assistant Professor of Public International Law at Trinity College Dublin's School of Law. She previously worked as a Legal Officer in the Office of Legal Affairs of the United Nations and the International Atomic Energy Agency (IAEA).

José E Alvarez is a Chaired Professor at NYU School of Law, was a former Co-Editor-in-Chief of the *American Journal of International Law*, and was a former President of the American Society of International Law (ASIL). A member of the Institut de Droit International, he has authored 7 books and over 170 shorter works and was awarded ASIL's highest honour, the Manley Hudson Medal, in 2024 for his contributions to scholarship and teaching.

Ana Balcazar-Moreno is an International Law PhD Research Associate at the Global Governance Centre and the Global Health Centre of the Graduate Institute of International and Development Studies (IHEID). She served as a Legal Officer in the Office of the Legal Counsel of the World Health Organization (WHO) and worked as a lawyer in various international entities, governments, and law firms in Belgium, Colombia, France, Switzerland, and the United Kingdom.

Michael Barnett is a University Professor of International Affairs and Political Science at the George Washington University. His research interests span the Middle East, humanitarianism, global governance, global ethics, and the United Nations. A former Associate Editor of *International Organization*, he previously taught at the University of Minnesota, the University of Wisconsin, Macalester College, Wellesley College, and the Hebrew University of Jerusalem; he was a Visiting Scholar at the New School for Social Research and the Dayan Center at Tel-Aviv University; and he was a Visiting Professor at the Graduate Institute of International and Development Studies (IHEID). Barnett is a member of the Council on Foreign Relations and the recipient of many grants and awards for his research.

Hannah Birkenkötter is an Assistant Professor of International Law at the Law Department of Instituto Tecnológico Autónomo de México (ITAM) and an Associated

Researcher at the Chair for Public Law and Jurisprudence, Humboldt University, Berlin as well as a member of the German United Nations Association's Research Council.

Niels Blokker is a Professor of International Institutional Law (Schermers Chair) at the Law Faculty of Leiden University since 2003. Previously, he has worked in the International Law Division of the Ministry of Foreign Affairs of the Netherlands, most recently as deputy legal adviser. He has published extensively on the law of international organizations and is co-editor-in-chief of the *International Organizations Law Review.*

Laurence Boisson de Chazournes is an Academic and a Practitioner in the field of international law. She is a member of the Institute of International Law and a member of the Curatorium of the Hague Academy of International Law. Following her career as Senior Counsel to the World Bank (1995–1999), she has been a Professor at the Law Faculty of the University of Geneva. She acts as an Expert with international organizations.

Nicola Bonucci is a French-Italian Lawyer. After five years at FAO, he then joined the OECD Legal Directorate, where he worked for 26 years including for more than 14 years as General Counsel. He left the OECD at the end of 2019. Following that he joined as a partner in the Global Trade and Investigations & White-Collar Defense practices of Paul Hastings, Paris. He is now an independent attorney and advises both public and private entities. Nicola Bonucci is also an associate professor at the University of Paris-Cité.

Fernando Lusa Bordin is an Associate Professor and a John Thornely Fellow in Law at Sidney Sussex College, University of Cambridge, and a Fellow of the Lauterpacht Centre for International Law.

Gian Luca Burci is a Senior Visiting Professor of International Law at the Graduate Institute of International and Development Studies (IHEID) and an Academic Adviser of its Global Health Centre. He previously served almost 30 years as a lawyer in various international organizations, including as the Legal Counsel of the World Health Organization (WHO) between 2005 and 2016.

Hassane Cissé is an International Lawyer, a Practitioner, and a Scholar with over 30 years of experience in international law, finance, and development, including a distinguished career at the International Monetary Fund and the World Bank in Washington, DC. He served as the Chief Counsel, Deputy General Counsel, and then Global Practice Director for Governance at the World Bank. He is a graduate of the universities of Harvard, Paris I, Paris II, and Dakar.

Jacob Katz Cogan is the Judge Joseph P Kinneary Professor of Law at the University of Cincinnati College of Law. He is also an Affiliate Faculty Member of the University's Department of History. He previously served as an Attorney-Adviser in the Office of the Legal Adviser at the US Department of State.

Charles Di Leva was a former World Bank Chief Officer of Environmental and Social Standards, and a Chief Counsel of Environmental and International Law. He is now a Partner at Sustainability Frameworks, LLP, and an Adjunct Professor at American University in Washington DC.

Janelle M Diller is a Senior Research Associate at the Graduate Institute of International and Development Studies (IHEID) and was a former Legal Counsel to the International Labour Organization. She has published extensively on international labour law and international organizations and taught international law courses in Canada, Switzerland, and the United States.

Henner Gött is a Legal and Policy Advisor at the German Federal Chancellery in Berlin and an Honorary Professor at Leuphana University, Lüneburg. His research focuses on international economic law, international organizations, international labour law, and EU and German constitutional law. He previously held positions as a legal advisor at the German Federal Ministry of Economic Affairs and Climate Action, a senior research fellow at Georg August University Göttingen, a guest lecturer at several other universities, and a Co-Founder and Co-Chair of the European Society of International Law's Interest Group on the European and International Rule of Law.

Mona Ali Khalil is the Director of MAK LAW International, an Affiliate of the Harvard Law School Program on International Law and Armed Conflict, was a former Senior Legal Officer of the UN Office of the Legal Counsel, and is a member of the Board of Directors of the Academic Council on the UN System.

Kyung Kwak is a Senior Legal Counsel of the IMF Legal Department. She provides legal advice and support to the IMF's Executive Board, management, and staff on various legal aspects of the IMF's operations and policies including lending, surveillance, and international trade.

David Lewis is the Managing Director and Global Head of anti-money laundering (AML) at Kroll and a Fellow of the Royal United Services Institute. He is recognized for his leadership in the fight against money laundering and illicit finance, voted Financial Crime Fighter of the Year by the Global Coalition to Fight Financial Crime, and a recipient of ACAMS public service award. As the former Financial Action Task Force Executive Secretary and G20 Deputy, Lewis led global AML efforts from 2015 to 2021.

Yan Liu is the General Counsel and Director of the IMF Legal Department. Liu oversees the department's work on all aspects of the IMF's operations and the development and implementation of IMF policies.

Huw Llewellyn recently retired from the United Nations Secretariat (2007–2024), where he was the Director of the Codification Division of the UN Office of Legal Affairs (2015–2024). In that role, he was the Secretary of the International Law Commission, the Secretary of the Sixth (Legal) Committee of the UN General Assembly, and the Secretary of the Special Committee on the Charter of the United Nations. He was previously a Legal Counsellor and a Diplomat with the United Kingdom Foreign and Commonwealth Office (1988–2007).

Jelena Madir is the Chief Compliance Officer at the European Bank for Reconstruction and Development. Between 2019 and 2023, she was the General Counsel of Gavi, the Vaccine Alliance.

Gabrielle Marceau is a Professor in the Department of Public International Law and International Organization at the Law Faculty of the University of Geneva, and a Hyman Soloway Visiting Professor at the University of Ottawa Law Faculty. She was also a Visiting Professor in several other universities and institutes. Marceau has been involved with associations and groups promoting international (economic) law, and she has published extensively in the same field. She worked for 30 years in the Secretariat of the WTO, in dispute settlement, in research, and in the Director-General's office.

Francis Maupain has a Docteur en droit (Paris Panthéon Sorbonne) LLM, MPA (Harvard University). He was formerly ILO Legal Adviser and once Special Adviser to the ILO Director-General. He has authored a number of articles, lectured at The Hague Academy in International Law in 1999, and authored a book titled *The Future of the International Labour Organization in the Global Economy*' (Hart 2013). Maupain is associated with a collection of essays entitled *Social Justice and the World of Work* (Hart 2023).

Margherita Melillo is an Independent Consultant specializing in global health and international trade law. Previously, she worked at Georgetown University's O'Neill Institute for National and Global Health Law, and at the Max Planck Institute Luxembourg. She completed her PhD at the European University Institute, and in 2021, she was awarded the Antonio Cassese Prize for the best thesis in international law.

Helen Mountford is the President and CEO of ClimateWorks Foundation, a global platform for philanthropy to innovate and scale high-impact climate solutions that benefit people and the planet. Mountford has almost three decades of global experience at the intersection of environmental action, economic development, and climate policy, including as Deputy Director of the OECD's Environment Directorate (2010–2014).

Namira Negm is the Director of the African Migration Observatory (from 2022 till date) and was a former Legal Counsel of the African Union (2017–2022). She is a seasoned diplomat. She served as the Ambassador of Egypt to Rwanda (2014–2017), the Head of the Anti-Corruption Unit at the Ministry of Foreign Affairs of Egypt (2013–2014), and the Legal Advisor and Counter Terrorism Expert of the Egyptian Mission to the United Nations, New York (2006–2010). She has also served as the Legal and Political Officer in the Embassy of Egypt to the Netherlands (1999–2003) and occupied several positions in the Department of Legal Affairs and International Conventions at the Egyptian Ministry of Foreign Affairs. Negm is currently the lead of the AU team for establishing the Hybrid Court for South Sudan. She had previously occupied the position of Vice-President of the Assembly of States Parties of the United Nations Convention on the Law of the Sea, Vice-Chairperson of the Ad hoc Committee on International Terrorism (Sixth Committee), and Coordinator of the African Group in New York for legal matters.

André-Philippe Ouellet is an International Law PhD Candidate at the Graduate Institute of International and Development Studies (IHEID) (Global Governance Centre), a Swiss National Science Foundation Doc.Ch Researcher, and a Doctoral Fellow of the Social Sciences and Humanities Research Council of Canada.

Kenneth Piercy is a Senior Legal Officer in international, constitutional, and global health law, in the Office of the Legal Counsel of the World Health Organization (WHO).

Prior to joining WHO, Piercy practiced law with a private firm in New York and with the Global Fund to fight AIDS, tuberculosis, and malaria. Piercy graduated from Harvard Law School (*cum laude*).

Gabriela Ramos is the Assistant Director-General for Social and Human Sciences of UNESCO, where she oversees the institution's contributions to building inclusive societies, tackling inequalities, and the ethics of science and technology. She was previously the Cabinet Director and the G20/7 Sherpa at the OECD.

Vivian Daniele Rocha Gabriel is a PhD Candidate in international law at the University of São Paulo (USP) and was a former Consultant within the Executive Cooperation Program between Economic Commission for Latin America and the Caribbean (ECLAC) and the Institute for Applied Economic Research (Ipea).

Guy Fiti Sinclair is an Associate Professor and an Associate Dean Pacific at Auckland Law School, the University of Auckland.

Steven A Solomon is a Principal Legal Officer in international, constitutional, and global health law, in the Office of the Legal Counsel of the World Health Organization (WHO). Prior to joining WHO, Solomon practised law with a private firm in Washington, DC, and in the Legal Office of the United States State Department. Solomon graduated from Georgetown Law School (*magna cum laude*).

Ronald Steenblik is a Senior Technical Advisor to the Quaker United Nations Office (QUNO), currently working on improving information on subsidies to the production of primary plastic polymers. A large part of his career has been focussed on subsidies to primary industries, including serving as the OECD's Special Counsellor for Fossil Fuel Subsidy Reform (2016–2018).

Naphtali Ukamwa is a Doctoral Researcher (Public International Law) at Trinity College Dublin's School of Law.

Akshaya Venkataraman is a Trade Lawyer with experience working at the Indian Government, WTO, and law firms in India and Switzerland. She is currently an Editorial Assistant for the *Journal of International Economic Law*. She completed her LLM in International Law at the Graduate Institute of International and Development Studies (IHEID) and is qualified to the bar in India. She has previously published on international trade, product standards, dispute settlement, and renewable energy subsidies.

Fady Zeidan was the former General Counsel of the Global Fund and is a legal professional with more than 30 years of experience in international finance and development. Before joining the Global Fund, Zeidan served as the Deputy General Counsel of the International Finance Corporation.

Introduction

Why Should We Care About IO Initiatives in Response to Needs?

José E Alvarez

Among the welter of current books dealing with international organizations (IOs) written by international lawyers, this collection of essays is distinguished by two unique attributes. First, its contributors and editors are dominated by legal practitioners, the majority of whom are or have been members of the secretariats of the organizations addressed, even though many have at least one foot in the academy as either part-time teachers or scholars. Second, its focus, unlike many publications relating to IOs by elite publishers, is not on high-level jurisprudential theory but on the ground-level operational practice of these institutions.

The goal of its 31 chapters is to examine 'IO initiatives' (defined as a pattern of events launched by an organization's secretariat that respond to needs that cannot easily be addressed within the confines of the organization's founding or prior activities, which in turn recalibrate the setting in which the organization operates thereafter). It brings to light organizational actions that have largely remained in the shadows without imposing or presuming a framework for explaining when such initiatives occur, which internal or external actors are necessary, or what structures, actors, or ideas contribute to or obstruct them. Most of its chapters are exemplars of what Hannah Birkenkötter calls 'historical institutionalism'.[1] They are deep accounts of how IOs change, and sometimes expand their mandates, over time without formal constitutional amendment.

The five chapters in Part I of the book briefly canvass potential 'theoretical and legal' foundations for *some* of these initiatives without committing to any one of them. Birkenkötter's chapter usefully surveys different 'theoretical and disciplinary vantage points' for understanding what 'IO change' is and when or how it occurs but asserts that '[t]here exists no generally accepted and unified theory of IO change'.[2] Guy Fiti Sinclair's contribution to that Part addresses the role

[1] Hannah Birkenkötter, 'Change in International Organizations', Chapter 1 in this volume.
[2] ibid, text accompanying n 54 (citing Ernst Haas).

José E Alvarez, *Introduction* In: *International Organization Initiatives.* Edited by: Gabrielle Marceau and Henner Gött, Oxford University Press. © Oxford University Press 2025. DOI: 10.1093/9780197803325.003.0001

of ideas, assumptions, and cognitive framings—which he calls 'imaginaries'—in motivating and guiding IO initiatives while acknowledging that these ideational factors are only one element underlying the phenomenon of IO change.[3] Christiane Ahlborn's chapter canvasses a number of theoretical and jurisprudential frameworks that may elucidate IO initiatives while, at the same time, disparaging suggestions that these frameworks actually motivate the leading actors since '[IO] practitioners generally do not use theories to justify new initiatives by IOs'.[4] The remaining two chapters in Part I, by Niels Blokker and Fernando Lusa Bordin, respectively, address the positivist legal rules deployed at least by the lawyers engaged in the underlying initiatives, that is, the significant roles played by the traditional rules of treaty interpretation, and the various techniques that govern the exercise of IOs' powers, including the important role accorded to the discrete powers specifically conferred to the organs and secretariats of distinct IOs in their respective charters. Given the prominent role of IO lawyers in many of the book's case studies, no one should be surprised by this level of attention to their common language. At the same time, neither Blokker nor Bordin suggest that lawyers alone—or legal positivism—determine when, how, or why IOs respond to change.

The chapters in Part I do not claim to be an exhaustive survey of the relevant jurisprudential or other frameworks. Those include 'orchestration',[5] global administrative law or global legal pluralism,[6] along with numerous theories within the broad labels of (neo) realism,[7] rationalist approaches (or law and economics),[8] critical theory,[9] and international relations.[10] Neither the five chapters

[3] Guy Fiti Sinclair, 'IO Initiatives, Ideology, and the Imaginaries of Liberal Reform', Chapter 2 in this volume.

[4] Christiane Ahlborn, 'From Functionalism to Constitutionalism: Translating Theories on IO Powers into Practice', Chapter 3 in this volume, text at n 11.

[5] Kenneth Abbott and others (eds), *International Organizations as Orchestrators* (CUP 2015).

[6] Lorenzo Casini, 'Global Administrative Law' in Jeffrey L Dunoff and Mark A Pollack (eds), *International Legal Theory* (CUP 2022) 199–220; Nico Krisch, 'Global Legal Pluralism' in Jeffrey L Dunoff and Mark A Pollack (eds), *International Legal Theory* (CUP 2022) 240–58.

[7] Gregory Shaffer, 'Legal Realism and International Law' in Jeffrey L Dunoff and Mark A Pollack (eds), *International Legal Theory* (CUP 2022) 82–100.

[8] Anne van Aaken, 'Rationalist and Behavioralist Approaches to International Law' in Jeffrey L Dunoff and Mark A Pollack (eds), *International Legal Theory* (CUP 2022) 261–81.

[9] Fleur Johns, 'Critical International Legal Theory' in Jeffrey L Dunoff and Mark A Pollack (eds), *International Legal Theory* (CUP 2022) 133–52; James Thuo Gathii, 'The Agenda of Third World Approaches to International Law (TWAIL)' in Jeffrey L Dunoff and Mark A Pollack (eds), *International Legal Theory* (CUP 2022) 153–73; Karen Engle, Vasuki Nesiah, and Dianne Otto, 'Feminist Approaches to International Law' in Jeffrey L Dunoff and Mark A Pollack (eds), *International Legal Theory* (CUP 2022) 174–95.

[10] Jeffrey L Dunoff and Mark A Pollack, *Interdisciplinary Perspectives on International Law and International Relations* (CUP 2013) (including chapters on 'institutionalism'; 'liberal theory', 'constructivism', 'discourse' theory, 'open economy law', 'reputation', 'network' theory, and theories on 'compliance' and 'legitimacy'). As this book demonstrates, international relations theories are far more complex than is suggested by the oft-cited binary between 'rationalist' and 'constructivist' approaches.

of Part I nor any of those other frameworks structure the rest of this book. Unlike, for example, a recent book defining the relatively new concept of IOs as 'orchestrators', this is not a monograph that uses IO case studies to present a unifying description of how IOs behave, or seeking generalizable prescriptions for more effective governance.[11]

Instead, the rest of this book consists of short chapters describing 'IO initiatives' (as defined above) launched by secretariats in general (Part II), the heads of organizations (Part III), or involving outsiders or third parties to IOs (Part IV). With the exception of the opening chapter of each of these three Parts (each of which attempts to put these types of actors in a more general context), the remaining chapters largely eschew theory in favour of the concrete. The chapters in Part II address, for example, the role of United Nations (UN) lawyers in establishing UN ad hoc war crimes tribunals; World Bank staff members who embrace environmental and social responsibilities; or global public health experts at the World Health Organization (WHO) exercising default 'global health authority' in response to the crisis of COVID-19. Part II captures the enormous range of 'needs' to which IOs respond: from new technological challenges (such as those involving the ethics of artificial intelligence (AI)) to contemporary political or moral concerns. The chapters in Part III either describe in more general terms the hitherto ignored roles of select organizational heads—namely the Secretaries-General of the UN or the Organisation for Economic Co-operation and Development and the Directors-General of the International Labour Organization (ILO) or the World Trade Organization—or canvass relevant initiatives by subject matter (as to counterterrorist financing or to address fossil fuel subsidies). Part IV focuses on IO interactions with outsiders to these organizations and addresses a wide gamut of IO initiatives. Its chapters canvass, for example, 'multi-stakeholder initiatives' within the ILO to advance its 'decent work' agenda in relation to the regulation of transnational supply chains, the 'catalytic' role of a diverse set of actors on initiatives taken by the World Bank's Management and Executive Directors, and the WHO's engagement with non-state actors in the wake of COVID-19 in governing body processes, including efforts to draft and negotiate a WHO convention on pandemic prevention, preparedness, and response, and to amend its International Health Regulations.

These chapters do not slot their accounts of IO initiatives into theoretical or jurisprudential frameworks. That would be a very different book, and given the considerable existing literature that already does that, it would probably be a less original one. One virtue of this book is that it does not force the considerable

[11] Compare, by contrast, Abbott and others (n 5). While that book contains empirical descriptions of some 40 cases of what might be considered 'IO initiatives' as defined in this volume, those case studies are used to define the contours of 'orchestration' as a mode of IO governance.

institutional practice that it describes into any one of those frameworks. It allows readers to appreciate the rich diversity of perspectives and to draw their own conclusions. One suspects that IO initiatives are likely to be supported by more than one theoretical framework in any case.

There is merit in empirical case studies that deflect theory or leave it to another day. This book's ground-level descriptions of what IOs have done to adapt to change are valuable in themselves. To answer my titular question: there are many reasons to care about the subject of this book.

Consider first the editors' decision to collect examples of IO initiatives that highlight why organizations are not opaque black boxes interacting only with other similarly opaque international legal persons, namely other IOs and states. Parts II, III and IV puncture the abstract concept of an IO. Their case studies puncture IOs to peek inside them: to consider the impact of their secretariats, including their lawyers and high officials, as well as third-party interlocutors. To be sure, a considerable body of IO literature has also addressed the role of their political bodies, particularly the UN Security Council. But to the extent legal commentators have previously paid attention to IO secretariats, it has usually been within the confines of examining IO administrative law, typically seen as purely 'internal' law of organizations *qua* organization (such as the rules governing the hiring and firing of their employees).[12] International administrative law is not the subject of this book. This book advances our knowledge of how IOs adapt to make a difference on substantive areas of the law, from global health law to international labour law.

Its case studies of IO initiatives are no less revelatory than liberal theorists' decisions to examine the impact of epistemic communities within states—including civil society groups—on the foreign policies pursued by 'abstract' states.[13] They complicate traditional conceptions of IOs. They foreground what is usually left in the background: the 'soft power' of IO bureaucrats, the singular importance of diverse forms of expertise both within IOs and within their chosen third-party interlocutors, and the often-exceptional role of lawyers even when they disclaim (as they often do) any responsibility for initiating legal change.[14]

This book uncovers a surprising number of initiatives not involving formal constitutional amendment and taken in the face of constitutional or other rules of the organization that do not accord the power to initiate change to either IO organs or to members of their secretariats. Instead, these initiatives have typically

[12] Niamh Kinchin, *Administrative Justice in the UN* (Elgar 2018).

[13] Andrew Moravcsik, 'Taking Preferences Seriously: A Liberal Theory of International Politics' (1997) 51 International Organizations 513.

[14] Joseph Nye, Jr, *Soft Power: The Means to Success in World Politics* (Public Affairs 2004).

been taken to respond to emerging needs through innovative operational activities, methods of work, or interpretations of IO mandates.

Many of the IO initiatives discussed in this book will be of interest to general international lawyers. They provide strong and direct evidence that certain concepts—like the doctrine of 'implied powers', the alleged 'teleological turn' in the law of IOs, and the value accorded to 'institutional practice'—are not figments of the academic imagination or limited to the interpretation of the UN Charter. The sheer fact that IO initiatives are so plentiful and varied has, to be sure, implications for certain theories about IOs, even if this book does not emphasize them. This book provides abundant examples of why the (mostly post-World War II) turn to institutions matters, complicates simplistic accounts that treat IOs either as the mere 'agents' of their state principals or as independent actors that pursue their own autonomous agendas, and compels re-examination of what constitutes 'authority' in international politics.[15]

The case studies here direct attention to how diverse institutions (including some that are not established by treaty or predominantly comprised of states) engage in forms of 'transnational' or 'global' governance that are not confined to the trilogy (treaties, custom, and general principles) contained in Article 38 of the Statute of the International Court of Justice.[16] Significantly, the contributors to this book do not limit their attention to traditionally defined IOs but include, for example, public–private partnerships such as Gavi, the Vaccine Alliance (Gavi),[17] and the Global Fund to Fight AIDS, Tuberculosis and Malaria (Global Fund), both established under Swiss law as not-for-profit organizations which have 'board members' that include representatives of states but also non-governmental organizations, UN system organizations, and entities from the private sector.[18] This blurring of traditional divides between 'private' and 'public' actors is suggested by the fact that the Global Fund, for example, enjoys privileges and immunities in a number of countries comparable to those enjoyed by formal IOs, and has even concluded bilateral treaties for this purpose.[19] Those looking

[15] Compare Kenneth Abbott and Duncan Snidal, 'Why States Act Through Formal International Organizations' (1998) 42 Journal of Conflict Resolution 3 (outlining a functionalist rationale for IOs based on states' needs for centralizing the actions of multiple states and also for establishing unique actors delegated with a certain degree of independence).

[16] Left largely unsaid are possible reasons why IOs resort to such 'initiatives' even when, in theory, hard-law treaty alternatives are possible. For an account of why institutional soft law has become an alternative to treaty-making in some cases, see Joost Pauwelyn, Ramses A Wessel, and Jan Wouters, 'When Structures Become Shackles: Stagnation and Dynamics in International Lawmaking' (2014) 25 European Journal of International Law 733.

[17] Jelena Madir, 'IOs' Initiatives: Gavi, The Vaccine Alliance', Chapter 28 in this volume.

[18] Fady Zeidan and Jean Abboud, 'The Global Fund to Fight AIDS, Tuberculosis, and Malaria: Partnerships, Collaborations, and Initiatives with International Organizations', Chapter 27 in this volume. See also Birkenkötter (n 1) nn 32–35.

[19] Agreement on Privileges and Immunities between Malawi and the Global Fund to Fight AIDS, Tuberculosis, and Malaria, 22 February 2018, 3300 UNTS.

for evidence that the category of de facto international legal persons seems to be expanding can find it here.

It is also important that even IO practitioners are taking seriously the idea that the legal impact of IOs is not limited to serving as venues for the negotiation of treaties or to serving as depositories for forms of state practice or *opinio juris* essential to the identification of custom. The case studies here provide empirical evidence that IO initiatives that have an impact on an IO's internal rules or international or national laws or regulatory practices might be described (as this author has suggested elsewhere) as 'law-making by subterfuge'.[20] In documenting instances of de facto IO law-making beyond the overly familiar (and now far less frequently deployed) example of Security Council action under Chapter VII of the UN Charter, this book suggests that even those organizations disparaged for their supposed absence of real-world impact may deploy power that cannot be reduced to the desires of its most powerful member (*pace* Hans Morgenthau).[21] Parts II and III contain multiple examples in which secretariats and high-level secretariat officials (including IO lawyers) engage in relatively autonomous action, even if their initiatives only take root if supported or approved subsequently (but sometimes only implicitly) by IO members. These examples demonstrate the soft and hard power of bureaucrats and expertise.

Those interested, on the other hand, in drawing analogies between IOs and the 'primary' law-making actors—states—will also find some of the case studies here of interest.[22] As Part IV demonstrates, like states, IOs seek allies and, like states, their effectiveness dims without them. Like states, IOs also operate under structures that contain some 'checks and balances'; even if these do not usually consist of judicial review by international courts but instead more closely resemble 'democratic checks' imposed by the need to solicit acquiescence from their members.

But these attempts to connect this book's case studies to certain theoretical concepts do not defend the book on its own terms. As indicated, this book is distinguished by what it generally avoids: theory. There are advantages to this avoidance.

Its case studies avoid the flattening of reality that tends to accompany more theory-bound compilations. The contributors here do not waste time waging internecine, discipline-defining battles with fellow theory-makers. Those principally interested in articulating or demonstrating the superior value of particular IO theories or frameworks spend a great deal of time delineating (often minute) distinctions between 'competing' frameworks. A considerable portion

[20] José Alvarez, *International Organizations as Law-Makers* (OUP 2005) 217.
[21] ibid 30.
[22] Compare Fernando Bordin, *The Analogy Between International Organizations and States* (CUP 2018).

of theoretically inclined work seeks to show the gaps or deficiencies of rival theories. Those intent on demonstrating, for example, how IOs enlist intermediary actors through ideational and material support feel the need to distinguish this 'orchestration' mode of governance from using normatively hard instruments for the same ends; orchestrators also distinguish their approach from mere 'collaboration' (defined to consist of the use of soft law instruments) or 'delegation' (where IOs directly control their agents).[23] Proponents of 'orchestration' use these distinctions to contend that their framework is superior to 'actor-centred' approaches that ostensibly ignore the 'institutional context' of the actors (including IOs), or to purely 'rational choice' or 'constructivist' conceptions.[24] Distinctions between these explanatory accounts for IO behaviour are used to highlight why 'orchestration' provides a 'richer understanding' than those who emphasize 'regime complexes' grounded in a purely 'functional' response to complex governance problems.[25] It is suggested that orchestration is also superior to a purely principal–agent model of functionalist IOs because states are not merely principals within IOs but, during orchestration, are the targets of IO intermediaries, who sometimes 'manage' states but sometimes 'bypass' them.[26]

In leaving theory for another day, the contributors here skilfully avoid these underlying inter-scholarly squabbles. In deflecting theory, the authors of these case studies also avoid the challenge of selecting any one framework as the most plausible. Such an attempt would probably be unwise in any case. Even while attempting to distinguish the merits or novelty of their preferred framework, those engaged in theory frequently acknowledge their reliance on 'rival' approaches. This suggests that those minute distinctions to justify their favoured model may not be so significant after all. Moshe Hirsch's description (and defence) of the 'sociological' perspective on international law, for example, acknowledges its debt to realism, functionalism, and legal positivism, as well as its capacity to absorb lessons from TWAILers' focus on social conflict.[27]

But whether as a source of distinction or acknowledgement of intellectual debt, the theoretical literature's self-reverential citations challenge outsiders, including practising lawyers. Entering the theoretical literature on how IOs ostensibly behave is akin to entering a hall of mirrors. Those without a conceptual map grounded in considerable prior reading will find themselves bumping their heads, particularly since even those aligned under a particular theory frequently

[23] Abbott and others (n 5) 3–4.
[24] ibid 17.
[25] ibid 32.
[26] ibid 16, 26, 32–35.
[27] Moshe Hirsch, 'The Sociological Perspective on International Law', in Jeffrey L Dunoff and Mark A Pollack (eds), *International Legal Theory* (CUP 2022) 282–304. Hirsch's description of the role of normative beliefs and social norms in constituting the social environments within IOs, ibid 289, echoes Guy Sinclair's reference to the importance of 'imaginaries' in Sinclair (n 3).

disagree on its essential elements. A room full of those who identify themselves as 'realists', for example, does not contain like-minded scholars. This book, by contrast, contains a wealth of knowledge of what IOs do, without distracting mirrors to defect from reality.

This book does not require that readers build the interdisciplinary bridges that are all the rage elsewhere. Without disparaging the merits of interdisciplinary collaborative scholarship, it is important to remember that there is a difference between achieving accurate descriptions and constructing useful lessons from them. Doing the first well may be more useful than doing both poorly. Theory-makers may deploy empirical examples from the real world to build their theories, but their core interest, inherent to many of the disciplines that generate them, is to build a *relatively parsimonious model for general behaviour inspired by, but not purely duplicative of, reality*. These models are drawn from real-world cases but intentionally ignore the real world's messiness in order to draw generalizable conclusions. A conclusion that legal practitioners might find to be most faithful to the actual IO initiatives that they find—namely that, in the end, everything matters in explaining whether a particular IO action is taken or gains traction (from the ideas valued by a Secretary-General to what they or others had for breakfast)—is simply not useful to those building theories in political science or other 'scientific' disciplines.

The different nature of the theoretical inquiry matters. The principal interlocutors of those engaged in theory-building are not legal practitioners or policymakers working in IOs. They are other theorists who need to be persuaded *in terms that the relevant discipline respects* that the framework under discussion fills a gap *in the literature on theory*. The self-referential nature of these internal monologues between theorists (which are built on 'ideal types' that, as the writers themselves acknowledge, may not actually exist outside their envisioned models)[28] helps to explain why most of the practitioner authors of chapters in this book do not engage with this literature or regard it as unduly academic.

Other aspects of the relevant theoretical literature—positive and negative—are also worth mentioning. Many, if not most, theoretical frameworks are accompanied by a normative agenda. This is obvious in some cases. Critical frameworks or accounts seek to deconstruct international institutions and their use of international law to reveal the underlying flaws of both. TWAILers point to the colonial origins of international law and its institutions, with some claiming that the discredited 'civilizing mission' of the nineteenth century is alive and well but is now subject to 'blue-washing' within UN system institutions that 'reform the world' by exporting ideological skewed agendas that favour the West

[28] Abbott and others (n 5) 10. See also ibid 19 ('the spare [orchestrator-intermediary-target] model does not reflect all the complexities of real-world relationships').

over the rest.[29] Feminist critics point to the hollowness, contradictions, or gaps in the UN 'gender main-streaming', the Security Council's Women, Peace and Security initiative, or efforts by the World Bank to promote Gender Equality.[30] Indeed, critical scholars often point out that rival jurisprudential frameworks for understanding the international legal system—from various schools of legal positivism to rationalist approaches grounded in law and economics to the approach endorsed by the Yale School of International Law—are tainted by ideological agendas that favour certain 'hegemonic' states.

Non-critical jurisprudential frameworks usually evince a more subtle normative agenda. To the extent these frameworks aspire to prescription—to finding generalizable recipes for reforming existing IOs or for building new ones—they tend to (silently) embrace international law's comforting 'progress narrative'.[31] Enthusiasts for the 'orchestration' mode of governance, for example, depict the empowerment of IOs that it enables in exceedingly positive terms—as if increasing the 'relative autonomy' of IOs, their use of intermediaries to outsource (and sometimes privatize) sources of expertise in favour of their normative projects, or the 'managing' or 'by-passing' of states that results—all constitute progressive advances in governing the world to the benefit of all.[32] Those attempting to describe IO initiatives more objectively may not want to adopt that kind of normative baggage.

Another one of the virtues of this book, in short, is that it does not try to convince us that all IO initiatives (or their consequences on the organization as a whole) are a good thing.

[29] Sinclair (n 3). Compare the discussion by Namira Negm, 'The African Union Commission's Endeavour with the International Court of Justice for Achieving the Complete Decolonization of Mauritius: The Case of the Chagos Archipelago', Chapter 11 in this volume (discussing the African Union Commission's effort to achieve the complete decolonization of Mauritius and its efforts before the International Court of Justice to secure the return of the Chagos Archipelago to Mauritius).

[30] Engle, Nesiah, and Otto (n 9). For a more general critique of the World Bank's aversion to human rights, see Galit Sarfaty, 'Why Culture Matters in International Institutions: The Marginality of Human Rights at the World Bank' (2010) 103 American Journal of International Law 657.

[31] Russell Miller and Rebecca Bratspies, *Progress in International Law* (Martinus Nijhoff 2008).

[32] Abbott and others (n 5). The opening chapter contains no mention that orchestration might be seen in less positive terms. That book says nothing about the possibility that IOs might use intermediaries to pursue the particular agendas of certain IO bureaucrats or to enable or advance the 'capture' of the underlying IOs by certain financial interests. The supporters of orchestration included in that volume express no fear that orchestration, to the extent it enables the by-passing of states, may also by-pass democratic governance. The proponents of orchestration in that volume praise the resort to expertise without acknowledging its downsides. See David Kennedy, 'Challenging Expert Rule: The Politics of Global Governance' (2005) 27 Sydney Law Review 2. Although *International Organizations as Orchestrators* devotes a chapter that purports to address the 'winners and losers' of orchestration governance (see Walter Mattli and Jack Seddon, 'Orchestration Along the Pareto Frontier: Winners and Losers' in Abbot and others (n 5) 315–48), that chapter focuses only on which parts of the orchestration partnership (IO, intermediary, or target) might benefit in particular cases. That chapter does not address what critical or TWAIL scholars might examine: namely, the consequences of orchestration on vulnerable groups within target states or on North/South distributional inequalities.

PART I

THEORETICAL AND LEGAL FOUNDATIONS OF IO INITIATIVES

1

Change in International Organizations

Hannah Birkenkötter

I. Introduction

What is change in international organizations (IOs), how does it occur, and who are the actors instigating change within IOs? What are the conditions that enable or obstruct change? These are some of the main questions that animate this book.

This chapter seeks to provide some conceptual common ground. It first reviews IO conceptualizations from different theoretical and disciplinary viewpoints. The chapter then proposes different dimensions of 'IO change' and which factors and actors drive or obstruct change within IOs. Acknowledging that different theoretical approaches help us understand different dimensions of IOs' reality today, the chapter offers a working definition and a set of scope conditions for change within IOs. Such conditions relate to the institutional set-up and the functioning of an IO's bureaucracy, the role of individuals, especially executive heads of IOs, the interests of member states and other constituencies, the overall legal–political environment, and the resources at an IO's disposal.

II. What Are IOs?

How we define IOs depends on whether we approach them from an internal or an external perspective,[1] our disciplinary rooting, and our general theoretical position. In turn, our understanding of an IO will inform how we conceptualize change in IOs and how we conceive of the roles of members and secretariats in fostering IO change. The question of what constitutes an IO is mainly treated by scholars from international relations (IR) and international law (IL), and differences in their respective conceptualizations can be traced mainly to different research questions. While much scholarship on IOs today straddles disciplinary boundaries, IR scholars are primarily interested in why IOs are created

[1] Jacob Katz Cogan, 'International Organizations' in Jean d'Aspremont and Sahib Singh (eds), *Concepts for International Law: Contributions to Disciplinary Thought* (Edward Elgar Publishing 2019) 540–48.

Hannah Birkenkötter, *Change in International Organizations* In: *International Organization Initiatives*. Edited by: Gabrielle Marceau and Henner Gött, Oxford University Press. © Oxford University Press 2025.
DOI: 10.1093/9780197803325.003.0002

in the first place and how they interact with other actors populating the global realm. Legal scholars, in turn, are primarily concerned with the rules that set up and govern IOs and IOs' legal boundaries.[2] Both IR and IL scholars are concerned with IOs' autonomy vis-à-vis their member states. In IL scholarship, it is widely accepted that independent will is a necessary condition for an IO to exist as a distinct legal subject. In IR scholarship, there has been a long-standing debate on the autonomy of IOs.

A. IOs and international institutions in IR scholarship: Different theoretical vantage points

Before addressing different theoretical vantage points on IOs, a terminological and conceptual note is needed. In IR scholarship, the field of IO study is often embedded in the broader field of the study of international institutions. International institutions, in turn, are standardly defined as 'persistent and connected sets of rules (formal and informal) that prescribe behavioural roles, constrain activity, and shape expectations'.[3] International institutions are then primarily understood as sets of rules and legal rules as one subset of rules, that is, a particular form of institutionalization.[4] IOs are the entities associated with specific institutions.[5] In contrast, international lawyers often use the term 'international institutional law' or 'institutional dimension of IL' when discussing IOs as an entity.[6] These two viewpoints are not incompatible but can lead to confusion where IR scholars focus on sets of *rules* that are embodied by a specific organizational entity, such as labour standards and the International Labour Organization (ILO) or climate change law and the United Nations Framework Convention on Climate Change, whereas IL scholars are interested in the *entity*.[7]

IR theory typically distinguishes rationalist and social constructivist approaches to international institutions and organizations, even though most scholars today acknowledge that different theoretical approaches coexist and

[2] Thanks to Gabriele Wadlig for reminding me of this point.

[3] Robert O Keohane, *International Institutions and State Power: Essays in International Relations Theory* (Westview Press 1989) 3.

[4] Kenneth W Abbott and others, 'The Concept of Legalization' (2000) 54 International Organization 401.

[5] Lisa Martin and Beth Simmons, 'International Organizations and Institutions' in Walter Carlsnaes, Beth A Simmons, and Thomas Risse (eds), *Handbook of International Relations* (2nd edn, SAGE Publications 2012) 326.

[6] Richard Collins, *The Institutional Problem in Modern International Law* (Bloomsbury Publishing 2016).

[7] Hannah Birkenkötter, 'International Law as a Common Language Across Spheres of Authority?' (2020) 9 Global Constitutionalism 318, 323–25.

communicate with one another.[8] Nonetheless, it is helpful to distinguish the different theoretical vantage points, as they conceptualize IOs, and therefore also IO change, differently.

Rationalist positions, which comprise realist and rational functionalist positions, view IOs as a function of states: states create and ultimately control IOs. Realists consider international institutions and IOs as epiphenomenal to states' interests.[9] In its most extreme form, this view explains IOs' existence by the fact that they serve (powerful) states' interests, and they will change and disappear if they no longer fulfil that goal.[10] In contrast, rational functionalism departs from the insight that there are problems of collective action that states can best address through mutual cooperation: it is in their best interest to set up IOs to solve certain collective action problems where individually beneficial state action would impede mutually beneficial cooperation.[11] This means that IOs are not epiphenomenal but central to realizing state interests. Both views are united in that IOs remain a function of the state—they exist because this is in states' interest, and their form, mandate, and tasks will hinge upon such interests.

Against this position, social constructivist approaches highlight IOs' nature as autonomously existing entities. Not only are IOs not entirely dependent on states' interests, but they have, in turn, a role in shaping states' interests. Indeed, state interests do not exist a priori but result from social interaction; international norms and actors' interests are mutually constitutive.[12] From this point of view, IOs are autonomous actors, which helps explain why IOs can exhibit pathological behaviour and have an impact on the world that is not willed by states.[13] One strand of research in this tradition focuses specifically on the bureaucratic nature of IOs and emphasizes the important role that bureaucrats can play, for example, in the setting up of new governance mechanisms.[14] International civil servants are considered bureaucratic actors with a certain level of autonomy from members, and relevant research enquires into the relationship between a bureaucracy's autonomy and their authority and, relatedly, their influence on the IO's agenda and decision-making.[15]

[8] Martin and Simmons (n 5) 336; Cogan (n 1) 547–48.

[9] Martin and Simmons (n 5) 329, referencing Hans Morgenthau and Edward Carr.

[10] Kenneth N Waltz, 'Structural Realism After the Cold War' (2000) 25 International Security 5, 18–27.

[11] For this characterization of the rational functionalist position, see Martin and Simmons (n 5) 331.

[12] Ian Hurd, 'Constructivism' in Christian Reus-Smit and Duncan Snidal (eds), *The Oxford Handbook of International Relations* (OUP 2008) 298–316.

[13] Michael Barnett and Martha Finnemore, *Rules for the World: International Organizations in Global Politics* (Cornell UP 2019).

[14] Tana Johnson, *Organizational Progeny: Why Governments Are Losing Control over the Proliferating Structures of Global Governance* (OUP 2014).

[15] Julia Fleischer and Nina Reiners, 'Connecting International Relations and Public Administration: Toward a Joint Research Agenda for the Study of International Bureaucracy' (2021) 23 International Studies Review 1230.

Thus, there are two competing theoretical views of IOs in IR theory: IOs as a function of states and IOs as autonomous, bureaucratic entities. This dichotomy has also been described as one between external and internal approaches to IOs,[16] or functionalist and constitutionalist conceptions of IOs.[17] This latter dichotomy is especially prominent amongst IL scholars.

B. IOs in public international law

In public international law, IOs are traditionally understood as intergovernmental organizations, that is, entities set up by states via an international treaty.[18] This conception highlights the importance of states and follows a largely functionalist paradigm that has been the predominant paradigm amongst IL scholars for many decades.[19] At the same time, it has long been acknowledged in IL that IOs are legal subjects in their own right,[20] and a standard definition of IOs posits that for an entity set up by treaty to qualify as an IO, the treaty needs to set up at least one organ with a will of its own.[21] This requirement reflects a constitutionalist idea of IOs as largely autonomous entities.

At face value, this distinction is similar to the distinction made in the previous section between rationalist approaches, which often focus on states, and social constructivist approaches, which often focus on bureaucracies. However, social constructivist and constitutional approaches to IOs only have in common that they both emphasize the existence of IOs as autonomous entities. Beyond that, the two approaches ask different questions and depart from different premises. Social constructivist approaches emphasize the mutually constitutive nature of international institutions and actors in IR and seek to provide explanations for puzzles that historically prior rationalist approaches—focusing on the role of

[16] Cogan (n 1).

[17] Jan Klabbers, 'Contending Approaches to International Organizations: Between Functionalism and Constitutionalism', in Jan Klabbers and Åsa Wallendahl (eds), *Research Handbook on the Law of International Organizations* (Edward Elgar Publishing 2011) 3–30; see also Christiane Ahlborn, 'From Functionalism to Constitutionalism: Translating Theories an IO Powers into Practice', Chapter 3 in this volume.

[18] See for such an understanding, eg Vienna Convention on the Representation of States in their Relations with International Organizations of a Universal Character (adopted 13 March 1975) UN Doc A/CONF.67/16 art 1(1)(i) or Vienna Convention on the Law of Treaties between States and International Organizations or between International Organizations (adopted 21 March 1986) UN Doc A/CONF.129/15 (VCLT-IO) art 2(1)(i).

[19] Jan Klabbers, 'The EJIL Foreword: The Transformation of International Organizations Law' (2015) 26 European Journal of International Law 9; Guy Fiti Sinclair, 'IO Initiatives, Ideology, and the Imaginaries of Liberal Reform', Chapter 2 in this volume.

[20] *Reparation for Injuries Suffered in the Service of the United Nations* (1949) (Advisory Opinion) ICJ Rep [1949] 174.

[21] Henry G Schermers and Niels M Blokker, *International Institutional Law* (6th rev edn, Brill 2018) 41.

states—could not. Social constructivism, while departing from certain normative premises, is thus, like most IR theory, a primarily explanatory theory.

In turn, legal and specifically constitutionalist approaches to IOs are perhaps best viewed as primarily normative approaches that aim at containing the powers exercised by IOs through rules of IL.[22] Several legal scholars today embrace the dual nature of IOs,[23] acknowledging that the agreements that establish IOs are international treaties amongst states, but at the same time also the constitutive instruments of independent entities—they are 'constitutional treaties' or 'treaty-constitutions'.[24] Whether one adopts a functionalist or constitutionalist perspective on IOs, IOs can be defined as entities with their own, formal structure established by agreement, with at least one organ with a will of its own.[25] In addition, most IL scholars require that the agreement establishing an IO be governed by public international law. There are two related indicators to determine whether an entity is governed by IL: the nature of the constitutive instrument and IO membership.

IOs are undoubtedly recognized as subjects of IL if states have set them up via an international treaty that explicitly provides for legal subjectivity or if the treaty is reasonably understood to entail a separate legal personality. However, the very definition of an international treaty contains a necessary condition that the agreement be governed by IL. There is thus a certain measure of circularity if we want to use the nature of the constitutive treaty to determine whether or not an entity is governed by IL.[26] One way of breaking this is to consider *who*

[22] Klabbers (n 17) 13–16. See also Anne Peters, 'International Organizations and International Law' in Jacob Katz Cogan, Ian Hurd, and Ian Johnstone (eds), *The Oxford Handbook of International Organizations* (OUP 2016) 43.

[23] Lorenzo Gasbarri, *The Concept of an International Organization in International Law* (OUP 2021).

[24] Peters (n 22) 34.

[25] The criterion of a formal structure established by agreement is taken from Clive Archer, *International Organizations* (4th edn, Routledge 2015) 30; whereas the criterion of at least one organ with its own distinct will is taken from Schermers and Blokker (n 21) 33, which also emphasized that IOs must be founded on an international agreement. See also International Law Commission (ILC), 'Report of the International Law Commission on the Work of Its 63rd Session' (26 April–3 June and 4 July–12 August 2011) UN Doc A/66/10, which contains the ILC's Draft Articles on the Responsibility of International Organizations (DARIO). DARIO Article 2(a) defines 'international organization' as 'an organization established by a treaty or other instrument governed by international law and possessing its own international legal personality'. Another example can be found in ILC, 'Settlement of International Disputes to which International Organizations are Parties. Titles and Texts of Draft Guidelines 1 and 2 Provisionally Adopted by the Drafting Committee' (15 May 2023) UN Doc A/CN.4/L.983, where Article 2(a) of the ILC's draft guidelines on settlement of international disputes to which IOs are parties defines 'international organization' more clearly as 'an entity possessing its own international legal personality, established by a treaty or other instrument governed by international law, that may include as members, in addition to States, other entities, and has at least one organ capable of expressing a will distinct from that of its members'.

[26] Vienna Convention on the Law of Treaties (adopted 22 May 1969, entered into force 27 January 1980) 1155 UNTS 331 art 2(a); Vienna Convention on Succession of States in Respect of Treaties (adopted 22 August 1996, entered into force 6 November 1996) 1946 UNTS 3 art 2(a); VCLT-IO (n 18) art 2(a).

sets up an IO: if an organization is set up exclusively by subjects of IL, then it is very likely that this organization will be governed by IL. This can include actors other than states if they undoubtedly possess international legal personality.[27] This comprises existing intergovernmental organizations, and there are several examples of IOs that are members of other IOs.[28]

The matter is more complicated for hybrid entities set up by actors who do not unequivocally possess international legal subjectivity. We will discuss this further in the next section. One decisive factor might be to what extent the parties to an agreement—if all of them are at least partial subjects of IL—choose explicitly or implicitly to be governed by IL. This depends on the interpretation of the document in question.

C. What makes an IO? The spectrum of IOs covered in this book

There are different ways in which IOs can be classified. This section focuses specifically on the difficulty of assessing organizations that are not unequivocally considered IOs because they do not satisfy all of the constitutive requirements in terms of being governed by IL. There is no doubt that organizations set up by states through international treaties and whose membership is predominantly comprised of states constitute IOs, irrespective of the theoretical or disciplinary perspective one adopts. This is the case for most of the IOs discussed in this book. The book covers initiatives from various task-specific organizations,[29] including the ILO, the World Trade Organization (WTO),[30] the World Bank, and the World Health Organization, as well as from general purpose organizations, including at the regional level the African Union and at the global level the United Nations (UN). These IOs, while different in their scope of activities, have in common the fact that they are undoubtedly IOs under IL.

The matter is more complicated for innovative organizational formats that are often characterized as 'public–private partnerships' (PPPs). This term emerged in the 1990s and is typically used for the various arrangements through which IOs interact with the private sector and other non-state actors; often, PPPs involve one or several IOs, states and non-state actors, both from the private sector

[27] DARIO (n 25) art 2(a). There is at least one IO that has been entirely set up by other IOs: see Jan Klabbers, *An Introduction to International Organizations Law* (3rd edn, CUP 2015) 9, fn 30.

[28] Eg the European Union is a member of the World Trade Organization and the Food and Agriculture Organization.

[29] On the distinction between task-specific and general-purpose organizations, see Tobias Lenz and others, 'Patterns of International Organization: Task Specific vs General Purpose' (2014) 49 PVS Politische Vierteljahresschrift 131.

[30] As previously mentioned, the European Union—itself formally an IO—is a member of the WTO, but the vast majority of WTO members are states.

and civil society, and they pursue some common policy and/or operational activity.[31]

Both Gavi, the Vaccine Alliance (Gavi),[32] and the Global Fund to Fight AIDS, Tuberculosis and Malaria (Global Fund), are examples of PPPs that show the difficulties of determining the legal status of a hybrid entity, that is, an entity that was not clearly established by subjects of IL via an international treaty.[33] Notably, the Global Fund exhibits some traits of a 'traditional' IO but cannot be unequivocally defined as such. As is explained more fully in the chapter on the Global Fund's partnerships and initiatives,[34] the Fund was set up in 2002, following a consultation process involving nearly 40 representatives of developing countries, donor countries, non-governmental organizations, the private sector, and the United Nations system (the so-called Transitional Working Group), based on a so-called framework document.[35] The framework document specifies that '[t]he Global Fund is a financial instrument, not an implementing entity' and provides for several organs, most importantly the Global Fund's Board and the Global Fund Secretariat.[36]

Is the framework document an 'agreement' that establishes an IO? It gave important indications as to the nature of the Global Fund and was instrumental in setting up the Fund's governance structure. But it is not the constitutive document of the Global Fund, strictly speaking, in that it did not establish the Fund's legal existence. Rather, the Global Fund was subsequently registered as a non-profit foundation under Swiss law[37] by the Board, elected by the Transitional Working Group. The Fund is governed by various documents, importantly by the by-laws adopted by the Global Fund's Board and various funding policies.[38] None of these documents have the formal characteristics usually associated with

[31] Kenneth W Abbott, 'Public Private Partnership', *Max Planck Encyclopedias of International Law* (2008) <https://opil.ouplaw.com/display/10.1093/law:epil/9780199231690/law-9780199231690-e1084> accessed 25 September 2024.

[32] Jelena Madir, 'IOs Initiatives: Gavi, the Vaccine Alliance', Chapter 28 in this volume.

[33] The Global Fund has been characterized as pertaining to a 'new class of dual and hybrid organizations': see Gerd Droesse, *Membership in International Organizations: Paradigms of Membership Structures, Legal Implications of Membership and the Concept of International Organization* (T.M.C. Asser Press 2020) 3, 58, 107.

[34] Fady Zeidan and Jean Abboud, 'The Global Fund to Fight AIDS, Tuberculosis, and Malaria: Partnerships, Collaborations, and Initiatives with International Organizations', Chapter 27 in this volume.

[35] 'The Global Fund to Fight AIDS, Tuberculosis and Malaria: The Framework Document' <https://www.theglobalfund.org/media/6019/core_globalfund_framework_en.pdf> accessed 25 August 2024 (Framework Document).

[36] ibid ss I, III(A) (specifying that the Global Fund is a financial instrument), IX(D).

[37] 'Bylaws of the Global Fund to Fight Aids, Tuberculosis & Malaria' <https://www.theglobalfund.org/media/6007/core_globalfund_bylaws_en.pdf> accessed 25 August 2024 (Bylaws).

[38] A full list is available at the Global Fund's website: 'Governance & Policies' <https://www.theglobalfund.org/en/governance-policies/> accessed 25 August 2024.

international treaties. This would indicate that the Global Fund is not an IO under IL but a domestic entity under Swiss law that acts transnationally.

At the same time, the by-laws in their current form explicitly state that the Global Fund has been recognized as an IO by various national governments.[39] It has concluded agreements with states in the form of international treaties, perhaps most prominently its Headquarter Agreement with Switzerland.[40] This agreement explicitly states that Switzerland recognizes 'for the purposes of this Agreement the international juridical personality and legal capacity in Switzerland of the Global Fund'[41] and contains various other provisions exhibiting properties typically associated with IOs. Importantly, the Global Fund benefits from immunity from jurisdiction, as do its Board members and officials.[42] This has led authors from within the Fund to assert that it 'has evolved, over time, into an IO'.[43]

Such an assessment is in line with the pragmatic approach to legal personality of IOs under IL that Jan Klabbers has called 'presumptive personality': as soon as an IO performs an act that necessitates international legal personality—for example ratifies an international treaty—it is presumed to possess such personality if there is no objection from other subjects of IL.[44] An IO is thus also considered as such under IL when other subjects of IL treat it as such.

In the context of this book, this is important for two reasons. First, the fact that we identify certain PPPs as IOs after a certain amount of time has passed says something about the importance of IO interaction with the 'outside world', discussed in Part IV of the book. The outside world comprises 'every actor other than the IO itself and its members',[45] and the example of the Global Fund shows

[39] Bylaws (n 37) art 1 states: 'The Global Fund to Fight AIDS, Tuberculosis and Malaria (the "Global Fund") is a multi-stakeholder international financing institution duly formed as a non-profit foundation under the laws of Switzerland and recognized as an international organization by various national governments.'

[40] 'Agreement Between the Swiss Federal Council and the Global Fund to Fight AIDS, Tuberculosis and Malaria in View of Determining the Legal Status of the Global Fund in Switzerland' <https://www.theglobalfund.org/media/8551/core_headquarters_agreement_en.pdf> accessed 25 August 2024 (Headquarters Agreement).

[41] ibid art 1. Similarly, several countries benefiting from Global Fund activities have accorded the Fund legal personality through the 'Agreement on Privileges and Immunities of the Global Fund to Fight AIDS, Tuberculosis and Malaria (adopted 14 December 2009, entered into force 17 April 2019) 3300 UNTS <https://treaties.un.org/Pages/showDetails.aspx?objid=080000028054a080&clang=_en> accessed 25 August 2024. Note that the treaty speaks of 'juridical personality' and not of 'international legal personality'.

[42] Headquarters Agreement (n 40) arts 5, 13–16. For an early criticism of the extension of privileges and immunities to the Global Fund, see Davinia Abdul Aziz, 'Privileges and Immunities of Global Public-Private Partnerships: A Case Study of the Global Fund to Fight AIDS, Tuberculosis and Malaria' (2009) 6 International Organizations Law Review 383.

[43] Zeidan and Abboud (n 34). Similarly, David Lewis, 'The Financial Action Task Force: Coming of Age: Becoming an International Organization', Chapter 15 in this volume.

[44] Klabbers (n 27) 49.

[45] Henner Gött, 'Interactions with the Outside World as a Factor of IO Initiatives', Chapter 22 in this volume.

that such interaction can sometimes lead to the emergence of new IOs altogether. Second, PPPs such as the Global Fund broaden the spectrum of organizations under scrutiny and allow for greater variation in governance structures. When we ask whether IO change is primarily driven by the secretariat or by an IO's members, we need to consider the varying membership structures across the spectrum of IOs. In the example of the Global Fund, the Fund does not have a traditional membership and organizational structure.[46] The decision-making body is the Global Fund Board, which comprises the Board members representing the different constituencies—these are the 'members' of the Global Fund from a formalistic perspective, but again, there is no traditional membership structure. One hypothesis might be that this non-traditional 'membership' provides greater leeway for the secretariat to initiate change.

At the same time, membership influence also varies considerably in traditional IOs. While traditional IOs are based on formal sovereign equality of their member states, states can play different roles within an IO, and voting rights are not necessarily equally distributed. The best-known example is the UN Security Council, which gives a veto right to its five permanent members. This voting structure has led to change initiatives by other UN organs.[47] One could ask whether the share votes system in the World Bank Group plays a role in determining which externally induced change initiatives are pursued and which ones are not.[48] The ILO has a unique tripartite structure where the constitutive treaty requires member states to include delegates representing a state's workers and employers in addition to government representatives. Each delegate votes individually, meaning workers' and employers' representatives vote independently of government officials. At the same time, the ILO has been considered too focused on its state-based tripartite structure, and PPPs, or multi-stakeholder partnerships, have been considered as one way to enhance representation.[49]

III. What Is IO Change and Who Drives It?

This book departs from an understanding of initiatives as 'systematic actions and programmes of IGOs with clear aims and outputs . . . which in turn push the boundaries of an organization, bringing new developments to its initial

[46] Droesse (n 33) 67.

[47] Mona Ali Khalil, 'The Evolution of UN Secretary-General Initiatives to Respond to Violent and Non-Violent Threats to International Peace and Security', Chapter 14 in this volume.

[48] On externally induced change in the World Bank, see Hassane Cissé, 'How Do External Factors Shape Institutional, Legal, Strategic, or Policy Change in International Organizations', Chapter 24 in this volume.

[49] Janelle M Diller, 'International Organization Interactions with Multi-stakeholder Initiatives: The International Labour Organization Experience', Chapter 23 in this volume.

functional activities.'[50] But what lies at the root of such systematic actions? To what extent is change primarily induced by factors outside of an IO, and what role do endogenous factors play? Does it matter whether change is initiated by an IO's membership, its secretariat, or through the cooperation of both? This section reviews existing scholarship on IO change. It emphasizes that the theoretical vantage point on IOs is crucial in formulating what change signifies, under which circumstances it occurs, and which actors are crucial to inducing change. While a general theory of IO change is elusive, the chapter proposes a combination of theoretical approaches, an 'eclecticism' that generally characterizes the study of IOs today, with a particular focus on historically informed case studies.[51]

A. What is 'IO change'?

What does 'IO change' mean? Change in IOs has at least three interrelated meanings: it can refer to (a) change in the overarching aim or mandate that an IO pursues; (b) change in the activities carried out by an IO, both at the policy and/or at the operational level; and (c) change in the organizational structure of an IO. These three types of change intersect in the following way: pursuing new activities typically necessitates new or altered organizational structures; a change in the overarching aim pursued by an organization will entail new activities in line with that newly defined aim;[52] and more often than not, pursuing new activities will gradually lead to shifts in an organization's mandate, even if formal amendments of an IO's constitutive document are rare. There exists no generally accepted and unified theory of IO change, and most scholars who have worked on change in IOs explicitly highlight that aiming at such a theory is somewhat futile.[53] Rather, existing scholarship almost always focuses on specific episodes

[50] Nicola Bonucci and others, 'IGOs Initiatives as a Response to Crises and Unforeseen Needs' (2022) 19 International Organizations Law Review 423, 427.

[51] See Cogan (n 1) 547, where the notion of eclecticism is used.

[52] I am deliberately using the broad term 'aim' to signal that I am concerned with the overall direction of an IO, rather than with a more narrowly defined 'purpose' or 'mandate' that is typically contained in the constituent instrument of an IO and therefore has a legal dimension. On the constituent documents of IOs, see Niels Blokker, 'Constituent Instruments', in Jacob Katz Cogan, Ian Hurd, and Ian Johnstone (eds), *The Oxford Handbook of International Organizations* (OUP 2016).

[53] See Ernst B Haas, *When Knowledge Is Power: Three Models of Change in International Organizations* (University of California Press 1992) 6, where it is stated: 'A typology is not a theory'; see also Devesh Kapur, 'Processes of Change in International Organizations' (2000) <https://wcfia.harvard.edu/files/wcfia/files/164_helsinki3.wcfia_.pdf> accessed 25 August 2024, where it is stated: 'The purpose of this paper is not to develop a general theory of change in international institutions.' For an excellent overview of recent approaches to IO change and the role of advocacy therein, see Kseniya Oksamytna, *Advocacy and Change in International Organizations: Communication, Protection, and Reconstruction in UN Peacekeeping* (OUP 2023) ch 1. Oksamytna also emphasizes that different conceptualizations of change in IOs respond to different theoretical approaches in international relations.

of IO change to suggest a typology or some other form of limited generalization. Similarly, this chapter aims to identify some of the most common factors driving IO change from existing research, not to propose a full theory of IO change.

In his pioneering study on change in IOs, Ernst Haas distinguishes between adaptation and learning through managed interdependence. Managing interdependence means that an IO consciously engages in a process to redefine its aim. In contrast, adaptation means that an organization adapts to a changed environment without explicitly redefining its aim by adding new tasks or designing new procedures. For Haas, these different models of change in IOs are Weberian ideal types, where the normatively desirable ideal type is managed interdependence, because only by redefining an organization's aim through an ordered process can the organization coherently (re-)act to a changed environment.[54]

At the same time, ideal types do not reflect empirical reality, and most case studies of IO change will unveil some combination of these different types of change or switches from a process of adaptation to managing interdependence and vice versa. Sometimes, change might even occur accidentally. This book focuses on IO initiatives, which, by definition, are deliberate. In line with this book's approach, Kseniya Oksamytna observes that change initiatives in IOs require advocacy, both when introducing them and for their institutionalization.[55] Such advocacy can come from an IO's secretariat, from members, from external actors, or a combination of these.[56] At the same time, it is not clear that change agents have complete control over the changes they initiate. Erin Graham has suggested that international institutions more often than not experience what she calls 'subterranean change': an action that was at one point in time considered as incremental change can show itself to have transformational consequences at a later point in time, consequences that were not intended and perhaps not even foreseeable to the original change agents.[57]

Our hypotheses on how change occurs within IOs also depend to some extent on our theoretical vantage point. Rationalist approaches will typically look for the origins of change outside of the IO: IOs will change when it is in the states' interest, and states' interests depend on the global environment.[58] In this conceptualization, change is driven by the IO's membership. Contrary to this view, Barnett and Coleman have conceptualized IO change as an organization's

[54] Haas (n 53).
[55] Oksamytna (n 53).
[56] For an example for change initiated by a coalition of different actors in the field of human rights, see Nina Reiners, *Transnational Lawmaking Coalitions for Human Rights* (CUP 2021).
[57] Erin Graham, *Transforming International Institutions: How Money Quietly Sidelined Multilateralism at the United Nations* (OUP 2023).
[58] For this characterization without embracing it, see Laurence R Helfer, 'Understanding Change in International Organizations: Globalization and Innovation in the ILO' (2006) 59 Vanderbilt Law Review 649, 661–62.

strategic response to its environment. They start from the assumption that IOs are autonomous entities that pursue three main goals: further their mandate as defined by their professional training and expert knowledge, protect their autonomy, and minimize organizational insecurity. According to this view, an IO will embrace or foster change if this is the best way to pursue one or several of these goals, and it will oppose change if such change is detrimental to them.[59]

Both approaches have in common that they understand change in IOs as a reaction to an exogenous phenomenon. Change is a *response* to something that happens outside the IO. This can include novel phenomena, for example transnational terrorism, global warming, or technological advances, and related novel knowledge, for example knowledge that the consequences of global warming are likely to entail far-reaching social consequences. Change can occur suddenly, especially in response to a crisis, such as a pandemic outbreak or a financial crisis.[60] But more often, change occurs gradually and incrementally through subtle shifts in everyday tasks, internal rearrangements, resource reallocation, and similar factors, which do not lead to immediately visible changes but, over time, can significantly alter the face of an organization. This is for example the case when an IO adjusts to a newly emerged norm, as neither norm emergence nor behaviour adjustment in view of a new norm happens overnight.[61] Take the gender equality norm, which emerged as an international norm throughout the twentieth century, including through the Convention on the Elimination of All Forms of Discrimination Against Women of 1979.[62] It is today considered a cross-cutting issue that needs to be mainstreamed into all fields of activity.[63] This has also induced change within IOs: almost all IOs today have a gender strategy and debates on gender parity, often the result of decades-long evolution rather than a clearly identifiable, singular change initiative, but with a significant impact on how an IO acts.

Rationalist and social constructivist approaches also differ in locating the actor or main driver of change: whereas rationalist approaches will locate the main driver of change outside of the organization, that is, in its membership, approaches that emphasize an IO's autonomy are more likely to assume

[59] Michael Barnett and Liv Coleman, 'Designing Police: Interpol and the Study of Change in International Organizations' (2005) 49 International Studies Quarterly 593.

[60] Bonucci and others (n 50).

[61] For a classical account of the norm life cycle, see Martha Finnemore and Kathryn Sikkink, 'International Norm Dynamics and Political Change' (1998) 52 International Organization 887.

[62] Convention on the Elimination of All Forms of Discrimination Against Women (adopted 18 December 1979, entered into force 3 September 1981) 1249 UNTS 13.

[63] Such an understanding of gender equality as a cross-cutting issue is evident in, eg, Transforming Our World: The 2030 Agenda for Sustainable Development, UNGA Res 70/1 (21 October 2015) para 20, which states: 'Realizing gender equality . . . will make a crucial contribution to progress across all the Goals and targets . . . The systematic mainstreaming of a gender perspective in the implementation of the Agenda is crucial.'

that change is driven from within the organization, that is, by its secretariat. Of course, this distinction is not black and white. It is difficult to distinguish exogenous and endogenous variables in institutional analysis. As Snidal puts it, 'while institutions are a consequence of human agency and history, they are valuable precisely because they lie outside the domain of short-term choice and thereby constrain it'.[64] This holds particularly true for static international institutions, of which an IO is perhaps the prototypical example. IOs may have been created by their members, but their appeal lies precisely in the fact that they have a measure of independence from their membership.[65] As Barnett and Finnemore have emphasized, IOs '*must* be autonomous actors in some ways simply to fulfil their delegated tasks'.[66] More often than not, cooperation between the membership and the secretariat will be necessary to foster change. While members, once they join an IO, occupy various positions within an organization (such as sitting on policy and executive organs or appointing staff, including the leaders of an IO) and generally in those functions, are bound to act within the interest of the organization, they still remain distinct actors vis-à-vis the organization as a whole.

The lack of a unified theory of IO change points to the fact that there is a certain measure of historical contingency at play. This has led to an increase in historically informed accounts of IO change, a methodological and theoretical orientation that is commonly labelled 'historical institutionalism'.[67] Historical institutionalism can account for multiple sources and context-specific factors of institutional change; its biggest disadvantage is perhaps that it comes with relatively limited predictive value.[68] At the same time, historically informed accounts of IO change often show how IO change results in task expansion and, connected with this, mandate expansion. This follows both a logic of path dependency and the functionalist logic that IOs were set up to fulfil a purpose that states individually and collectively could not, and then use their expert and moral authority to expand their tasks and influence.[69] Erin Graham has suggested that historical institutionalism helps shed light on long-term, transformational change that started as incremental change but has resulted in transformational shifts, that is, change that involves reorganizing fundamental relationships and principles of governance.[70]

64 Duncan Snidal, 'The Politics of Scope: Endogenous Actors, Heterogeneity and Institutions' (1994) 6 Journal of Theoretical Politics 449, 457.

65 Kenneth W Abbott and Duncan Snidal, 'Why States Act Through Formal International Organizations' (1998) 42 Journal of Conflict Resolution 3.

66 Barnett and Finnemore (n 13) 22.

67 Helfer (n 58) 666–68.

68 ibid 668.

69 Barnett and Finnemore (n 13) 44. For a recent historically informed study on why the expansion of powers of IOs becomes viewed largely as both legal and legitimate, see Guy Fiti Sinclair, *To Reform the World: International Organizations and the Making of Modern States* (OUP 2017).

70 Graham (n 57).

B. Who or what drives IO change? IO initiatives and the respective roles of the secretariat and the members

IO initiatives need not be deliberately aimed at transformational change but often will be. Who or what is at the root of such initiatives? Bonucci, Marceau, Ouellet, and Walker define an IO initiative as one 'undertaken or implemented by the Secretariat'[71] but clarify that acceptance or rejection by an IO's memberships is an important factor in assessing the viability of any IO initiative.[72] What are 'the membership' and 'the Secretariat', and what are common factors that constrain or enable both actors to foster IO change?

As mentioned, membership in IOs traditionally consists of states and sometimes other intergovernmental organizations, with most IO members normally being states. Where membership of an IO is exclusively or majorly composed of states, domestic politics of powerful member states play an important role in a member's willingness to instigate or hinder change and can have important consequences for IOs' room of manoeuvre. One example is withholding funding for IOs, which often depends on domestic politics.[73] Another example is impending domestic elections within powerful member states, especially where the election is contested or considered high stakes. Electoral campaigns in such situations can lead to inertia in a state's international relations because the focus is elsewhere. To what extent domestic politics affect IO change depends in no small measure on each member's importance. While states enjoy formal sovereign equality in IOs, their impact varies depending on economic power and engagement with a given IO.[74]

One interesting question is whether a membership structure that comprises diverse actors and separates the organization's existence from its members results in more leeway for the secretariat. Let's take once again the example of the Global Fund. The Board is the supreme governing organ of the Global Fund but not a plenary organ in the traditional understanding. It does not consist solely of a specific type of actor (eg states) but rather of different constituencies: developing countries, donors, civil society, the private sector, and communities affected by the diseases. Board members are appointed by their respective constituencies,

[71] Bonucci and others (n 50).
[72] ibid 6 and 18–19.
[73] The United States severely cut funding for several UN agencies, including the United Nations Populations Fund, during the administration of Donald Trump; and at the time of writing was in arrears for assessed contributions for UN peacekeeping missions (assessed at 27 percent of the overall budget), because the US Congress caps contributions at 25%; see 'Funding the United Nations: How Much Does the U.S. Pay?' (*Council on Foreign Relations*, 29 February 2024) <https://www.cfr.org/article/funding-united-nations-what-impact-do-us-contributions-have-un-agencies-and-programs> accessed 25 August 2024.
[74] Eg Kapur (n 53) 18–19, identifying domestic politics as one source of change to exclusively use examples of US domestic politics.

and each constituency determines its selection process. As Fady Zeidan and Jean Abboud point out in this volume, this process and the composition of the Board reflect the principle of partnership and collaboration that animates the Fund's work (Chapter 27). At the same time, in the view of this author, the kind of power imbalance that characterizes many IO membership structures also exists at the Global Fund, in the form of donors and recipients, even if the Global Fund has put into place several procedural rules intended to counter such imbalances, in particular in terms of voting rights.[75] To what extent this translates into more impact for donors than other stakeholders would be interesting to study.

Under which conditions do IO secretariats respond proactively to change? As Barnett and Coleman point out, secretariats seek to preserve their autonomy and further their mandate. However, to do so, they need resources, which are generally allocated by the member states. An IO's response to changes in the external environment can, therefore, depend on a trade-off between resources and the organization's autonomy.[76] Put differently: change typically occurs as a response to a changed environment, but this is not a sufficient condition for change to occur. Rather, several endogenous factors must be present for change to occur successfully, including a certain measure of organizational security, resource availability, and congruence of interests and organizational culture between different actors.

In the same way that states are not monolithic blocks, and therefore, domestic politics can impact quests for change, IO secretariats are not monolithic either. Specific attention has been paid to IOs' executive heads.[77] A clearly defined leadership role in the secretariat opens ways of influencing if and when change occurs, inter alia through agenda-setting power and discretionary power in organizational matters.[78] This includes how departments and divisions within a secretariat are organized.[79] Depending on IO size and mandate, there might be conflicts within the secretariat in the form of struggles over resources or disagreement as to whether certain topics and activities should be pursued or fall outside the organization's mandate. Further opening the 'Secretariat' black box to include different actors within a bureaucracy is then needed to assess international secretariats' role in initiating change.[80]

[75] Zeidan and Abboud (n 34). For a Board decision to pass, this requires an affirmative two-thirds majority vote both from the implementer group and from the donor group.

[76] Barnett and Coleman (n 59) 595.

[77] Nina Hall and Ngaire Woods, 'Theorizing the Role of Executive Heads in International Organizations' (2018) 24 European Journal of International Relations 865.

[78] Kapur (n 53) 21.

[79] Bonucci and others (n 50) 16, highlighting that internal initiatives such as restructuring of departments or amending administrative practices are effective ways of fostering change.

[80] Nicola Bonucci, 'The Driving Role of the Heads of Intergovernmental Organizations: A Case Study Around the Organisation for Economic Cooperation and Development', Chapter 20 in this volume.

In this context, the rules governing the legal relationship between the secretariat and the membership are important. Does the constitutive document of an IO accord explicit powers to the executive head, and if so, which ones? Lastly, it is evident on the surface, but difficult to study in detail, to what extent executive leaders' personal convictions, ethics, and personality traits impact change initiatives.[81]

IV. Conclusion

What is 'IO change'? Change occurs when an IO responds to a change in its environment in such a way that its mandate and/or its operations are affected by said response. Such a change can be triggered by a once-off 'event' in the form of a crisis, a new development such as a technological advance, new global norms, or new information about the world, amongst others. An IO's response can take place at multiple levels: the IO can adjust its overall aim or mandate, it can take up new activities and tasks, and it can change its institutional structure. Often, change will likely occur at different levels at once. Sometimes, a change in the institutional structure will have immediate effects. In other cases, it might take decades until the consequences become visible. Sometimes, incremental change ushers in transformational consequences that the relevant actors did not foresee when the change was made.

Change is traditionally thought of as a deliberate response to exogenous factors. IO change will probably be considered successful if the IO is viewed as having adequately responded to the changes in its environment through some form of concerted action. Such concerted action will consider existing norms and regulations, resource allocation, and bureaucratic concerns, amongst other factors. For a response to be regarded as adequate, a certain measure of acceptance is required. This means that we ought to expect those change initiatives that garner support from both the membership and the secretariat to be the most successful.

[81] For a study of the ethics of UN Secretary-General Dag Hammarskjöld, see Manuel Fröhlich, *Political Ethics and The United Nations: Dag Hammarskjöld as Secretary-General* (Routledge 2010).

2
IO Initiatives, Ideology, and the Imaginaries of Liberal Reform

Guy Fiti Sinclair

I. Introduction

What role do ideas, assumptions, and cognitive framings play in motivating and guiding the initiatives taken by the executive heads and secretariats of international organizations (IOs) to extend their mandates beyond initial understandings and expectations? Is it possible to identify any common or shared rationalities, narratives, or structures of legitimation for 'IO initiatives', as defined in the Preface?[1] And how do these ideational elements connect with the various other factors explored in this volume? What is their relationship to legal doctrines and theories, on the one hand,[2] and the enormous diversity of practices observed in innumerable IOs, on the other?

This chapter argues that answering these questions requires us to consider the dynamics and imaginaries that give meaning to everyday practices of reform in IOs. The chapter begins by arguing that IO initiatives cannot be explained or understood through a simple ideology of 'functionalism'. It then identifies a dynamic of liberal reform that helps to make sense of many, if not all, of the IO initiatives explored in this volume. Finally, it proposes the conceptual category, and examines two specific examples, of 'socio-legal imaginaries' which embody elements of the dynamic of liberal reform and which have been widely used to explain and legitimize IO initiatives.

[1] Gabrielle Marceau and Henner Gött, 'Preface' in this volume. I have previously examined how the legal powers of IOs have expanded through processes of discourse, practice, and (re)interpretation, rather than by formally amending their constituent instruments, which I defined as 'IO expansion'. Many instances of 'IO expansion' originate in 'IO initiatives', as defined in this volume, though I also attempted to show how 'IO expansion' drew on and integrated projects of reform led by a wider variety of state and non-state actors. See generally Guy Fiti Sinclair, *To Reform the World: International Organizations and the Making of Modern States* (OUP 2017).

[2] Fernando Lusa Bordin, 'Interpreting Constituent Instruments to Justify the Evolving Powers of International Organizations', Chapter 5 in this volume; Christiane Ahlborn, 'From Functionalism to Constitutionalism: Translating Theories on IO Powers into Practice', Chapter 3 in this volume.

Guy Fiti Sinclair, *IO Initiatives, Ideology, and the Imaginaries of Liberal Reform* In: *International Organization Initiatives*.
Edited by: Gabrielle Marceau and Henner Gött, Oxford University Press.
DOI: 10.1093/9780197803325.003.0003

II. Forget 'Functionalism'!

One response to the questions with which this chapter began might start with something called 'functionalism', which has been described as the dominant 'theory' or 'ideology' of the law of international organizations (IOs law).[3] As an 'ideal type' reconstructed from many sources, if never fully realized in any particular IO, 'functionalism' in this sense posits that IOs are created by states to carry out specific tasks or functions, generally understood to serve their common needs.[4] This is a principal–agent theory, focusing exclusively on the relationship between IOs and their member states and embedding an assumption that IOs are neutral, apolitical, and presumptively good.

Understood in these broad terms, however, the ideology of 'functionalism' does not offer much by way of descriptive or explanatory insight into IO initiatives.[5] It does not help to explain, for example, what *kinds* of novel activities the executive head and secretariat of an IO might lead in any particular circumstances. Perhaps the most it would suggest is that any such change would likely be motivated by the goal of fulfilling the IO's overall functions or purposes—though it says nothing about how or in what direction these might evolve—and would need to be authorized by express or implied delegations of power from its members. Indeed, recent scholarship seeking to excavate the theoretical foundations of IOs law has revealed what would be better described as a variety of 'functionalisms', in the plural, rather than a 'single body of thought'.[6] While this might be interpreted as evidence of 'functionalism's' ideological strength—its relatively few, theoretically thin components permitting multiple reworkings in diverse configurations, making it difficult to challenge or dismantle—it simultaneously makes this conception of 'functionalism' much less useful for gaining insight into IO initiatives.

The chapters in this volume give us some sense of what the posited definition of 'functionalism' cannot describe or explain in IO initiatives. First, IOs

[3] Jan Klabbers, 'The EJIL Foreword: The Transformation of International Organizations Law' (2015) 26 European Journal of International Law 9; Jan Klabbers, 'What Role for International Organizations in the Promotion of Community Interests? Reflections on the Ideology of Functionalism' in Eyal Benvenisti and Georg Nolte (eds), *Community Interests Across International Law* (OUP 2018). See also Hannah Birkenkötter, 'Change in International Organizations', Chapter 1 in this volume. The law of international organizations (IOs law) is assumed here to be synonymous with international organizations law or international institutional law.

[4] Klabbers, 'What Role' (n 3) 98.

[5] Guy Fiti Sinclair, 'The Original Sin (and Salvation) of Functionalism' (2015) 26 European Journal of International Law 965.

[6] Klabbers, 'What Role' (n 3) 97. See generally Jan Klabbers and Guy Fiti Sinclair (eds), 'Symposium: Theorizing International Organizations Law' (2020) 31 European Journal of International Law 489; Devika Hovell, Jan Klabbers, and Guy Fiti Sinclair (eds), 'Year-Long Symposium: Re-Theorizing International Organizations Law: Reconsiderations, Hidden Gems, and New Perspectives' (2023) 34 European Journal of International Law 899.

interact—and *change* in interacting—with other IOs and a wide variety of non-state actors, informal IOs, non-governmental organizations (NGOs), public–private partnerships, networks, markets, and so on.[7] A narrow focus on the principal–agent relationship between IOs and their members accordingly excludes much of the complex, interacting ecology of global governance today, not to mention the 'tripartite' relationships underpinning one of the oldest 'functional' IOs, the International Labour Organization (ILO).[8] Second, for the same reason, 'functionalism' in this IOs law sense does not have anything to say about the role of executive heads or the secretariats of IOs more broadly in leading IO initiatives.[9] Third, the core tenets of functionalism do not really capture how different modes of authority, beyond delegation, work together to frame and legitimize change in IOs. These include appeals to moral authority, including the purposes of IOs; the invocation of norms and concepts that run deep in legal culture, beyond simply rules; and the different forms of expertise that IOs draw on, channel, and apply.[10]

In short, the purported ideology of IO 'functionalism' seems much too thin to say anything meaningful about the diverse sources and dynamics of IO initiatives. It certainly doesn't reflect much of the *texture* of the self-understandings or justifications of IO initiatives that we see in practice, including appeals to 'constitutionalism', which is often taken to be a polar opposite to 'functionalism'.[11] The next part of this chapter suggests an alternative framing which might afford greater descriptive and explanatory purchase on IO initiatives.

[7] Fady Zeidan and Jean Abboud, 'The Global Fund to Fight AIDS, Tuberculosis, and Malaria: Partnerships, Collaborations, and Initiatives with International Organizations', Chapter 27 in this volume; Henner Gött, 'Interactions with the Outside World as a Factor for IO Initiatives', Chapter 22 in this volume; Charles Di Leva, 'The World Bank Bank's Evolution Towards Environmental and Social Responsibilities', Chapter 8 in this volume; Hassane Cissé, 'How Do External Factors Shape Institutional, Legal, Strategic, or Policy Change in International Organizations: Review of Selected Examples in World Bank Practice', Chapter 24 in this volume.

[8] Janelle M Diller, 'International Organization Interactions with Multi-stakeholder Initiatives: The International Labour Organization Experience', Chapter 23 in this volume.

[9] IOs functionalism thus differs significantly from the 'functionalism' or 'neo-functionalism' of international relations theory, which does indeed give a central place to the agency of international civil servants and bureaucracies. See, eg, Ernst Haas, *Beyond the Nation State: Functionalism and International Organization* (Stanford UP 1964).

[10] Guy Fiti Sinclair, 'The International Civil Servant in Theory and Practice: Law, Morality, and Expertise' (2015) 26 European Journal of International Law 747. For alternative typologies of authority in IOs, see Michael Barnett and Martha Finnemore, *Rules for World: International Organizations in Global Politics* (Cornell UP 2004); Deborah D Avant, Martha Finnemore, and Susan K Sell (eds), *Who Governs the Globe?* (CUP 2010). On expertise in IOs, see Margherita Melillo, 'IO Secretariats as Knowledge Actors', Chapter 6 in this volume; Jens Steffek, *International Organization as Technocratic Utopia* (OUP 2021).

[11] Ahlborn (n 2); cf Klabbers, 'Transformation' (n 3).

III. A Dynamic of Liberal Reform

A second set of responses to this chapter's opening questions might take a different tack in describing the great variety of ideational elements embodied in different IO initiatives, rather than attempting to reduce them to a single ideology. The multiple ideologies motivating quintessential examples of IO initiatives, such as 'Uniting for Peace' and United Nations (UN) peacekeeping, have thus been described (and denounced) in terms coloured by the conflicting worldviews of the Cold War.[12] Similarly, the complex legitimating ideas underpinning (and opposing) the New International Economic Order—a set of IO initiatives pursued by, among others, the executive head and secretariat of the UN Conference on Trade and Development—have been cogently analysed in terms of competing and partially overlapping 'opinion clusters'.[13] A burgeoning literature on neoliberalism in IOs has further examined the role of these and related ideas, and resistance to them, in the expanding range of activities undertaken by the General Agreement on Tariffs and Trade (GATT) and the World Trade Organization (WTO),[14] the World Bank and other development banks,[15] the Organisation for Economic Co-operation and Development (OECD),[16] the International Monetary Fund (IMF),[17] and the World Health Organization (WHO).[18]

What set of ideas could possibly unite the heterogeneous IO initiatives in all these organizations, arising in very different eras and under the influence of such disparate bodies of thought? Rather than a single ideology, I suggest that IO initiatives can be better understood as profoundly interconnected with cultural processes of state formation through a dynamic of liberal reform that continually defines and redefines what it means for a state to be 'modern'.[19] The

[12] Guy Fiti Sinclair, 'International Organisations During the Cold War: Reconsidering Institutional Rivalries', in Matt Craven, Sundhya Pahuja, and Gerry Simpson (eds), *Cambridge History of International Law, Volume XI: International Law During the Cold War (1945–1990)* (forthcoming, CUP 2025). On the 'Uniting for Peace' resolution, also see Mona Ali Khalil, 'The Evolution of UN Secretary-General Initiatives to Respond to Violent and Non-Violent Threats to International Peace and Security', Chapter 14 in this volume.

[13] Robert W Cox, 'Ideologies and the New International Economic Order: Reflections on Some Recent Literature' (1979) 33 International Organization 257; Craig Murphy, *Emergence of NIEO Ideology* (Westview Press 1984). See also Christopher RW Dietrich, *Oil Revolution: Anticolonial Elites, Sovereign Rights, and the Economic Culture of Decolonization* (CUP 2017).

[14] Kristen Hopewell, *Breaking the WTO: How Emerging Powers Disrupted the Neoliberal Project* (Stanford UP 2016); Quinn Slobodian, *Globalists: The End of Empire and the Birth of Neoliberalism* (Harvard UP 2018).

[15] Sinclair (n 1) ch 6; Sarah Babb, *Behind the Development Banks: Washington Politics, World Poverty, and the Wealth of Nations* (University of Chicago Press 2009).

[16] Matthias Schmelzer, *The Hegemony of Growth: The OECD and the Making of the Economic Growth Paradigm* (CUP 2016).

[17] Jeffrey M Chwieroth, *Capital Ideas: The IMF and the Rise of Financial Liberalization* (Princeton UP 2010); Richard Peet, *Unholy Trinity: The IMF, World Bank and WTO* (Zed Books 2009).

[18] Nitsan Chorev, *The World Health Organization Between North and South* (Cornell UP 2012).

[19] Guy Fiti Sinclair, 'State Formation, Liberal Reform, and the Growth of International Organizations' (2015) 26 European Journal of International Law 445.

argument here is not that IO initiatives and state reform are analogous, but rather that they are deeply imbricated processes that share a common dynamic. Thus, IO initiatives that may appear very different on their face—indeed, that may seem to push in contrary directions—are explicable as manifestations of the same dynamic of liberal reform that drives modern state formation on a broadly Western model.

It is worth pausing to describe this dynamic in general terms before illustrating its operations in IO initiatives more concretely. As a critical ethos and practice that defines modern state rule, liberalism is constantly concerned with the problem of 'governing too much'.[20] Taking individual freedom as the principle and limit of governmental action, liberalism posits a number of domains of liberty—including civil society, the market, economy, and family—which are subject to their own 'natural' laws and dynamics and with which the state should interfere to the least extent possible.[21] Paradoxically, however, liberalism also endorses and legitimizes numerous interventions at the level of both society and the individual. Accordingly, certain 'social' mechanisms—such as health insurance schemes, old age pensions, public health, and hygiene programmes—are seen as necessary to guarantee and support individual freedom and security in the face of a whole range of risks inherent in modern life. Moreover, freedom itself can only be exercised by individuals who have acquired the capacities for autonomous action and self-mastery; where such capacities are lacking, they must be instilled through the application of appropriate disciplinary techniques, even to the point of requiring interventions that would otherwise be considered despotic or authoritarian.[22] Together, these contradictory pulls produce the endlessly recursive, reiterative dynamic of liberal reform.

This dynamic may be seen in the IO initiatives examined in this volume. Consider, for example, economic IOs such as the World Bank, the GATT/WTO, the IMF, and the OECD, whose founding and earliest activities—not to mention many of whose subsequent initiatives—were motivated by the goals of promoting capitalist models of political economy, reducing state interference in markets, and to that end disciplining governments and domestic political actors.[23] Yet, several chapters in this volume reveal how a rising consciousness of the risks associated with unchecked market liberalization, privatization, and deregulation has also impelled IOs such as these to pursue initiatives intended to support individual freedom through a range of interventions in the social and

[20] Michel Foucault, *Security, Territory, Population* (Graham Burchell tr, Macmillan 2007) 385.

[21] Nikolas Rose, *Powers of Freedom: Reframing Political Thought* (CUP 1999); Peter Miller and Nikolas Rose, *Governing the Present: Administering Economic, Social and Personal Life* (Polity 2008).

[22] Mariana Valverde, '"Despotism" and Ethical Liberal Governance' (1996) 25 Economy and Society 3.

[23] See, eg, Quinn Slobodian (n 14); Sinclair (n 1); Babb (n 15); Schmelzer (n 16); Chwieroth (n 17); Peet (n 17).

environmental spheres. Thus, the chapters by Di Leva and Cisse both show how, even though the World Bank's Articles of Agreement make no mention of environmental purposes, that IO has nevertheless responded to criticisms of its projects and lending practices to establish new policies and institutions, and to become deeply invested in activities associated with climate change and biological diversity.[24] Similarly, the chapter by Liu and Kwak reveals that the IMF, notwithstanding its rather narrow mandate focused on balances of payments, has become engaged in efforts to address social and environmental issues such as climate change, pandemic preparedness, and the global food crisis.[25]

Conversely, initiatives undertaken by the ILO, the WHO, and other relatively more socially oriented IOs have long aimed to buttress the 'social' dimensions of freedom through the expansion of state functions and services, indeed by constructing welfare states.[26] These governmental interventions, too, have entailed mechanisms that work to construct, responsibilize, and discipline individual subjectivities and actions. However, the push–pull dynamic of liberal reform has meant that even these IOs have *also* been drawn into advancing reforms that have the effect of constraining state power, introducing market mechanisms, and enhancing the role of civil society actors. The chapter by Solomon and Piercy, for example, shows how the WHO responded to the COVID-19 pandemic by adopting a 'town hall' approach to consultation with relevant stakeholders 'outside' the WHO, including private sector actors and NGOs.[27] The chapters by Zeidan and Abboud and by Madir likewise highlight how hybrid public–private organizations, such as the Global Fund and Gavi, bring socially oriented IOs into a complex array of partnerships and other forms of continuous interaction with civil society, private foundations, and corporations.[28] These relations serve to legitimize the role of private actors in global governance and impel socially oriented IOs to accommodate the mechanisms and logic of neoliberal capitalism.[29]

The heterogeneity of IO initiatives—and their social legitimacy—thus derives from the diverse ways they are seen to connect with and support projects of liberal reform. Law, technical expertise of various kinds, and visions of moral improvement all play important roles in articulating and enacting new technologies of liberal government, implemented in the initiatives of IOs and

[24] Di Leva (n 7); Cisse (n 7).
[25] Yan Liu and Kyung Kwak, 'IMF's Responses to New Challenges in the Global Economy: Recent Reforms of Its Financing Toolkit', Chapter 25 in this volume.
[26] Guy Fiti Sinclair, 'A "Civilizing Task": The ILO, International Social Reform, and the Genealogy of Development' (2018) 20 Journal of the History of International Law 145; Chorev (n 18).
[27] Steven A Solomon and Kenneth Piercy, 'Interactions with the "Outside World" and the Work of the World Health Organization in Revising the Global Health Architecture for Pandemic Prevention, Preparedness, and Response', Chapter 26 in this volume.
[28] Zeidan and Abboud (n 7).
[29] Chorev (n 18).

state bureaucracies alike. To be clear, this is not just another version of the 'functionalist' claim that IOs are created and have evolved to meet state needs. Rather, it is an interpretive claim about the web of meanings—the background assumptions, beliefs, and discourses—that are embodied in, and make sense of, institutional practices. To describe those practices and meanings is not to endorse them; instead, it is to seek a fuller understanding of the motivations, and thereby a better explanation, of IO initiatives.[30]

IV. Socio-legal Imaginaries of IO Initiatives

Law is integral to all these IO initiatives, both in how they are formally authorized and legitimated and in the means by which they are implemented. But it is also important to recognize that law's operations are made effective in each case in connection with moral purposes (liberty, social reform, peace, welfare, etc) and a variety of expert vocabularies (economics, public health, diplomacy, public administration, etc). It is therefore necessary to adopt a socio-legal lens that seeks to analyse how these three modes of practice are enacted and connected, how they intersect and interact, in each IO initiative. In the remainder of this chapter, I argue that one useful way to approach such analysis is to consider the socio-legal *imaginaries* that embody the dynamic of legal reform outlined above and through which participants in IO initiatives implicitly understand and legitimize those processes.

Drawing on the work of the philosopher Charles Taylor, I propose to think of 'imaginaries' as the complex 'common understandings', which make IO initiatives possible in 'common practices and a widely shared sense of legitimacy'.[31] Two points should be emphasized here. The first is that imaginaries operate in the symbolic realm: they are expressed in shared narratives, legends, images, metaphors, and analogies. Imaginaries of this kind thereby 'structure what we perceive, how we get around in the world, and how we relate to other people'.[32] The second point is that this symbolic realm of imaginaries occupies a 'fluid middle ground between embodied practices and explicit doctrines'; I take the latter to include both legal doctrines and articulated theories.[33] So the socio-legal imaginaries of IO initiatives can be analysed in two ways: first, by considering the theories, doctrines, and rationalities by which international lawyers

[30] Mark Bevir and Roderick AW Rhodes, 'Defending Interpretation' (2006) 5 European Political Science 69.

[31] Charles Taylor, 'Modern Social Imaginaries' (2002) 14 Public Culture 91, 106.

[32] George Lakoff and Mark Johnson, *Metaphors We Live By* (University of Chicago Press 2003) 3.

[33] Dilip Parameshwar Gaonkar, 'Toward New Imaginaries: An Introduction' (2002) 14 Public Culture 1, 11.

and international civil servants seek to justify IO initiatives; and second, by examining the practices or technologies within which IO initiatives take shape materially.

Let me then outline two such socio-legal imaginaries, which I think give us better access to understanding the ideas, assumptions, and cognitive framings underpinning IO initiatives.

The first is the metaphor of the 'living constitution'. This has a long lineage in IOs, drawing upon traditions of thought about 'living constitutions' and 'constitutional growth' in domestic legal systems. It can be found, for example, in Albert Thomas' descriptions of the ILO as a 'really living' institution and his comparison of the ILO's expected evolution to transformations in the constitution of France.[34] In the merging of moral purposes (social reform) and legal authority with the possibility of adaptation to crises and changing needs, the image of a 'living constitution' helped to explain and legitimize a wide range of institutional innovations in the ILO. These included, cumulatively, the growth of the International Labour Office and construction of a network of branch offices and national correspondents; missions and inquiries; opinions on the interpretation of conventions and recommendations; the provision of technical assistance; and practices of national and international economic planning.[35] The 'living constitution' imaginary also informed a liberal, progressive, and purposive hermeneutics of the ILO's constituent instrument and a broad view of its competences, both within the International Labour Office and in the jurisprudence of the Permanent Court of International Justice.[36] Later IO innovations in the UN, including 'Uniting for Peace' and peacekeeping, likewise came to be understood as expressions of the UN Charter's nature as a 'living instrument', 'living organism', or 'living constitution', and were linked with ideas of 'de facto amendment' and the emerging doctrine of implied powers.[37]

The same imaginary animates, sometimes explicitly but more often implicitly, several of the IO initiatives examined in this volume. Lewis' initiatives as head of the Financial Action Task Force, which he describes as 'intended to transform the organisation from a caterpillar to a butterfly'—including by reviewing its legal status, strengthening its leadership, developing its governance structure, seeking greater recognition and participation, and formalizing its mandate—are strikingly similar in substance and imagination to those undertaken by Thomas in the ILO a century earlier.[38] Blokker's contribution describes the 'legal

[34] Albert Thomas, *International Social Policy* (ILO 1948) 7–8; Albert Thomas, 'The International Labour Organisation: Its Origins, Development, and Future' (1921) 1 International Labour Review 5, 7–8.

[35] Sinclair (n 1) chs 1 and 2.

[36] ibid ch 1.

[37] ibid ch 3. On implied powers, see Bordin (n 2).

[38] David Lewis, 'The Financial Action Task Force: Coming of Age: Becoming an International Organization', Chapter 15 in this volume.

framework' for the 'evolution of powers and activities' of IOs, bearing in mind that 'unlike its legal framework, an international organization's life cannot be pre-agreed'.[39] Bordin's chapter analyses the case law of the International Court of Justice, identifying concepts of implied powers and institutional practice that enable IO initiatives, and concludes: 'The picture that emerges is one of a purposive, dynamic approach to interpretation which regards IOs as living institutions that must be equipped to perform their functions effectively over time.'[40] Birkenkötter underscores the continuing attraction of the 'constitutional' metaphor in thinking about IO initiatives.[41]

The second socio-legal imaginary I want to highlight is captured in the idea of 'international administration'. This, too, can also be traced back at least as far as the early inter-war period. Invoking an analogy to the emerging national government bureaucracies of the time, 'international administration' carried with it connotations of professionalization and expert authority.[42] IO initiatives have often been rationalized and justified through a more or less self-consciously administrative mode, drawing on and transplanting the image of national civil services (and servants) to the international realm. One of the most effective deployments of the 'international administration' imaginary was by Dag Hammarskjöld, the second UN Secretary-General, who explicitly linked constitutional growth in the UN—particularly in the proliferation of specialized agencies and other entities, with the attendant 'risk of disintegration of the international framework'—to the need for greater integration in the activities of the UN and other IOs.[43] Hammarskjöld's solution to this problem was to launch a further series of initiatives, engaging the exercise of novel forms of international executive authority by the UN Secretary-General when faced with crises or emergencies, such as those in the Suez and the Congo.[44]

Perhaps because this volume focuses on IO initiatives led by secretariats and their executive heads, elements of the 'international administration' imaginary are present in many of the chapters. Burci and Balcazar-Moreno emphasize the 'epistemic authority' of the WHO secretariat,[45] while Melillo argues that IO

[39] Niels Blokker, 'The Evolution of IO Powers and Activities: A Legal Framework', Chapter 4 in this volume.
[40] Bordin (n 2).
[41] Birkenkötter (n 3).
[42] See, eg, Francis Bowes Sayre, *Experiments in International Administration* (Harper & Brothers 1919); Cecil Delisle Burns, 'International Administration' (1926) 7 British Yearbook of International Law 54; Norman L Hill, *International Administration* (McGraw-Hill 1931).
[43] Dag Hammarskjöld, 'The Development of a Constitutional Framework for International Cooperation' in Andrew W Cordier and Wilder Foote (eds), *Public Papers of the Secretaries-General of the United Nations, vol IV* (Columbia UP 1974) 583, 590.
[44] See generally Sinclair (n 1) ch 4.
[45] Gian Luca Burci and Ana Balcazar-Moreno, 'WHO's Reactions to COVID-19: Between Politics and Managerialism', Chapter 9 in this volume.

secretariats draw on expertise as the basis of their authority and use it 'in various ways to de-politicize their actions'.[46] Liu and Kwak depict the IMF's management as 'initiating nimble and innovative responses' to global crises.[47] Marceau and Venkataraman presents a narrative of successive Directors-General of the WTO exercising 'creativity and innovation in undertaking initiatives' in responding to a similar set of crises.[48] Bonucci depicts the OECD's Secretary-General, Ángel Gurría, as taking bold action in response to the Global Financial Crisis and then bravely defending the prerogatives of his office and organization against the 'wrath' of member states.[49] Finally, Maupain lauds Wilfred Jenks' 'analytical and practical capacity to build institutional bridges towards the future' and 'true sense of purpose', while describing his impartiality and self-sacrifice in taking actions that would 'safeguard the rule of law and the future of the ILO' and 'leave to the younger generations a strong organization for the future'.[50]

These two imaginaries—of the 'living constitution' and 'international administration'—have proved highly adaptable to different circumstances and epochs, often in tandem, in advancing diverse projects of liberal reform. Both had close affinities to the rise of administrative states and welfare states in the early and mid-twentieth century, in the context of crises such as the Great Depression and the two World Wars. In the post-war period of decolonization, both imaginaries aligned well with the modernization narrative, which legitimized IOs' expanding activities in newly independent states. Both thereby seemed intuitively to offer solutions to the changing needs of different times, extending into the eras of globalization and global governance, the Washington Consensus and beyond. Reflecting on over four decades of IO initiatives in the World Bank, Ibrahim Shihata once again compared the charters of IOs to the constitutions of states, both of them being adaptable through processes of 'evolution of consistent practice in new directions, supported by creative interpretation of the text'.[51] At the same time, Shihata acknowledged the leadership of the Bank's executive heads, from Robert McNamara to James Wolfensohn, on its evolution.[52]

Both imaginaries should be treated with caution. A powerful articulator of the 'living constitution' imaginary, Hammarskjöld himself has been seen by many as the ideal embodiment of international administration, merging personal

[46] Melillo (n 10).
[47] Liu and Kwak (n 25).
[48] Akshaya Venkataraman, 'Taking Initiatives in the WTO: The Role of an Executive Head in Steering Change', Chapter 18 in this volume.
[49] Nicola Bonucci, 'The Driving Role of the Heads of International Organizations: A Case Study Around the Organisation for Economic Co-operation and Development', Chapter 20 in this volume.
[50] Francis Maupain, 'Is Too Much Vision a Handicap for an Executive Head? Some Thoughts on W Jenks' Curtailed Mandate as ILO Director-General', Chapter 17 in this volume.
[51] Ibrahim FI Shihata, 'The Dynamic Evolution of International Organizations: The Case of the World Bank' (2000) 2 Journal of the History of International Law 217, 217.
[52] ibid 228.

virtue, administrative expertise, and legal authority in a way that has proved enduringly attractive.[53] Yet his example offers several object lessons on the dangers and dark sides of IO initiatives. In combination, the 'living constitution' and 'international administration' imaginaries are easily mustered to legitimize the exercise of emergency powers, pushing the boundaries or suspending the operation of law, as Hammarskjöld appears to have countenanced and approved in the Congo. The image of the international civil servant as self-disciplined, neutral, and morally responsible—as depicted in Hammarskjöld's Oxford address on 'The International Civil Servant in Law and in Fact'[54]—can incline sympathetic observers to draw a contrast with national political actors, as when UN officials described Congolese leaders in racialized terms as corrupt, irrational, lazy, and inept.[55] To facilitate the growth of a 'living constitution' is not an automatic moral good: everything will depend on what is made of that life.

V. Conclusion

Socio-legal imaginaries of IO initiatives continue to appear in new forms and under new labels. The 'living constitution' metaphor has re-emerged in theories of global constitutionalism and the constitutionalization of international law,[56] while the image of 'international administration' lies at the heart of concepts such as 'global administrative law', 'global experimental governance', 'global government networks', 'orchestration' by IOs, and more.[57] In different ways, all of these imaginaries embody and express the dynamic of liberal reform that drives and legitimizes IO initiatives. Of course, these are not the only imaginaries of IO initiatives one could analyse; they might not even be the most important ones today. As recent scholarship has suggested, 'new ways of seeing like a state' that have recently emerged entail the use of novel technologies of liberal government, such as prototypes, algorithmic regulation, digital (and other) infrastructures,

[53] Sinclair (n 10).

[54] Hammarskjöld, 'The International Civil Servant in Law and in Fact' in Wilder Foote (ed), *Servant of Peace: A Selection of Speeches and Statements of Dag Hammarskjöld* (Harper & Row 1962) 329.

[55] Kevin C Dunn, *Imagining the Congo* (Palgrave Macmillan 2003) 83–97; Sinclair (n 1) 186–87.

[56] Jan Klabbers, Anne Peters, and Geir Ulfstein, *The Constitutionalization of International Law* (OUP 2009); Anne Peters, 'The Merits of Global Constitutionalism' (2009) 16 Indiana Journal of Global Legal Studies 397.

[57] Nico Krisch and Benedict Kingsbury, 'Introduction: Global Governance and Global Administrative Law in the International Legal Order' (2006) 17 European Journal of International Law 1; Gráinne de Búrca, Robert O Keohane, and Charles Sabel, 'Global Experimentalist Governance' (2014) 44 British Journal of Political Science 477; Anne-Marie Slaughter, *A New World Order* (Princeton UP 2005); Kenneth W Abbott and Duncan Snidal, 'International Regulation Without International Government: Improving IO performance Through Orchestration' (2010) 5 Review of International Organizations 315.

and risk management.[58] Consider, for example, the complex technologies assembled in areas of practice as disparate as border security[59] or forecasting the effects of climate change on sea levels.[60] As each of these is adapted and applied in new IO initiatives, my suggestion is that a productive line of inquiry will be to investigate the socio-legal imaginaries they enable and enact.

I would like to close, then, by suggesting that we need to be more attentive to the stories we tell ourselves, the metaphors we live by,[61] and the assumptions and teleologies we internalize in thinking about and enacting change in IOs. In doing so, the executive heads of IOs, their secretariat staff, and international lawyers working in the field might do well to ask themselves the following questions: What work do our imaginaries do in legitimizing IO initiatives? How do they relate to our explicit theories, legal doctrines, and practices of change in IOs? Do they offer a comforting narrative of progress—the forward 'march of institutions'—that continues despite, or perhaps because of and through, the crises that punctuate it? Do they naturalize and reinforce existing regimes of moral, expert, and legal authority, which entrench inequalities and injustices? Do they encourage us to act as if our moral ends justify our technocratic means? Or could we revisit our imaginaries—*reimagine* them—so as to open up new pathways for transformation in IOs that lead in different and more emancipatory directions?

[58] Fleur Johns, 'From Planning to Prototypes: New Ways of Seeing Like a State' (2019) 82 Modern Law Review 833–63; Fleur Johns and Caroline Compton, 'Data Jurisdictions and Rival Regimes of Algorithmic Regulation' (2022) 16 Regulation & Governance 63; Benedict Kingsbury, 'Infrastructure and InfraReg: On Rousing the International Law "Wizards of Is"' (2019) 8 Cambridge International Law Journal 171; Dimitri Van Den Meerssche, 'Deformalizing International Organizations Law: The Risk Appetite of Anne-Marie Leroy' (2023) 34 European Journal of International Law 141.

[59] Dimitri Van Den Meerssche, 'Virtual Borders: International Law and the Elusive Inequalities of Algorithmic Association' (2023) 33 European Journal of International Law 171.

[60] Pacific Islands Regional Climate Assessment, 'Sea Level Forecasts for Pacific Islands' <https://pacificislandsclimate.wordpress.com/2016/07/02/sea-level-forecasts-for-pacific-islands/> accessed 26 September 2024.

[61] Lakoff and Johnson (n 32).

3

From Functionalism to Constitutionalism

Translating Theories on IO Powers into Practice

Christiane Ahlborn

I. Introduction

The law of international organizations (IOs) is a discipline shaped by practitioners. The discipline was born in the 1950s and 1960s, with the first textbooks being written by Bowett, Seidl-Hohenveldern, and Schermers in the 1960s and 1970s.[1] Those textbooks were mainly based on the practice of IOs, comparing different organizations in terms of their technical nature, membership, and scope of activities. Given the diversity of IOs, it has been challenging to identify common legal principles that apply to all of them in their various shapes and sizes. Schermers' and Blokker's 'International Institutional Law', which has grown considerably in size and detail since the first edition, highlights this tension between 'unity' and 'diversity' in the law of IOs particularly well.[2] Finn Seyersted, who was a domestic and international civil servant before becoming an academic, made a remarkable attempt to develop a *Common Law of International Organizations*;[3] however, his work was not widely appreciated.[4] In general, the rise of IOs has seen very little conceptualization until recently.

The current trend towards theorizing IOs has been driven by their increasing exercise of significant powers coupled with their changing structures, which seems to lack a proper theoretical foundation in the law of IOs. José Alvarez captured this phenomenon by characterizing *International Organizations as*

[1] For a 'very brief history', see Jan Klabbers, 'Theorizing International Organizations' in Anne Orford and Florian Hoffmann (eds), *The Oxford Handbook of the Theory of International Law* (OUP 2016) 618, 621. For the first editions of the relevant textbooks, see Derek W Bowett, *The Law of International Institutions* (Stevens & Sons 1963); Ignaz Seidl-Hohenveldern, *Das Recht der internationalen Organisationen einschliesslich der supranationalen Gemeinschaften* (Heymann 1967); and Henry G Schermers, *International Institutional Law* (Sijthoff 1972).

[2] Henry G Schermers and Niels Blokker, *International Institutional Law: Unity Within Diversity* (6th rev edn, Brill Nijhoff 2018).

[3] Finn Seyersted, *Common Law of International Organizations* (Brill Nijhoff 2008).

[4] Fernando Lusa Bordin, 'The Quest for International Legal Status: On Finn Seyersted and the Challenges of Theorizing International Organizations Law' (2023) 34(1) European Journal of International Law 169–94.

Christiane Ahlborn, *From Functionalism to Constitutionalism* In: *International Organization Initiatives*. Edited by: Gabrielle Marceau and Henner Gött, Oxford University Press. © Oxford University Press 2025.
DOI: 10.1093/9780197803325.003.0004

Law-Makers based on their complex roles in developing international law.[5] The Project on the Exercise of Public Authority by International Institutions set out to scrutinize the exercise of unilateral powers by international institutions.[6] And Global Administrative Law (GAL) was launched to explore their increasing use of administrative-type mechanisms, such as those related to transparency, participation, accountability, and review.[7] Both the Project on the Exercise of Public Authority and GAL consider the growing diversity of 'international institutions', which is a concept that is broader than 'international organizations'.[8] International institutions may comprise actors other than states, for instance, in the form of public–private partnerships such as the Global Fund to Fight AIDS, Tuberculosis and Malaria (the Global Fund) or Gavi, the Vaccine Alliance (Gavi).[9] The trend towards theorizing IOs has also picked up among traditional international institutional lawyers, such as Klabbers, who have taken issue with the 'leading' legal approach to IOs, namely functionalism.[10]

Although the evolution of the law of IOs has been practice-driven, these theoretical debates are mostly foreign to practising IO lawyers. Apart from judges serving on apex courts of IOs,[11] practitioners generally do not use theories to justify new IO initiatives. This is evidently not because the staff in IO secretariats or in other parts of the IO are not frequently faced with tough decisions on whether a certain course of action lies within the IO's mandate. As this book highlights, situations in which IO secretariats have to find a legal basis for the exercise of their powers are aplenty.[12] Scholars typically discuss prominent examples such as the inclusion of peacekeeping into the United Nations (UN) activities, the creation of the World Bank's Inspection Panel, or the European Union's (EU)

[5] José E Alvarez, *International Organizations as Law-Makers* (OUP 2005).

[6] Armin von Bogdandy, Philipp Dann, and Matthias Goldmann, 'Developing the Publicness of Public International Law: Towards a Legal Framework for Global Governance Activities' (2008) 9 German Law Journal 1375.

[7] Benedict Kingsbury, Nico Krisch, and Richard B Stewart, 'The Emergence of Global Administrative Law' (2005) 68(3) Law & Contemporary Problems 15.

[8] See Jan Klabbers, 'The Paradox of International Institutional Law' (2008) 5 International Organizations Law Review 151, 154.

[9] Fady Zeidan and Jean Abboud, 'The Global Fund to Fight AIDS, Tuberculosis, and Malaria: Partnerships, Collaborations, and Initiatives with International Organizations', Chapter 27 in this volume; Jelena Madir, 'IOs' Initiatives: Gavi, the Vaccine Alliance', Chapter 28 in this volume.

[10] Jan Klabbers, 'The EJIL Foreword: The Transformation of International Organizations Law' (2015) 26(1) European Journal of International Law 9, 9. But see Guy Fiti Sinclair, 'The Original Sin (and Salvation) of Functionalism' (2016) 26(4) European Journal of International Law 965.

[11] Sondre Torp Helmersen, *The Application of Teachings by the International Court of Justice* (CUP 2021) (discussing references to teachings in the opinions of the judges).

[12] IDI, 'Report (Rapporteur M Arsanjani): Are there Limits to the Dynamic Interpretation of the Constitution and Statutes of International Organizations by the Internal Organs of such Organizations (with Particular Reference to the UN System)?' (7th Commission, 2019) 100 ('In practice, the constituent instruments of international organizations are interpreted almost on a daily basis, by their organs, for the performance of their functions.') <https://www.idi-iil.org/app/uploads/2019/06/Commission-7-Interpretation-constitution-of-international-organizations-Arsanjani-Travaux-La-Haye-2019.pdf> accessed 15 May 2023.

powers in external relations.[13] Yet, the different practitioners' chapters in this book illustrate that difficult decisions on the limits of an organization's mandate arise not only in high-profile cases but also on a daily basis and at the lower echelons of institutional decision-making.

Given the variety of theoretical approaches, it may not be surprising that practising lawyers generally do not resort to theory when initiating novel IO activities. As Birkenkötter discusses, international law and international relations (IR) studies offer diverse theories on IOs.[14] Both in IR and international law scholarship, theoretical approaches diverge on the question of how much autonomy IOs have. Considering the mainstream legal theories, functionalists see IOs as vehicles or agents to fulfil state interests. While acknowledging that the constituent instruments of IOs have a constitutional dimension, functionalists emphasize the contractual nature of those instruments. The powers of IOs are limited by the will of their member states and the rules created by the organization may be characterized as international law.[15] In contrast, constitutionalists put greater emphasis on the constituent instruments' constitutional nature. They recognize that IOs may exercise powers not explicitly foreseen by their founders, allowing them to create legal orders separate from international law. The traditional legal theories on IOs oscillate between functionalism and constitutionalism to different degrees.[16] Often, this oscillation takes place without awareness, even among scholars and international lawmakers who draft rules on IOs. Being faced with a plethora of different approaches, practitioners will likely rather abstain from than engage with legal theory.

This chapter discusses whether and how theories or—to use a more modest term—approaches to the exercise of powers by IOs could be applied in the practice of IO secretariats to explain and justify IO initiatives. To translate legal theory into practice, this chapter suggests that legal theory on IOs should become more coherent and accessible to practitioners. After exploring the reasons

[13] Alexander Orakhelashvili, 'The Legal Basis of the United Nations Peace-Keeping Operations' (2003) 43(2) Virginia Journal of International Law 485; Daniel D Bradlow and Sabine Schlemmer-Schulte, 'The World Bank's New Inspection Panel: A Constructive Step in the Transformation of the International Legal Order' (1994) 54 Zeitschrift für ausländisches öffentliches Recht und Völkerrecht 392; Piet Eckhout, *EU External Relations Law* (2nd edn, OUP 2011) ch 3 ('The doctrine of implied powers').

[14] Hannah Birkenkötter, 'Change in International Organizations', Chapter 1 in this volume. See also Jeffrey L Dunhoff, 'The Law and Politics of International Organizations' in Jacob Katz Cogan, Ian Hurd, and Ian Johnstone (eds), *The Oxford Handbook of International Organizations* (OUP 2016) 60.

[15] On the nature of the so-called rules of the organization, see Niels Blokker, 'The Evolution of IO Powers and Activities: A Legal Framework', Chapter 4 in this volume. See also Christiane Ahlborn, 'The Rules of International Organizations and the Law of International Responsibility' (2011) 8(2) International Organizations Law Review 397.

[16] Lorenzo Gasbarri, *The Concept of an International Organization in International Law* (OUP 2021) chs 2 ('Functionalism') and 3 ('Constitutionalism').

why theories on IOs are usually not invoked in their everyday activities (Section II), the chapter discusses the advantages and disadvantages of applying theory in practice (Section III). The chapter argues that theories on IOs could be made more coherent by recognizing that functionalism and constitutionalism are not as different as commonly perceived (Section IV).[17] In fact, constitutionalism may be seen as an advanced version of functionalist theory, which would allow for a more nuanced and practical understanding of the internal and external dimensions of IOs.

II. Why is Theory Not Invoked in Practice?

After their establishment, IOs develop through their practice. The constituent instrument of the organization forms the basic framework for this development, but it typically does not expressly cover the various daily acts by IO officials and organs.[18] As the constituent instruments are typically treaties, it is assumed that Vienna Convention on the Law of Treaties (VCLT) serves as the basis to interpret the practice of the organization.[19] This view was confirmed by the UN International Law Commission (ILC) in its Conclusions on Subsequent Agreements and Subsequent Practice in Relation to the Interpretation of Treaties,[20] and by the *Institut de droit international* (IDI) in its 2021 resolution on the question 'Are there Limits to the Dynamic Interpretation of the Constitution and Statutes of International Organizations by the Internal Organs of such Organizations?'.[21] The view reflects the functionalist image of IOs, which permeates general international law scholarship. While IO lawyers may certainly refer to the VCLT in their practice, this is typically not based on theoretical awareness but because the VCLT might be useful to justify a particular decision. In yet other situations, IO lawyers will refer to the unique nature of the practice of the organization, which speaks in favour of constitutionalism.[22]

[17] Fiti Sinclair (n 10) 972.

[18] For a discussion, see the chapter by Blokker (n 15).

[19] Vienna Convention on the Law of Treaties (adopted 23 May 1969, entered into force 27 January 1980) 1155 UNTS 331. See Fernando Lusa Bordin, 'Interpreting Constituent Instruments to Justify the Evolving Powers of International Organizations', Chapter 5 in this volume.

[20] ILC, 'Report of the International Law Commission on the Work at its 70th session' (30 April–1 June and 2 July–10 August 2018) UN Doc A/73/10, 15, para 52.

[21] IDI, 'Resolution: Limits to Evolutive Interpretation of the Constituent Instruments of the Organizations within the United Nations System by their Internal Organs' (7th Commission, 4 September 2021) 7 RES EN.

[22] IDI (n 12) 234 ('The competence to interpret authoritatively their own constitutive instruments has permitted a broad and permissive jurisprudence of "constitutional" interpretation to flourish within each organization, subject only to infrequent—and merely advisory—oversight'). On relevant principles of constitutional interpretation, see Ibrahim FI Shihata, *The World Bank Legal Papers: Interpretation as Practiced at the World Bank* (M Nijhoff Publishers 2000) xliii, xliv–xlv.

Various reasons may explain why theories on IOs do not figure prominently in the practice of secretariats when initiating new activities that push the boundaries of an IO's mandate. These reasons are not necessarily specific to international law. The most obvious reason is that theories are abstract. According to *Black's Law Dictionary*, a theory is a '[s]et of propositions, assumptions or facts attempting to provide a rational explanation of cause and effect of observed phenomenon'.[23] Implied in this definition is the assumption that theories explain practice based on past events. But in law, the purpose of theories does not end here. Legal theories are part of a broader 'normative enterprise'[24] and, at the international level, convey certain 'normative ideals of "world order"'.[25] Accordingly, theories should explain earlier events in a way that will guide practice in the future.[26] Still, practitioners often see 'theory as a useless speculation of theorists, irrelevant to the administration of law . . . [and] "metaphysical speculation"'.[27] Theories may press practice that cannot be explained rationally into constructs that do not reflect reality.

Applying an abstract approach like functionalism to complicated real-life situations in IO practice may be unhelpful. At a very basic level, the concept of 'function' is ambiguous.[28] Accordingly, member states and staff may have different views on what constitutes the function of an IO and the limits of its mandate. As Di Leva discusses in his chapter, the World Bank's Articles of Agreement do not refer to environmental protection, which was not high on the international agenda after the Second World War.[29] When the Bank's President and management began addressing environmental issues following demands from civil society and the United States (US) Congress, some member states, particularly from the Global South, expressed concerns that this new environmental focus would make loans more expensive and shift the Bank's attention away from poverty reduction.[30] More recently established institutions such as the Global Fund are arguably more flexible in adapting and expanding their functions to new circumstances. As Zeidan and Abboud explain, in November 2023, the Global Fund and the World Bank concluded a memorandum of understanding

[23] The Law Dictionary, 'Theory' (*Free Online Legal Dictionary—Featuring Black's Law Dictionary*, 2nd edn) <https://thelawdictionary.org/theory/> accessed 15 May 2023.

[24] Cass R Sunstein, 'On Legal Theory and Legal Practice' (1995) 37 Nomos 267.

[25] Martti Koskenniemi, *From Apology to Utopia: The Structure of International Legal Argument. Reissue with New Epilogue* (CUP 2009) 1.

[26] Michael J Detmold, 'Law as Practical Reason' (1989) 48(3) The Cambridge Law Journal 436, 436–37.

[27] Wolfgang Friedmann, 'Legal Theory and the Practical Lawyer' (1941) 5(2) The Modern Law Review 103, 103.

[28] Klabbers (n 10) 26.

[29] Charles Di Leva, 'The World Bank's Evolution Towards Environmental and Social Responsibilities', Chapter 8 in this volume.

[30] ibid.

(MoU) stipulating that both institutions will, *inter alia*, collaborate regarding climate change and health.[31] The MoU highlights the Global Fund's recognition of the increasing importance of 'blended finance' and its emphasis on climate change and health.

These practical examples relate to a second reason why theories on IO are typically not invoked in everyday practice: they are unclear because they are often dissociated from practice, and they may even be outdated. As pointed out above, theories on IOs have been controversial. Legal scholarship oscillates between functionalism and constitutionalism, which is palpable in the rules of general international law meant to apply to all IOs. A pertinent example is the Articles on the Responsibility of International Organizations (ARIO), which the ILC adopted in 2011.[32] IOs across the board have been critical of the ARIO,[33] and neither of the main IO theories seem to be able to quell that criticism. How can functionalism explain why IOs incur separate international responsibility when they are actually only agents of their member states? Conversely, constitutionalism seems to go too far in its claim that IOs are completely autonomous from their creators, especially when an IO is not able to provide remedies. Also, neither of the two theories adequately clarifies why IOs, which may differ significantly in their mandates, structures, size, and composition, should be subjected to the same law of international responsibility.[34] Each IO has its own legal, political, and social norms that govern questions of accountability. Those norms might exert a stronger pull on IO practitioners than general theoretical approaches developed by scholars.[35]

A third reason for the possible lack of references to theories is pragmatic: decisions must be made fast, and there is not much room for theoretical discussions. An example in this regard is the World Health Organization's (WHO) handling of the Severe Acute Respiratory Syndrome (SARS) crisis. In February 2003, non-governmental sources had warned the WHO of the outbreak

[31] Zeidan and Abboud (n 9).

[32] ILC, 'Draft Articles on Responsibility of International Organizations, with commentaries' (2011) II(2) ILC Yearbook 46.

[33] Joint submission by a group of IOs as part of the comments and information received from governments and international organizations, UNGA, 'Responsibility of international organizations: Report of the Secretary General' (26 April 2017) UN Doc A/72/80, 6. See also the comments received on the Draft ARIO on first reading from governments, 'Responsibility of international organizations' (14 February, 13 April, and 8 August 2011) UN Doc A/CN.4/636 and add.1–2; comments received from IOs, UNGA, 'Responsibility of international organizations' (14 and 17 February 2011) UN Doc A/CN.4/637 and add.1.

[34] In this regard, see the comments referred to in n 33 above. See also Gerhard Hafner, 'Is the Topic of Responsibility of International Organizations Ripe for Codification? Some Critical Remarks' in Ulrich Fastenrath and others (eds), *From Bilateralism to Community Interest: Essays in Honour of Bruno Simma* (OUP 2011) 695, 704; and Klabbers (n 10) 50, pointing to functionalism's structural inability to accommodate third parties.

[35] I am grateful to Henner Gött for this observation.

of a new disease, SARS, which was not covered by the 1969 International Health Regulations (IHR).[36] 'In an unprecedented move, WHO went on the offensive against China',[37] and directly alerted travellers—instead of its member states—to avoid Toronto, Hong Kong, Taiwan, and parts of China to stop the spread of the disease.[38] Resort to theoretical considerations might have prevented the WHO to take such urgent action. As Burci and Balcazar-Moreno discuss in this volume, the WHO Secretariat also took swift action when the COVID-19 pandemic broke out,[39] in cooperation with other actors such as Gavi, the Vaccine Alliance (Gavi), which facilitated the equitable development, procurement, and delivery of COVID-19 vaccines worldwide.[40]

A fourth reason for the lack of references to theories in IO practice is political or policy-oriented: policymakers in IOs might already envisage certain outcomes, or a theory would point to an outcome that is not desirable considering the political circumstances. IOs operate frequently in politically difficult environments, and their secretariats have to balance different interests. In view of the continued grave breaches of international humanitarian law in the Balkans conflicts, the United Nations Security Council (UNSC), in resolution 808 (1993), decided to establish 'an international tribunal for the prosecution of persons responsible for serious violations of international humanitarian law committed in the territory of the former Yugoslavia since 1991'.[41] Although the UNSC adopted the resolution unanimously, several of its members were critical of the Council's authority under the UN Charter to establish an international criminal tribunal as a subsidiary organ. Being charged with elaborating 'specific proposals and where appropriate options for the effective and expeditious implementation of the decision' to create a tribunal,[42] the UN Office of Legal Affairs (OLA) decided not to refer to theories on IO powers. As Llewellyn observes, OLA 'focused rather on the fact that, given the urgent circumstances, a multilateral treaty negotiation among States would simply not be sufficiently expeditious or effective'.[43] A more

[36] World Health Assembly, *International Health Regulations (1969): Adopted by the Twenty-Second World Health Assembly in 1969 and Amended by the Twenty-Sixth World Health Assembly in 1973 and the Thirty-Fourth World Health Assembly in 1981* (World Health Organization 1983).

[37] David P Fidler, *SARS, Governance, and the Globalization of Disease* (Palgrave Macmillan 2004) 96.

[38] Andrew P Cortell and Susan Peterson, 'Dutiful Agents, Rogue Actors, or Both? Staffing, Voting Rules, and Slack in the WHO and WTO' in Darren G Hawkins and others (eds), *Delegation and Agency in International Organizations* (CUP 2008) 270.

[39] Gian Luca Burci and Ana Balcazar-Moreno, 'WHO's Reactions to COVID-19: Between Politics and Managerialism', Chapter 9 in this volume.

[40] Madir (n 9).

[41] UNSC, 'Resolution 808: Adopted by the Security Council at 3175th meeting' (22 February 1993) UN Doc S/RES/808, para 1.

[42] ibid para 2.

[43] Huw Llewellyn, 'The Establishment of the UN Criminal Tribunals: The Role of the UN Secretariat', Chapter 7 in this volume.

recent example is the creation of the International, Impartial and Independent Mechanism for Syria by the UN General Assembly (UNGA), which took place despite the resistance of Syria, the Russian Federation, and China.[44] The reference to theory could have jeopardized the desired political outcome in both cases.

III. Should Theory Be Invoked in Practice?

While IO lawyers may not invoke theories in their practice, theory is inseparable from practice. As law is inherently a 'normative enterprise',[45] legal practice relies on rules, principles, and precedents that are geared towards common normative goals. Such reliance fosters legal certainty and, hence, the rule of law.[46] However, the tectonic shifts in IOs covered in this book demonstrate that IOs have been frequently faced with novel situations in which they could not rely on existing rules or precedents to find a solution. In those situations, a lack of awareness of theoretical assumptions underlying certain positions might lead to adverse consequences. Some would even go as far as claiming that 'it can hardly be denied that those lawyers who are unconscious of their legal theory, are apt to do more harm than their more conscious colleagues'.[47] The lawyer that is unaware of legal theory might feel less burdened by the implications of their decisions,[48] but the repercussions of such unawareness could be far-reaching.

Some degree of theoretical awareness might indeed have benefits. When in need of pragmatism, legal theory could enable IO decision-makers to decide and act faster. For example, an IO could find itself in a situation where it has to decide whether an activity is within its mandate so that funds can be allocated. When UN Secretary-General Dag Hammarskjold developed the concept of 'UN peacekeeping' in the wake of the Israeli–British–French invasion of Egypt in 1956, he did not stand on solid legal foundations as the UN Charter does not refer to peacekeeping forces. Almost 60 years later, UN Secretary-General Ban Ki-moon expressed his intention 'to immediately establish a United Nations Mission for Ebola Emergency Response (UNMEER)' to fight the Ebola outbreak in several Western African states. As Khalil discusses in her chapter, the UNSC

[44] UNGA, 'Resolution adopted by the General Assembly on 21 December 2016' (11 January 2017) UN Doc A/RES/71/24 (adopted by 105 votes to 15, 52 abstentions), establishing the 'International, Impartial and Independent Mechanism to assist in the Investigation and Prosecution of those Responsible for the Most Serious Crimes under International Law committed in the Syrian Arab Republic since March 2011'.

[45] Sunstein (n 24) 267.

[46] On the application of the rule of law to IOs, see Ahlborn (n 15).

[47] Friedmann (n 27) 103–04.

[48] ibid.

and the UNGA both endorsed the Secretary-General's intention.[49] In addition to an established practice of UN peacekeeping, the Secretary-General could also base his plans to establish UNMEER on the case law of the International Court of Justice (ICJ). In its *Certain Expenses* advisory opinion, the ICJ was requested to answer the question whether the expenditures authorized by the UNGA regarding the UN Operation in the Congo and the UN Emergency Force in the Middle East were 'expenses of the Organization' within the meaning of Article 17, paragraph 2, of the UN Charter.[50] The ICJ's confirmation that the UNGA had the authority to approve expenses for peacekeeping forces has allowed for a broad reading of the implied powers doctrine in other contexts,[51] and it could justify the *ad hoc* expansion of powers in emergency situations.

Theories can also be beneficial in shedding light on the potential costs and benefits of different courses of action. Before the United Nations Educational, Scientific and Cultural Organization (UNESCO) admitted Palestine as a full member, the US and Israel threatened punitive measures.[52] Following Palestine's admission, the US withheld its membership contributions as previously announced.[53] From a functionalist perspective, the US withholding of funds undermined UNESCO's ability to fulfil its functions.[54] This is why in a comparable situation in 1989, the Director-General of the WHO had negotiated a compromise to avoid that the World Health Assembly would recognize the Palestinian Liberation Organization with the aim 'to put the health of the agency before politics'.[55] Framing this situation in constitutionalist terms, this approach prevented a violation of the WHO Constitution and kept the WHO operational with the necessary US funding. Regarding UNESCO, the US ultimately withdrew from the organization in 2017 due to 'mounting arrears at UNESCO, the need for fundamental reform in the organization, and continuing "anti-Israel bias"'.[56] In functionalist and constitutionalist terms, the US left UNESCO

[49] Mona Ali Khalil, 'The Evolution of UN Secretary-General Initiatives to Respond to Violent and Non-Violent Threats to International Peace and Security', Chapter 14 in this volume.

[50] *Certain Expenses of the United Nations* (Advisory Opinion) [1962] ICJ Rep 151.

[51] Andrzej Gadkowski, 'The Doctrine of Implied Powers of International Organizations in the Case Law of International Tribunals' (2016) 6 Adam Mickiewicz University Law Review 45, 55. See also Alvarez (n 5) 127.

[52] UN, 'UNESCO votes to admit Palestine as full member' (*UN News*, 31 October 2001) <https://news.un.org/en/story/2011/10/393562> accessed 15 May 2023.

[53] Harriet Sherwood, 'US Pulls UNESCO Funding after Palestine Is Granted Full Membership' *The Guardian* (31 October 2011) <https://www.theguardian.com/world/2011/oct/31/unesco-backs-palestinian-membership> accessed 15 May 2023.

[54] On the broader repercussions, see Larry D Johnson, 'Palestine's Admission to UNESCO: Consequences within the United Nations' (2011) 40 Denver Journal of International Law & Policy 118.

[55] Cortell and Peterson (n 38) 267.

[56] Daniel Marwecki, 'Why Did the U.S. and Israel Leave UNESCO?' *E-International Relations* (14 February 2019) <https://www.e-ir.info/pdf/77622> accessed 15 May 2023.

to avoid continuously violating the UNESCO Constitution and because it was of the view that UNESCO was not fulfilling its functions.[57]

Nonetheless, the fact that theories on IOs are typically not invoked could indicate that theory should not be applied in practice. An argument against the explicit application of theory is that practitioners may not completely understand complicated theoretical constructs developed by scholars, who have more time for research and analysis.[58] The risk of not fully comprehending a theory and its implications is likely even higher in situations of fast decision-making. In the case of the SARS outbreak, WHO officials might have thought that their acts were necessary to fulfil the WHO's mandate of 'the attainment by all peoples of the highest possible level of health'.[59] In that process, they assumed powers that went beyond what was foreseen in the already ongoing reform efforts of the IHR,[60] thus disregarding the constitutional constraints of the organization. The revised 2005 IHR give the WHO Director-General the power to determine a public health emergency of international concern (PHEIC), in consultation with the state party involved and based on the views of an Emergency Committee composed of experts.[61] Despite these new powers, however, the WHO was criticized for acting too carefully in declaring COVID-19 a PHEIC out of deference to China.[62]

With the evolution of IOs, the need to refer to theory has become less pressing because of available precedents, which hold the promise of coherence, legitimacy, and stability in legal relations. Whenever possible, IO secretariat staff, member states, and political organs rely on the previous practice of the organization. Where no direct precedent exists, reasoning by analogy might offer an appropriate solution.[63] The contemporary law on IO immunities is seen to be very different from state immunity,[64] but in the early days of IOs, the law of state immunity served as a frame of reference for the interpretation of their immunities.[65] Today, legal advice on the immunities of the UN is standardized

[57] Jan Klabbers, *Advanced Introduction to the Law of International Organizations* (Edgar Elgar 2015) 48 (confirming that functionalist theory is often seen as useful in explaining withdrawals from IOs).

[58] Sunstein (n 24) 271.

[59] Constitution of the World Health Organization (adopted 22 July 1946, entered into force 7 April 1948) 14 UNTS 186 art 1.

[60] Cortell and Peterson (n 38) 270.

[61] WHO, *International Health Regulations (2005)* (3rd edn, WHO 2016) art 12.

[62] Srinivas Mazumdaru, 'What influence does China have over the WHO?' (*Deutsche Welle*, 17 April 2020) <https://www.dw.com/en/what-influence-does-china-have-over-the-who/a-53161220> accessed 15 May 2023.

[63] See generally Fernando Lusa Bordin, *The Analogy between States and International Organizations* (CUP 2018).

[64] Michael Wood, 'Do International Organizations Enjoy Immunity Under Customary International Law?' (2013) 10 International Organizations Law Review 287.

[65] UN, 'Inter-Office Memorandum to the Acting Director of the Legal Department, Concerning the Waiver of Immunity—Actual and Implied' (United Nations Juridical Yearbook Special Edition 1948) <https://legal.un.org/unjuridicalyearbook/pdfs/english/by_chapter/chpVI/legal_opinions/

in most scenarios.[66] Still, the existence of precedents does not mean that legal theory does not matter at all. Precedents are based on principles underlying the IO legal order as a whole. Accordingly, it could be said 'that legal practice is simply a form of legal theory without the requisite self-consciousness or ambition'.[67]

Although IOs have developed into increasingly complex and dense legal systems, they continue to face new challenges not covered by existing rules. In some situations, however, the political stakes are so high that decision-makers might prefer indeterminacy in the law to shape outcomes to their liking. It might also not be possible to reach solutions reflecting general principles that would find future application.[68] In 1991, based on UNSC resolution 687,[69] the Secretary-General convened a five-member UN Iraq–Kuwait Boundary Demarcation Commission, whose final report was submitted to the UNSC.[70] The Council, acting under Chapter VII, reaffirmed that the Commission's decisions regarding the boundary demarcation were final in resolution 833.[71] The Minister of Foreign Affairs of Iraq only retroactively accepted the terms of the UNSC resolution in a letter addressed to the Secretary-General and the President of the Council. It is telling that UNSC members speaking before and after the adoption of resolution 833 emphasized 'the unique situation of which there has been no parallel since the establishment of the United Nations; hopefully, there will be none in the future'.[72]

While a certain degree of indeterminacy in the law is unavoidable, it might lead to outcomes that are undesirable from a broader policy perspective. For instance, regarding the responsibility of IOs as codified in the ARIO, the lack of clarity as to whether IOs are principals or agents of their members may be problematic when the IO's activities cause damage to third parties. To avoid responsibility, an IO may make the (functionalist) argument that its wrongful conduct is

1948.pdf> accessed 15 May 2023. See also Cornelis van Vollenhoven, 'Diplomatic Prerogatives of Non-Diplomats' (1925) 19(3) American Journal of International Law 469.

[66] UN, 'United Nations Juridical Yearbook' (2015) ST/LEG/SER.C/53, ch VI.A.1 ('Privileges and immunities') <https://legal.un.org/unjuridicalyearbook/pdfs/english/volumes/2015.pdf> accessed 17 September 2024.

[67] Sunstein (n 24) 278.

[68] ibid 281.

[69] UNSC, 'Resolution 687 (1991) adopted by the Security Council at its 2891st meeting' (8 April 1991) UN Doc S/RES/687.

[70] UN, 'Letter Dated 21 May 1993 from the Secretary-General addressed to the President of the Security Council' (21 May 1993) UN Doc S/25811 and Add.1 (1993) <https://documents.un.org/doc/undoc/gen/n93/295/64/pdf/n9329564.pdf> accessed 17 September 2024.

[71] UNSC, 'Resolution 833 (1993) adopted by the Security Council at its 3224th meeting' (27 May 1993) UN Doc S/RES/833.

[72] UNSC, 'Provisional Verbatim Record of the Two Thousand Nine Hundred and Eighty-First Meeting' (3 April 1991) UN Doc S/PV/2981, 72–78 (statement by India). For a full discussion, see IDI (n 12) 150–53.

ultimately the result of the decision of its members. In contrast, members could counter with the (constitutional) point that the IO has autonomy and is, therefore, the responsible actor. The result of this situation is the well-known debate on the lack of responsibility of IOs and their member states because this responsibility shifting exercise might leave injured parties without a remedy.[73]

Unawareness or ignorance of theory might have some merit, particularly when theory could be misunderstood and then misapplied in practice. Also, it is safer to rely on precedent in straightforward and uncomplicated cases, which fosters the coherence of the legal order and the legitimacy of the IO's exercise of powers. Legal offices in established IOs typically have streamlined working methods in which staff make decisions based on precedent and reasoning by analogy. However, the application of precedent has its limits. When IOs are faced with novel challenges, the resort to theory may be helpful to develop new rules that do not contradict the existing IO law or practice. In the absence of precedent, theory takes a crucial place in ensuring coherence in decision-making. In turn, insufficient resort to theory in IO practice might lead to adverse outcomes for the IO, its members, and other stakeholders.

IV. How Can Theory Be Translated into Practice?

To translate theories on the exercise of IO powers into practice, it would be useful to develop a more coherent approach on what constitutes an IO and which powers it may exercise. Such an approach would have to consider the important role of member states in establishing and running an IO while recognizing the autonomy of the organization from its founders regarding the exercise of its powers in its internal and external relations. This approach would need to strike a more conciliatory tone between the two mainstream theories of functionalism and constitutionalism, while incorporating their basic tenets. And at a more pragmatic level, this approach should be easily accessible to IOs practitioners and to the representatives of member states that interact with IOs in domestic legal orders and internationally. In this context, inspiration could be drawn from theories on statehood: some theoretical variations exist, but practitioners and scholars agree on the basic characteristics of the state and its role in the international legal order.

While functionalism and constitutionalism are often portrayed as opposing approaches to IOs, they share many characteristics. Once constituted to fulfil certain functions, IOs enjoy a degree of autonomy from their member states.

[73] See generally Carla Ferstman, *International Organizations and the Fight for Accountability: The Remedies and Reparations Gap* (OUP 2017).

Notwithstanding the substantial differences between states and IOs, the process of constituting an IO by political agreement has parallels with that of establishing a state. Based on political theory, states could be characterized as a constituting power when creating an IO, which becomes the *pouvoir constitué*. Within the overall legal framework of its constitution, the IO has autonomy to develop its legal order. Some of its powers may be explicitly stated in the constitution through attributed competences. Other powers may be implied as the IO is faced with unforeseen challenges, which will increase as the constitution grows older. In this sense, 'there is room for some analogy with constitutional law because there exist certain structural similarities between national constitutions and the constitutions of international organizations'.[74]

Constitutionalism does not mean that states lose control of the organization, which is one of the basic premises of functionalism. Member states remain in control of the IO through its constitutional framework, which includes rules on decision-making. Those rules may allow the organization to push forward certain initiatives despite the opposition of some member states (see, eg, the International, Impartial and Independent Mechanism for Syria). Although the constitutional frameworks of most organizations are rudimentary in comparison with those of states, the checks and balances within those organizations do not only operate between the IO's organs but they also work in the relations between member states and IO secretariats (eg through reporting obligations and budgetary review).[75] If member states disapprove a decision, they can try to resolve the dispute informally before resorting to more formal decision-making such voting, or judicial dispute settlement. The ultimate step is for a member to exit the organization,[76] as the US and Israel did after Palestine became a full member of UNESCO.

Instead of pitting different IO theories against each other, constitutionalism could be seen as an advanced version of functionalism to better explain the internal and external dimensions of IOs. Drawing more explicit parallels with the state is then useful in understanding that IOs have internal law, which is exclusively applicable between the organization and its members. At the same time, IOs, through their secretariats, interact with the external world by engaging in multistakeholder relations, as discussed in Part IV of this book. As the most integrated IO, the EU illustrates that international law may be incorporated into the internal legal order of the organization either automatically or based on set rules

[74] Krzysztof Skubiszewski, 'Implied Powers of International Organizations' in Yoram Dinstein (ed), *International Law at a Time of Perplexity* (Brill Nijhoff 1989) 855.
[75] Jan Klabbers, 'Checks and Balances in the Law of International Organizations' in Mortimer Sellers (ed), *Autonomy in the Law* (Springer 2007) 141.
[76] In this regard, see Albert O Hirschman, *Exit, Voice, and Loyalty. Responses to Decline in Firms, Organizations and States* (Harvard UP 1970).

of incorporation, which can also be found in dualist domestic legal orders.[77] A particularity of IOs is that their law and practice might not only have an external effect due to their own institutional conduct but also as a result of their member states wearing 'different hats'.[78] As members in different organizations and subjects of international law, states create institutional and legal linkages between IOs and international law, which leads to not only cross-fertilization but also conflict.[79]

The reluctance to compare states with IOs is deep-seated, making it difficult to accept such an approach with all its possible implications. This is evident in advisory opinions of the ICJ, and also in the work of codification bodies such as the ILC and the IDI. The ICJ already stated in its *Reparation for Injuries* advisory opinion that the UN is not a 'super-State',[80] and the Court has shifted between emphasizing the constitutional and treaty nature of IO constituent instruments.[81] A further example are the ILC's conclusions on subsequent agreements and subsequent practice, which state in conclusion 12, paragraph 3, that the '[p]ractice of an international organization in the application of its constituent instrument *may contribute* to the interpretation of that instrument when applying articles 31 and 32'.[82] In this reading, it appears that IO constituent instruments are primarily treaties, and that their role as constitutions is only secondary. Similarly, the IDI emphasized the rules on treaty interpretation in the VCLT before noting the possible relevance of specific interpretative rules of the organization.[83]

From the perspective of IO law and practice, comparing the constituent instruments of IOs with the constitutions of states is not groundbreaking. However, a certain degree of unawareness of the main theoretical streams has created an ambiguous twilight zone that does not clearly delineate between the

[77] Fernando Lusa Bordin, 'General International Law in the Relations between International Organizations and Their Members' (2019) 32(4) Leiden Journal of International Law 653. See also Tawhida Ahmed and Israel de Jesús Butler, 'The European Union and Human Rights: An International Law Perspective' (2006) 17(4) European Journal of International Law 771.

[78] This is reminiscent of Georges Scelle's theory of 'dédoublement fonctionnel' (see, eg, Georges Scelle, 'Le phénomène juridique du dédoublement fonctionnel' in Walter Schätzel and Hans Jürgen Schlochauer (eds), *Rechtsfragen der internationalen Organisation, Festschrift für Wehberg* (V Klostermann 1956) 324).

[79] A well-known example is the *Kadi* cases, see Case T-315/01 *Yassin Abdullah Kadi v Council of the European Union and Commission of the European Communities* [2005] ECR II-3649, and Joined Cases C-402/05 P and C-415/05 P *Yassin Abdullah Kadi and Al Barakaat International Foundation v Council of the European Union and Commission of the European Communities* [2008] ECR I-06351.

[80] *Reparation for Injuries Suffered in the Service of the United Nations* (Advisory Opinion) [1949] ICJ Rep 174, 179. The Court also noted that its conclusion that the UN is an international legal person 'is not the same thing as saying that it is a State' (at 179). In *Legality of the Use by a State of Nuclear Weapons in Armed Conflict* (Advisory Opinion) [1996] ICJ Rep 66, 78, the ICJ observed: 'International organizations . . . do not, unlike States, possess a general competence.'

[81] See, eg, the *Certain Expenses* case (n 50) 157 (characterizing the UN Charter as 'a multilateral treaty, albeit a treaty having certain special characteristics').

[82] ILC (n 20) (emphasis added).

[83] IDI (n 21).

internal and external dimensions of IOs.[84] Most practitioners in IOs acknowledge that IOs are part of international law. Even so, they witness first-hand how IOs develop into their own legal orders that are very different from the international legal order. As the various initiatives discussed in this book demonstrate, this development is decisively driven by IO secretariats, which are not parties to the IO's constituent instruments. Secretariat staff only experience those instruments as 'living constitutions',[85] establishing the IO as its own legal universe. Accordingly, the law and practice of different IOs are quite distinct from each other. Like states, IOs may be connected through formal institutional cooperation, such as within the UN Common System, or informal reliance on each other's practices in the sense of comparative institutional law.[86]

A more coherent IO theory based on constitutionalism has several advantages regarding the further evolution of IO theory and practice. Conceptually, it would provide more fertile ground to distil and develop the rules of international law that are common to all IOs—in short, to establish more 'unity within diversity' among IOs.[87] This includes some of the foundational rules of international law, such as those on the law of responsibility, treaties, and immunities, but it could also extend to common practices in the law on international civil service or disputes with third parties.[88] Seeing IOs as constituted legal orders will also allow for a more nuanced analysis of the various degrees of institutional linkages and cooperation between organizations.[89] At a pragmatic level, a constitutional approach to IOs is likely more accessible to IO lawyers, which will be beneficial in translating theory into practice. These practitioners may not have a background in public international law at all, but they will have likely studied constitutional law at the domestic level.

V. Conclusion

This chapter is based on the observation that lawyers in IOs generally do not refer to theories in their daily work. However, as Sunstein rightly notes, 'the

[84] Seyersted (n 3) 5.

[85] On the metaphor of the 'living constitution' in international organizations law, see Guy Fiti Sinclair, 'IO Initiatives, Ideology, and the Imaginaries of Liberal Reform', Chapter 2 in this volume.

[86] George A Bermann, 'Comparative Law and International Organizations' in Mauro Bussani and Ugo Mattei (eds), *The Cambridge Companion to Comparative Law* (CUP 2012) 241.

[87] Schermers and Blokker (n 2).

[88] See, eg, the ILC's current consideration of the topic of 'Settlement of international disputes to which international organizations are parties' (see ILC, 'Report of the International Law Commission on the Work of its 73rd Session' (18 April–3 June and 4 July–5 August 2022) UN Doc A/77/10, para 238.

[89] Laurence Boisson de Chazournes, *Interactions between Regional and Universal Organizations—A Legal Perspective* (Brill 2016).

practice of law is theory-laden . . . [M]any lawyers and judges are actually making theoretical claims'.[90] The lack of references to theory in practice has advantages and disadvantages. On the one hand, it allows practitioners to decide more rapidly and to prioritize pragmatic considerations, which is important in an often politically charged IO environment. Also, theories are typically complex and abstract and thus difficult to understand and apply to real-life cases. On the other hand, resort to theory can contribute to better and sometimes even faster decision-making, while taking into account potential costs and benefits for the IO, member states, and other relevant stakeholders. In novel situations without a precedent, an understanding of theory is essential in developing the law coherently, which serves the overall stability of the legal system and the rule of law.

To translate theories on IO powers into practice, this chapter suggested an understanding of constitutionalism as an advanced version of functionalism. For theory to be accessible to practising IO lawyers, simplicity is key. While functionalism and constitutionalism are often understood as opposing poles on a spectrum, it may be possible to reconcile them into one approach. The challenge is that this might mean letting go of entrenched beliefs, such as that IOs cannot be compared with states. However, reconciling the different theories on IOs into one coherent framework will serve both academics and practitioners. It will free academics from what Koskenniemi has called 'the prison-house of irrelevance' in which their scholarly work has limited practical impact.[91] And it will help decision-makers in IOs to make more legally sound and coherent decisions that will support—rather than undermine—the fulfilment of the IO's functions.

[90] Sunstein (n 24) 285.
[91] Koskenniemi (n 25) 4.

4

The Evolution of IO Powers and Activities

A Legal Framework

Niels Blokker

I. Introduction

The evolution of powers and activities of international organizations (IOs) is not taking place in a lawless limbo but within a legal framework. This legal framework is comprehensive and multilayered. It includes both general international law and the domestic law of the states where an organization performs its activities. However, above all, at the heart of this legal framework are the so-called rules of the organization. This notion is mentioned in the 1969 Vienna Convention on the Law of Treaties[1] and was subsequently defined in the 1975 Vienna Convention on the Representation of States in Their Relations with International Organizations of a Universal Character,[2] in the 1986 Vienna Convention on the Law of Treaties Between States and International Organizations or Between International Organizations,[3] and in the 2011 International Law Commission (ILC) Draft Articles on Responsibility of International Organizations (DARIO).[4]

The definition of 'rules of the organization' adopted in the DARIO is the following: '"rules of the organization" means, in particular, the constituent instruments, decisions, resolutions and other acts of the international organization adopted in accordance with those instruments, and established practice

[1] Vienna Convention on the Law of Treaties (adopted 23 May 1969, entered into force 27 January 1980) 1155 UNTS 331 art 5.

[2] Vienna Convention on the Representation of States in Their Relations with International Organizations of a Universal Character (adopted 14 March 1975) UN Doc A/CONF.67/16 art 1.1(34). This Convention has not yet entered into force.

[3] Vienna Convention on the Law of Treaties Between States and International Organizations or Between International Organizations (adopted 21 March 1986) art 2.1(j). This Convention has not yet entered into force.

[4] ILC, 'Report of the International Law Commission on the Work of Its 63rd Session' (26 April–3 June and 4 July–12 August 2011) UN Doc A/66/10, which contains the ILC's Draft Articles on the Responsibility of International Organizations (DARIO). See 52, DARIO art 2(b). In UNGA Res 66/100, the UN General Assembly 'takes note' of the DARIO.

Niels Blokker, *The Evolution of IO Powers and Activities* In: *International Organization Initiatives.* Edited by: Gabrielle Marceau and Henner Gött, Oxford University Press. © Oxford University Press 2025. DOI: 10.1093/9780197803325.003.0005

of the organization'.[5] It is clear that this definition does not provide an exhaustive enumeration of 'rules of the organization' ('in particular') and that it lays down a hierarchy between its elements. The organization's constituent instrument is mentioned first; it is the foundation of its legal framework. It is at the apex of the organization's legal order: the 'decisions, resolutions and other acts' to which the definition refers must be adopted in accordance with it. This is not required for the organization's 'established practice', the last mentioned element of the rules of the organization.[6] While this gives considerable flexibility to IOs, it also raises the question how a particular 'established practice' that is not in accordance with an organization's constituent instrument relates to the fundamental principle governing the legal powers of IOs: the attribution principle, also named the principle of speciality or the principle of conferral. IOs only have those powers that have been attributed to them.[7] If a power is not attributed in the organization's constituent instrument, can 'established practice' (as a rule of the organization) be its legal basis? If this is the case, how robust should such a practice be, and when can it be considered 'established'? The notion of 'established practice' is neither defined in the aforementioned Vienna Conventions that refer to it nor in the DARIO. At the same time, it may be questioned whether it would be necessary or wise to define this notion. In the meantime, it is regularly used in practice.[8]

[5] ibid. The definition given in the 1986 Vienna Convention (n 3) is largely similar. The definition in the 1975 Vienna Convention (n 2) is different (in particular, the words 'adopted in accordance with them' are absent).

[6] Christopher Peters, 'Subsequent Practice and Established Practice of International Organizations: Two Sides of the Same Coin' (2011) 3 Goettingen Journal of International Law 617, 617–42. Christopher Peters, *Praxis Internationaler Organisationen: Vertragswandel und völkerrechtlicher Ordnungsrahmen* (Springer 2016); Niels Blokker, 'Legal Facets of the Practice of International Organizations' (2024) 435 Recueil des cours 73–324, in particular 95–130.

[7] As the ICJ has observed:

> [t]he Court need hardly point out that international organizations are subjects of international law which do not, unlike States, possess a general competence. International organizations are governed by the "principle of speciality", that is to say, they are invested by the States which create them with powers, the limits of which are a function of the common interests whose promotion those States entrust to them.'

Legality of the Use by a State of Nuclear Weapons in Armed Conflict (Advisory Opinion) [1996] ICJ Rep 226, paras 66, 78 specifically para 25. See also, earlier, the separate opinion of Judge Gros in the ICJ, *Interpretation of the Agreement of 25 March 1951 Between the WHO and Egypt* (Advisory Opinion) [1980] ICJ Rep 73, 103.

[8] For instance, by the UN Secretariat. See the *United Nations Juridical Yearbook* (UNJY) for examples; eg UN, 'Treaty Provisions Concerning the Legal Status of the United Nations and Related Inter-governmental Organizations' (1962) United Nations Juridical Yearbook, 59; UN, 'Selected Legal Opinions of the Secretariat of the United Nations and Related Intergovernmental Organizations' (1973) United Nations Juridical Yearbook, 133, 143, 160, and 176; UN, 'Selected Legal Opinions of the Secretariats of the United Nations and Related Intergovernmental Organizations' (2001) United Nations Juridical Yearbook 387–88; UN OLA, 'Treaties Concerning the Legal Status of the United Nations and Related Intergovernmental Organizations' (2016) United Nations Juridical Yearbook 111; UN OLA, 'Selected Legal Opinions of the Secretariats of the United Nations and Related Intergovernmental Organizations' (2016) United Nations Juridical Yearbook 412.

The DARIO definition of 'rules of the organization' reflects a fundamental tension that is inherent in the law and life of any IO. First, the organization is a product of law; it is normally established by a treaty concluded between states (and sometimes also (other) IOs), inter alia defining the functions and powers of the organization. Such a treaty, the constituent instrument of the organization, needs the consent of the participating states. In an international society in which the state is the primary form of political organization, IOs do not come into being without states taking the initiative. Such an initiative has been taken in the hundreds of cases in which IOs have been created. In these cases, the participating states considered it in their own and common interest not only to conclude a treaty with mutual rights and obligations but also to establish a dynamic framework within which their future cooperation in the area of activity of the organization would be structured. This framework is a reflection of the rule of law in international society. Future cooperation between the states concerned and the functioning of 'their' organization should not take place in a lawless limbo, following the law of the jungle and the 'rule of power', but rather governed by the rule of law, within a legal framework.

Second, unlike its legal framework, an IO's life cannot be pre-agreed. The founding states of an IO cannot foresee the unforeseeable. Some crises may occur in an area in which an IO performs its functions. If the organization is to be effective, also during such a crisis, it should be sufficiently flexible. Flexibility is needed, as the future is by definition uncertain. In spite of this uncertainty, or perhaps because of it, the founding states choose to face that future in the area of activity of the organization together rather than alone, essentially because 'there is no sovereignty in solitude', to use the words of former Prime Minister of Italy Draghi.[9]

II. Balancing and Governing IOs Exercise of Powers

The aforementioned fundamental tension between the requirement of a legal framework and the need for flexibility may be illustrated by taking the United Nations (UN) Security Council as an example. The Security Council is widely regarded as a (very) political organ of the UN, dominated by the five permanent members. It was deliberately created as the enforcement body of the UN, with primary responsibility for the maintenance of international peace and security, having unprecedented powers. It is for the Security Council to determine

[9] In the original text: 'Non c'è sovranità nella solitudine' (speech before the Italian Senate, see *Corriere della sera / Politico*, 17 February 2021).

whether there is a threat to the peace, breach of the peace, or act of aggression.[10] These three notions, in particular the notion 'threat to the peace', are very broad. This has allowed the Security Council to qualify particular acts or situations as threats to the peace of which it is unlikely that the drafters of the Charter had this in mind and take a wide array of enforcement measures.

At the same time, the Security Council's powers are not unlimited. The International Criminal Tribunal for the former Yugoslavia (ICTY) stated in 1995, when scrutinizing the power of the Security Council to establish this Tribunal, that the Council:[11]

> plays a pivotal role and exercises a very wide discretion under this Article. But this does not mean that its powers are unlimited. The Security Council is an organ of an international organization, established by a treaty which serves as a constitutional framework for that organization. The Security Council is thus subjected to certain constitutional limitations, however broad its powers under the constitution may be. Those powers cannot, in any case, go beyond the limits of the jurisdiction of the Organization at large, not to mention other specific limitations or those which may derive from the internal division of power within the Organization. In any case, neither the text nor the spirit of the Charter conceives of the Security Council as *legibus solutus* (unbound by law).

Quoting Article 24(2) of the Charter, the Tribunal concluded: '[t]he Charter thus speaks the language of specific powers, not of absolute fiat'.[12] Much earlier, in 1948, the International Court of Justice (ICJ) had already observed something similar: '[t]he political character of an organ cannot release it from the observance of the treaty provisions established by the Charter when they constitute limitations on its powers or criteria for its judgment'.[13]

Perhaps such observations were to be expected, as both the ICJ and the ICTY are judicial organs. However, the fact that the Security Council is bound by the Charter has also often been emphasized in statements in the Council from the very beginning. Already in its first meeting on 17 January 1946 in London, the President, the Australian Minister of Navy Makin stated: '[o]ur work must be based on the Charter. We are not permitted to go beyond it, but we shall not

[10] Charter of the United Nations (adopted 26 June 1945, entered into force 24 October 1945) 1 UNTS XVI art 39.

[11] ICTY, *Prosecutor v Tádic* (1995) Case No IT-94-1-AR72 (decision of 2 October 1995 on the defence motion for interlocutory appeal on jurisdiction) para 28.

[12] ibid.

[13] *Admission of a State to the United Nations (Charter, Art. 4)* (Advisory Opinion) [1948] ICJ Rep 57 (quotation at 64).

fail to exercise to the full the very great powers which have been given to this Council'.[14]

The essence of these observations regarding the Security Council is also true for organs of IOs generally. Since this book is focusing in particular on the role of secretariats of IOs, a second example illustrating the fundamental tension between the requirement of a legal framework and the need for flexibility relates to the UN Secretariat.[15] In 1965, the UN concluded an agreement with Belgium 'relating to the settlement of claims filed against the United Nations in the Congo by Belgian nationals', in the context of the operations of UN peacekeeping force UN Operation in the Congo (ONUC). In this exchange of letters, the UN Secretary-General agreed to pay the Belgian government 'without prejudice to the privileges and immunities enjoyed by the United Nations, . . . one million five hundred thousand United States dollars in lump-sum and final settlement of all claims' arising from the operations of ONUC, particularly those which took place in Katanga. The Union of Soviet Socialist Republics (Soviet Union) protested against this claims settlement, stating inter alia, that 'this action by the United Nations Secretariat is unlawful and contrary to decisions taken by the United Nations'.[16] In addition, it stated that

> Belgium, as is well known, committed aggression against the Republic of the Congo and as an aggressor has no moral or legal basis for making claims against the United Nations either on its own behalf or on behalf of its citizens. Belgium is responsible to the Congo and the United Nations for its aggression against that country, and not vice versa.[17]

In the opinion of the Soviet Union, the Secretariat 'has no right in this case to enter into any agreements on behalf of the United Nations concerning the payment of compensation without the authorization of the Security Council'.[18] UN Secretary-General U Thant replied to this four days later. In his reply, the Secretary-General stated that he had acted 'in his capacity of chief administrative officer of the Organization, consistently with the established practice of the United Nations under which claims addressed to the Organization by private individuals are considered and settled under the authority of the Secretary-General'.[19] The Secretary-General did not further elaborate on the origin or legal

[14] UNSC, 'Security Council Official Records, First Meeting' (1946) 5 <https://digitallibrary.un.org/record/636510?v=pdf> accessed 26 September 2024.

[15] This example is mentioned in Blokker (n 6) 110–11. The description is largely reproduced from this publication.

[16] 'Letter of 2 August 1962' (1965) United Nations Juridical Yearbook 40–41, quotation at 40.

[17] ibid.

[18] ibid 41.

[19] 'Letter of 6 August 1962' (1965) United Nations Juridical Yearbook 42.

basis of this established practice, aside from the reference to his capacity of chief administrative officer of the organization, a status bestowed on him in Article 97 of the Charter. While there may not have been a clearly established specific power for the Secretary-General, there was broad support for the view that, overall, it was within his powers to conclude the claims settlement agreement with Belgium. Without such flexibility, without a sufficiently broad interpretation of the powers of the Secretariat, the UN would not be able to perform its functions and meet urgent needs.

These two examples, relating to the UN Security Council and to the UN Secretariat, could be supplemented by many others. No matter how urgent the need to take initiatives, in all these examples, the organs concerned can only act within the limits of their powers. They only have attributed powers. These are explicit and implied, they may be wide and can be fully used, but they are not unlimited. In this respect, not much has changed since the Permanent Court of International Justice observed almost a century ago, with respect to the European Commission of the Danube, one of the oldest IOs:[20]

> As the European Commission is not a State, but an international institution with a special purpose, it only has the functions bestowed upon it by the Definitive Statute with a view to the fulfilment of that purpose, but it has power to exercise these functions to their full extent, in so far as the Statute does not impose restrictions upon it.

Not much has changed since then. Given the fact that IOs do not have general powers, and only have the specific powers attributed to them, they regularly face the dilemma that a situation arises, or a crisis occurs, in which a new task is considered for the organization, but in which it is questioned whether it has the necessary powers. There are countless examples. The beginning of UN peacekeeping during the 1956 Suez crisis: Was it within the powers of the General Assembly to establish a peacekeeping operation? In 1965, was it within the powers of the Secretary-General of the UN to conclude a claims settlement agreement with Belgium? In the 1990s, was the creation of criminal tribunals by the UN Security Council within its powers?[21] Was the 2018

[20] *Jurisdiction of the European Commission of the Danube* (Advisory Opinion) [1972] PCIJ Series B No. 14, 64. The French version of this sentence uses the word 'attribution':

> Comme la Commission européenne n'est pas un État, mais une institution internationale pourvue d'un objet spécial, elle n'a que les attributions que lui confère le Statut définitif, pour lui permettre de remplir cet objet; mais elle a compétence pour exercer ces fonctions dans leur plénitude, pour autant que le Statut ne lui impose pas de restrictions.

[21] Huw Llewellyn, 'The Establishment of the UN Criminal Tribunals: The Role of the UN Secretariat', Chapter 7 in this volume, devoted to the role of the UN Secretariat in the establishment of UN criminal tribunals.

decision of the Organisation for the Prohibition of Chemical Weapons (OPCW) Conference to identify the perpetrators of the use of chemical weapons within the organization's powers? As a final example, the Preparatory Commission for the Comprehensive Nuclear-Test-Ban Treaty Organization (PrepCom) has established installations all over the world to verify compliance with the 1996 Comprehensive Nuclear-Test-Ban Treaty, but these installations are now also used for tsunami warning, a purpose that is entirely outside the scope of the PrepCom's constituent instrument. A myriad of further examples may be given where IOs have taken initiatives when a crisis occurred,[22], including cases in which they seem to fall short of powers necessary to meet a crisis and in which, nevertheless, action was taken.

In these situations, what is the role of law and of the legal framework? Should the law merely facilitate, accommodate whatever is agreed at the political level? Should the legal advisers act as 'corporate lawyers'? But then, what is left of the attribution principle and of the rule of law? Are there certain limitations? If so, how are these implemented in practice? How do, and how should IOs sail between the Scylla of too much rigour and the Charybdis of too much flexibility? A number of techniques and legal doctrines exist to guide IOs, their members, their secretariats, the legal advisers involved, and, at times, international courts and tribunals to sail the right course.

First, the constituent instruments of some IOs include, in addition to specific powers, a rather open-ended more general power for the organization or for one of its organs. A few examples are the following:

- Constitution of the World Health Organization (1946)
  - Article 2: In order to achieve its objective, the functions of the Organization shall be: . . . (v) generally to take all necessary action to attain the objective of the Organization.
  - Article 18: The functions of the Health Assembly shall be: . . . (m) to take any other appropriate action to further the objective of the Organization.
- Agreement on the Status and Functions of the International Commission on Missing Persons (2014), Article 6 (Powers): In furtherance of the foregoing purposes and activities, the Commission shall have the following powers: . . . e. to take other lawful action necessary to accomplish the purposes of the Commission.
- Articles of Agreement of the Asian Infrastructure Investment Bank (2015), Article 16 (General Powers), paragraph 9: The Bank may exercise such

[22] Some further examples (and the action undertaken by IOs) are mentioned in Nicola Bonucci and others, , 'IGO's Initiatives as a Response to Crises and Unforeseen Needs' (2022) 19 International Organizations Law Review 2, 423–82.

> other powers and establish such rules and regulations as may be necessary or appropriate in furtherance of its purpose and functions, consistent with the provisions of this Agreement.

These examples, and many others, demonstrate how flexibility may be given to (organs of) IOs while staying within their attributed powers. Exceptionally, the Treaty on the Functioning of the European Union (EU) prescribes a specific decision-making procedure when the EU intends to take action outside the existing powers of the Union. This decision-making procedure provides for the involvement of the European Commission and the European Parliament; such far-reaching decisions cannot simply be taken by the Council alone. According to Article 352, paragraph 1:

> If action by the Union should prove necessary, within the framework of the policies defined in the Treaties, to attain one of the objectives set out in the Treaties, and the Treaties have not provided the necessary powers, the Council, acting unanimously on a proposal from the Commission and after obtaining the consent of the European Parliament, shall adopt the appropriate measures. Where the measures in question are adopted by the Council in accordance with a special legislative procedure, it shall also act unanimously on a proposal from the Commission and after obtaining the consent of the European Parliament.

The inclusion of such broad 'catch-all clauses' as in the four examples mentioned above may compensate to a certain extent for the inherent constitutional constraint that not all powers necessary for the performance of the organization's functions can be anticipated and enumerated in detail. Nevertheless, even if the constituent instrument of an IO includes a 'catch-all clause', it is unavoidable that sometimes, in practice, situations occur in which there is a demand for action by an IO, but in which the necessary constitutional powers are lacking.[23]

Another example is the doctrine of implied powers. It is generally recognized that IOs do not only have the powers that are laid down explicitly in their constituent instrument but that they also have implied powers. As the ICJ observed in 1996[24]:

> the necessities of international life may point to the need for organizations, in order to achieve their objectives, to possess subsidiary powers which are not expressly provided for in the basic instruments which govern their activities. It

[23] Blokker (n 6), in particular 138–56.

[24] Nuclear Weapons Advisory Opinion (n 7) 66, quotation at 79.

is generally accepted that international organizations can exercise such powers, known as 'implied' powers.

It has furthermore been suggested that IOs have inherent powers[25] and customary powers,[26] but these are not generally recognized. Finally, if none of such doctrines and techniques provide relief, constituent instruments may be amended to give new powers to an IO. However, this does not happen very often[27], because there is no agreement about such an amendment, because it is feared that a proposal to amend the constituent instrument could open Pandora's box, or for other reasons. Moreover, normally it takes a long period of time before an amendment enters into force. An organization facing a crisis may not have such time to do what is necessary to respond to the crisis.

III. The Role of International Secretariats During Crises

So far, this chapter has discussed the powers of IOs as such. It did not lift their veil to 'look inside' these organizations to analyse powers of specific types of organs such as their secretariats (hereinafter also referred to as 'international secretariats'). However, the focus of this book is very much on initiatives taken by these secretariats, and it is therefore appropriate to make some introductory observations about their powers and composition, and the relationship of an international secretariat with the members of IOs (IOs members).

[25] Most well known in this context are the publications by Seyersted. See Finn Seyersted, 'Can the United Nations Establish Military Forces and Perform Other Acts Without Specific Basis in the Charter?' (1962) 1 Österreichische Zeitschrift für Öffentlicher Recht 12, 190–229, in particular at 201–14, at 210–11:

> while intergovernmental organizations, unlike states, are restricted by specific provisions in their constitutions as to the aims for which they shall work, such organizations are, like states, in principle free to perform any sovereign acts, or any act under international law, which they are in a factual position to perform, to attain these aims, provided that their constitutions do not preclude such acts. . . . Thus, it is not necessary to look for specific provisions in the constitution or to resort to strained interpretations of texts and intentions or to other constructions to justify legally the performance by an intergovernmental organization of a sovereign or an international act not specifically authorized in its constitution. As an intergovernmental organization it has an *inherent power* to do so, which need not be justified by construing a special delegation in each case. (italics in the original)

See also Finn Seyersted, *Common Law of International Organizations* (Nijhoff 2008) 31.

[26] Blokker (n 6) 168–77.

[27] Examples are some of the amendments to the Articles of Agreement of the International Monetary Fund (adopted 27 December 1945, entered into force 27 December 1945) 2 UNTS 39, the first (1969) amendment creating the Special Drawing Right as an international reserve asset and giving powers to the Fund in that context (eg the power to allocate SDRs to members), the 1990 amendment introducing new penalties, and the 2008 amendment expanding the investment authority of the International Monetary Fund.

In practice, when reference is made to an IO, what is really meant is sometimes the organization's secretariat. To take a conspicuous example: references to the UN are sometimes, in fact, references to the UN Secretariat or the UN Secretary-General. The reverse may also happen, references being made to the secretariat as a *pars pro toto*, the intention being to refer to the organization as a whole. Studies in international law and in international relations, therefore, generally distinguish between the two, the organization as a whole and its secretariat as one of its organs. For example, in this context, Inis Claude once emphasized the need to 'distinguish between the two identities of the UN, which I shall call the "First UN" and the "Second UN"'.[28] The 'First UN' 'is constituted by its staff, an international secretariat or bureaucracy located in New York, Geneva, and other regional headquarters'.[29] The 'Second UN' is 'a collectivity formed by almost all the states of the world; it consists of its member states, who employ an international secretariat to support their joint deliberations and activities'.[30] In these two identities '– as an organization *for* states and as an organization *of* states – the UN's role is to help in remedying the deficiencies of the pluralistic state system, in coping with the problems that the system presents, and in exploiting the opportunities that it provides'.[31] In practice, reference is sometimes made to 'the UN' while in fact it is intended to refer to one of the UN's two identities: the UN Secretariat or one of the UN's policy-making organs composed of all or some of the member states (eg the General Assembly or the Security Council). While both the First and the Second UN may play a role in dealing with a crisis in the world, this book focuses in particular on initiatives by international secretariats such as the UN Secretariat in that context.

What Claude has observed in relation to the UN is also true for most other IOs; they also have two different identities that are not always neatly distinguished in practice. Taking into account this distinction, the second part of this chapter 'looks within' IOs; it focuses on the role of Claude's 'First UN' and its brothers and sisters, the secretariats of other IOs. Their relationship with the member states of the organization is of particular relevance. It is these international secretariats that may be essential when an IO faces a crisis within its fields of activities, where it is competent to act. It is therefore useful, for the purpose of this book, to not only consider IOs generally but also their secretariats.

When analysing international secretariats, the two key aspects are their tasks and their composition. Both aspects play a key role for the potential for international secretariats to take initiatives in crisis situations. There is great diversity

[28] Inis L Claude, 'Peace and Security: Prospective Roles for the Two United Nations' (1996) 2 Global Governance 289.

[29] ibid 290.

[30] ibid 291.

[31] ibid 297.

in the tasks of international secretariats and great unity in their composition, as will now be elaborated.

A. The tasks and powers of international secretariats

Often, the constituent instruments of IOs do not, or only to a limited extent, detail the specific tasks, functions, duties, and powers of their secretariats (different terms are used for what they need to do).[32] Details may be included in other rules of the organization, and policy-making organs of the organization usually give specific instructions as to what the secretariat needs to do. While these tasks, functions, duties, and powers are specific and different for each secretariat of an IO, their nature is often similar. All secretariats have administrative functions, and for some secretariats these are their only functions. Acting as 'conference managers', they provide the necessary services (from administration to interpretation and translation) for the meetings of policy-making organs of an IO. For example, the Technical Secretariat of the Organisation for the Prohibition of Chemical Weapons (or just OPCW, this acronym was announced above) 'shall . . . [p]rovide administrative and technical support to the Conference, the Executive Council and subsidiary organs'.[33]

Some international secretariats have considerable policy-making tasks themselves. For instance, some have the power to take various kinds of initiatives. Perhaps most well known is the power of the Secretary-General of the UN to 'bring to the attention of the Security Council any matter which in his opinion may threaten the maintenance of international peace and security'.[34] This power has hardly been used in practice, but the wider significance of this Charter provision is the general political authority it gives to the Secretary-General.[35]

Constituent instruments of several other IOs also attribute the power to the organization's Secretary-General (Director-General, etc) to take initiatives or

[32] UN Charter (n 10) ch XV; Constitution of the World Health Organization (adopted 22 July 1946, entered into force 7 April 1948) 14 UNTS 185 ch VII; Marrakesh Agreement Establishing the World Trade Organization (adopted 15 April 1994, entered into force 1 January 1995) 1867 UNTS 3 art VI. Constitution of the ILO, Part XIII of the Treaty of Versailles (1919 as amended since): the Constitution of the ILO is somewhat more specific, see art 10.

[33] Convention on the Prohibition of the Development, Production, Stockpiling and Use of Chemical Weapons and on Their Destruction (adopted 3 September 1992, entered into force 29 April 1997) 1975 UNTS 45 art VIII.D.38(c).

[34] UN Charter (n 10) art 99.

[35] Simon Chesterman, 'Art. 99' in Bruno Simma and others (eds), *The Charter of the United Nations: A Commentary* (4th edn, OUP 2024) vol II, 2627–41 (at 2628: '[Art. 99] represents the most important delegation of political discretion to an international civil servant in the history of international organizations'); Simon Chesterman (ed), *Secretary or General? The UN Secretary-General in World Politics* (CUP 2007).

make proposals.[36] By using this power, the Secretary-General may contribute in a useful way to how her or his organization is performing its functions in a particular area and, more specifically, is dealing with a particular crisis, in the common interest of the member states. Even when such a power of initiative is not explicitly mentioned in an organization's constituent instrument, a Secretary-General may still use her or his authority in practice, for example, to trigger an organization's reaction to a particular crisis, as a kind of indirect initiative.[37] He or she may informally persuade representatives of the member states to take an initiative or support a particular approach. No matter whether it is based on formal or informal authority, the usefulness of the active involvement of a Secretary-General is mainly explained by her or his independence from the members of the organization, to be discussed next.

B. The composition of international secretariats and their relationship with IOs members

In contrast to the wide diversity in tasks of international secretariats, there is considerable unity as far as their composition is concerned. Since some 100 years ago, it is widely considered necessary for international secretariats to be composed of independent international civil servants, not representatives from member states. This basic choice was made in particular when, after the First World War, the League of Nations and the International Labour Organization (ILO) were established.[38] At the time, this characteristic of their secretariats was not laid down in the constituent instruments of these organizations; it was based on decisions taken subsequently in practice. Its rationale is that the work done by the secretariat, whatever it is, should really be done in the common interest of membership as a whole, and should not be partisan, favouring the interest of (a) particular member states. An international secretariat must be independent and must also be seen to be independent. The experiences of the League and of the ILO did not lead to another conclusion, and the requirement of an independent secretariat and an independent staff was therefore firmly codified in the UN Charter. It is laid down in Article 100 of the Charter, as follows:

[36] FAO Constitution, art VII.5; Convention on the Organisation for the Economic Co-operation and Development (with Supplementary Protocols Nos 1 and 2) (adopted 14 December 1960, entered into force 30 September 1961) 888 UNTS 179 art 10.2.

[37] Various examples are mentioned in Part III of this volume. See, eg, Akshaya Venkataraman, 'Taking Initiatives in the WTO: The Role of an Executive Head in Steering Change', Chapter 18 in this volume; Jane Aeberhard-Hodges, 'Concluding Commentary: Reflections on IO Leaders' Approaches', Chapter 21 in this volume.

[38] As demonstrated by Reinalda, early roots of the independent international civil service can already be found in the nineteenth century. See Bob Reinalda, *International Secretariats: Two Centuries of International Civil Servants and Secretariats* (Routledge 2020) 175–76.

1. In the performance of their duties the Secretary-General and the staff shall not seek or receive instructions from any government or from any other authority external to the Organization. They shall refrain from any action which might reflect on their position as international officials responsible only to the Organization.
2. Each Member of the United Nations undertakes to respect the exclusively international character of the responsibilities of the Secretary-General and the staff and not to seek to influence them in the discharge of their responsibilities.

This text makes clear that the independence of the UN staff is based on two pillars. On the one hand, a firm obligation on the staff (paragraph 1) and, on the other hand, an equally firm obligation for the member states. Provisions similar to Article 100 were included in the constituent instruments and/or in other rules of all major organizations established during or immediately after the Second World War.[39] The constituent instruments of many more recently created IOs also contain such provisions, with the relevant obligations both for the staff of the organization and for the member states.[40] This happened even in the face of a considerable number of serious violations of these obligations (or perhaps *because* of such violations),[41] reflecting the perceived need to underline their continued relevance for the successful functioning of IOs. The key importance of this characteristic of international secretariats has also been underlined in judgments of international administrative tribunals. For example, the ILO Administrative Tribunal stated in 2003: 'the independence of international civil servants is an essential guarantee, not only for the civil servants themselves, but also for the proper functioning of IOs'.[42]

In order to establish and effectuate an independent position of an international secretariat vis-à-vis the member states of the organization, two types of member states are of particular importance: First, the host state, on whose

[39] WHO Constitution (n 32) art 37; Convention of the World Meteorological Organization (adopted 11 November 1947, entered into force 23 March 1950) 77 UNTS 143 art 22(b).

[40] Marrakesh Agreement (n 32) art VI.4; Chemical Weapons Convention (n 33) arts VIII.D.46–47; Asian Infrastructure Investment Bank Articles of Agreement (adopted 29 June 2015, entered into force 25 December 2015) 3218 UNTS art 31.3.

[41] Jacques Lemoine, *The International Civil Servant: An Endangered Species* (Brill Nijhoff 1995).

[42] ILO Administrative Tribunal, '*Judgment No. 2232*' (16 July 2003) para 16 <https://webapps.ilo.org/dyn/triblex/triblexmain.fullText?p_lang=en&p_judgment_no=2232&p_language_code=EN> accessed 26 September 2024. On this judgment, see Jan Klabbers, 'The Bustani Case Before the Iloat: Constitutionalism in Disguise?' (2004) 53 The International and Comparative Law Quarterly 455; Ana Stanic, 'Bustani v. Organisation for the Prohibition of Chemical Weapons' (2004) 98 American Journal of International Law 810; Chanaka Wickremasinghe, 'Casenote: The Bustani Case Before the ILOAT' (2004) 1 International Organizations Law Review 197.

territory the secretariat is located.[43] It is also for this reason that headquarters agreements concluded between an IO and its host state usually contain the most detailed rules on the status, privileges, and immunities of the organization.[44] Second, member states whose nationals work for international secretariats as international civil servants. The history of IOs is abounding with examples of member states unlawfully influencing their nationals working for international secretariats, and with examples of such nationals not acting as independent international civil servants in this context. It is not a coincidence that the only two Advisory Opinions of the ICJ dealing with the 1946 UN General Convention concerned disputes between a UN member state and one of its nationals working for the UN.[45]

Member states may be somewhat ambivalent about the independence of international secretariats. On the one hand, they want international secretariats to be independent; on the other hand, they may not want them to become too independent. On the one hand, they may fully support the independence of international secretariats and their staff, when a new organization is created and hopefully also later, in practice. On the other hand, they may want to control what an international secretariat is doing, and how it is performing its functions. On the one hand, it is in the common interest of members that international secretariats have the necessary knowledge and experience to serve the organization. On the other hand, members may also be wary of secretariats becoming new centres of power.[46] International secretariats are expected to act in the common interest of membership as a whole, but their acts may not necessarily be perceived by each member to be also in its *individual* interest.[47] In addition, member states may not have the same views as to the proper balance between

[43] The secretariat of an international organization is normally located on the territory of one of its member states. An exception is the Organization of Petroleum Exporting Countries; its Secretariat is based in Vienna.

[44] Alexander Muller, *International Organizations and Their Host States: Aspects of Their Legal Relationship* (Springer 1995). For a more recent study focusing on the role of Switzerland as a host state, see Pierre-Yves Marro, *Rechtsstellung internationaler Organisationen* (Dike 2021), in particular 81–143.

[45] *Applicability of Article VI, Section 22, of the Convention on the Privileges and Immunities of the United Nations* (Advisory Opinion) [1989] ICJ Rep 177; *Difference Relating to Immunity from Legal Process of a Special Rapporteur of the Commission on Human Rights* (Advisory Opinion) [1999] ICJ Rep 62. Strictly seen, these cases did not concern staff of an international secretariat but experts on mission (Mr Mazilu from Romania and Mr Cumaraswamy from Malaysia).

[46] eg see Margherita Melillo, 'IO Secretariats as Knowledge Actors', Chapter 6 in this volume; Ronald Steenblik and Helen Mountford, 'Fossil Fuel Subsidies at the Organisation for Economic Co-operation and Development', Chapter 10 in this volume.

[47] eg Francis Maupain, 'Is Too Much Vision a Handicap for an Executive Head? Some Thoughts on W Jenks' Curtailed Mandate as ILO Director-General', Chapter 17 in this volume. Partly for this reason, some international organizations have a so-called tenure policy, limiting the total length of service of secretariat staff (eg OPCW and the Preparatory Commission for the Comprehensive Nuclear-Test-Ban Treaty Organization; both have a seven-year tenure policy).

these two different attitudes. It is in this somewhat ambivalent setting that secretariats must perform their functions and take initiatives. They must do so in a rapidly changing world that is rather different from the one existing at the time of the creation of the organization.

IV. Conclusion

This brief contribution has only touched upon a few aspects of the legal framework within which powers and activities of IOs and their secretariats evolve. The contributions that follow in Parts II, III, and IV discuss a number of specific examples and address some of the relevant questions and complexities more in depth.

5

Interpreting Constituent Instruments to Justify the Evolving Powers of International Organizations

Fernando Lusa Bordin

I. Introduction

There are at least three ways in which the evolving powers that international organizations (IOs) claim as they respond to unexpected circumstances or situations of crisis can be justified legally. The first is by inserting clauses in constituent instruments to provide for that possibility.[1] The second is by amending constituent instruments after matters arise in the practice of the organizations. The third is through the purposive interpretation of constituent instruments. Because member states do not always have the desire or foresight to go for the first option when they conclude constituent instruments, and because the second option typically involves cumbersome and time-consuming processes both at the international and domestic levels, interpretation takes on an important role in the practice of IOs.

That puts pressure on interpretation as a technique of law application. The question arises, both from a doctrinal and a normative point of view, as to whether, how, and to what extent legal interpretation can sufficiently accommodate change. This chapter offers some reflections on that question in two steps. First, it explores how treaty interpretation has been adapted to cater to the context in which IOs operate. Second, it discusses issues of legality and legitimacy.

II. Treaty Interpretation as Applied to Constituent Instruments

In the absence of any special rules, the starting point for the interpretation of constituent instruments of IOs has been Articles 31 and 32 of the 1969 Vienna

[1] As discussed in Niels Blokker, 'The Evolution of IO Powers and Activities: A Legal Framework', Chapter 4 in this volume.

Fernando Lusa Bordin, *Interpreting Constituent Instruments to Justify the Evolving Powers of International Organizations*
In: *International Organization Initiatives*. Edited by: Gabrielle Marceau and Henner Gött, Oxford University Press.
 DOI: 10.1093/9780197803325.003.0006

Convention on the Law of Treaties (VCLT 1969).[2] The interpreter is instructed to start with 'the ordinary meaning to be given to the terms of the treaty in their context and in the light of its object and purpose', also taking into account subsequent agreements regarding the interpretation of the treaty, subsequent practice in the application of the treaty establishing an agreement on how it is to be construed, and any 'relevant rules of international law applicable in the relations between the parties'.[3] To confirm the meaning reached at that first step, or to determine that meaning further in cases where it is either left 'ambiguous or obscure' or leads to a 'manifestly absurd or unreasonable' result, the interpreter is directed to 'supplementary means of interpretation', including the preparatory work of the treaty.[4]

This analytical framework, which invites the flexible weighing of several hermeneutic factors, is capable of accommodating the contexts of different subfields and regimes of international law.[5] An illuminating synthesis of how the 'rules' of interpretation have been adapted to make sense of the peculiarities of IOs is offered by the International Court of Justice (ICJ) in *Legality of the Use by a State of Nuclear Weapons in Armed Conflict.* The Court started by observing that '[f]rom a formal standpoint, the constituent instruments of international organizations are multilateral treaties, to which the well-established rules of treaty interpretation apply'.[6] At the same time, it acknowledged that constituent instruments are 'treaties of a particular type' because they 'create new subjects of law endowed with a certain autonomy, to which the parties entrust the task of realizing common goals'.[7] Due to this dual character of constituent instruments—'conventional and at the same time institutional', in the Court's words—interpretation must take into account the 'nature of the organization created', the 'objectives' assigned to the organization, 'the imperatives associated with the effective performance of [the organization's] functions', and the practice of the organization itself.[8]

That synthesis encapsulates two bespoke hermeneutic factors which, together with its predecessor, the Court played a crucial role in developing over the

[2] Vienna Convention on the Law of Treaties (adopted 22 May 1969, entered into force 20 January 1980) 1155 UNTS 331 (VCLT). That is envisaged in Article 5, which provides that the rules in the Convention apply to 'any treaty which is the constituent instrument of an international organization', though 'without prejudice to any relevant rules of the organization'. See further Henner Gött, *Law of Interactions Between International Organizations* (Springer 2020) 233ff.

[3] VCLT (n 2) art 31.

[4] ibid art 32.

[5] Campbell McLachlan, 'The Principle of Systemic Interpretation and Article 31(3)(c) of the Vienna Convention' (2005) 54 International and Comparative Law Quarterly 279, 291.

[6] *Legality of the Use by a State of Nuclear Weapons in Armed Conflict* (Advisory Opinion) [1996] ICJ Rep 66 para 19.

[7] ibid.

[8] ibid.

decades. The first is the so-called implied powers doctrine, according to which an IO 'must be deemed to have those powers which, though not expressly provided in the [constituent instrument], are conferred upon it by necessary implication as being essential to the performance of its duties'.[9] This is an applied form of teleological interpretation, which puts a premium on the nature, objectives, and effective functioning of the organization. It is also an expression of the principle of effectiveness in treaty interpretation,[10] which is illustrated by the Permanent Court of International Justice's suggestion that an 'international institution with a special purpose' has 'the power to exercise [its] functions to their full extent, in so far as [its] Statute does not impose restrictions upon it'.[11]

The second factor is established institutional practice. This factor can be viewed as an application of the prompt found in Article 31(3)(b) VCLT 1969, which invites the interpreter to consider the subsequent practice of the parties to the extent that it reveals an agreement on the interpretation of the treaty. In the case of IOs, the relevant practice regarding the application of the constituent instrument and other internal rules often comes from the organization itself, through action taken not only by political organs but also by secretariats. That practice is then compounded by the practice of the member states, *qua* parties to the constituent instrument, as they react to what the organization is doing by endorsing it, rejecting it, or remaining silent. It is by appraising this synergy between IOs and their members that the interpreter can determine whether and to what extent a practice is 'established' so as to shed light on the meaning of the constituent instrument.[12] Significantly, the 'established practice of the organization'

[9] *Reparation for Injuries Suffered in the Service of the United Nations* (Advisory Opinion) [1949] ICJ Rep 174, 182. See also Blokker (n 1); Naphtali Ukamwa, 'The Role of Heads of Secretariats in Initiating Change: Functional Formalism and Pluralism', Chapter 13 in this volume.

[10] A sophisticated discussion of the principle of effectiveness as a mode of teleological reasoning is pursued by Tim Clark, *Teleology in the Law of International Organizations* (PhD Dissertation, University of Cambridge 2023), on file with the author.

[11] *Jurisdiction of the European Commission of the Danube* (Advisory Opinion) [1927] PCIJ Series B No 14, 64.

[12] International Law Commission (ILC), 'Report of the International Law Commission on the Work of Its 70th Session' (30 April–1 June and 2 July–10 August 2018) UN Doc A/73/10, which includes the ILC's 'Draft Conclusions on Subsequent Agreements and Subsequent Practice in Relation to the Interpretation of Treaties'. In Conclusion 12 of its 2018 Conclusions on Subsequent Agreements and Subsequent Practice in Relation to the Interpretation of Treaties, the ILC recognizes that '[s]ubsequent agreements and subsequent practice of the parties under article 31, paragraph 3, or subsequent practice under article 32, may arise from, or be expressed in, the practice of an international organization in the application of its constituent instrument'. It states further that '[p]ractice of an international organization in the application of its constituent instrument may contribute to the interpretation of that instrument when applying articles 31 and 32'. The ILC thus distinguishes between the practice of the member states and the practice of the organization and, while acknowledging that the two types of practice may be connected, it suggests that they may provide independent hermeneutic factors for the interpretation of constituent instruments. But whether it can be established that there is established institutional practice without no regard to the attitude of the member states is an interesting doctrinal question that the Commission does not tackle: see Report of the International Law Commission (2018) 93–104 <https://legal.un.org/ilc/reports/2018/english/a_73_10_advance.pdf> accessed 25 September 2024. For a sophisticated discussion of the

has come to be accepted as part of the definition of the internal law of IOs (the so-called rules of the organization) found in the 1986 Vienna Convention on the Law of Treaties Between States and International Organizations and Between International Organizations and in the 2011 Draft Articles on the Responsibility of International Organizations (DARIO).[13]

By resorting to the implied powers doctrine and established institutional practice, the International Court has confirmed a few 'evolving powers' that the organs of the United Nations (UN) asserted as the organization faced novel situations. For example, in *Reparation for Injuries*, when the UN was considering how to react to the assassination of its envoy to the Middle East, the Court found that the power to espouse an official's claim on the international plane against a non-member state was implied in the Charter.[14] In *Certain Expenses*, at a time when the UN Security Council was unable to agree on enforcement action because of the onset of the Cold War, the Court confirmed the power of the General Assembly (UNGA) and the Security Council to set up peacekeeping operations, the costs of which had to be borne by the member states as apportioned by the UNGA.[15] Recourse to established institutional practice has also led the Court to validate procedural deviations from the letter of the Charter that had consolidated through the functioning of political organs of the UN. In the *Namibia* advisory opinion, the Court found that an abstention from a permanent member of the Security Council qualifies as a 'concurring vote' for the purposes of applying Article 27(3) of the Charter, given that such a procedure had been 'generally accepted by Members of the United Nations and [evidenced] a general practice of that Organization'.[16] In the *Wall* advisory opinion, the Court did not think that Article 12(1) of the Charter, according to which the General Assembly may not make recommendations '[w]hile the Security Council is exercising in respect of any dispute or situation the functions assigned to it', prevented the Assembly from requesting an advisory opinion, because it had

continuities and discontinuities of the practice of the parties and the practice of the organization, see Julian Arato, 'Treaty Interpretation and Constitutional Transformation: Informal Change in International Organizations' (2013) 38 Yale Journal of International Law 290, 318–27.

[13] Vienna Convention on the Law of Treaties Between States and International Organizations or Between International Organizations (1986) 25 ILM 543 art 2(j), '"rules of the organization" means, in particular, the constituent instruments, decisions and resolutions adopted in accordance with them, and established practice of the organization'. DARIO Article 2(b) provides an almost identical definition. See further Christopher Peters, 'Subsequent Practice and Established Practice of International Organizations: Two Sides of the Same Coin?' (2011) 3 Goettingen Journal of International Law 617.

[14] *Reparation for Injuries Suffered in the Service of the United Nations* (n 9) 182–84.

[15] *Certain Expenses of the United Nations* (Advisory Opinion) [1962] ICJ Rep 151.

[16] *Legal Consequences for States of the Continued Presence of South Africa in Namibia (South West Africa) Notwithstanding Security Council Resolution 276 (1970)* (Advisory Opinion) [1971] ICJ Rep 16 para 22.

become an 'accepted practice' that the Council and the Assembly '[dealt] in parallel with the same matter concerning the maintenance of international peace and security'.[17]

The picture that emerges is one of a purposive, dynamic approach to interpretation, which regards IOs as living institutions that must be equipped to perform their functions effectively over time. While the case law of the ICJ barely scratches the surface, as interpretation takes place in the day-to-day operations of organizations and in the form of legal advice that is often not public or at least not publicized widely, the Court's approach has become influential.[18] That is certainly the case among academics,[19] and presumably also among legal advisors and other practitioners.[20] It has also been recognized in a recent resolution of the *Institut de Droit international*, which provides both that '[i]nternational organizations may resort to evolutive interpretation of their constituent instruments to address current challenges and to fill unforeseen gaps' and that 'when there is a general agreement among the membership of the international organization as to an interpretation, the interpretation should be presumed to be valid and *intra vires*'.[21]

III. The Doctrinal and Normative Challenges of Justifying Evolving Powers Through Interpretation

Recourse to a purposive approach to the interpretation of constituent instruments may create doctrinal and normative concerns. In particular, the question arises of whether reliance on teleological interpretation under the guise of 'implied powers' and similar notions does not take the reasoning too far from

[17] *Legal Consequences of the Construction of a Wall in the Occupied Palestinian Territory* (Advisory Opinion) [2004] ICJ Rep 136 paras 25–27.

[18] Blokker (n 1).

[19] As reflected in leading textbooks and monographs on the law of IOs. See, eg, José E. Alvarez, *International Organizations as Law-Makers* (OUP 2005) 82–100; Henry Schermers and Niels M Blokker, *International Institutional Law: Unity Within Diversity* (6th edn, Nijhoff 2018) 872–85.

[20] On the role that purposive reasoning has played within the World Bank, see Ibrahim FI Shihata, 'The Dynamic Evolution of International Organizations: The Case of the World Bank' (2000) 2 Journal of the History of International Law 217, especially 223–24 and 246–47. For a rich study of 'IO expansion', including analyses of how interpretation was deployed within the International Labour Organization, the United Nations, and the World Bank, see Guy Fiti Sinclair, *To Reform the World: International Organizations and the Making of Modern States* (OUP 2017). See also Hassane Cissé, 'How Do External Factors Shape Institutional, Legal, Strategic, or Policy Change in International Organizations: Review of Selected Examples in World Bank Practice', Chapter 24 in this volume.

[21] Institut de Droit international, 'Limits to Evolutive Interpretation of the Constituent Instruments of the Organizations Within the United Nations System by Their Internal Organs' (Resolution of 4 September 2021) <https://www.idi-iil.org/en/publications/limites-a-linterpretation-evolutive-des-actes-constitutifs-des-organisations-du-systeme-des-nations-unies-par-leurs-organes-internes/> accessed 25 September 2024.

the realm of law-application into the realm of law-making. In legal practice, the line between law application and law-making can be fine, especially when, as it is often the case with IOs, questions are posed for which existing rules provide no immediate answer. Yet, even if interpretation in such cases will always imply an element of innovation, those carrying it out are expected to provide an answer that fits well within the legal system in which they operate.[22] That is required from anyone who acts under the political ideal of the rule of law.[23] A solution that extrapolates from, and is coherent with, existing rules or legal practice is superior to a solution that can only be justified on the basis of the policy preferences of the interpreter.

Timothy Clark has commented on the 'teleological turn' in the law of IOs, arguing that the use of purposive reasoning by the ICJ in some of its advisory opinions has broken down 'the link between text and outcome', to the point that what the Court has done looks more like law-making than interpretation.[24] His analysis does indeed throw into relief shortcomings of the reasoning of the Court, especially when one compares the test that the Court purports to apply with the outcome that the Court reaches. In *Reparation for Injuries*, for example, the Court observed that the UN 'must be deemed to have those powers which, though not expressly provided in the Charter, are conferred upon it by necessary implication as being essential to the performance of its duties'. Based on the need to 'ensure the efficient and independent performance of [its] missions and to afford effective support to its agents', the Court went on to find that 'the capacity of the Organization to exercise a measure of functional protection of its agents arises by necessary intendment out of the Charter'.[25] It may be plausible to suggest that the power to exercise functional protection furthers the purposes of the UN and that it presents a solution that fits well within the system established by the UN Charter. But describing that solution as a 'necessary implication as being essential', or as arising 'by necessary intendment out of the Charter', is a stretch.[26]

At the same time, to look for a link between text and outcome in a scenario where the interpreter simply does not have a specific textual basis to work with is

[22] Fernando Bordin, *The Analogy Between States and International Organizations* (CUP 2019) 17–35.

[23] Neil McCormick, *Legal Reasoning and Legal Theory* (OUP 1978) 246–55.

[24] Timothy Clark, 'The Teleological Turn in the Law of International Organisations' (2021) 70 International and Comparative Law Quarterly 533, 556.

[25] *Reparation for Injuries Suffered in the Service of the United Nations* (n 9) 182 –84.

[26] Clark is not alone in taking issue with how the ICJ has articulated and applied the implied powers doctrine. See, eg, the well-known and scathing assessment offered by Finn Seyersted, *Common Law of International Organizations* (Nijhoff 2008) 30, for whom:

> in order to avoid a conflict with practice and to escape the consequences of their point of departure without admitting its falseness, the formula of 'implied powers' has had to be applied whenever the need was felt – in such a wide, fictitious and undefined manner that it offers no guidance, merely an escape from the false point of departure.

a futile exercise. It is telling that in cases where the Court has had to pronounce on the powers of IO organs as laid down in a particular provision from the constituent instrument, considerations regarding the most expedient functioning of the organization did not prevail over the text. Thus, in *Competence of the General Assembly for the Admission of a State to the UN*, the Court gave effect to the wording of Article 4(2) of the Charter, observing that '[t]o hold that the General Assembly has power to admit a State to membership in the absence of a recommendation of the Security Council would deprive the Security Council of an important power which has been entrusted to it by the Charter'.[27] Similarly, in the *Inter-Governmental Maritime Consultative Organization (IMCO)* advisory opinion, the Court gave effect to the wording of Article 28(a) of the Inter-Governmental Maritime Consultative Organization's constituent instrument, according to which the largest ship-owning nations were to occupy no less than eight seats at the IMCO Maritime Safety Committee; it denied the possibility that the IMCO Assembly could exercise discretion in determining who those largest ship-owning nations were, even if that approach could have potentially served the interest of maritime safety better.[28] In contrast, in cases where the constituent instrument gives no specific indication as to whether a power that an IO asserts is permitted or proscribed, the interpreter's task is to articulate the appropriate interpretative test and apply it faithfully to the case, ensuring that there is a link between the test and the outcome reached. In this respect, the Court's reasoning in *Certain Expenses* is more convincing than that in *Reparation for Injuries*. Instead of asking whether the setting up of peacekeeping missions such as the United Nations Emergency Force (UNEF) and United Nations Operation in the Congo (ONUC) arose 'by necessary intendment out of the Charter', the Court relied on a presumption that 'action which warrants the assertion that it was appropriate for the fulfilment of one of the stated purposes of the United Nations . . . is not *ultra vires* the Organization'.[29]

At the same time, a broad test such as that articulated in *Certain Expenses* raises further concerns. Unlike states, which are presumed to be free to act in the absence of constraints imposed by international law, IOs are established

[27] *Competence of Assembly Regarding Admission to the United Nations* (Advisory Opinion) [1950] ICJ Rep 4, 9.

[28] *Constitution of the Maritime Safety Committee of the Inter-Governmental Maritime Consultative Organization* (Advisory Opinion) [1960] ICJ Rep 150, 166. As the Court noted in its very first advisory opinion, concerning the interpretation of Article 4 of the UN Charter, '[t]o warrant an interpretation other than that which ensues from the natural meaning of the words, a decisive reason would be required, which [needs to be] established': *Admission of a State to the United Nations* (Advisory Opinion) [1948] ICJ Rep 57, 63. When the Court accepted an 'interpretation other than that which ensues from the natural meaning of the words' in *Namibia* and *Wall*, the 'decisive reason' was provided by established institutional practice.

[29] *Certain Expenses of the United Nations* (n 15) 168.

under international law to fulfil predefined purposes and exercise predefined functions. They are, as such, expected to 'show their powers' before taking action, at least vis-à-vis their members. If a casual analogy between international law and the domestic legal systems of liberal democracies can be allowed to illustrate the point, international law treats states like liberal democracies treat individuals, putting a premium on their freedom of action; conversely, it treats IOs like liberal democracies treat public bodies, requiring them to justify any encroachment on their member's freedoms.[30] In this spirit, the ICJ may well have wished to employ a narrow test of 'necessary intendment' in some of its advisory opinions to reassure states that it was serious about reviewing UN action. There is some merit in Clark's suggestion that overly purposive approaches not only create 'the risk of State backlash' but also ignore the fact that the contractual (conventional) dimension of constituent instruments remains an 'ultimate source of democratic legitimacy' for IOs.[31]

The question then becomes what test would be appropriate for those interpreting constituent instruments to apply in situations of uncertainty. That is a difficult question to answer in the abstract. As Viljam Engström has persuasively argued, there can be no 'inherent meaning' to concepts such as 'functional necessity' that are 'detached from the interpreters' conception of what [each] organization should do and why'.[32] Different IOs will necessarily invite different hermeneutic sensibilities. Thus, while commonalities between IOs mean that a general analytical framework is useful, the interpretation of constituent instruments is ultimately a question of institutional law, specific to the internal law and constitutional culture of each IO. The balance to be struck between the need to allow the IO to react to novel situations in ways that allow it to fulfil its purposes and the need to ensure that IOs do not encroach upon the rights of their members will vary from organization to organization.[33]

[30] In reality, both states and IOs, as institutions governed by forms of public law, are created, empowered, and constrained by their constitutions. However, the constitutions of states are typically viewed as falling outside the purview of international law, whereas the constitutions of IOs, which derive their validity from international law, naturally attract the attention of international lawyers who may be required to look, or interested in looking, into the rules that govern the relations between organization and members. At the same time, a distinction between the rules of international law that apply to IOs on the international plane and the 'rules of the organization' that apply between IOs and its members on the institutional plane must be made. The expectation 'to show powers' referred here characterizes the relations on the institutional plane but is of little, if any, consequence on the international plane. See further Christiane Ahlborn, 'The Rules of International Organizations and the Law of International Responsibility' (2012) 8 International Organizations Law Review 397; Fernando Bordin, 'General International Law in the Relations Between International Organizations and Their Members' (2019) 32 Leiden Journal of International Law 653.

[31] Timothy Clark (n 24) 565–66.

[32] Viljam Engström, 'Reasoning on Powers of Organizations' in Jan Klabbers and Åsa Wallendahl (eds), *Research Handbook on the Law of International Organizations* (Edward Elgar 2011) 56, 65–66.

[33] Compare, eg, the initiatives described in Mona Ali Khalil, 'The Evolution of UN Secretary-General Initiatives to Respond to Violent and Non-Violent Threats to International Peace and Security', Chapter 14 in this volume; Gian Luca Burci and Ana Balcazar-Moreno, 'WHO's Reactions

Yet, in pondering this question of balance, it is useful to turn to the interplay between purposive interpretation and institutional practice. The interaction between those two factors offers a system of checks and balances, for member states are always in a position to push back against interpretations that they find exorbitant.[34] An example is provided in the ICJ's opinion in *Legality of the Use by a State of Nuclear Weapons in Armed Conflict*, where the Court did not view the resolution of the World Health Assembly requesting the advisory opinion as 'establishing an agreement between the members of the Organization to interpret its Constitution as empowering it to address the question of the legality of the use of nuclear weapons', noting that it had been adopted 'not without opposition'.[35] The Court likewise saw the absence of any previous real engagement with the question in the practice of the World Health Organization (WHO) as evidence that the WHO Constitution did not empower the organization to deal with it.[36] An even more eloquent example of member state pushback against purposive action within the WHO concerns the adoption of the International Health Regulations in 2005. Eyal Benvenisti has suggested that the Regulations, for all their merits, were a regressive reaction against the WHO Director-General's robust and purposive exercise of her powers when the organization tackled the SARS epidemic.[37] By adopting them, the member states have favoured an approach that is more deferential to state sovereignty and limits independent WHO action.[38]

It is thus a mistake to discount the agency that members of IOs exercise. Indeed, it can be misleading to picture member states as being at the receiving end of evolving powers, as if the organization was always, or even often, imposing those powers on them against their will. Rather, member states are frequently drivers of change, either when the initiative originates in the political organs of the organization or when those political organs are quick to endorse initiatives proposed by secretariats or other organs where members do not sit. An example, discussed in Mona Ali Khalil's chapter in this volume (Chapter 14), is the establishment by UN Secretary-General Ban Ki-Moon of the UN Mission for Ebola Emergency Response. By launching the UN's first health-keeping mission,

to COVID-19: Between Politics and Managerialism', Chapter 9 in this volume; and Akshaya Venkataraman, 'Taking Initiatives in the WTO: The Role of an Executive Head in Steering Change', Chapter 18 in this volume.

[34] Schermers and Blokker refer to this as a 'reality check', Schermers and Blokker (n 19) 882. The effectiveness of that 'reality check' will depend, among other things, on the existence of a critical mass of members objecting to the potentially unlawful IO action.

[35] *Legality of the Use by a State of Nuclear Weapons in Armed Conflict* (n 6) para 27.

[36] ibid.

[37] Eyal Benvenisti, 'The WHO—Destined to Fail?: Political Cooperation and the COVID-19 Pandemic' (2020) 114 American Journal of International Law 588, 594–97.

[38] ibid.

the Secretary-General purported 'to make maximum use of the authority provided to [him], including in the area of human resources, in order to promote the timely and effective response to the Ebola crisis'.[39] In a resolution adopted without a vote, the UNGA reacted to the Secretary-General's articulation of an evolving power by not only welcoming that power but also requesting him to exercise it.[40] Another example, also discussed in Khalil's chapter, concerns the General Assembly's acceptance, also unanimously, of the proposition that the UN Security Council may use force to prevent or stop genocide, war crimes, and crimes against humanity under the doctrine of the responsibility to protect, which had been championed by Secretary-General Kofi Annan.[41] While the Security Council enjoys wide discretion under Chapter VII of the Charter, the recognition by the entirety of the UN membership that those international crimes may constitute a threat to international peace and security (even when committed in a non-international armed conflict) places enforcement action in those scenarios on firmer constitutional ground. That is one of the reasons why established institutional practice can be legitimately viewed as forming part of the rules of the organization—one way or another, it reveals an agreement of the 'masters of the treaty' on how the constituent instrument is to be construed and on which novel initiatives taken by discrete organs, and secretariats in particular, fall within the organization's remit.

In short, institutional practice both grounds and constrains purposive interpretation. When concurring with that interpretation, it provides evidence that the evolving power is plausible. But when member states are divided about the evolving power, or where the evolving power comes across as completely divorced from the organization's track record, the burden to show its plausibility through purposive interpretation becomes more onerous.[42]

IV. Concluding Remarks

This chapter has shown how an analytical framework for the interpretation of the constituent instruments of IOs has emerged that is capable of accommodating change and justifying the evolving powers of those organizations. That

[39] UNGA, 'Identical Letters Dated 17 September 2014 from the Secretary-General Addressed to the President of the General Assembly and the President of the Security Council' (18 September 2024) UN Doc S/2014/679.

[40] UNGA, 'Measures to Contain and Combat the Recent Ebola Outbreak in West Africa' (23 September 2014)) UN Doc A/RES/69/1.

[41] UNGA, '2005 World Summit Outcome' (24 October 2005) UN Doc A/RES/60/1 paras 138–39.

[42] At least in theory: for a discussion of the ICJ's willingness to rely on institutional practice even in the face of (at least some) disagreement among UN member states in *Certain Expenses* and *Wall*, see Arato (n 12) 318–21 and 324–27.

analytical framework is not without doctrinal and normative challenges, but it derives some stability and plausibility from a synergy between purposive reasoning and institutional practice.

Academic approaches to this topic, like the one attempted here, tend to suffer from an empirical blind spot: that of relying too heavily on the case law of the ICJ, when it corresponds to just a little fragment of the practice of interpretation of constituent instruments. A full account must also consider the day-to-day activities of legal advisors and other stakeholders that engage in interpretation, both for the IOs and for the members. Is the analytical framework described useful and used, especially in times of crisis? Do the hermeneutic sensibilities that the case law of the ICJ encapsulate remain appealing to practitioners, if they ever were?

Many of the IO initiatives discussed in this volume could be rationalized as confirming the traditional legal account of how the powers of IOs evolve: secretariats take bold action in situations of crisis without a clear mandate (that is, invoke implied powers), which are later confirmed (or, more rarely, rejected) by the practice of the political organs of the organizations concerned. At the same time, the extent to which legal considerations play a part in the taking of those initiatives is not easy to determine, and details of the legal thinking behind them are not easy to find (at least in the public domain). Still, regardless of the role that the analytical framework plays in actual decision-making, doctrines of interpretation provide a valuable technique to evaluate IO initiatives from the perspective of the political ideal of the rule of law.

PART II

THE ROLE OF SECRETARIATS IN INITIATING IO CHANGE

6

IO Secretariats as Knowledge Actors

Margherita Melillo

I. Introduction

This chapter deals with the question of 'how' change occurs in international organizations (IOs). Focusing on the secretariats of IOs, it conceptualizes their role as one of 'knowledge actors'.[1] Accordingly, it reviews how secretariats of IOs use their knowledge authority to instigate or support change in IOs.

That expertise is one of the main characteristics of IOs and has long been recognized by international relations (IR) scholarship. Early IO scholars like Ernst B Haas and Peter Haas highlighted the importance of knowledge in the life of IOs.[2] However, consistent with the theoretical underpinnings of their work, their principal focus was on how knowledge shapes the beliefs and attitudes of their member states (and, only consequently, international governance). With some notable exceptions,[3] in fact, IO secretariats had been mostly neglected by realist and liberal IR scholarship.

It is only with the explicit embrace of constructivist theory that the role of expertise in IO secretariats becomes a discrete investigative topic.[4] In their breakthrough book, Barnett and Finnemore have provided the first formal conceptualization of IO secretariats as international bureaucracies that can act autonomously from their member states.[5] IO secretariats, they argue, derive authority from three sources: delegation (from their member states), the moral character of their values and goals (which helps them present themselves

[1] In this chapter, 'knowledge' is used in a broad meaning, as any 'understanding of or information about a subject that you get by experience or study' (*Cambridge Dictionary* 2023). It is used interchangeably with 'expertise', 'specialized knowledge', and 'expert knowledge'.

[2] Ernst B Haas, *Beyond the Nation State: Functionalism and International Organization* (ECPR Press 2008); Ernst B Haas, *When Knowledge Is Power: Three Models of Change in International Organizations* (University of California Press 1990); Peter M Haas, 'Introduction: Epistemic Communities and International Policy Coordination' (1992) 46 International Organization 1.

[3] Robert W Cox and others, *The Anatomy of Influence: Decision Making in International Organization* (Yale UP 1973).

[4] Peter M Haas and Ernst B Haas, 'Learning to Learn: Improving International Governance' (1995) 1 Global Governance 255.

[5] Michael Barnett and Martha Finnemore, *Rules for the World: International Organizations in Global Politics* (Cornell UP 2004).

Margherita Melillo, *IO Secretariats as Knowledge Actors* In: *International Organization Initiatives.* Edited by: Gabrielle Marceau and Henner Gött, Oxford University Press. © Oxford University Press 2025.
DOI: 10.1093/9780197803325.003.0007

as impartial), and expertise.[6] Following this groundbreaking book, in the past 20 years, IR scholars have continued studying the autonomy and activities of IO secretariats and the role of expertise.[7]

Legal scholarship has taken even longer to recognize the fundamental role of expertise in IO secretariats. This reflects the discipline's long-standing limited role in theorization of IOs.[8] Captured 'in the grip of a positivistic preoccupation with an ostensibly sacrosanct doctrine of sources', in fact, international legal scholars have long failed to appreciate the normative role of IOs in international law.[9] Moreover, a lingering functionalist view of IO has long hindered international lawyers in effectively addressing legal questions on the relationship of IOs with actors that are not their member states.[10]

Once these conceptual barriers are revealed, however, expertise emerges as a key characteristic of IO secretariats. In his landmark article, Klabbers has described two ubiquitous 'concepts' of IOs in international law: one is managerial, which highlights the expert role of IOs ('[l]eave it to the experts . . . and shortsighted things such as sovereignty will be overcome by pure reason'), and the other *agora*, which emphasizes their political nature as intergovernmental fora.[11] Despite being sometimes seen in contraposition, Klabbers argues, the two dimensions are interdependent and complementary in the life of IOs. The two concepts of IOs can be also seen reflected in how IOs exercise their normative authority: through formal instruments (such as treaties and resolutions) and through informal instruments (such as guidelines and technical briefings) whose main source of authoritativeness rests on the expert knowledge of the IO producing them.[12]

[6] ibid 16–27.

[7] Steffen Bauer, 'Does Bureaucracy Really Matter? The Authority of Intergovernmental Treaty Secretariats in Global Environmental Politics' (2006) 6 Global Environmental Politics 23; Frank Biermann and Bernd Siebenhüner (eds), *Managers of Global Change: The Influence of International Environmental Bureaucracies* (MIT Press 2009); Diane Stone, *Knowledge Actors and Transnational Governance: The Private-Public Policy Nexus in the Global Agora* (Springer 2013); Sikina Jinnah, *Post-Treaty Politics: Secretariat Influence in Global Environmental Governance* (MIT Press 2014); Louisa Bayerlein, Christoph Knill, and Yves Steinebach, *A Matter of Style?: Organizational Agency in Global Public Policy* (CUP 2020).

[8] Jan Klabbers and Guy Fiti Sinclair, 'On Theorizing International Organizations Law: Editors' Introduction' (2020) 31 European Journal of International Law 489.

[9] José E Alvarez, *International Organizations as Law-Makers* (OUP 2006) x–xi.

[10] Jan Klabbers, 'The EJIL Foreword: The Transformation of International Organizations Law' (2015) 26 European Journal of International Law 9; Namira Negm, 'The African Union Commission's Endeavour with the International Court of Justice for Achieving the Complete Decolonization of Mauritius: The Case of the Chagos Archipelago', Chapter 11 in this volume; Part IV of this volume, 'Interaction with the Outside World and IO Change'; Laurence Boisson de Chazournes and others, 'Conclusion: Adaptation, Change, and International Organizations: An Inside–Outside Perspective' in this volume.

[11] Jan Klabbers, 'Two Concepts of International Organization' (2005) 2 International Organizations Law Review 277, 281–82.

[12] Jan Klabbers, 'The Normative Gap in International Organizations Law: The Case of the World Health Organization' (2019) 16 International Organizations Law Review 272, 279.

The recognition of the autonomy of IO secretariats has challenged some of the traditional tenets of the discipline and led to new investigations. A new field, Global Administrative Law, has emerged to fill the normative gap created by the expansion of power of IOs.[13] Among these studies, the role of expertise of IO secretariats has been highlighted as a key innovation. For example, one renowned IO textbook now states that expertise is one of the main reasons why IO secretariats have become 'centers of power', leading to calls for more accountability.[14] The call has not gone unanswered, and accountability of experts in international governance has been the subject of various investigations.[15] On the other hand, the increase in resort to experts has been seen as a tool to enhance legitimacy, either in its output dimension (by improving quality) or in the input dimension (by making processes and thus decisions more transparent).[16] This strand of legal scholarship looks at ways of how expert involvement can be improved by formalizing their roles and strengthening the related legal frameworks. Finally, they make the point that legal expertise is a form of expertise, despite usually not being regarded as such by IR scholarship.[17]

Against this background, this chapter investigates the role of IO secretariats as knowledge actors. The chapter begins by tracing the intellectual and historical origin of the technocratic character of IOs as a whole. It then turns to analysing the role of IO secretariats as international bureaucracies. It shows that, like for all bureaucracies, knowledge is a key component of the authority of IO secretariats and that IO secretariats routinely rely on their technical expertise to depoliticize their actions. Addressing the question of change, the chapter reviews the role that knowledge can play in the strategic actions of IO secretariats.[18] It concludes that expertise is an important but not sufficient condition for IO secretariats to influence policy outcomes. Moreover, the amount, quality, and type of expertise also matter in influencing policy change. Nonetheless, qualifying IO secretariats as knowledge actors is an important step towards better understanding their role in global governance, as well as their links to other relevant actors.[19]

[13] Benedict Kingsbury and Lorenzo Casini, 'Global Administrative Law Dimensions of International Organizations Law' (2009) 6 International Organizations Law Review 319.

[14] Henry G Schermers and Niels M Blokker, *International Institutional Law: Unity Within Diversity* (5th rev edn, Nijhoff 2011) 404–05.

[15] Alessandra Arcuri and Florin Coman-Kund, *Technocracy and the Law: Accountability, Governance and Expertise* (Routledge 2021).

[16] Mónika Ambrus and others, *The Role of 'experts' in International and European Decision-Making Processes: Advisors, Decision Makers or Irrelevant Actors?* (CUP 2014) 5–6.

[17] ibid 10–14.

[18] Gian Luca Burci and Ana Balcazar-Moreno, 'WHO's Reactions to COVID-19: Between Politics and Managerialism', Chapter 9 in this volume.

[19] Negm (n 10); Part IV of this book (n 10); Boisson de Chazournes and others (n 10).

II. The Indissoluble Link Between IOs and Specialized Knowledge

The link between IOs and expertise is arguably as old as IOs themselves. Examining the intellectual history of the idea of IOs, Jens Steffek has showed how from the early nineteenth-century writers from different backgrounds envisioned creating technocratic institutions that would manage transnational cooperation and its problems.[20] What is remarkable about this intellectual history is that the necessity of international institutions with specialized knowledge is at the same time unexplained and common to authors from very different traditions of thought—an 'ideology', in Steffek's words.[21] Paul Reinsch, David Mitrany, Ernst B Haas, but also Hans Morgenthau are some of the familiar names that can be found in Steffek's work along the writings of many less-known authors.[22]

Part of the reason why IOs with a technical focus became widely embraced is probably the fact that many of the first embryonic forms of modern IOs established in the nineteenth century had a narrow and technical focus: river commissions (like the Rhine Commission and the European Commission of the Danube) as well as international administrative unions (like the International Telegraph Union and the International Postal Union).[23] Peters and Peter have submitted that these so-called technical IOs were used as 'path-clearers' for general and more political IOs like the League of Nations.[24]

The distinction between more and less technical areas of international cooperation is often referred to as the one between 'high' and 'low' politics.[25] Different traditions of thought in IR have described these categories differently, with some challenging the very idea that low politics can be truly differentiated from high politics.[26] But even discounting the criticism, one should recognize that, historically, the move from 'low' to 'high' politics IOs has been limited to a few major political projects: the United Nations, and the European Union and some other

[20] Jens Steffek, *International Organization as Technocratic Utopia* (OUP 2021).

[21] ibid 185.

[22] Margherita Melillo, 'Jens Steffek, International Organizations as Technocratic Utopia, Oxford University Press, 2021, ISBN 9780192845573, 256pp' (2023) 36 Leiden Journal of International Law 219.

[23] Anne Peters and Simone Peter, 'International Organizations: Between Technocracy and Democracy' in Bardo Fassbender and Anne Peters (eds), *The Oxford Handbook of the History of International Law* (OUP 2012) 176.

[24] ibid 194–95.

[25] Garrett W Brown, Iain McLean, and Alistair McMillan, *A Concise Oxford Dictionary of Politics and International Relations* (OUP 2018), specifically 'High and Low Politics' <https://www.oxfordreference.com/display/10.1093/acref/9780199670840.001.0001/acref-9780199670840-e-1672> accessed 25 September 2024.

[26] Jeremy Youde, 'High Politics, Low Politics, and Global Health' (2016) 1 Journal of Global Security Studies 157, 158–59.

regional integration projects. The whole post-war era, with an acceleration in the 1990s, has instead focused on the establishment of IOs with a technical focus.[27]

While it is beyond the scope of this chapter to give a full account of the debate related to the proliferation of specialized IOs and regimes, it seems crucial to note that the move has been met with criticism. Koskenniemi has described the proliferation of technically focused regimes (and their related IOs) as an attempt to depoliticize international politics and outsource the resolution of political problems to experts, also called 'managerialism'.[28] As he put it, '[m]anagerialism was the dark side of the inter-war project of imagining international law in technical terms'.[29] Following this insight and the science and technology (STS) literature, critical legal scholars posit that expertise cannot be effectively decoupled from politics.[30]

III. The Use of Expert Knowledge by IO Secretariats

If the establishment of IOs is based on an idea of international governance by experts, IO secretariats are the bedrock upon which this idea has been built. IO secretariats, in fact, are nothing else than international bureaucracies, and in the Weberian ideal type, bureaucracy is the exercise of authority through knowledge.[31]

The nature of bureaucracies as a locus of expertise has only increased since Weber wrote about it in 1922. The twentieth century has witnessed an increased expansion and professionalization of bureaucracies, at the national as well as international level.[32] This has happened in parallel with an increase in delegation of decisions from policymakers to experts. The reasons for this shift are manifold and cannot be fully discussed in this chapter. However, suffice to say that, at least for IOs, it can be easily observed that international governance has moved into areas posing more complex and more technical problems characterized by a high degree of uncertainty, thus (ostensibly, according to the critics) calling for more expertise.[33]

But there is more. Unlike most of their national counterparts (ie national government officials in IO member-driven bodies), IO secretariats are often the only

[27] Jan Klabbers, *An Introduction to International Organizations Law* (4th edn, CUP 2022).

[28] Martti Koskenniemi, 'The Fate of Public International Law: Between Technique and Politics' (2007) 70 The Modern Law Review 1.

[29] ibid 29.

[30] Jacqueline Peel, *Science and Risk Regulation in International Law* (CUP 2010); Burci and Balcazar-Moreno (n 18).

[31] Barnett and Finnemore (n 5) 29.

[32] Peter Haas (n 2) 8–11.

[33] ibid 12.

IO bodies with permanent staff.[34] This gives IO secretariats a unique advantage in terms of authority through expertise. Governmental delegations, in fact, may be comprised of professionals and experts, but they are more likely to participate in the work of the IO on a rotating basis. Moreover, governmental delegates do not always have multinational experience. Hence, in many regimes, IO secretariats become an authoritative repository of institutional and specialized knowledge. IO secretariats, nonetheless, act often as more than repositories. As noted in the Introduction, expertise is one of the main sources of IO secretariats' authority.[35] Expert knowledge, in this view, becomes a vital resource for IO secretariats' actions: it is the cornerstone of IOs' authority and of the secretariats' authority within IOs. It is the IO secretariats' magic bullet.

Saying that IO secretariats act based on expert knowledge, however, should not be mistaken for saying that they confine their actions to a small set of technical problems. Reconfiguring the dividing line between the technical and the political is a well-known strategy to reduce the margin of political contestation.[36] As Louis and Maertens have recently illustrated, IO secretariats routinely use expertise to depoliticize their practices.[37] They describe two main techniques used by IOs to this end: claiming expertise and providing technical interpretations.[38] Examples of these techniques can be found routinely in IO practices and are increasingly made visible in academic literature.

The effort to depoliticize international politics with expertise is best underscored by the growing use of numerical indicators in global governance. Using indicators such as rankings and targets can mask political decisions and priorities under the guise of objective and technical measures.[39] A notable example of the political tensions that can be disguised by numerical indicators is the World Bank's 'Doing Business' report. Published annually, the report ranked countries according to whether their regulatory framework was more or less business-friendly. In 2021, an investigation found that senior World Bank officials pressured their staff to alter data to favour certain countries.[40] The report was discontinued.

[34] Jinnah (n 7) 27.

[35] Barnett and Finnemore (n 5) 16–27.

[36] Sheila Jasanoff, *The Fifth Branch: Science Advisors as Policymakers* (Harvard UP 1990) 14.

[37] Marieke Louis and Lucile Maertens, *Why International Organizations Hate Politics: Depoliticizing the World* (Routledge 2021) 27–46.

[38] ibid.

[39] Kevin Davis and others, *Governance by Indicators: Global Power Through Classification and Rankings* (OUP 2012); Sally Engle Merry, Kevin E Davis, and Benedict Kingsbury, *The Quiet Power of Indicators: Measuring Governance, Corruption, and Rule of Law* (CUP 2015).

[40] Andrea Shalal, 'External Review Finds Deeper Rot in World Bank "Doing Business" Rankings' *Reuters* (21 September 2021) <https://www.reuters.com/business/external-review-finds-deeper-rot-world-bank-doing-business-rankings-2021-09-20/> accessed 25 September 2024.

A different but prominent example of the attempt to isolate expertise from politics can be seen in the World Health Organization's (WHO) management of the COVID-19 pandemic.[41] Although the Director-General insisted that the WHO was acting solely on expertise ('my focus is saving lives, we don't do politics in the WHO'[42]), in reality, the risk management recommendations that the organization was adopting were not only evidence based, but also value based—and, as such, political.

Recognizing that expert knowledge can be used to depoliticize international politics introduces the possibility of autonomous IOs taking action in politicized issues based on knowledge. By the same token, the use of expert knowledge by IO secretariats should not be seen as an act of passive reliance on existing resources. IOs can produce and mobilize knowledge.[43] Cecilia Cannon provides an interesting classification of the different modes of knowledge mobilization 'by/for international bureaucracies': advocacy; solicitation of experts; knowledge translated in forms that are more accessible by policymakers; and use of standard forms of expert knowledge (ie journal articles, books, conferences).[44] In two of these modes, the initiative is taken by experts (directly with advocacy or indirectly through translation of knowledge), while in the other two, the initiative is taken by IO secretariats (in direct engagement through solicitation or indirectly through use of standard forms of expert knowledge).

Cecilia Cannon's classification helps us understand *how* IO secretariats use expert knowledge. However, they do not tell us *why*. Why do IO secretariats take the initiative to produce and mobilize knowledge? And, in line with the focus of the present book, can expert knowledge be used by IO secretariats to initiate or support change?

IV. IO Secretariats and Change: Expert Knowledge as a Necessary but Insufficient Condition

Different authors have provided different conceptualizations of the ways knowledge can be used by public organizations. Although the exact definitions

[41] Lukasz Gruszczynski and Margherita Melillo, 'The Uneasy Coexistence of Expertise and Politics in the World Health Organization: Learning from the Experience of the Early Response to the COVID-19 Pandemic' (2022) 1 International Organizations Law Review 1; Burci and Balcazar-Moreno (n 18).

[42] WHO, 'COVID-19 virtual press conference: 8 April 2020 (transcript)' <www.bit.ly/3aNWqoI> accessed 15 September 2021.

[43] Annabelle Littoz-Monnet, *The Politics of Expertise in International Organizations: How International Bureaucracies Produce and Mobilize Knowledge* (Taylor & Francis 2017).

[44] Cecilia Cannon, 'Modes of Knowledge Mobilization by/for International Bureaucracies Throughout International Policy Process', in Annabelle Littoz-Monnet (ed), *The Politics of Expertise in International Organizations* (Routledge 2017).

may vary, it is generally recognized that knowledge can be used in three main ways: instrumentally, symbolically, and strategically.[45] In this view, instrumental use corresponds to a plain, ordinary, problem-solving approach: when knowledge is used to solve an existing problem.[46] Symbolic use, conversely, has to do with enhancing legitimacy: producing a report, for example, to signal that the organization has relevant expertise and is working on a topic.[47] Strategic use, finally, can have two goals: advocating for a (predefined or preferred) policy option or backing an expansion of powers.[48] Under this classification, strategic use is what would mostly correspond to the idea of initiatives for change that is the focus of the present book.

Production and mobilization of knowledge have been often associated with strategic uses by IO secretariats.[49] In my own work, I have argued that use of expertise was one of the main strategies employed by the WHO Secretariat to support the development of the Framework Convention on Tobacco Control.[50] Relying on a vast set of empirical sources, I have illustrated different modalities in which expertise was strategically employed by the WHO Secretariat: borrowing, mobilization, and framing. Arguably, it is precisely this strategic use of expertise that allowed the WHO Framework Convention on Tobacco Control to be successfully concluded and become an 'evidence-based treaty'.[51]

Several of the chapters in Parts II, III, and IV of this volume provide examples of strategic use of expertise to foster change. Rocha Gabriel provides an interesting example of how the United Nations Economic Commission for Latin America and the Caribbean used external consultants to integrate sustainable development in its work.[52] Ukamwa contends that the expertise and personality of the Executive Heads are key in determining the success of IOs' initiatives.[53] Bonucci describes how, in the aftermath of the 2007–2008 financial crisis, the Secretary-General of the Organisation for Economic Cooperation and

[45] Lorna Schrefler, 'Reflections on the Different Roles of Expertise in Regulatory Policy Making' in Ellen Hey and others (eds), *The Role of 'Experts' in International and European Decision-Making Processes: Advisors, Decision Makers or Irrelevant Actors?* (CUP 2014) 66–69.

[46] ibid 68.

[47] ibid 70.

[48] Schrefler (n 45) ibid 69.

[49] Littoz-Monnet (n 43).

[50] Margherita Melillo, *Weaponising Evidence: A History of Tobacco Control in International Law* (CUP 2024).

[51] 'WHO Framework Convention on Tobacco Control', Foreword, v <https://iris.who.int/bitstream/handle/10665/42811/9241591013.pdf?sequence=1> accessed 25 September 2024.

[52] Vivian Daniel Rocha Gabriel, 'The Role of Outside Experts in Anchoring Sustainable Development and Climate Protection in ECLAC's Work', Chapter 29 in this volume.

[53] Naphtali Ukamwa, 'The Role of Heads of Secretariats in Initiating Change: Functional Formalism and Pluralism', Chapter 13 in this volume.

Development was able to launch the development of a technocratic but ambitious initiative named 'New Approaches to Economic Challenges'.[54]

Recent research in IO secretariats has started to assume expertise as a precondition for IO secretariats' influence.[55] Additionally, this literature unpacks the notion of expertise to shed light on how the type of expertise of IO secretariats impacts their ability to wield influence. Can the IO secretariat's expertise be easily substitutable by other actors?[56] Can the homogeneity of the professional expertise of IOs' staff reduce internal challenges?[57] Understanding how the expertise of IO secretariats can bring about change requires understanding the nature of said expertise.

In the same vein, scholars have recognized that the expertise of the staff of IO secretariats can also act as a bias and affect the interpretation of their mandates and of the means to implement them.[58] In other words: an organization mostly staffed by economists will tend to frame problems as economic problems, while an organization mostly staffed by lawyers will tend to frame problems as legal problems. Among the chapters in this book, Di Leva's chapter best illustrates this point.[59] His description of the evolution of the World Bank's environmental and social responsibility framework reveals how the World Bank has responded to external pressures by developing a more comprehensive and effective framework. However, despite some notable advancements like the inclusion of rights of people with disabilities and gender-based violence, the new environmental and social framework of the World Bank remains in line with the institutional culture of the organization, leaving little room for human rights language.[60] Knowledge, nevertheless, is not sufficient for IOs to be able to bring about change. In his monograph, Fiti Sinclair has identified expertise, along with morality and the law, as one of the three 'modes of discourse and practice' that have been employed to justify expansion of IOs' powers.[61] It is interesting to observe a parallel between Fiti Sinclair's three modes of discourse of IOs (morality, expertise, and law) and Barnett and Finnemore's three sources of authority of IOs (moral character, expertise, and delegation). Whereas their works belong to different fields

[54] Nicola Bonucci, 'The Driving Role of the Heads of International Organizations: A Case Study Around the Organisation for Economic Co-operation and Development', Chapter 20 in this volume.

[55] Jinnah (n 7); Christoph Knill and others, 'Bureaucratic Influence and Administrative Styles in International Organizations' (2019) 14 The Review of International Organizations 83.

[56] Jinnah (n 7) 56–65.

[57] Knill and others (n 55) 90–91.

[58] Michael Barnett and Liv Coleman, 'Designing Police: Interpol and the Study of Change in International Organizations' (2005) 49 International Studies Quarterly 593, 597.

[59] Charles Di Leva, 'The World Bank's Evolution Towards Environmental and Social Responsibilities', Chapter 8 in this volume.

[60] Galit A Sarfaty, *Values in Translation: Human Rights and the Culture of the World Bank* (Stanford UP 2012).

[61] Guy Fiti Sinclair, *To Reform the World: International Organizations and the Making of Modern States* (OUP 2017) 288.

of investigation (legal scholarship and IR, respectively) and pursue different research agendas, they seem to agree that expertise is one of the main—but not the only—mode of action of IO secretariats.

Other researchers have come to similar conclusions. In their empirical work on IO bureaucracies,[62] Biermann and Siebenhüner explain the variation in IO secretariats' capacity to wield influence with recourse to three main variables: the structure of the problems, the polity (or institutional, financial, and legal frameworks), and the staff that comprise the IOs.[63] In this framework, expertise comes into play as one of the factors shaping one of the three variables (the capacity of the staff).[64] However, expertise can do little to address the other two variables (the polity and the structure of the problem they face).

My investigation on the Framework Convention on Tobacco Control comes to a similar conclusion. Reviewing the outcome of the treaty negotiation, I argued that the strong focus on scientific evidence advanced by the WHO Secretariat enabled the treaty to incorporate strong provisions on the scientific evidence supporting tobacco control measures. However, at the same time, the focus on evidence could not do much to get States to agree on important treaty features such as financing and implementation mechanisms.[65]

V. Conclusion

IO secretariats are recognized as important actors in initiating or supporting change in IOs. But how do they wield their influence? To answer this question, this chapter has reviewed the IR and legal scholarship on IO secretariats as knowledge actors and has shown that expertise is a key but not sufficient feature in IO secretariats' strategic actions.

IOs as a whole have been conceived and established as technocratic organizations. The idea—common to many authors with different epochs and backgrounds—was to establish a supranational framework for experts to address and solve problems related to transnational cooperation. This move has been supported by the fact that the very first IOs, as well as some of the most recent, have been established with a very narrow, technical focus. Critical legal literature

[62] The term 'international bureaucracy' is used here as a more comprehensive and less rigid alternative to 'international organizations'; see Biermann and Siebenhüner (n 7) 37–39. However, the distinction appears immaterial for our purposes, since the present book investigates a broad array of 'IOs' beyond the traditional and rigid distinction (see Hannah Birkenkötter, 'Change in International Organizations', Chapter 1 in this volume).

[63] Biermann and Siebenhüner (n 7) 327–46.

[64] ibid 340–41.

[65] Melillo (n 50).

has criticized the proliferation of multiple, technocratic regimes as a form of 'managerialism' of international affairs that tries to conceal their political nature.

IO expertise is considered an essential characteristic of IO secretariats. These actors, in fact, are conceptualized as international bureaucracies, and knowledge is the basis of the authority of any bureaucracy. Drawing from existing literature, I have shown that IO secretariats use expertise in various ways to depoliticize their actions by, inter alia, producing and mobilizing knowledge, isolating expertise from politics, and providing technical interpretation of political problems such as quantifications.

The last part of this chapter has tried to assess the role of IO secretariats' use of knowledge in initiating or supporting change. It has illustrated that IO secretariats can use knowledge in three main ways: instrumentally, symbolically, and strategically—with the latter category mostly overlapping with the notion of initiating or supporting change. Several of the chapters of this book demonstrated that expertise can be critical in initiating or supporting change. However, expertise alone is not sufficient to influence policy outcomes.

Where does this picture leave us? While the assessment of the exact role of IO secretariats' knowledge in influencing change is more a matter of study for IR scholarship, international legal scholarship has something to learn from the characterization of IO secretariats as knowledge actors. Examining IO secretariats' practices in detail, as the present book does, is an important step towards a better understanding of the intricate links between IO secretariats, experts, and expertise—and thus, applicable legal frameworks. On the other hand, from the perspective of practitioners and policymakers, understanding the importance, but also the limits, of IO secretariats' role as knowledge actors can also help shed light on their overall role in international governance and demystify some myths.

7
The Establishment of the UN Criminal Tribunals
The Role of the UN Secretariat

Huw Llewellyn

I. Introduction

The United Nations (UN) Secretariat played a key, but often overlooked, role in the establishment of the UN criminal tribunals: the International Criminal Tribunal for the former Yugoslavia (ICTY) in 1993,[1] the International Criminal Tribunal for Rwanda (ICTR) in 1994,[2] the Special Court for Sierra Leone (SCSL) in 2002,[3] the Extraordinary Chambers in the Courts of Cambodia (ECCC) in 2003,[4] and the Special Tribunal for Lebanon (STL) in 2007.[5] Although the establishment of each of the UN criminal tribunals was mandated by a UN principal organ, initiatives by the Secretariat, acting primarily through the UN Office of Legal Affairs (OLA), were critical in triggering the UN's engagement in the

[1] The ICTY was established by UNSC Res 898 (22 February 1993) UN Doc S/RES/808 and UNSC Res 827 (25 May 1993) UN Doc S/RES/827, which approved UNSC, 'Report of the Secretary General' (3 May 1993) UN Doc 25704 and add.1 containing the provisions of the Statute for the ICTY.

[2] The ICTR was established by UNSC Res 955 (8 November 1994) UN Doc S/RES/955.

[3] Established by the Agreement between the United Nations and the Government of Sierra Leone on the Establishment of a Special Court for Sierra Leone, with annexed Statute (adopted 16 January 2002, entered into force 12 April 2002) 2178 UNTS 137.

[4] Although 2003 is given as the relevant date here, the ECCC was first established by the Law on the Establishment of the Extraordinary Chambers in the Courts of Cambodia, 10 August 2001, which is Cambodian national legislation. This was amended by the Law to Amend the 2001 law on the Establishment of the Extraordinary Chambers in the Courts of Cambodia, 27 October 2004: Law on the Establishment of the Extraordinary Chambers, with inclusion of amendments as promulgated on 27 October 2004 (NS/RKM/1004/006). See the ECCC website at <https://www.eccc.gov.kh/en/about/legal-framework>.

Agreement between the United Nations and the Royal Government of Cambodia concerning the prosecution under Cambodian law of crimes committed during the period of Democratic Kampuchea (adopted 6 June 2003, entered into force 29 April 2005) 2329 UNTS 117.

[5] UNSC Res 1757 (30 May 2007) UN Doc S/RES/1757 with annexed draft Agreement and draft Statute.

Huw Llewellyn, *The Establishment of the UN Criminal Tribunals* In: *International Organization Initiatives*. Edited by: Gabrielle Marceau and Henner Gött, Oxford University Press. © Oxford University Press 2025.
DOI: 10.1093/9780197803325.003.0008

prosecution of serious international crimes, which paved the way for the establishment of the International Criminal Court (ICC).[6]

This chapter focuses on three prominent examples of OLA initiatives. They illustrate differing aspects of the relationship between the UN Secretariat and other UN principal organs (the Secretariat itself being a principal organ[7]), and the Secretariat's ability, and in some instances, inability, to influence the course of events.

Section II concerns the role of OLA in the establishment of the ICTY by the Security Council in 1993, despite doubts about its authority to do so having been expressed by some Council members. Section III concerns OLA's initiation of negotiations with the Government of Cambodia and the unique institutional structure of the ECCC crafted by OLA. Section IV discusses the role of OLA in influencing the way in which the STL was negotiated and established by the Council. Section V sets out concluding remarks.

This chapter demonstrates how the UN Secretariat is not merely an implementing agent for the Security Council and the General Assembly but acts with a will distinct from that of these political organs and of member states[8] and is a key and influential player in its own right.

II. The Secretariat's Role in the Establishment of the ICTY

The establishment of the ICTY by the Security Council in 1993 on the basis of an OLA report pushed the boundaries of what had previously been considered possible. It took place against a background of long-term efforts to create an international criminal court dating back to the First World War,[9] which came to fruition in the wake of the Second World War with the establishment of the Nuremberg[10] and Tokyo[11] International Military Tribunals. Efforts within the

[6] Rome Statute of the International Criminal Court (adopted 17 July 1998, entered into force 1 July 2002) 2187 UNTS 90.

[7] Charter of the United Nations (adopted 26 June 1945, entered into force 24 October 1945) 1 UNTS XVI art 7.1.

[8] For the phrase 'a will distinct', see Draft Guideline 2(a) and the commentary thereto, International Law Commission (ILC), 'Report of the International Law Commission on the Work of Its 74th Session' (24 April–2 June and 3 July–4 August 2023) UN Doc A/78/10, which contains the ILC's Draft Guidelines on Settlement of Disputes to which International Organizations are parties: see para 49, which sets out an updated definition of 'international organization'.

[9] Treaty of Peace with Germany (Treaty of Versailles) (signed 28 June 1919) art 227. The tribunal was never in practice established.

[10] Agreement for the Prosecution and Punishment of Major War Criminals of the European Axis (adopted 8 August 1945, entered into force 8 August 1945) 82 UNTS 280, 284.

[11] Special Proclamation by the Supreme Commander for the Allied Powers at Tokyo, 19 January 1946, TIAS No. 1589, 4 Bevans 20 <https://digital-commons.usnwc.edu/cgi/viewcontent.cgi?article=2132&context=ils> accessed 27 September 2024.

newly established UN to create a truly international criminal jurisdiction were unsuccessful for many years but came to life in 1993 when the Council was released from its Cold War paralysis.

Responding to the report of a Secretary-General appointed Commission of Experts that highlighted grave breaches of international humanitarian law in the conflicts in the Balkans,[12] the Council took a decision in principle in its resolution 808 (1993), adopted unanimously, to establish an international criminal tribunal.[13]

Despite this unanimity, doubts were voiced by three Security Council members (Brazil, China, and Venezuela) questioning the Council's authority to establish the ICTY as its subsidiary organ with criminal investigation, prosecution, and judicial powers—powers that the Council did not itself possess.[14] Before moving to the next stage of establishment, therefore, the Secretary-General was handed a hot potato when requested by the Council to prepare a report within 60 days with 'options for the effective and expeditious implementation of the decision' to establish a tribunal.[15]

In preparing the report, it would have been open to OLA, of course, to address the question whether the UN, and therefore the Security Council, possessed the authority to establish an international criminal tribunal. It is clear that states, in exercise of their sovereign powers, may establish international criminal courts and tribunals by agreement with other states.[16] It is not the case that all international organizations (IOs) necessarily have authority to establish international criminal courts and tribunals, and indeed, the UN Organization had not previously done so. Further, it is an established principle of international institutional law (and it has a certain inescapable force of logic) that parent organs cannot bestow upon subsidiary organs more powers or functions than they themselves possess.[17] This principle has been

[12] Interim report of the Commission of Experts submitted under the cover of a letter from the Secretary-General to the President of the Security Council dated 9 February 1993: UNSC, 'Letter Dated 9 February 1993 from the Secretary-General to the President of the Security Council' (10 February 1993) UN Doc S/25274.

[13] UNSC Res 808 (n 1) para 1.

[14] Doubts expressed by Brazil, China, and Venezuela in the Council meetings leading to the establishment of the ICTY: UNSC, 'Provisional Verbatim Record of the Three Thousand One Hundred and Seventy-Fifth Meeting' (22 February 1993) UN Doc S/PV.3175; UNSC, 'Provisional Verbatim Record of the Three Thousand Two Hundred and Seventeenth Meeting' (25 May 1993) UN Doc S/PV.3217.

[15] UNSC Res 808 (n 1) para 2

[16] The Nuremberg and Tokyo IMTs provide precedents, albeit criticized, as does the ICC.

[17] Case 9-56 *Meroni & Co., Industrie Metallurgiche, SpA v High Authority of the European Coal and Steel Community* [1958] ECR 1957–58, 151–52, discussed in Henry G Schermers and Niels M Blokker, *International Institutional Law, Unity Within Diversity* (5th rev edn, Martinus Nijhoff 2011) 173–76; *Tadic Case* (Decision on the defence motion for interlocutory appeal on jurisdiction) Case No IT-94-1-AR72 (2 October 1995) para 37; Jose E Alvarez, 'Nuremberg Revisited: The Tadic Case' (1996) 7 European Journal of International Law 245.

confirmed in the context of the UN, including in opinions of the UN Legal Counsel.[18]

In its report, OLA did not address the question of the Security Council's authority nor advance any theories based on implied powers to explain why the Council may have authority to establish a subsidiary organ with criminal prosecutorial and judicial powers.[19] It focused on the fact that given the urgent circumstances, a multilateral treaty negotiation among member states would not be sufficiently expeditious or effective. Only the Council acting under Chapter VII of the UN Charter to establish a tribunal would meet this imperative.[20] The report considered this 'legally justifiable' as an enforcement measure under Chapter VII aimed at restoring international peace and security, and in light of 'past Security Council practice'.[21]

The report was careful to distinguish the limited and temporary nature of the proposed ad hoc tribunal from an international criminal jurisdiction in general or the creation of an international criminal court of a permanent nature, which were under active consideration at that time by the International Law Commission and the General Assembly. The Council would not be 'legislating' for the applicable law before the tribunal, which would have the task of applying only existing rules of international humanitarian law that were beyond any doubt part of customary international law.[22]

OLA's report, in effect, lowered the temperature by not engaging in the 'hot' question of the extent of the Security Council's powers. If the report had done so, it may have been more difficult for the three States expressing doubts to join the consensus in the Council.

Through a combination of sound political judgement and pragmatism by OLA, therefore, together with the confidence of the Security Council in OLA's legal technical expertise in the preparation of the ICTY draft Statute, the Council was able to endorse the Secretary-General's report in its entirety in resolution 827 (1993).[23] The delegations of China, Brazil, and Venezuela were able to cast positive votes, limiting themselves to explanations of their positions.[24]

[18] UNGA, 'Summary of Internal Secretariat Studies of Constitutional Questions Relating to Agencies Within the Framework of the United Nations' A/C.1/758, 13, paras 1–2; and also the Repertory of Practice of United Nations Organs vol 1 (1945–1954) 228.

[19] Report of the Secretary-General (n 2). See Christiane Ahlborn, 'From Functionalism to Constitutionalism: Translating Theories on IO Powers into Practice', Chapter 3 in this volume, regarding the tendency of practicing lawyers in IOs not to engage in theorizing about organizations' powers.

[20] ibid para 28.

[21] ibid para 24. This was a reference to previous occasions when the Council had established subsidiary organs aimed at restoring international peace and security, in particular, UNSC Res 687 (3 April 1991) UN Doc S/RES/687 paras 18–19.

[22] ibid paras 29, 34.

[23] See Verbatim Record of 25 May 1993 (n 14).

[24] ibid 33, 36–37.

A year later, in 1994, although Rwanda voted against the Security Council resolution 955 (1994) that established the ICTR, and China abstained,[25] these were for reasons unconnected with the doubts and criticisms regarding the powers of the Council that had been voiced at the time of establishment of the ICTY. There were no further statements on the lines of those previously made by China, Brazil, and Venezuela. Nor were any such doubts or objections of principle voiced within the Council in 2000 when it adopted resolution 1315 (2000) mandating the establishment of the SCSL by a treaty to be negotiated by OLA with the Government of Sierra Leone.[26] OLA's key role in enabling the Council's novel exercise of powers in establishing the ICTY had helped to establish an accepted practice that the UN has authority to establish international criminal tribunals, at least in situations that the Council has determined to constitute threats to international peace and security.

III. The Secretariat's Role in the Establishment of the ECCC

OLA similarly played an innovative role in the establishment of the ECCC, albeit one that encountered differences of approach with the General Assembly. The ECCC was established to prosecute the wide scale crimes committed during the period of the former Khmer Rouge regime, which held power in Cambodia from April 1975 to January 1979. In June 1997, the co-Prime Ministers of Cambodia wrote to the Secretary-General to request assistance in establishing a tribunal to prosecute those most responsible for the atrocities.[27] The Security Council was unable to react because China, which had had close ties with Democratic Kampuchea, was considered likely to veto any resolution mandating negotiations.[28] The General Assembly accordingly took the lead through its Third (Human Rights) Committee.[29]

The General Assembly asked the Secretary-General to examine the Cambodian request and to appoint a group of experts to evaluate the evidence and propose further measures.[30] The group of experts, led by OLA, visited

[25] UNSC Res 995 (n 2) was adopted by 13 votes, with Rwanda voting against and China abstaining. See the views of Rwanda and China set out in the UNSC Verbatim Record (8 November 1994) UN Doc S/PV.3453.

[26] UNSC Res 1315 (14 August 2000) UN Doc S/RES/1315.

[27] UNGA and UNSC, 'Letter Dated 21 June 1997 from the First and Second Prime Ministers of Cambodia to the Secretary-General' (21 June 1997) UN Docs A/51/930 and S/1997/488.

[28] Daphna Shraga, 'The Second Generation UN-based Tribunals: A Diversity of Mixed Jurisdictions' in Cesare Romano, A Nollkaemper, and J Kleffner (eds), *Internationalised Criminal Courts* (OUP 2004) 15–38.

[29] Lindsey Raub, *Positioning Hybrid Tribunals in International Criminal Justice* (2009) 41 New York University Journal of International Law and Politics 1045; Shraga (n 28) 17–19.

[30] UNGA Res 52/135 (1998) UN Doc A/RES/52/135.

Cambodia in November 1998 and proposed a UN-supported international tribunal, established either by agreement with the Government (the SCSL model) or by Security Council resolution under Chapter VII of the UN Charter (the ICTY and ICTR model).[31] Neither the General Assembly nor the Security Council reacted. The Secretary-General therefore took the initiative, under his general authority to offer 'good offices', to discuss (through OLA) the establishment of a tribunal with the Government of Cambodia.

Discussions took place between July 1999 and February 2002, at which point the Secretary-General and the UN Legal Counsel decided that the UN should withdraw.[32] Many legal and institutional issues had been contentious, including the Government's opposition to an international rather than a national tribunal. The UN Legal Counsel considered that the model of an international tribunal on the lines of that being negotiated at that time with the Government of Sierra Leone should be followed.[33] Other contentious issues included whether the majority of judges in each Chamber should be Cambodian or international and the primacy of the potential UN/Cambodia Agreement over Cambodian legislation to establish the ECCC.[34]

The negotiations had revealed what OLA regarded as two visions of justice: on the one hand, a tribunal meeting international standards of independence and impartiality through a decisive international majority in judicial decision-making; and on the other hand, the risk of a politically controlled judicial process.[35] In withdrawing from the negotiations, the Secretary-General made clear that the tribunal as envisaged by the Government 'would not guarantee the independence, impartiality and objectivity that a court established with the support of the United Nations must have'.[36]

In response to this withdrawal, the General Assembly mandated the Secretary-General to resume negotiations and to conclude an agreement with the Government based on the preceding negotiations and the Cambodian

[31] Report of the Group of Experts for Cambodia established pursuant to General Assembly Res 52/135 (18 February 1999), annexed to 'Identical Letters Dated 15 March 1999 from the Secretary-General to the President of the General Assembly and the President of the Security Council' (16 March 1999) UN Doc A/53/850.

[32] Press statements by the Secretary-General on 8 February and 20 August 2002 concerning negotiations between the Secretary-General and the Government of Cambodia on the establishment of ECCC, referred to in the preamble of UNGA Res 57/228 (2003) UN Doc A/RES/57/228, see also UN, 'Daily Press Briefing by the Office of the Spokesman for the Secretary-General' (08 February 2002) <www.un.org/press/en/2002/db020802.doc.htm> accessed 27 September 2024.

[33] ibid; Letter of 17 June 1999 from Prime Minister Hun Sen to the Secretary-General, on file with the author.

[34] Letter dated 23 November 2001 from Prime Minister Hun Sen to the UN Legal Counsel, on file with the author. See also the press statements by the Secretary-General (n 32).

[35] Shraga (n 28) 18.

[36] UNGA, 'Report of the Secretary-General on the Khmer Rouge Trials' (31 March 2003) UN Doc A/57/69.

ECCC Law[37]—in effect, on Cambodian terms. Remarkably, on the same day, the Assembly also adopted a resolution[38] on the situation in Cambodia which noted with concern 'the continued problems related to the rule of law and the functioning of the judiciary resulting from, inter alia, corruption and interference by the executive with the independence of the judiciary'.[39]

In the subsequent negotiations, the UN Legal Counsel was unable to change the position of the Government on key issues[40] and remained unconvinced that the draft agreement with Cambodia would ensure an independent and impartial process given the 'precarious state of the judiciary in Cambodia'.[41] Nevertheless, the General Assembly in its resolution 57/228B of 13 May 2003[42] approved the draft agreement and urged the Secretary-General and the Government to bring it into force and implement it. With serious misgivings on the part of the UN Secretary-General and the Legal Counsel, therefore, the ECCC Agreement was signed on 6 June 2003.[43]

A remarkable aspect of the structure of the ECCC that emerged from OLA's efforts to ensure that it would meet international standards was the UN component embedded within it, known as UN Assistance to the Khmer Rouge Trials (UNAKRT), comprising UN judges, prosecutors, and administrative UN staff members. UNAKRT forms part of the UN Secretariat.[44] In other words, part of a principal organ of the UN, its Secretariat, is embedded within a Cambodian national court as an essential and integral part of its structure.

This unique dual component structure positions the ECCC at the institutional boundary between national and international tribunals and is one aspect of the many safeguards built into this agreement by OLA, along with numerous express references to the rights of the accused and the International Covenant on Civil and Political Rights. The agreement contains express provision for withdrawal by the UN should the Government of Cambodia cause the ECCC to function in a manner that does not conform with its terms.[45]

37 UNGA Res 228 A (2002) UN Doc A/RES/57/228A.
38 UNGA Res 57/225, 'Situation of Human Rights in Cambodia' (2002) UN Doc A/RES/57/225.
39 ibid s II, para 2.
40 UNGA, 'Report of the Secretary-General on Khmer Rouge Trials' (3 December 2003) UN Doc A/58/617.
41 ibid para 79.
42 UNGA 228 B (2003) UN Doc A/RES/57/228B.
43 ECCC Agreement (n 4).
44 UNAKRT, 'About Us' <www.unakrt-online.org/about-us> accessed 30 August 2024.
45 ECCC Agreement (n 4) arts 12–13.

IV. The Secretariat's Role in the Establishment of the STL

The STL was established to prosecute those responsible for carrying out the attack of 14 February 2005 in Beirut that killed 22 people, including the former Lebanese Prime Minister, Rafiq Hariri, and related attacks.[46] The assassination was one of a series of politically motivated attacks in Lebanon linked to growing tensions over Syria's presence and involvement in the country, and there was speculation at that time of involvement by the Syrian security service.[47] These acute political sensitivities and divisions were also reflected among the Security Council members.

The Prime Minister of Lebanon wrote to the Secretary-General in December 2005 to request the UN to establish 'a tribunal of international character' to try those found responsible for the attacks.[48] Following a visit to Lebanon, the UN Legal Counsel in March 2006 set out the scope and nature of a possible tribunal.[49] A week later, the Council decided unanimously to request the Secretary-General to negotiate an agreement on this basis.[50] The UN Legal Counsel and his OLA team conducted the negotiations, reaching a conclusion with the Lebanese authorities on the draft Agreement and draft Statute for the STL in November 2006.[51]

Consultations in New York, The Hague, and Beirut in the period March to November 2006 between OLA and the Lebanese authorities were shadowed by OLA consultations in New York with, on the one hand, the main Security Council proponents of the STL, particularly France, the United States of America (USA), and the United Kingdom of Great Britain and Northern Ireland (UK), and on the other hand, the Russian Federation.[52] These latter consultations led in particular to the inclusion by OLA of two innovations in the draft Statute of the STL that had not featured in the Statutes of any of the four previous UN criminal tribunals. First, the inclusion of a Defence Office as an organ in its own right of the STL and a post of Head of the Defence Office[53] to meet Russian concerns. Second, given that there was little expectation among the proponents that any accused would surrender themselves to the STL, or be so surrendered, the inclusion of the possibility of trial *in absentia*.[54] OLA had thus worked behind the

[46] UNSC Res 1757 (n 5) STL Statute art 1.

[47] UNSC, 'Report of the International Independent Investigation Commission' (20 October 2005) UN Doc S/2005/662.

[48] UNSC, 'Letter from the Prime Minister of Lebanon to the Secretary-General' (13 December 2005) UN Doc S/2005/783.

[49] UNSC, 'Report of the Secretary-General' (21 March 2006) UN Doc S/2006/176.

[50] UNSC Res 1664 (2006) UN Doc S/RES/1664.

[51] UNSC, 'Report of the Secretary-General' (15 November 2006) UN Doc S/2006/893.

[52] The author was the Legal Counsellor at the UK Mission in New York at the time participating in these negotiations.

[53] UNSC Res 1757 (n 5) STL Statute arts 7(d), 13.

[54] UNSC Res 1757 (n 5) STL Statute art 22.

scenes to ensure an outcome acceptable not only to the Lebanese authorities but also to the main protagonists in the Council.

In Lebanon, the question of a tribunal led to a constitutional crisis which prevented the Parliament meeting to ratify the draft STL Agreement. The Prime Minister nevertheless requested that the Security Council take action to bring the STL into effect.[55] A visit by the UN Legal Counsel to Lebanon failed to break the constitutional impasse, and France, the UK, the USA, Belgium, Italy, and Slovakia presented a draft resolution to the Council in May 2007. Two weeks later, following negotiations among Council members, the Security Council adopted a resolution under Chapter VII of the UN Charter to bring 'the provisions of' the draft STL Agreement and draft STL Statute, annexed to the resolution, into effect.[56] As explained by the sponsors, this provision was formulated to give mandatory force under Chapter VII to the words contained in the draft documents, not to bring the Agreement as such into force as a treaty between the UN and Lebanon.[57]

As originally drafted, the proponents, led by France, had formulated the above paragraph in terms that could be read to purport to bring the draft STL Agreement as such into effect under Chapter VII of the UN Charter. The controversy of an approach that appeared to involve the Council acting to override the internal constitutional processes of a member state of the UN, and to bring a treaty into force in the absence of an 'international agreement' as required by the Vienna Convention on the Law of Treaties,[58] was apparent to those involved in the negotiation. It was also apparent to the UN Legal Counsel and his OLA team, who remained actively engaged behind the scenes. The lawyers representing member states who were not members of the Council at that time heard about it 'on the grapevine', as did their legal departments at Foreign Ministries in capitals. The collective raised eyebrows by this broad legal community were sufficient to persuade the drafters of the Council resolution to pause, to re-think, and to amend the text in question.

Even so, the Council resolution was adopted with only ten positive votes, one more than the minimum requirement under the Charter.[59] There were five abstentions: China, Indonesia, Qatar, Russia, and South Africa. These States

[55] Letter of 14 May 2007 from the Prime Minister of Lebanon to the Secretary-General, annexed to UNSC, 'Letter Dated 15 May 2007 from the Secretary-General to the President of the Security Council' (16 May 2007) UN Doc S/2007/281.

[56] UNSC Res 1757 (n 5) para 1.

[57] UNSC 'The Situation in the Middle East' (30 May 2007) UN Doc S/PV.5685, in particular the statement of the Permanent Representative of France.

[58] Vienna Convention on the Law of Treaties (adopted 23 May 1969, entered into force 27 January 1980) 1155 UNTS 331.

[59] Charter of the United Nations (n 7) art 27.3.

did not accept the explanation of the proponents. As the Russian Permanent Representative expressed it:

> The treaty between ... Lebanon and the United Nations ... by definition cannot enter into force on the basis of a decision by only one party. The constituent documents for the Tribunal, imposed by a unilateral decision of ... a Security Council resolution ... represent an encroachment upon the sovereignty of Lebanon.[60]

The STL Appeals Chamber later confirmed in a 2012 decision that '[t]he Tribunal is purely a creature of a Security Council resolution' and that resolution 1757 (2007), adopted under Chapter VII of the Charter, was the sole legal basis of the STL's establishment. The Agreement that had been negotiated with the Government of Lebanon was not the legal basis of the STL.[61]

OLA thus played an instrumental role, along with others, in influencing decision-making by the Security Council. Scholars have described the importance of the 'iterative process of discourse'[62] and 'the power of deliberation' among States.[63] In IOs in particular, international law operates through a process of 'justificatory discourse' in which claims are made and criticized, actions approved and condemned, with legal argumentation featuring prominently.[64] Discourse plays out within the organization's 'interpretative community', which includes its political organs but also extends to the Secretariat and to government lawyers in capitals.[65] The lawyers involved in negotiations in the Security Council do not make decisions with one eye on a 'judge over their shoulder', but rather through a discursive process involving 'checks and balances within the system'.[66] OLA lawyers are influential actors in this discursive process.

[60] The situation in the Middle East (n 57).

[61] *Prosecutor v Ayyash et al., Decision on the Defence Appeals Against the Trial Chamber's Decision on the Defence Challenges to the Jurisdiction and Legality of the Tribunal,* ICL 1065 (STL 2012) Appeals Chamber, paras 46, 53.

[62] Abram Chayes and Antonia Chayes, *The New Sovereignty: Compliance with International Regulatory Agreements* (CUP 1995) 25.

[63] Ian Johnstone, *The Power of Deliberation, International Law, Politics and Organisations* (OUP 2011).

[64] ibid 7.

[65] ibid 8–9.

[66] Michael Wood, *The Security Council's Powers and Their Limits* (8 November 2006) Lauterpacht Lectures: Second Lecture, transcript on file with the author.

V. Concluding Remarks

The role of the Secretariat in important developments at the UN is often overlooked. As is clear from the account in this chapter, the UN Secretariat, acting primarily through OLA, has been much more than a mere implementing agent for the Security Council and the General Assembly in the initiation of the era of UN criminal tribunals. It played this role in a way that, as Ahlborn underlines in Chapter 3 of this book,[67] is typical of lawyers in IOs, without reference to theory, but driven by pragmatic considerations and political imperatives in situations that had been determined by the Council to be threats to international peace and security. OLA's ability to play this role is based on a combination of sound political judgement together with a recognized and respected high level of technical legal expertise. OLA's institutional knowledge and recognized expertise enables its lawyers to be particularly influential participants in the discursive process that shapes decision-making within the UN.

[67] Ahlborn (n 19).

8

The World Bank's Evolution Towards Environmental and Social Responsibilities

Charles Di Leva

I. Introduction

British former Prime Minister Gordon Brown recently asserted that the World Bank (Bank) should become a 'global public goods bank'.[1] United States (US) Treasury Secretary Janet Yellen has called for the Bank to reform its lending practices to help deal with global threats, particularly climate change[2]. It may be ironic that these voices calling for evolution come from England and the United States, two key founding member countries that led the drafting of the Bank's Articles of Agreement (Articles) and their adoption in 1945.[3]

Focusing on the impacts of the Second World War , the Bank's Articles did not refer to the environment, or sustainability, unlike some multilateral development banks (MDBs) that emerged after the Bank.[4] Article I, 'Purpose', succinctly states that Bank investments are for 'productive purposes' and contains no reference to environmental or social goals. Similarly, Article III, 'General Provisions

[1] Gordon Brown, 'Rich Nations Have Promised to Pay for the Climate Crisis: But Will They?' *The Guardian* (26 November 2022) <https://www.theguardian.com/commentisfree/2022/nov/26/rich-nations-climate-crisis-cop28-gordon-brown> accessed 5 July 2023.

[2] Leigh Thomas, 'World Bank Should Add Disaster Clauses to Debt Agreements, Yellen Says' *Reuters* (22 June 2023) <https://www.reuters.com/sustainability/world-bank-should-add-disaster-clauses-debt-agreements-yellen-2023-06-22/> accessed 5 July 2024.

[3] Articles of Agreement of the International Bank for Reconstruction and Development (adopted 22 July 1944, entered into force 27 December 1945, as amended effective 27 June 2012) 2 UNTS 134 art IV s 10 (IBRD Articles of Agreement). See also Edward Mason and Robert Asher, *The World Bank Since Bretton Woods* (Brookings Institution Press, 2010).

[4] eg the EBRD, whose Article 2(1)(vii) 'Functions' includes 'to promote in the full range of its activities environmentally sound and sustainable development', Agreement Establishing the European Bank for Reconstruction and Development [1991] OJ L 372, <https://eur-lex.europa.eu/legal-content/EN/ALL/?uri=CELEX%3A21990A1231%2801%29> accessed 12 September 2024; AIIB art I includes in its Purpose 'to foster sustainable economic growth', Article of Agreement of the Asian Infrastructure Development Bank (29 June 2015) OXIO 510 <https://www.aiib.org/en/about-aiib/basic-documents/_download/articles-of-agreement/basic_document_english-bank_articles_of_agreement.pdf> accessed 12 September 2024; the African Development Bank includes in its Article 'Purpose' 'sustainable economic development' and 'social progress', Agreement Establishing the African Development Bank (10 September 1964) https://www.afdb.org/fileadmin/uploads/afdb/Documents/Legal-Documents/Agreement_establishing_the_African_development_bank_-_2016_edition.pdf accessed 12 September 2024.

Charles Di Leva, *The World Bank's Evolution Towards Environmental and Social Responsibilities* In: *International Organization Initiatives*. Edited by: Gabrielle Marceau and Henner Gött, Oxford University Press. © Oxford University Press 2025.
DOI: 10.1093/9780197803325.003.0009

Relating to Loans and Guarantees', notes the ambition to benefit members for 'projects for development and projects for reconstruction alike' and the 'purpose of facilitating the restoration and reconstruction of the economy of members whose metropolitan territories have suffered great devastation from enemy occupation or hostilities'.

Since its inception, however, the Bank has engaged in roles not originally envisioned.[5] Often, such activities led to questions whether these new roles required too much elasticity from the Articles. Thus, it is unsurprising that developing countries have been concerned that views such as Brown's and Yellen's could make borrowing more expensive or move the focus away from poverty reduction.[6] As well, it is understood that there has been occasional chafing within UN agencies when the financially endowed Bank may be seen by them to intrude in subjects covered under their charters. Nevertheless, the Bank's eventual embrace of the importance of protecting the environment has become embedded in the Bank, as a matter of both law and policy.

This chapter portrays how the Bank became engaged in environmental matters and the largest source of multilateral environmental finance. It discusses two initiatives that were not contemplated at the time of the Bank's foundation: setting and being accountable for environmental standards, and providing climate finance. Given that neither of these roles were contemplated in 1945, it is not surprising that the journey to this point was challenging.

II. The Origins of Concern About the Bank and the Environment

At the Bank's founding, fears about the environment were not prominent.[7] Concerns about climate change and loss of biodiversity had been voiced by a scarce number of prescient scientists.[8] Nevertheless, strategic competition over international waters led the Bank in 1956 to develop its first environment-related

[5] Among these, the 'Green Revolution' launched by World Bank President Robert McNamara is seen as the first major evolution in the Bank's roles. Ernest Feder, 'McNamara's Little Green Revolution: World Bank Scheme for Self-Liquidation of Third World Peasantry' (1976) 11 Economic and Political Weekly 532 <https://www.jstor.org/stable/4364513> accessed 12 September 2024.

[6] Charles Kenny, Vijaya Ramachandran, and Riddhi Kankaria, 'Do Clients Want the World Bank to Focus on Climate?' (*Center For Global Development*, 23 February 2023) <https://www.cgdev.org/blog/do-clients-want-world-bank-focus-climate> accessed 5 July 2023. Indeed, during the Presidency of James Wolfensohn, the Bank's 'twin goals' were promoting shared prosperity and ending poverty.

[7] Macrotrends, 'World Population 1950–2024' <https://www.macrotrends.net/global-metrics/countries/WLD/world/population> accessed 5 September 2024.

[8] The website for the US National Air and Space Administration provides a history of the unfolding knowledge about climate change. NASA, 'Evidence' <https://climate.nasa.gov/evidence> accessed 12 September 2024.

measure.[9] The Bank's Operational Memorandum (OM) on projects in international waters arose due to India and Pakistan disputing how hydropower projects should be developed on their shared rivers. The OM did not, however, address the environmental or social impacts of hydro development, and no policy-related instrument of the Bank directly addressed the environment throughout the 1970s.

As the Bank approached its fiftieth anniversary, a segment of civil society viewed that some Bank-financed projects were harmful to the environment. Some questioned whether the Bank had reached the end of its useful life. Civil Society's campaign against the Bank, 'Fifty Years is Enough, caught on, including with some in the US Congress, the legislative body key to authorizing the funds needed for maintaining the United States as the Bank's largest shareholder.[10]

Environmental groups, particularly those tackling domestic issues, were now also concerned about broader, global problems. This concern was particularly focused on the developing world where the Bank had been the largest source of infrastructure finance. Many in this environmental movement were motivated by the 1972 Stockholm Conference on the Human Environment. With this awareness, environmentalists began documenting harm associated with Bank-financed projects.[11] Further, the US Congress linked demands for environmental changes with the release of funds for future appropriations to the Bank.

A. Incremental measures towards environmental concerns

To satisfy its critics, the Bank President and management[12], with encouragement from some Board members, began to address environmental issues. President

[9] Operational Memorandum 8, 'Projects on International Waterways'. This memorandum and subsequent revisions did not deal with the substance of environmental concerns but addresses possible conflict between riparian states if the Bank were financing a project of one of its member states. For full treatment of this issue, see Salman MA Salman, *The World Bank Policy for Projects on International Waterways: An Historical and Legal Analysis* (World Bank Publications 2009) 32; Christina Leb, *Cooperation in the Law of Transboundary Water Resources* (CUP 2013).

[10] Ian A Bowles and Cyril F Kormos, 'Environmental Reform at the World Bank: The Role of the US Congress' (1994) 35 Virginia Journal of International Law 777.

[11] The views of adverse environmental impact of projects underway in the 1980s are discussed in Bruce Rich, *Mortgaging the Earth: World Bank, Environmental Impoverishment and the Crisis of Development* (Earthscan 1994); David Reed, *Structural Adjustment, the Environment and Sustainable Development* (Earthscan 1992).

[12] As noted in Hassane Cissé, 'How Do External Factors Shape Institutional, Legal, Strategic, or Policy Change in International Organizations: Review of Selected Examples in World Bank Practice', Chapter 24 in this volume, unlike other IOs, the Bank does not use the term 'Secretariat' for the internal entity that makes management decisions. It has a Board that makes decisions related to Policy, and Management, including the President, that makes management decisions on how policy is implemented.

McNamara appointed an environmental advisor in the early 1970s.[13] It was acknowledged, however, that the Bank had few staff with neither sufficient resources nor influence to alter the Bank's impact on the environment. In 1984, it issued its first specific environment-related operational manual statement (OMS).[14] This OMS asserted that since 1970, the Bank had 'steadily increased its attention to the environmental opportunities and risks introduced by the development process'. It encouraged assessment of the impact of Bank projects on the environment, but was considered as 'guidance', and lacked the environmental staffing necessary for its implementation. Supporting 'Environmental Guidelines' were also issued at that time.[15]

In 1987, the need for the Bank and other international organizations (IOs) to take environmental concerns more seriously grew with the release of 'Our Common Future'.[16] This report emphasized the responsibilities of IOs to integrate concerns for the protection of the environment into economic planning and stated the expectation that the World Bank would demonstrate 'a fundamental commitment to sustainable development'. Just one month later, Bank President Barber Conable announced an increase in staffing devoted to environment. By the fall of 1988, the Bank's Legal Department foresaw demand for building internal environmental capacity, noting among other matters the growth in international environmental law.[17]

These actions did not quiet the reform efforts of the US Congress, and in 1989, it passed legislation that included the 'Pelosi Amendment' after its sponsor, Congresswoman Nancy Pelosi.[18] The provision remains in effect and requires US Executive Directors at the World Bank and all the regional MDBs to abstain or vote against any proposed action with significant environmental effects if it has not received an appropriate environmental assessment, or if the assessment has not been made available to the Executive Directors and the public for 120 days before a vote.

The Pelosi Amendment instituted the possibility that the United States could vote against a project that, in its view, failed to have adequate environmental assessment. This possibility led the Bank, in turn, to enhance environmental

[13] The World Bank Archives, 'Fonds of the Environment Sector' <https://archivesholdings.worldbank.org/records-of-environment-sector> accessed 3 June 2023.

[14] The World Bank, 'Environmental Aspects of Bank Work: Operational Manual Statement' (May 1984) s 2.36, 1–5.

[15] The World Bank Archives, 'Environmental Guidelines: Office of Environmental Affairs' <https://documents1.worldbank.org/curated/en/106411467998481297/pdf/multi-page.pdf> accessed 12 July 2023.

[16] World Commission on Environment and Development, *Our Common Future* (*UN*, March 1987) <https://cclr.lexxion.eu/article/CCLR/2017/4/7> accessed 12 July 2023.

[17] Internal Memo of Barbara Lausche, 9 November 1988.

[18] Assessment of environmental impact of proposed multilateral development bank actions, US Public Law 101–240, 22 USC 262m-7.

assessment and information access procedures. Thus, in 1989, the Bank adopted an Operational Directive that required all projects under consideration for Bank loans be screened for potential environmental and social impact.[19] However, internal evaluations and reports by US Government and non-governmental organizations identified continuing problems in the use by Bank of environmental assessment data. Environmental assessments were still often performed on a 'parallel track', not as an integral part of project design and decision-making.[20] As a result, despite these changes, views persisted that the Bank still failed to fully address the environmental impact of its lending. Thus, the US foreign appropriations legislation added new provisions instructing the US executive directors of the World Bank and other MDBs to set benchmarks in the areas of sustainable energy development, forest conservation, forced displacement of populations, and procedures for environmental impact assessment.[21] Moreover, this law required the US Senate appropriations committee to consider 'appropriate actions, including withholding a portion of World Bank and other MDB appropriations' unless these benchmarks were met or there had been appropriate progress.

The US Congress was also aware of critical reviews of Bank performance relevant to the environment and social impacts of Bank lending. The 1992 Morse Berger Commission report,[22] launched by Bank President Lewis Preston, was the first independent commission reviewing World Bank performance. The Commission reviewed the Sardar Sarovar project in India, a project of hydropower development along the Narmada River that displaced over 100,000 people. The report criticized the Bank's failure to address the environmental and social issues related to the project, including impacts related to indigenous peoples and a failed approach to properly resettle the displaced communities. In this same time frame, a troubling report was led by Willi Wapenhans, Vice President of an internal watchdog group. The 'Wapenhans Report' asserted continuing challenges at the project level and regarding internal procedures.[23] Indeed, it

[19] The World Bank, 'Operational Directive 4.00 Environmental Assessment' in *Environmental Assessment Sourcebook* (October 1989) Annex A, 27 <https://documents1.worldbank.org/curated/en/223391468174870007/pdf/Environmental-assessment-sourcebook-volume-1-policies-procedures-and-cross-sectoral-issues.pdf> accessed 12 September 2024.

[20] Jonathan Sanford, 'CRS Report for Congress: Multilateral Development Banks Environmental Assessment and Information Policies: Impact of the Pelosi Amendment' (12 February 1998) <http://congressionalresearch.com/98-180/document.php> accessed 1 June 2024.

[21] Making appropriations for foreign operations, export financing, and related programmes for the fiscal year ending 30 September 1993, US Public Law 102–391 (6 October 1992).

[22] Bradford Morse and Thomas R Berger, *Sardar Sarovar: Report of the Independent Review* (Resource Futures International 1992) <https://ielrc.org/Content/c9202.pdf> accessed 12 July 2023.

[23] Alison Evans and Ramus Heltberg, 'How the Wapenhans Report Came to Change the World Bank 30 Years Ago' (*World Bank Independent Evaluation Group*, 21 September 2022) <https://ieg.worldbankgroup.org/blog/how-wapenhans-report-came-change-world-bank-30-years-ago> accessed 10 June 2023.

castigated the Bank's 'approval culture' and its tendency towards unnecessarily large and complex projects. While the Morse Berger report was commissioned to understand the adverse impacts of a singular project and the Bank's due diligence, the Wapenhans Report was particularly valuable because President Preston also wanted to help understand the basis for continuing criticism about the quality of a large number of projects. Thus, while not focusing on the environment per se, the report underscored the credibility of the concerns in the Morse report and the need for stronger accountability.

B. An evolution in accountability: The creation of the Independent Inspection Panel

The Wapenhans and Morse Commission reports convinced critics that earlier initiatives to improve environmental performance were inadequate.[24] To help address this concern, the Bank created the World Bank Independent Inspection Panel. As the Bank's General Counsel, Ibrahim Shihata, stated:

> Both the 'Wapenhans Report' and the Narmada [Sardar Sarovar] case received wide attention inside and outside the Bank, with a new focus on the debate over the adequacy of existing control mechanisms. The debate triggered a number of proposals in the course of 1993, some originating within the Bank and others from member governments and external critics. All contributed, no doubt, to the process culminating in the establishment of the Inspection Panel.[25]

Since 1993, the Panel has investigated complaints in all geographic regions and inspired the creation of accountability mechanisms across other multilateral, regional, and bilateral development entities. The Panel can investigate the Bank's compliance with Bank policies provided:

> The affected party must demonstrate that its rights or interests have been or are likely to be directly affected by an action or omission of the Bank as a result of a failure of the Bank to follow its operational policies and procedures with respect to the design, appraisal and/or implementation of a project financed by the Bank ... provided in all cases that such failure has had, or threatens to have, a material adverse effect.[26]

[24] Bruce Rich, *Mortgaging the Earth: The World Bank, Environmental Impoverishment, and the Crisis of Development* (2nd edn, Island Press 2013).

[25] Ibrahim FI Shihata, *The World Bank Inspection Panel: In Practice* (2nd edn, OUP 2000) 16–17.

[26] IBRD and IDA, 'Resolution No. IBRD 2020-0004 and Resolution No. IDA 2020-0003' (The World Bank Inspection Panel, 8 September 2020) para 13 <https://www.inspectionpanel.org/sites/default/files/documents/InspectionPanelResolution.pdf> accessed 20 June 2023.

Despite this innovation, accountability was still hindered by a lack of clarity on Bank and borrower responsibilities under the relevant 'operational policies and procedures', particularly environmental and social. Thus, despite the Panel's establishment, the US Center for Strategic and International Studies (CSIS) noted that there was 'confusion over accountability' and MDBs should be accountable to their shareholders for the results of their projects. In their view, if the borrower is not implementing the project adequately, the Bank should help correct the problem or stop funding the project.[27]

Due to the Pelosi Amendment, and new environmental policies, the CSIS Task Force had originally considered that environmental concerns had been resolved. However, 'the task force encountered much evidence that many of the improved policies had not been translated into changes in how the MDBs were functioning, especially in how projects were being implemented on the ground'.[28]

This lack of clarity became more apparent during the Panel investigation concerning the Western Poverty Reduction project in China.[29] As the Panel noted:

> During the course of examining some 20 projects over the past five years, the Panel has encountered certain differences in views among staff on just how the Bank's operational policies and procedures should be applied. In this case, however, the Panel's interviews revealed an unusually and disturbingly wide range of divergent and, often, opposing views. These large differences pervade all ranks of the staff, from senior management to front-line professionals. And they apply to virtually all of the major decisions required by the policies. The implications of this for a reasonable application of the Bank's policies and procedures became a matter of serious concern to the Panel, and ought to be of concern to the Bank generally since there is no way that the policies can be applied with reasonable consistency in the face of such wide divergences of opinion.[30]

These findings, along with frustration at the Bank's approach towards environmental risk classification in the Western Poverty project, led Bank Management to recognize the need for more clarity.

[27] CSIS US and the Multilateral Development Banks Task Force, *The United States and the Multilateral Development Banks: Final Report* (Center for Strategic and International Studies 1997) 61.

[28] ibid 18.

[29] The World Bank Group, 'Inspection Panel Investigation Report: Western Poverty Reduction Project' (1999) <https://www.inspectionpanel.org/sites/default/files/ip/PanelCases/16-Investigation%20Report%20%28English%29.pdf> accessed 15 June 2023.

[30] ibid xiv.

C. Strengthening accountability: Revisions to environmental and social policies

Following the Panel report on Western Poverty, Bank management restructured its environmental directives and created a 'Safeguards Team' to help projects 'do no harm' and to establish standards for a uniform approach to environmental and social risk.[31] The Safeguards Team fortified a standardized approach towards environmental and social risk, and centralized the Bank's approach towards Panel investigations. This team launched the 2018 World Bank Environmental and Social Framework (ESF) under which the Bank addresses a wider range of environmental and social issues related to its investment operations.[32] The ESF's Environmental and Social Policy sets out the Bank's binding responsibilities in its due diligence during project preparation.

Moreover, the ESF addresses new environmental and social risks in a manner that allows Bank operational teams to be more risk-responsive.[33] For example, following Inspection Panel findings of gender-based violence (GBV), tools were added to help prevent this from occurring in Bank projects.[34] The ESF also mandates measures to mitigate and adapt to climate change. In addition, the new standards recognize that leading causes of mortality in developing countries include lack of appropriate road safety and design. As a result, project design must take road safety into account. New provisions also recognize the near universal adoption of the Convention on the Rights of People with Disabilities and, as a result, include adaptive design.[35]

[31] Ole Kristian Fauchald, 'Hardening the Legal Softness of the World Bank Through an Inspection Panel?' (2013) 58 Scandinavian Studies in Law 101.

[32] World Bank Group, 'Environmental and Social Framework' <https://www.worldbank.org/en/projects-operations/environmental-and-social-framework> accessed 28 June 2023.

[33] Charles E Di Leva, 'The Challenge and Promise at the Intersection of Environmental and Social Policies: How the World Bank Established a Policy Framework That Fully Integrates Environmental and Social Concerns' (2021) 21 Global Social Policy 344.

[34] See, eg, World Bank Group, 'Strengthening Prevention of Gender-Based Violence (GBV): Contractor Accountability and Disqualification' (*World Bank*, 10 August 2022) <https://www.worldbank.org/en/projects-operations/products-and-services/brief/prevention-of-gender-based-violence-contractor-accountability-and-disqualification> accessed 12 September 2024. More recently, the World Bank has added to the Environmental and Social Framework a Good Practice Note to address GBV and Sexual Exploitation and Abuse and Sexual Harassment in Human Development Operations: World Bank, 'Good Practice Note' (30 September 2022) https://thedocs.worldbank.org/en/doc/e2ff01be0f07c82d73bc0c5e7ddf394f-0290032022/original/ESF-Good-Practice-Note-on-Addressing-SEA-SH-in-HD-Operations-First-Edition-September-16-2022.pdf accessed 12 September 2024.

[35] Other examples can be found on the ESF website, including in the ESF series of Good Practice Notes. World Bank, 'Environmental and Social Framework Resources' <https://www.worldbank.org/en/projects-operations/environmental-and-social-framework/brief/environmental-and-social-framework-resources#guidancenotes> accessed 12 September 2024.

III. How International Environmental Law Helped the Evolution Towards Climate Finance

Today, the Bank is the world's largest provider of climate finance to developing countries.[36] Yet, similar to its role as an environmental and social standard setter, providing climate finance was not envisioned during most of its first half-century. Nevertheless, this role began with the growth of international environmental law and recognition that global environmental problems could only be solved if developing countries receive the necessary financial support to move away from harmful practices and products. Thus, for example, in 1991 the World Bank began funding the costs for developing countries to transition to less ozone-depleting substances.[37]

One year later, at the Rio Conference on Environment and Development, the Bank was called on to support the Conference's Program of Action and have 'an important role to play in the implementation of relevant parts of agenda 21 and other decisions of the conference'.[38] Coincidentally, at Rio, the UN Framework Convention on Climate Change (UNFCCC) and the Convention on Biological Diversity were adopted and formally established financial mechanisms to function under the guidance of and be accountable to the Conventions' member states.[39] The two mechanisms became embodied in the Global Environment Facility, an independent entity hosted by the Bank, and of which the Bank remains a key implementing entity.

Since 1992, the Bank has regularly participated in the Conventions and is an important source of finance and knowledge to help implement them. For example, even before the 1997 Kyoto Protocol to the UNFCCC, the Bank collaborated with several member states to develop an 'early action' mechanism to reduce carbon emissions and became the first multilateral bank to launch

[36] World Bank Group, 'A Closer Look at Climate Finance' (31 October 2022) <https://www.worldbank.org/en/news/factsheet/2022/10/31/a-closer-look-at-world-bank-group-climate-finance#:~:text=Over%20the%20past%20seven%20years,include%20a%20climate%20finance%20component> accessed 28 June 2023.

[37] Lauren Kelly, 'The Multilateral Fund for the Implementation of the Montreal Protocol: Addressing Challenges of Globalization—An Independent Evaluation of the World Bank's Approach to Global Programs—Case Study (English)' (2004) OED Working Paper No 32914 <https://documents.worldbank.org/en/publication/documents-reports/documentdetail/804261468321262499/the-multilateral-fund-for-the-implementation-of-the-montreal-protocol-addressing-challenges-of-globalization-an-independent-evaluation-of-the-world-banks-approach-to-global-programs-case-study> accessed 23 January 2025.

[38] United Nations Conference on Environment and Development, 'Agenda 21: Program of Action for Sustainable Development' (12 August 1992) [ST/] DPI/1344 (Agenda 21).

[39] United Nations Framework Convention on Climate Change (adopted 9 May 1992, entered into force 21 March 1994) 1771 UNTS 107 (UNFCCC) art 11 <https://unfccc.int/resource/docs/convkp/conveng.pdf> accessed 12 September 2024; Convention on Biological Diversity (adopted 5 June 1992, entered into force 29 December 1993) 1760 UNTS 69 art 22 <https://www.cbd.int/convention/text/> accessed 25 June 2023.

carbon market initiatives.[40] This support has helped drive global public goods finance to the point where Gordon Brown suggested the Bank should be a climate bank.

To address climate change, the Bank must assume greater risk and stretch its capital to incentivize private capital investment. Prominent voices have promoted major debt relief to help developing countries deal with climate change, and shareholders appear to have agreed to move in this direction.[41] Thus, the exigencies of climate change have also broadened the Bank's approach to financial risk.[42]

Some analysts have questioned the efficacy of the World Bank's climate finance and the accuracy of its projection of climate co-benefits associated with each Bank-financed project.[43] Nevertheless, the trend towards increasing climate support seems embedded.[44] This is evident in the World Bank Group's pledge to make all of its operations be 'Paris Aligned' in its new Climate Change Action Plan covering 2021–2025. This means all operations 'will be consistent with the objectives of the Paris Agreement and a country's pathway towards low greenhouse gas emissions and climate-resilient development'.[45] Moreover, at a 2023 summit in Paris, the Bank's new President Ajay Banga made clear his commitment to follow through on the Bank's recent 'Evolution Roadmap'—which, inter alia, includes commitments to enhance and expand the Bank's climate funding.[46] The roadmap states that 'The World Bank Group must evolve in response to the unprecedented confluence of global crisis that has upended development progress and threatens people on the planet'.[47] The actions that may stretch the Bank's balance sheet to meet the Roadmap might include pausing

[40] The World Bank Internal Evaluation Group, 'Climate Change and the World Bank Group' (2010) <https://documents1.worldbank.org/curated/en/636081468330899831/pdf/Climate-change-and-the-World-Bank-Group-climate-adaptation-Approach-Paper.pdf> accessed 12 July 2023. For discussion about joint implementation initiatives, see ibid 5, 73.

[41] John Irish and Leigh Thomas, 'Rich Nations Pledge to Unlock Hundreds of Billions of Dollars for Climate Fight' (*Reuters*, 23 June 2023) <https://www.reuters.com/sustainability/sustainable-finance-reporting/frances-macron-says-leaders-finalised-accord-100-bln-climate-finance-2023-06-23/> accessed 12 September 2024.

[42] Admittedly, this is not the first time the Bank has been asked to use risk mitigation more effectively and optimize its balances sheet. Charles Di Leva, 'Financing Climate Mitigation and Adaptation' (2017) 11 Carbon & Climate Law Review 314, 323.

[43] Aime Williams, 'Hundreds of World Bank Climate Projects Have No Direct Connection to Climate, Research Finds' (*Financial Times*, 15 June 2023) <https://www.ft.com/content/ba416b81-afa2-41be-aa3b-e86b8b3136e0> accessed 12 September 2024.

[44] World Bank (n 36).

[45] World Bank, 'The World Bank Group and Paris Alignment' <https://www.worldbank.org/en/publication/paris-alignment> accessed 12 September 2024.

[46] Development Committee of the World Bank and the International Monetary Fund, 'Evolution of the World Bank Group: A Report to Governors' (30 March 2023) <https://consultations.worldbank.org/content/dam/sites/consultations/doc/2023/Development-Committee-paper-2023.pdf> accessed 23 January 2025.

[47] ibid iv.

debt repayments by countries that are faced with climate-related disasters and drought as well as ways to stretch the Bank's risk appetite as a means to attract more private capital to renewable energy projects that have a longer gestation period for financial return.

IV. Conclusion

Reflection upon the Bank's history helps explain the evolution of its relationship with the environment. This history reveals that environmental goals were never part of the Bank's original mission, and it took time and evidence of environmental and social impacts for many of those charged with supporting that mission to understand the connection between development and the environment and to implement effective policies and project finance.

9

WHO's Reactions to COVID-19

Between Politics and Managerialism

Gian Luca Burci and Ana Balcazar-Moreno

I. Introduction

The outbreak of the severe acute respiratory syndrome coronavirus 2 (SARS-CoV-2) causing the coronavirus disease 2019 (COVID-19) took the world by surprise and overwhelmed most international governance systems. The World Health Organization (WHO) and its global health security mechanisms were no exception. The speed and ferocity of the spread of the disease, the lack of preparedness, and the hesitancy of most countries impacted by its initial wave created a 'perfect storm' that affected the role, performance, and reputation of the WHO. It also led it to take several reactive actions, largely at the initiative of the Secretariat and its Director-General, Dr Tedros Adhanom Ghebreyesus, that created a complex legal and political dynamic with WHO's intergovernmental bodies and key member states.

At the time of writing, the main legal instrument defining the role of WHO in detecting and controlling international disease outbreaks are the International Health Regulations (2005) (IHR), which not only lay out obligations and conditions for states parties but also grant significant authority to the Secretariat. The latter, in particular, can carry out surveillance alongside states parties,[1] rely on non-governmental sources for that purpose,[2] declare a 'public health emergency of international concern' (PHEIC) including a pandemic emergency (introduced through the May 2024 amendments),[3] and issue temporary recommendations addressed to States and other stakeholders.[4]

Despite this impressive formal authority, the IHR proved inadequate to prevent and stem the spread of COVID-19. Many states were slow to comply, or they often adopted disproportionate unilateral measures that made international co-ordination impossible and fostered an image of the Regulations as toothless and

[1] International Health Regulations (2005), Article 5(4).
[2] ibid art 9ff.
[3] ibid art 12.
[4] ibid art 15ff.

Gian Luca Burci and Ana Balcazar-Moreno, *WHO's Reactions to COVID-19* In: *International Organization Initiatives*. Edited by: Gabrielle Marceau and Henner Gött, Oxford University Press. © Oxford University Press 2025.
DOI: 10.1093/9780197803325.003.0010

too permissive.[5] The Secretariat's role was also questioned, as it was criticized for being too cautious and deferential to important member states instead of using its legal authority to pressure them into compliance.

The magnitude of the crisis focused the expectations of the world on WHO as the default global health authority. These expectations have not evaporated with the end of the PHEIC[6] but continue to define in complex and, at times, politically controversial ways the role played by the Director-General and his self-assertion of authority vis-à-vis the positions adopted by WHO's governance organs and key member states. Such dynamic has to be assessed against the context of the mandates entrusted to the Secretariat by the World Health Assembly in 2020 and 2021, as well as of the negotiations towards a new binding instrument on pandemic prevention, preparedness and response (pandemic agreement)[7] and the amendments to the IHR adopted in June 2024.[8]

Indeed, these two legal processes represent the main normative initiatives taken by the World Health Assembly in response to the COVID-19 pandemic. They were respectively launched in December 2021, led by the Intergovernmental Negotiating Body (INB), and in May 2022, led by the Working Group on Amendments to the International Health Regulations (2005) (WGIHR). Their negotiations proceeded on parallel tracks and were only finalized by the 77th World Health Assembly with regard to the IHR. However, negotiations on the pandemic agreement have been slow and more complex, with clashing positions between developing and developed countries and are still ongoing at the time of writing.

[5] Gian Luca Burci. 'The Legal Response to Pandemics: The Strengths and Weaknesses of the International Health Regulations' (2020) 11 Journal of International Humanitarian Legal Studies 2 <https://brill.com/view/journals/ihls/11/2/article-p204_204.xml?language=en> accessed 4 September 2023.

[6] WHO, 'Statement on the fifteenth meeting of the IHR (2005) Emergency Committee on the COVID-19 pandemic' (5 May 2023) <https://www.who.int/news/item/05-05-2023-statement-on-the-fifteenth-meeting-of-the-international-health-regulations-(2005)-emergency-committee-regarding-the-coronavirus-disease-(covid-19)-pandemic> accessed 27 September 2024.

[7] See WHO (Decision of the World Health Assembly), 'Special session of the World Health Assembly to consider developing a WHO convention, agreement or other international instrument on pandemic preparedness and response' (31 May 2021) WHA74(16). WHO (Decision of the World Health Assembly), 'The World Together: Establishment of an intergovernmental negotiating body to strengthen pandemic prevention, preparedness and response' (1 December 2021) SSA2(5). WHO (Decision of the World Health Assembly) 'Intergovernmental Negotiating Body to draft and negotiate a WHO convention, agreement or other international instrument on pandemic prevention, preparedness and response' (1 June 2024) WHA77(20). See also Ana Balcazar-Moreno, Gian Luca Burci, and Adam Patryk Strobejko, 'Taxonomy of Substantive Proposals for a New Instrument on Pandemic Prevention, Preparedness and Response' (*Global Health Centre*, 2022) <https://www.graduateinstitute.ch/sites/internet/files/2022-01/taxonomy-paper.pdf> accessed 2 September 2023.

[8] WHO (Resolution of the World Health Assembly), 'Strengthening preparedness for and response to public health emergencies through targeted amendments to the International Health Regulations (2005)' (1 June 2024) WHA77.17.

The legal and constitutional basis for the measures taken by the Secretariat can be found in the specific decisions adopted by the World Health Assembly in response to the COVID-19 pandemic, in the previous resolutions establishing the WHO Emergency Programme or, more generally, in WHO's constitutional mandate. Significantly, while some of the initiatives under consideration have been criticized for interfering with the aforementioned intergovernmental negotiations or being too far 'ahead' of member states, there has never been a suggestion that they were ultra vires the constitutional or programmatic mandates of the Organization.

The Secretariat's actions can be roughly divided between reactive measures adopted in the immediacy of the COVID-19 emergency and more strategic and political initiatives connected to the efforts by WHO to build a stronger system for pandemic prevention, preparedness, and response (PPR).[9] The difference between the two is not only chronological but also thematic and functional.

II. Emergency Reactive Initiatives

The WHO Secretariat adopted a series of immediate and tactical measures in response to the COVID-19 outbreak emergency. Those initiatives were taken in a policy and normative vacuum as they did not have a clear basis on a mandate by the governing bodies and were adopted during intense political pressures.

A. Recommendations and guidance

The Secretariat aggressively used its website as an outreach and communication tool during the COVID-19 pandemic. It constantly published data, statistics, advice, technical guidance, and a wide range of recommendations, from coordinating clinical trials on vaccines to advising policymakers and the general public, as well as mobilizing ground-level engagement.[10]

Even though the Director-General issued temporary recommendations for COVID-19 response under the authority of the IHR,[11] their relevance and

[9] See generally Independent Panel for Pandemic Preparedness and Response, 'COVID-19: Make It the Last Pandemic' (2021) <https://theindependentpanel.org/wp-content/uploads/2021/05/COVID-19-Make-it-the-Last-Pandemic_final.pdf> accessed 27 September 2024. See also Independent Oversight and Advisory Committee for the WHO Health Emergencies Programme, 'Public health emergencies: preparedness and response' (*WHO*, 17 May 2023) <https://apps.who.int/gb/ebwha/pdf_files/WHA76/A76_8-en.pdf> accessed 27 September 2024.

[10] See generally WHO, 'Coronavirus disease (COVID-19) pandemic' <https://www.who.int/emergencies/diseases/novel-coronavirus-2019> accessed 4 September 2023.

[11] On 30 January 2020, the WHO Director-General declared that the outbreak of COVID-19 constitutes a PHEIC and issued temporary recommendations. WHO, 'WHO Director-General's statement on IHR Emergency Committee on Novel Coronavirus (2019-nCoV)' (30 January

normative impact paled when confronted with the growing mass of material developed outside the IHR framework and without the input of identified groups of experts. While it is within the WHO's constitutional mandate to advise member states on all sorts of public health issues, the scope and volume of COVID-19 material surpassed other sources without formal endorsement by WHO governing bodies.

B. Exercise of epistemic authority

The impact of the aforementioned guidance points to the epistemic authority WHO enjoys, particularly at times of crisis, as the international authority on global health matters, acting based on science and evidence.[12]

The aggressive use of media and social media by the Secretariat and the regular press briefings presided over by the Director-General throughout the COVID-19 emergency produced empirically visible reactions from governmental officials and other stakeholders that played into the political controversies characterizing the pandemic. The best example of this observation is the effects of the statement by the Director-General on 11 March 2020 that COVID-19 had become a pandemic.[13] Even though the Director-General was careful at couching that statement in factual terms, the reactions worldwide were much more extreme than after the declaration of a PHEIC on 30 January 2020. They raised in graphic terms how the actual normative impact of WHO was not necessarily reliant on its legal mandate.

C. Participation in establishing new governance tools

Perhaps the most far-reaching instance of the independent exercise of power by the Secretariat was WHO's direct engagement in establishing complex public–private platforms to manage the development, procurement, and equitable global allocation of scarce medical countermeasures (MCM). In April

2020) <https://www.who.int/director-general/speeches/detail/who-director-general-s-statement-on-ihr-emergency-committee-on-novel-coronavirus-(2019-ncov)> accessed 4 September 2023.

[12] See generally Jan Klabbers, 'The Normative Gap in International Organizations Law: The Case of the World Health Organization' (2019) 16 International Organizations Law Review 272–98. See also Christian Kreuder-Sonnen, *Emergency Powers of International Organizations: Between Normalization and Containment* (OUP 2019).

[13] WHO, 'Director-General's opening remarks at the media briefing on COVID-19' (11 March 2020) <https://www.who.int/director-general/speeches/detail/who-director-general-s-opening-remarks-at-the-media-briefing-on-covid-19---11-march-2020> accessed 1 September 2023.

2020, the Director-General joined France, the European Commission, the Gates Foundation, the World Bank, and several public–private partnerships in creating the Access to COVID-19 Tools Accelerator (ACT-A) and its vaccine pillar—COVID-19 Vaccines Global Access, better known as COVAX.[14] The Director-General also joined the President of Costa Rica in May 2020 in establishing the COVID-19 Technology Access Pool (C-TAP) to collect voluntary pledges to share intellectual property and knowledge related to COVID-19 countermeasures.[15]

While these initiatives were of mixed success, the Secretariat took extraordinary measures of great normative and political significance in the absence of a specific mandate in response to an acute emergency requiring an immediate response. The ACT-A (and COVAX in particular) developed an elaborated governance structure that oversaw complex financial and procurement transactions attempting to shape the COVID-19 vaccine market. The World Health Assembly, in its resolutions at its 2020 and 2021 sessions, limited itself to highlight the ACT-A initiative and the role played by WHO.[16] The Assembly, therefore, seemed to either acquiesce to what the Director-General had already undertaken or implicitly recognize that he had the authority to engage the Organization in those initiatives based on its constitutional mandate.

III. Longer-Term and Strategic Initiatives

The initiatives under consideration in this section interact, or even 'compete', with policy decisions articulated in the context of the negotiations mentioned in the Introduction. They are not limited to the institutional framework of WHO but see the Secretariat taking an active role in discussions and negotiations in other intergovernmental organizations and forums. It is not surprising that member states' reactions have been mixed, ranging from acquiescence or support to disapproval, the reassertion of political space for member states, and a narrower delimitation of the legitimate exercise of power by the Secretariat.

[14] WHO, 'Access to COVID-19 Tools (ACT) Accelerator' (24 April 2020) <https://www.who.int/publications/m/item/access-to-covid-19-tools-(act)-accelerator> accessed 1 September 2023.

[15] WHO, 'Operationalizing the COVID-19 Technology Access Pool (C-TAP): A Concept Paper' <https://cdn.who.int/media/docs/default-source/essential-medicines/intellectual-property/who-covid-19-tech-access-tool-c-tap.pdf?sfvrsn=1695cf9_36> accessed 2 September 2023.

[16] WHO (Resolution of the World Health Assembly) 'COVID-19 response' (19 May 2020) WHA73(1). See also WHO (Resolution of the World Health Assembly) 'Strengthening local production of medicines and other health technologies to improve access' (31 May 2021) WHA74(6) and WHO (Resolution of the World Health Assembly) 'Strengthening WHO preparedness for and response to health emergencies' (31 May 2021) WHA74(7).

A. Creation of global hubs

Beyond the immediate response to COVID-19, WHO has remained at the centre of international efforts to strengthen PPR capacities to reduce the risk of further pandemics and, as importantly, to strengthen equity and fairness in favour of developing countries that have found themselves at the receiving end of the pharmaceutical market.

The lack of coordination and leadership in crucial aspects of PPR, such as generating and sharing timely and accurate information and data, as well as accelerating the production and equitable allocation of MCM, was evident during the COVID-19 outbreak. These are also central aspects of the negotiations on a pandemic agreement. Despite the parallel intergovernmental negotiations until June 2024, the Director-General did not hesitate to exercise leadership by establishing—or supporting the establishment of—'hubs' through bilateral agreements with selected member states to incentivize international co-operation on PPR.

In particular, following a statement by the Director-General in favour of a global system for sharing pathogens and clinical samples,[17] the Secretariat proposed[18] setting up a WHO BioHub System as a voluntary mechanism for sharing biological materials with epidemic or pandemic potential.[19] In May 2021, the Director-General and Switzerland signed a Memorandum of Understanding and launched the first WHO BioHub Facility.[20] Despite the expectations generated by that initiative, there has not been consistent communication about it, and it is unclear whether the Swiss laboratory has been receiving samples.

In April 2021, the WHO announced the launch of the COVID-19 mRNA Vaccine Technology Transfer Hubs to boost the capacity of low and middle-income countries (LMIC) to produce COVID-19 vaccines.[21] In July 2021, the

[17] WHO, 'WHO Director-General's closing remarks at the World Health Assembly' (13 November 2020) <https://www.who.int/director-general/speeches/detail/who-director-general-s-closing-remarks-at-the-world-health-assembly---13-november-2020> accessed 4 September 2023.

[18] WHO, 'The WHO BioHub System for Preparedness and Response to Epidemics and Pandemics: Concept note' (22 June 2021) <https://cdn.who.int/media/docs/default-source/2021-dha-docs/210617_whobiohubconceptnote_brochure-(1).pdf?sfvrsn=5e5a06f3_1&download=true> accessed 4 September 2023.

[19] WHO, 'WHO Director-General's opening remarks at the World Health Assembly' (9 November 2020) <https://www.who.int/director-general/speeches/detail/who-director-general-s-opening-remarks-at-the-world-health-assembly---9-november-2020> accessed 4 September 2023.

[20] WHO, 'WHO and Switzerland launch global BioHub for pathogen storage, sharing and analysis' (24 May 2021) <https://www.who.int/news/item/24-05-2021-who-and-switzerland-launch-global-biohub-for-pathogen-storage-sharing-and-analysis> accessed 4 September 2023.

[21] WHO, 'Establishment of a COVID-19 mRNA vaccine technology transfer hub to scale up global manufacturing' (16 April 2021) <https://www.who.int/news-room/articles-detail/establishment-of-a-covid-19-mrna-vaccine-technology-transfer-hub-to-scale-up-global-manufacturing> accessed 4 September 2023.

WHO launched the South African mRNA hub at Afrigen Biologics in Cape Town[22] to share technology and technical know-how with local producers.[23] Afterwards, two countries from the WHO region of the Americas received mRNA technology from the global hub in South Africa.[24]

In September 2021, with Germany's support, the Director-General inaugurated the WHO Hub for Pandemic and Epidemic Intelligence in Berlin[25] to improve surveillance, gather high-quality data, and use collaborative intelligence to help leaders make better decisions.[26] In February 2022, the WHO announced the selection of the Republic of Korea as a global biomanufacturing training hub to support LMIC in producing their own vaccines and therapies by providing training in vaccine and biologics manufacturing.[27]

In general terms, these initiatives aim to enhance global preparedness and response to health emergencies and ensure equity and access through local and regional manufacturing capacity of MCM and other technologies. Yet, it remains unclear whether and how they relate to the pandemic agreement negotiations over access to health products, technologies and know-how, cross-border sharing of pathogen samples or sequence information, and the equitable distribution of the benefits of their use, including for research and development (R&D) activities.

B. G20 and the creation of the Pandemic Fund

During the COVID-19 outbreak, the interactions between the Director-General and political networks, such as the G20, intensified—once more

[22] 'The selected consortium comprises Afrigen Biologics, the South African Medical Research Council (SAMRC) and Biovac, a South African vaccine producer. Within this consortium, Afrigen is the entity mandated to establish mRNA vaccine production technology, SAMRC is providing the research and Biovac is the first manufacturing "spoke".' WHO, 'FAQ - The mRNA vaccine technology transfer hub' <https://www.who.int/initiatives/the-mrna-vaccine-technology-transfer-hub/faq> accessed 4 September 2023.

[23] WHO, 'The mRNA vaccine technology transfer hub' <https://www.who.int/initiatives/the-mrna-vaccine-technology-transfer-hub> accessed 4 September 2023.

[24] Pan American Health Organization, 'Latin American manufacturers complete first training in mRNA technology in bid to improve regional vaccine production' (24 March 2022) <https://www.paho.org/en/news/24-3-2022-latin-american-manufacturers-complete-first-training-mrna-technology-bid-improve> accessed 4 September 2023.

[25] WHO, 'WHO, Germany open Hub for Pandemic and Epidemic Intelligence in Berlin' (1 September 2021) <https://pandemichub.who.int/news-room/news/item/01-09-2021-who-germany-open-hub-for-pandemic-and-epidemic-intelligence-in-berlin> accessed 4 September 2023.

[26] WHO, 'The WHO Hub for Pandemic and Epidemic Intelligence: Strategy Paper' (13 December 2022) <https://pandemichub.who.int/publications/m/item/the-who-hub-for-pandemic-and-epidemic-intelligence-strategy-paper> accessed 4 September 2023.

[27] WHO, 'WHO and Republic of Korea sign landmark agreement to boost biomanufacturing capacity' (26 May 2023) <https://www.who.int/news/item/26-05-2023-WHO-and-Republic-of-Korea-sign-landmark-agreement-to-boost-biomanufacturing-capacity> accessed 4 September 2023.

without a specific mandate from the World Health Assembly. Through the Rome Declaration of 2021,[28] the leaders of the G20 supported WHO's role, the value of all pillars of the ACT-A, the newly created WHO hubs, and the need to ensure adequate and sustained financing for PPR within a One Health approach. The idea of a new financing mechanism to mobilize and channel funds into national pandemic preparedness was discussed and negotiated by the G20 during its Italian presidency. The WHO actively participated in those discussions and advocated to ensure its technical leadership.

Subsequently, at the Second Special Session of the World Health Assembly in November–December 2021, the President of the European Commission announced the creation of a financial intermediary fund at the World Bank for global health security and pandemic preparedness. The Director-General echoed the need for a new robust and predictable financing mechanism for global health security 'supported by a Secretariat based at WHO, housed at the World Bank, and financed by countries and regional organizations on a burden-sharing basis'.[29]

In September 2022, the Financial Intermediary Fund for Pandemic Prevention, Preparedness and Response (Pandemic Fund) was formally established.[30] The World Bank serves as the Fund's trustee and hosts its Secretariat, which includes technical staff seconded from WHO which also chairs the Technical Advisory Panel charged with assessing and making recommendations on the technical merits of investment proposals.[31] The Director-General highlighted that 'WHO will play a central role [. . .], providing technical leadership for [the Pandemic Fund's] work in close collaboration with the World Bank to realize this ambitious vision'.[32]

The G20 has been criticized for allegedly becoming a global directorate controlled by the most powerful countries. Thus, WHO's involvement in the creation and governance of the Pandemic Fund, without a specific mandate from

[28] EU, 'Rome Declaration' (21 May 2021) <https://global-health-summit.europa.eu/rome-declaration_en> accessed 4 September 2023.

[29] WHO, 'WHO Director-General's opening remarks Global Health Landscape Symposium - 9 December 2021' (9 December 2021) <https://www.who.int/director-general/speeches/detail/who-director-general-s-opening-remarks-global-health-landscape-symposium---9-december-2021> accessed 4 September 2023.

[30] World Bank Group, 'Establishment of a Financial Intermediary Fund for Pandemic Prevention, Preparedness and Response. World Bank Group' (17 June 2022) <https://documents1.worldbank.org/curated/en/733191656685369495/pdf/Establishment-of-a-Financial-Intermediary-Fund-for-Pandemic-Prevention-Preparedness-and-Response.pdf> accessed 4 September 2023.

[31] World Bank, 'G20 hosts Official Launch of The Pandemic Fund' (13 November 2022) <https://www.worldbank.org/en/news/press-release/2022/11/12/g20-hosts-official-launch-of-the-pandemic-fund> accessed 4 September 2023.

[32] WHO, 'World Bank Board Approves New Fund for Pandemic Prevention, Preparedness and Response (PPR)' (30 June 2022) <https://www.who.int/news/item/30-06-2022-world-bank-board-approves-new-fund-for-pandemic-prevention--preparedness-and-response-(ppr)> accessed 4 September 2023.

its governing bodies, carried political risks. This criticism also characterized the first round of financing in early 2023, including the insufficient funds mobilized compared with previous estimates of minimum financial needs. Even though WHO's role is formally limited to the technical evaluation of proposals, the reputational and political risks are evident.

C. 'One Health' and inter-agency coordination

In March 2022, the Executive Heads of the Food and Agriculture Organization of the United Nations, World Organisation for Animal Health, United Nations Environment Programme,[33] and WHO signed a Quadripartite Memorandum of Understanding[34] providing a formal framework to strengthen their cooperation in tackling the challenges of disease spread at the human, animal, and ecosystem interface. This goes beyond the narrower scope of the IHR (2005) by strengthening cross-sectoral capacities and coordination among human and animal health as well as environmental management.

In October 2022, the 'Quadripartite' launched the One Health Joint Plan of Action[35] to create an integrated framework in order to collectively better prevent, predict, detect, and respond to health threats by 'achieving sustainable health and food systems, reduced global health threats and improved ecosystem management'.[36] The Plan of Action was adopted by the four Secretariats, once again without a specific mandate by their respective governing bodies. The other defining event was the establishment in May 2021 of the One Health High-Level Expert Panel (OHHLEP)[37] as a joint advisory body to improve the understanding of, inter alia, how zoonoses with the potential to trigger pandemics emerge and spread, and to prevent and prepare for zoonotic outbreaks.

[33] WHO, 'UN Environment Programme joins alliance to implement One Health approach' (18 March 2022) <https://www.who.int/news/item/18-03-2022-un-environment-programme-joins-alliance-to-implement-one-health-approach> accessed 4 September 2023.

[34] WHO, 'Quadripartite Memorandum of Understanding (MoU) signed for a new era of One Health collaboration' (29 April 2022) <https://www.who.int/news/item/29-04-2022-quadripartite-memorandum-of-understanding-(mou)-signed-for-a-new-era-of-one-health-collaboration> accessed 4 September 2023.

[35] WHO, Food and Agriculture Organization of the United Nations, World Organisation for Animal Health, and United Nations Environment Programme, 'One Health Joint Plan of Action (2022-2026): Working together for the health of humans, animals, plants and the environment' (2022) <https://apps.who.int/iris/bitstream/handle/10665/363518/9789240059139-eng.pdf?sequence=1&isAllowed=y> accessed 4 September 2023.

[36] ibid.

[37] WHO, 'One Health High-Level Expert Panel (OHHLEP)' <https://www.who.int/groups/one-health-high-level-expert-panel> accessed 4 September 2023.

D. Piloting of Universal Health and Preparedness Review

The lack of compliance and accountability mechanisms in the IHR (2005) has emerged as one of the main flaws in PPR. Since 2020, the Director-General has advocated for a peer-reviewed, member states-led, voluntary Universal Health and Preparedness Review (UHPR).[38] The Secretariat has actively developed an overall concept and operational modalities for the UHPR and piloted it with a number of volunteering member states.[39] Yet, the Director-General's initiative is similar to some of the proposed review mechanisms examined during the same period by the INB[40] and eventually included in the amended IHR.[41] The parallel unfolding of these proposals generated confusion because some of the earlier negotiating proposals for the pandemic agreement refer to UHPR without clarifying whether the reference is equivalent to a delegation of authority to the Director-General's initiative.

In reaction, some member states underlined the importance of avoiding duplications[42] and cautioned in 2023 that the 'substance of the proposals [was] an integral part of the [. . .] discussion at the INB and the WGIHR, with the difference that these processes have been developing in a much more transparent and inclusive way, with participation by non-state actors and guidance offered by member states'.[43]

E. Conceptualization of an MCM platform

As part of a comprehensive set of proposals on PPR, the Director-General announced at the 152nd session of the Executive Board in January 2023 that the Secretariat was 'convening a process to create an end-to-end platform for equitable access to MCM, building on lessons from the ACT-A, the Pandemic

[38] WHO, 'Technical Advisory Group (TAG) for Universal Health and Preparedness Review (UHPR)' <https://www.who.int/groups/technical-advisory-group-for-universal-health-and-preparedness-review> accessed 9 September 2023.

[39] WHO, 'Universal Health and Preparedness Review' <https://www.who.int/emergencies/operations/universal-health---preparedness-review> accessed 9 September 2023.

[40] INB, 'Bureau's text of the WHO convention, agreement or other international instrument on pandemic prevention, preparedness and response (WHO CA+)' (2 June 2023) Document A/INB/5/6 <https://apps.who.int/gb/inb/pdf_files/inb5/A_INB5_6-en.pdf> accessed 4 September 2023.

[41] See generally World Health Assembly (n 8), Annex, arts 13, 54, and 54 bis.

[42] Statement submitted by the United Kingdom of Great Britain and Northern Ireland, 'Item 12.1: Summary' <https://apps.who.int/gb/statements/eb152/PDF/UK-12.1.pdf> accessed 4 September 2023.

[43] Statement submitted by Brazil, 'Item 12.1. Strengthening WHO preparedness for and response to health emergencies: Strengthening the global architecture for health emergency preparedness, response and resilience' (7 February 2023) <https://apps.who.int/gb/statements/eb152/PDF/Brazil-12.1.pdf> accessed 4 September 2023.

Influenza Preparedness (PIP) Framework and other mechanisms'.[44] The Secretariat later issued a Concept Note on the consultative process to design a multi-disease, multitool, end-to-end platform for coordinating the rapid development and equitable access to MCM.[45] That process unfolded in parallel to the measures negotiated by the INB and the WGIHR, both of which featured provisions on equitable access to MCM. However, the Secretariat emphasized that the 'WHO-led process [would] not get ahead of the INB and WGIHR processes and [would] instead work towards informing the design of an "interim" or "working" coordination platform, drawing on [. . . their] deliberations and negotiations'.[46] That reassurance was offered again by the Director-General in his report to the 2023 World Health Assembly.[47]

In this case, the Secretariat framed its initiative based on extensive consultations with member states (both outside and in parallel to WHO's governance) as an interim arrangement to avoid an operational and policy vacuum in case of a new pandemic before new international rules enter into force and without prejudice to the latter. At the same time, the proposals influenced the negotiations and elicited the same mixed reactions as the UHPR.

IV. Concluding Remarks

Given its broad technical mandate, the WHO Secretariat exemplifies many types of authority that Barnett and Finnemore[48] argue are characteristic of IOs as bureaucracies. For example, WHO's normative function to adopt legal instruments such as agreements, regulations, and recommendations enables it to exercise rational, epistemic, and legal authority. The constitutional objective of improving the world's health grants WHO a measure of moral authority,

[44] WHO, 'WHO Director-General's remarks at the 152nd session of the Executive Board' (30 January 2023) <https://www.who.int/director-general/speeches/detail/who-director-general-s-remarks-at-the-152nd-session-of-the-executive-board> accessed 4 September 2023.

[45] WHO, 'Concept Note: Developing a new platform for equitable access to medical countermeasures in pandemics: Design & consultation process' (2 February 2023) <https://cdn.who.int/media/docs/default-source/documents/emergencies/countermeasures-platform_who-consultative-process---concept.pdf?sfvrsn=7f23de34_2> accessed 4 September 2023.

[46] WHO, 'WHO Medical Countermeasures Platform Design & Consultation Process: Q&A' (7 March 2023) <https://cdn.who.int/media/docs/default-source/documents/emergencies/countermeasures-platform-design-and-consultation-process-qa.pdf?sfvrsn=2d98b641_7> accessed 27 September 2024.

[47] WHO (Report by the Director-General) 'Strengthening WHO preparedness for and response to health emergencies: Strengthening the global architecture for health emergency preparedness, response and resilience' (19 May 2023) Document A76/10 <https://apps.who.int/gb/ebwha/pdf_files/WHA76/A76_10-en.pdf> accessed 4 September 2023.

[48] Michael Barnett and Martha Finnemore, *Rules for the World: International Organizations in Global Politics* (Cornell UP 2004).

while the strong preference for staffing the Secretariat with medical professionals reinforces WHO's technical authority.[49]

Arguably, the Secretariat deployed a wide array of mechanisms by using some constitutional flexibilities and (re)interpreting them during the COVID-19 pandemic. For example, according to preambular paragraph 8 of the WHO Constitution, '[i]nformed opinion and active co-operation on the part of the public are of the utmost importance in the improvement of the health of the people'. Hence, the Secretariat has communicated directly with the general public and adapted its outreach using media, social media platforms, and other mechanisms. This approach reflects an evolution of how IOs interact directly with civil society and the general public rather than limiting themselves to direct their communication to their member states.

Although WHO member states delegated a measure of authority to the Secretariat when they established the WHO in 1948, this authority has been exponentially developed during the recent health crises, which facilitated the Director-General's innovative launch of new institutional activities, bodies, and programmes, as well as partnerships with other international actors. Indeed, the constitutive documents of the WHO have provided its Director-General with certain powers for the fulfilment of its mandate. Yet, an explicit comprehensive or general right of initiative was not enshrined in the WHO Constitution, unlike, for example, in Article 99 of the UN Charter in favour of the UN Secretary-General. However, subsequent Director-Generals have interpreted the broad constitutional mandate of WHO as granting them the authority not only to respond to health emergencies but also to prevent them and to strive for, inter alia, equitable and fair conditions of access to life-saving MCM.

[49] Adam Kamradt-Scott, 'The International Health Regulations (2005): Strengthening Their Effective Implementation and Utilisation' (2019) 16 International Organizations Law Review 256.

10

Fossil Fuel Subsidies at the Organisation for Economic Co-operation and Development

Ronald Steenblik and Helen Mountford[*]

I. Introduction

On 25 September 2009, at their summit in Pittsburgh, Pennsylvania, the political leaders of the Group of Twenty (G20) nations issued a joint communiqué that, among other objectives, committed themselves to 'Rationalize and phase out over the medium term inefficient fossil fuel subsidies that encourage wasteful consumption'.[1] Ten months earlier, the International Energy Agency (IEA) had estimated that subsidies for the consumption of fossil fuels provided by 20 non-OECD countries (accounting for over 80% of total non-OECD primary energy demand) amounted to about USD 310 billion in 2007.[2] Such subsidies were the result of pricing policies in mainly petroleum-exporting countries that kept domestic prices for oil products or coal below world market prices, or natural gas and fossil fuel-generated electricity prices below export or import prices or, if not traded, below the costs of supplying them. A joint analysis by the IEA and the Organisation for Economic Co-operation and Development (OECD), using the OECD's ENV-Linkages computable general equilibrium (CGE) model, showed that 'eliminating [such] fossil fuel subsidies by 2020 would reduce global greenhouse gas emissions in 2050 by ten percent'.[3]

One of the requests contained in the G20's Pittsburgh Communiqué was that 'relevant institutions', such as the IEA, the Organization of Petroleum Exporting Countries (OPEC), OECD, and the World Bank, 'provide an analysis of the scope of energy subsidies and suggestions for the implementation of

* The authors would like to thank Christiane Ahlborn, Assia Elgouacem, Jacob Cogan, Doug Koplow, Gabrielle Marceau, Mark Mateo, and Jehan Sauvage for their helpful information, feedback, or both.

[1] G20, 'G20 Leaders Statement: The Pittsburgh Summit, 24–25 September 2009' para 29 <http://www.g20.utoronto.ca/2009/2009communique0925.html> accessed 19 October 2023.

[2] IEA, *World Energy Outlook 2008* (OECD 2008) 62.

[3] G20 (n 1) para 29; based on OECD, *The Economics of Climate Change Mitigation: Policies and Options for Global Action beyond 2012* (OECD 2009) 104.

Ronald Steenblik and Helen Mountford, *Fossil Fuel Subsidies at the Organisation for Economic Co-operation and Development* In: *International Organization Initiatives.* Edited by: Gabrielle Marceau and Henner Gött, Oxford University Press. DOI: 10.1093/9780197803325.003.0011

their commitment to phase out inefficient fossil fuel subsidies and report back to the next summit'[4] (which took place in Toronto, Canada, 26–27 June 2010). To coordinate the OECD's contributions to the report, the then Deputy Director of the Environment Directorate[5] formed an internal task force comprised of staff from the Environment Directorate, the Centre for Tax Policy, and the Trade and Agriculture Directorate. The task force members also attended regular convenings (most of which took place via telephone conference calls) of the G20's Energy Sustainability Working Group.

The reaction of environmental activist groups to the G20's non-binding commitment to phase out 'inefficient fossil fuel subsidies' had been positive but cautious. Both they and members of the G20 who were not OECD member countries pointed to a crucial missing piece of the puzzle: estimates of fossil fuel subsidies provided by OECD countries. How much were *they* subsidizing fossil fuels? Nobody knew.

Initially, the G20 tried to fill the gap by asking members of its Energy Sustainability Working Group to report on how they planned to carry out fossil fuel subsidy reform and to describe the policies each believed relevant to that goal. The first set of responses, dated 11 June 2010, was patchy at best.[6] Koplow, in reviewing those notifications, observed:[7]

> Of the 20 member countries, eight stated that they have no fossil-fuel subsidies at all subject to phase out, of which two (United Kingdom and Japan) provided no information at all. Only one of the twelve countries (the United States) reported more than ten subsidies subject to reform. Three countries discussed energy subsidies in a general sense without listing any specific subsidy policies (Indonesia, Russia, and Mexico).

Eighteen months later, Koplow observed that the G20's results of self-reporting their subsidies had worsened:[8]

[4] G20 (n 1) para 30.

[5] Ms Helen Mountford.

[6] This document, which was titled 'Annex of the G20 Initiative on Rationalizing and Phasing out Inefficient Fuel Subsidies', appears to have disappeared from the Internet. See G20 Research Group, '2010 Seoul G20 Interim Compliance Report' (2011) <https://g20.utoronto.ca/compliance/2010seoul-interim/index.html> accessed 18 September 2024.

[7] Doug Koplow and Steve Kretzmann, 'G20 Fossil Fuel Subsidy Phase-Out: A Review of Current Gaps and Needed Changes to Achieve Success' [2010] Earth Track <https://www.earthtrack.net/sites/default/files/uploaded_files/OCI.ET_.G20FF.FINAL_.pdf> accessed 18 September 2024.

[8] Doug Koplow, 'Phasing Out Fossil-Fuel Subsidies in the G20' [2012] Earthtrack <https://www.earthtrack.net/sites/default/files/uploaded_files/FIN.OCI_Phasing_out_fossil-fuel_g20.pdf> accessed 18 September 2024.

Although Japan and the United Kingdom again opted out of reporting in October 2011, they were joined by four additional countries: Australia, France, Saudi Arabia, and South Africa. This means that nearly one-third of G20 member countries have now determined they have no requirement at all to report.

Could a different body fill the information gap? The logical international organization (IO) to have turned to would have been the IEA.[9] It was already the most active IO in both estimating fossil fuel subsidies and in calling for their reform. But the types of subsidies it was measuring—consumer price support—were not being provided by any IEA members at the time and by only a couple of OECD members (the IEA's membership comprised only OECD member countries but at the time did not include Chile or Mexico). By contrast, the forms of support that OECD countries provided to their producers and consumers were mainly tax breaks, concessional credit, and some direct payments. Although in the late 1980s and throughout the 1990s the IEA had estimated support to coal production provided by its members, that work had ended several years earlier. The experience with measuring government support more broadly resided in the OECD.[10]

There was potentially a bureaucratic obstacle to the OECD taking on this work. From the establishment of the IEA in 1974 until well into the 1990s, there had been both formal and informal agreements between the two organizations that effectively prevented the OECD from working on almost any topic related to energy.[11] As more OECD members joined the IEA, however, and climate policy grew in importance, restrictions on the OECD involving itself in matters related to energy began to loosen. That opening, plus the IEA's limited experience with subsidies that were not conferred through pricing, provided an opportunity for the OECD to start compiling information on its members' fossil fuel subsidies.

[9] The other logical source of information on fossil fuel subsidies was the World Trade Organization (WTO). Under Article 25.2 of the WTO Agreement on Subsidies and Countervailing Measures, WTO Members are required to 'notify any subsidy . . . which is specific within the meaning of Article 2, granted or maintained within their territories'. But the comprehensiveness and timeliness of these notifications has been routinely poor. See WTO, 'Transparency concerns highlighted during discussions at subsidies committee meeting' (*WTO*, 27 October 2023) <https://www.wto.org/english/news_e/news23_e/scm_27oct23_e.htm> accessed 11 December 2023.

[10] The OECD was already a regularly invited observer to the meetings of the G20. OECD staff, as well as staff from the IEA and other IOs, participated in and often contributed substantively to meetings of G20 specialist groups, including those focusing on energy or climate change.

[11] OECD, *The History of the International Energy Agency – The First 20 Years: Origins and Structure Volume 1* (OECD 2004) 134–35 <https://www.iea.org/reports/the-history-of-the-international-energy-agency-the-first-20-years> accessed 3 February 2024.

II. Innovative Fast-Track Approval of Data Collection

Normally, work on a new topic at the OECD emerges via an 18-month process that involves initial discussions between the Secretariat Directorates and the Committees or the subgroups they serve, the translation of those ideas into a work proposal by the Secretariat, a review and ranking of all the work proposals by the responsible Committees, and eventually a set of recommendations to the highest standing body, the OECD Council, which after further deliberation approves the Organisation's agreed biennial programme of work and budget.

Approval of work to produce an inventory of government support for fossil fuels (henceforth, the OECD Inventory), however, was fast-tracked. During a discussion with the Council on the outcomes of the 2009 G20 Summit, and how the OECD should follow-up on the G20's request to the OECD and three other IOs for a joint analysis of the scope of energy subsidies and suggestions for the implementation of their commitment, the Deputy Director of the Environment Directorate pointed out that it was embarrassing that public data on fossil fuel subsidies (produced by the IEA) existed for emerging and developing countries but not for OECD countries. She suggested that the OECD should provide the missing data on fossil fuel subsidies for OECD countries. The Council agreed and assigned joint responsibility to the Trade Committee, the Committee on Fiscal Affairs, and the Environmental Policy Committee (EPOC).[12] Funding of the work initially came out of the Secretary-General's discretionary fund, but eventually the activity was folded into the Organisation's recurring programme of work.[13]

The actual task of producing an inventory of government support policies had to be done by somebody, however, and the experience in doing that resided mainly in the Directorate for Trade and Agriculture (TAD). TAD had hundreds of staff-years of experience identifying and estimating government support to agriculture and to marine capture fishing. The senior staff member put in charge of that task—one of the co-authors of this chapter[14]—himself had 22 years earlier produced the aforementioned estimates of coal producer subsidies for the IEA[15] and, after transferring to the OECD, had worked on agricultural support and later led the OECD's initial work on estimating subsidies to marine capture fishing.

[12] The latter two Committees then assigned responsibility for reviewing the work to their joint sub-committee, the Joint Meetings of Tax and Environment Experts (JMTEE).

[13] In practical terms, that required that the Council agree to a 'permanent reallocation', which meant that funding for some lower-priority activity in the organization had to be reduced.

[14] Mr Ronald Steenblik.

[15] IEA, *Coal Prospects and Policies in IEA Countries: 1987 Review* (OECD 1988).

Identifying hundreds of support measures and obtaining information on their value across several previous years was a big task. Moreover, unlike the IEA's estimates of consumer price subsidies (which look only at one type of policy: the setting of domestic end user prices for fossil fuels or fossil fuel-generated electricity below their opportunity costs of supply), the goal in developing the OECD Inventory was to identify, document, and measure the value of each (non-price) support policy benefitting both producers and consumers, including by subnational governments.[16]

This task involved scouring official government sources, such as budget documents and tax expenditure reports. Initially, the work of compiling the inventory was carried out by one senior staff member and one junior staff member (who was recruited to work on the project in April 2010). Within a few months, the team had added two additional junior staff members, plus a statistical assistant. Between them, they could navigate budget documents and tax expenditure reports written in at least eight languages (Dutch, French, English, Polish, Portuguese, Spanish, and Turkish), but that still left others like Italian, Greek, Hebrew, Hungarian, and Japanese for which local consultants had to be recruited.

The OECD's Secretary-General at the time, Angel Gurría,[17] was particularly keen on advancing this work to support the G20's discussions and so he set a deadline for producing a report and a first set of estimates of government support to fossil fuels provided by OECD countries in time for the meeting of the G20 Finance Ministers and Central Bank Governors (Paris, 14–15 October 2011), which would be followed three weeks later by the G20 Leaders' Summit (Cannes, France, 3–4 November 2011). The G20 Finance Ministers' meeting was also the deadline for a second four-IO report to the G20, which, unlike the first one, could now contain information on fossil fuel support provided by OECD countries.[18] That meant that a more or less complete Inventory had to be ready for circulation to OECD Member-country delegates to the Joint Meetings of Tax and Environment Experts[19] for review by early in 2011.

The review process went as smoothly as could be expected through the technical (subcommittee) stages, though at the political (Council) stage, a

[16] Jehan Sauvage, Ronald Steenblik, and Jagoda Egeland, 'Counting Thy Numbers: Defining and Measuring Fossil Fuel Subsidies' (*CEPR*, 15 September 2012) <https://cepr.org/voxeu/columns/counting-thy-numbers-defining-and-measuring-fossil-fuel-subsidies> accessed 12 December 2023.

[17] Angel Gurría's work in the OECD as Secretary-General is discussed in some detail in Niccola Bonucci, 'The Driving Role of the Heads of International Organizations: A Case Study Around the Organisation for Economic Co-operation and Development', Chapter 20 in this volume.

[18] IEA, OPEC, OECD, and World Bank, 'Joint Report by IEA, OPEC, OECD and World Bank on Fossil-Fuel and Other Energy Subsidies: An Update of the G20 Pittsburgh and Toronto Commitments' <https://www.oecd.org/env/49090716.pdf> accessed 3 January 2024.

[19] The work was also presented to the Joint Working Party on Trade and the Environment for their information.

few member countries tried—unsuccessfully—to block the report's release, questioning the inclusion of some types of tax expenditures as 'government support'. A preliminary version of the report, providing data on 250 individual support mechanisms used by 24 of the OECD's 34 member countries at the time, was released in early October 2011, in time for the two G20 meetings.[20] Already, in the first year after public release of the data, a number of OECD countries initiated new efforts to reform the subsidies reported in the Inventory, and think tanks and civil society were able to use the data to engage governments on subsidy reform.

III. Evolution of the Inventory's Coverage

The next edition, published in January 2013, was expanded to cover all 34 OECD member countries,[21] and in September 2015, the OECD expanded its country coverage again, adding data on six 'partner countries', which were all non-OECD members of the G20: Brazil, the People's Republic of China, India, Indonesia, the Russian Federation, and South Africa.[22] In that year, the detailed data and metadata were moved from the paper report (henceforth called the *OECD Companion to the Inventory of Support Measures for Fossil Fuels*) to the OECD's online public database, *OECD Data Explorer*.[23]

The addition of non-OECD countries to the OECD Inventory risked confusion with the subsidy estimates being reported by the IEA, however.[24] While the IEA measures consumer price support by comparing domestic prices with world market prices, the OECD looks at the budgetary and tax-revenue implications (if any) of these policies. Even though the OECD estimates were meant to complement the IEA's, there was some double counting if the two sets of estimates were added together. Negotiations between the OECD and IEA staff over whether and how to present combined estimates that eliminated double counting started in

[20] OECD, *Inventory of Estimated Budgetary Support and Tax Expenditures for Fossil Fuels* (OECD 2012) <https://www.oecd.org/fossil-fuels/48805150.pdf> accessed 18 September 2024.

[21] ibid.

[22] OECD, *OECD Companion to the Inventory of Support Measures for Fossil Fuels 2021* (OECD 2021).

[23] OECD, 'Data Explorer' <https://data-explorer.oecd.org> accessed 18 September 2024.

[24] As of August 2024, the OECD Inventory covers 48 economies: 38 OECD members countries, 6 non-OECD members of the G20 (three of which—Argentina, Brazil, and Indonesia—are in the process of acceding to the OECD), and 4 European Union Eastern Partnership (EaP) economies. Data from the EaP economies emerged from a separate effort under the GREEN Action Task Force hosted by the OECD and financially supported by Germany, see OECD, 'Green Action Task Force' <https://www.oecd.org/en/networks/green-action-task-force.html> 18 September 2024.

2016. It was not until 2018, however, in a report to the G20, that the OECD and IEA started providing combined estimates based on each organization's work.[25]

In March 2019, the United Nations Environment Programme (UNEP), which is the custodian of the UN Sustainable Development Goal Target 12.c ('rationalise inefficient fossil-fuel subsidies that encourage wasteful consumption'), published a report that set out the methods it would use to estimate and report the corresponding indicator, 12.c.1 ('Amount of fossil-fuel subsidies per unit of GDP (production and consumption)').[26] OECD staff[27] had been active in the advisory group overseeing the preparation of that document and took the lead in drafting the methodological chapter. The establishment of an agreed method was necessary before UNEP could begin collecting data from UN members. Not long thereafter, the International Institute for Sustainable Development (IISD)[28] proposed to the OECD that they jointly establish a dedicated website that would compile subsidy estimates being produced by the OECD, the IEA, and the International Monetary Fund (IMF),[29] as a contribution to UNEP's efforts to establish a truly global inventory of fossil fuel subsidies and 'to bridge any reporting gap on the indicator'.[30] Negotiations over the reporting format and other details of the website took almost two years to resolve, but on 6 May 2021 the joint IISD and OECD FossilFuelSubsidyTracker.org website was officially launched. The database was updated just before the twenty-sixth Conference of Parties (COP26) of the United Nations Framework Convention on Climate Change (UNFCCC) (Glasgow, 31 October–12 November 2021)[31] and continues to be updated following the release of new data from each IO.

[25] IEA and OECD, 'Update on Recent Progress in Reform of Inefficient Fossil Fuel Subsidies That Encourage Wasteful Consumption' <https://www.oecd.org/fossil-fuels/publicationsandfurtherreading/update-progress-reform-fossil-fuel-subsidies-g20.pdf> accessed 10 December 2023.

[26] Ronald Steenblik, Peter Wooders, and Anna Zinecker, 'Measuring Fossil Fuel Subsidies in the Context of the Sustainable Development Goals' (UNEP 2019) <https://wedocs.unep.org/bitstream/handle/20.500.11822/28111/FossilFuel.pdf?sequence=1&isAllowed=y> accessed 18 September 2024.

[27] Ronald Steenblik, with the assistance of Meryem Torun.

[28] The IISD had worked collaboratively with the OECD and other IOs from the beginning of the OECD's work on the Inventory, providing external consultants to compile several countries' estimates, including later those for the EaP economies; in 2017 it had compiled a two-page document: OECD, 'Comparison of Fossil Fuel Subsidy and Support Estimates' compiled by itself, the IEA, the IMF, and the OECD <https://www.iisd.org/gsi/sites/default/files/ffs_methods_estimationcomparison.pdf≥ accessed 3 January 2024; and it had co-authored the 'methodology report' for SDG Indicator 12.c.1, see Steenblik and others (n 26).

[29] The data that are used are only the IMF's estimates of consumer price support for countries not reported by the IEA, the main component of what the IMF calls 'explicit subsidies'. The IMF database can be accessed here, IMF, 'External Fuel Subsidies Template' <https://www.imf.org/-/media/Files/Topics/energy-subsidies/external-fuel-subsidies-template-2023-10-02.ashx> accessed 18 September 2024.

[30] OECD and IISD, 'Fossil Fuel Subsidy Tracker: Methodology' <https://fossilfuelsubsidytracker.org/methodology/> accessed 18 September 2024.

[31] OECD, 'Energy Price Surge Underlines Need to Accelerate Clean Energy Transitions rather than Subsidise Fossil Fuels: OECD & IEA' (*OECD*, 2 November 2021) <https://www.oecd.org/

Reporting data via the FossilFuelSubsidyTracker.org website necessitated that the OECD shift from the previous biennial reporting cycle to an annual one, to keep pace with the IEA's annual cycle. Thus, in May 2023, the OECD released separate updates of its data for each country included in its database,[32] and in December 2023—timed for release at the UNFCCC COP28 in Dubai—it published a short summary document of data on 48 countries for 2022.[33]

In the latter document, the OECD changed the way it had been referring to the total support estimate from 'overall government support for fossil fuels' to 'the fiscal cost of government support for fossil fuels'.[34] This subtle change was made in response to long-running concerns from some OECD member countries with the way the OECD had been dealing with tax expenditures. The data, derived from countries' own tax expenditure reports, are not strictly comparable because each country defines its benchmark tax system differently.[35] Thus, in the case of excise taxes—the levels of which vary widely from fuel to fuel and across countries—the revenue forgone of a tax exemption (eg to agricultural consumers of diesel) will be larger for the same volume of exempted fuel consumed in a country with a high benchmark excise tax than it would be in a country with a lower one. Moreover, the value of a tax expenditure can increase as a result of an increase in the offered concession (relative to the benchmark tax system), an increase in the affected volume, or an increase in the benchmark tax itself.[36] Complementary indicators such as the effective marginal tax rate (EMTR) have been proposed but none implemented yet.[37]

newsroom/energy-price-surge-underlines-need-to-accelerate-clean-energy-transitions-rather-than-subsidise-fossil-fuels.htm> accessed 4 January 2024.

[32] Accessible at the following website: OECD (n 23), applied filter 'fossil fuel support' <https://data-explorer.oecd.org/?tm=Fossil%20Fuel%20Support&pg=0&fs[0]=Topic%2C3%7CTrade%23TRD%23%7CTrade%20policy%23TRD_POL%23%7CSubsidies%20and%20government%20support%23TRD_POL_SUB%23%7CFossil%20fuel%20support%23TRD_POL_SUB_FOS%23&fc=Topic&snb=49&si=1> accessed 18 September 2024.

[33] OECD, *OECD Inventory of Support Measures for Fossil Fuels 2023* (OECD Publishing 2023).

[34] ibid 2.

[35] Ronald Steenblik and Tara Laan, 'Tax Expenditures Related to the Consumption of Fossil Fuels', in C von Haldenwang, A Redonda, and F Aliu (eds), *Tax Expenditures in an Era of Transformative Change: GTED Flagship Report 2023* (German Inst of Development and Sustainability and Council on Economic Policies, 2023) 52–58 <https://www.cepweb.org/wp-content/uploads/2023/11/von-Haldenwang-et-al-2023-_-TEs-in-an-era-of-transformative-change.pdf> accessed 13 December 2023.

[36] ibid 1.

[37] Assia Elgouacem, 'Designing Fossil Fuel Subsidy Reforms in OECD and G20 Countries: A Robust Sequential Approach Methodology' (OECD Environment Working Papers No. 168, OECD 2020).

IV. Concluding Remarks

It would be an exaggeration to credit the OECD's foray into the measurement of government support to fossil fuels as wholly the result of Secretariat action, but the OECD Secretariat certainly drove the process and drew on its expertise in the area of subsidy identification and measurement. Exploiting, in a sense, economies of scope,[38] the Secretariat's initiative pushed the boundaries of the mandate of the Organisation into an activity that was beyond its founding operational activities. By proposing such work soon after the G20 Leaders' Summit that established a high-level commitment to phase out fossil fuel subsidies, the Secretariat was able to respond to new needs of the OECD members, filling in a timely way an important information gap. It was enabled by the fortunate circumstance of having staff in place with experience both in energy policy and subsidy identification and measurement. The OECD Inventory's immediate value for the OECD members was to quell charges that the G20 exercise was unfairly focused on non-OECD members' subsidies. It also provided transparency publicly on these subsidies, enabling others to call on governments to reduce or reform them. Longer term, it provided a template for G20 and other members to prepare their own national inventories of fossil fuel support, particularly in support of the G20's peer reviews of their members' fossil fuel subsidy reform efforts. The detailed nature of the OECD Inventory was an important reason why the OECD was invited to chair those G20 peer reviews, as it facilitated discussion of specific policies and programmes. Within the OECD itself, country-level data from the Inventory have been cited in the Organisation's *Economic Surveys*, *Environmental Performance Reviews*, and *Environment at a Glance* country profiles.[39]

One indirect but important fruit of preparing the OECD Inventory was the training it provided for a new generation of staff in the Trade and Agriculture Directorate, who, since 2017, have carried out groundbreaking work to identify and analyse subsidies benefitting leading manufacturers of several industrial products, including automobiles, aluminium smelting, aerospace, semiconductors, shipbuilding, and solar photovoltaic modules.[40]

The OECD Inventory has also had a large influence on national and international discussions on fossil fuel subsidies beyond the OECD and G20. It remains the only database compiled by an IO that provides information on government support policies benefitting producers as well as consumers of

[38] Essentially, the efficiencies gained by diversifying into an activity that can draw on existing resources, in this case a knowledge base. See John C Panzar and Robert D Willig, 'Economies of Scope' (1981) 71 The American Economic Review 268.

[39] OECD and IEA (2021) ch 5.

[40] This work, led by Mr Jehan Sauvage, who played an important role in developing the OECD Inventory, is summarized in OECD, 'Government Support in Industrial Sectors: A Synthesis Report' (OECD Trade Policy Papers No. 270, OECD 2023).

fossil fuels, including at the subnational level, and for each individual support measure. The G7 Climate, Energy and Environment Ministers, in their 16 April 2023 Communiqué, recognized the OECD Inventory as an important tool for facilitating 'greater transparency on inefficient fossil fuel subsidies globally'.[41] It has informed discussions in the World Trade Organization (WTO)'s Working Group on Subsidies[42] and its Fossil Fuel Subsidy Reform working group[43]; indeed, the design of the OECD Inventory anticipated the needs of a possible future international negotiation on fossil fuel subsidies. Data contained in the OECD Inventory form an important part of the joint OECD–IEA estimate of support for fossil fuels, of the Fossil Fuel Subsidy Tracker, and of the IMF's estimates of 'explicit subsidies' for countries covered by the Inventory.[44] Independent researchers also have drawn on the data when undertaking in-depth analyses of the effects of government support policies on fossil fuel production.[45]

At this juncture, the future of the OECD Inventory is uncertain, owing to strong centrifugal forces. Unlike subsidy accounts for other primary sectors such as agriculture and fisheries, for which the subsidy definition and methods of producing aggregate numbers are settled, fossil fuel subsidies are described by a wide variety of terms and reflect different types of government support in different combinations.[46] Attempts to produce new compilations of fossil fuel subsidies appear on a regular basis.[47] It remains to be seen whether such efforts will strengthen the OECD's relative position among the IO community, or provide a rationale for undertaking new work on fossil fuel subsidies elsewhere. Meanwhile, turning the data into action remains politically challenging, even as the urgency of tackling the climate crisis grows.

41 G7, 'G7 Climate, Energy and Environment Ministers' Communiqué' (*meti.go.jp*, 16 April 2023) 28 <https://www.meti.go.jp/press/2023/04/20230417004/20230417004-1.pdf> accessed 18 September 2024.

42 See Grégoire Garsous, 'Getting Started on Phasing Out Fossil Fuel Subsidies' (May 2022) <https://www.wto.org/english/tratop_e/tessd_e/oecd_18may22.pdf> accessed 12 December 2023

43 See WTO, 'Fossil Fuel Subsidy Reform Meeting Advances Work in Lead-Up to MC13' (*WTO*, 24 November 2023) <https://www.wto.org/english/news_e/news23_e/ffsr_24nov23_e.htm> accessed 18 September 2024.

44 Regarding the IMF's reliance on the OECD Inventory, see Simon Black and others, 'IMF Fossil Fuel Subsidies Data: 2023 Update' (2023) IMF Working Paper No 2023/169, 25.

45 See in particular Peter Erickson and others, 'Effect of Subsidies to Fossil Fuel Companies on United States Crude Oil Production' (2017) 2 Nature Energy 891; Ploy Achakulwisut, Peter Erickson, and Doug Koplow, 'Effect of Subsidies and Regulatory Exemptions on 2020–2030 Oil and Gas Production and Profits in the United States' (2021) 16 Environmental Research Letters 084023.

46 For example, the G20 and numerous other forums speak of 'inefficient' fossil fuel subsidies; the part of the IMF that produces the Fund's estimates of fossil fuel subsidies classifies them as either 'explicit' or 'implicit' (the latter category actually represents externalities); and many journalists speak of 'direct' and 'indirect' subsidies.

47 See, eg, COP28, 'Joint Statement on Fossil Fuel Subsidies' to the UNFCCC' (*Government.NL*, 9 December 2023) <https://www.government.nl/documents/publications/2023/12/09/joint-statement-on-fossil-fuel-subsidies> accessed 11 February 2025.

11

The African Union Commission's Endeavour with the International Court of Justice for Achieving the Complete Decolonization of Mauritius

The Case of the Chagos Archipelago

Namira Negm

I. Introduction

The journey towards seeking justice and rectifying historical injustices connected with the European colonization of the African continent has been a long and arduous one. One case in point has been the long-standing conflict between Mauritius and the UK of Great Britain and Northern Ireland (UK) over the Chagos Archipelago. Since Chagos's separation from Mauritius in 1965, the issue has remained a contentious point, emblematic of broader struggles for sovereignty and self-determination across the African continent.

The African Union (AU) and its predecessor, the Organisation of African Unity (OAU), have always been committed to achieving an Africa free of colonization, a goal that is reflected in the founding Charter of the OAU[1] and the Constitutive Act of the AU[2], and has shaped its practice from the beginning. In his inaugural speech at the first OAU conference in Addis Ababa, Ethiopia, in 1963, the late President Kwame Nkrumah, founding father of African unity and one of the leading figures behind the establishment of the OAU, said:

[1] Charter of the Organization of African Unity (adopted 25 May 1963, entered into force 13 September 1963) 479 UNTS 39, Preamble, para 6: 'Determined to safeguard and consolidate the hard-won independence as well as the sovereignty and territorial integrity of our states, and to fight against neo-colonialism in all its forms' and also art II.1(d): '1. To Organization shall have the following purposes: [. . .] (d) To eradicate all forms of colonialism from Africa.' <https://www.sahistory.org.za/archive/charter-organization-african-unity-479-unts-39-entered-force-sept-13-1963> accessed 17 May 2024.

[2] Constitutive Act of the African Union (adopted 10 July 2000, entered into force 26 May 2001) 2158 UNTS 3 (OAU) Preamble, para 3, as well as arts 3(b) and 4(b) <https://au.int/sites/default/files/pages/34873-file-constitutiveact_en.pdf> accessed 17 May 2024.

Namira Negm, *The African Union Commission's Endeavour with the International Court of Justice for Achieving the Complete Decolonization of Mauritius* In: *International Organization Initiatives.* Edited by: Gabrielle Marceau and Henner Gött, Oxford University Press. © Oxford University Press 2025. DOI: 10.1093/9780197803325.003.0012

> How, except by our united efforts, will the richest and still enslaved parts of our continent be freed from colonial occupation and become available to us for the total development of our continent? Every step in the decolonization of our continent has brought greater resistance in those areas where colonial garrisons are available to colonialism. This is the great design of the imperialist interests that buttress colonialism and neo-colonialism, and we would be deceiving ourselves in the most cruel way were we to regard their individual actions as separate and unrelated.[3]

With regard to the Chagos Archipelago, the AU/OAU has passed several decisions and resolutions,[4] denouncing the British presence in Chagos as continued British colonization and requesting the UK to end this colonization and return Chagos to its rightful owner, Mauritius.[5]

One might be shocked to learn that an African nation is still fighting for full independence at this age of freedom and democracy. This, while the UK, the old colonial power, claims that colonization came to an end long ago. Even more astoundingly, the UK had the audacity to defend its continued colonization through different means, such as the declaration of a so-called Marine Protected Area around Chagos[6], which obstructed a return of the native Chagossian population to the Archipelago.

In light of this historical context, Africa stands united more than ever in solidarity with Mauritius, advocating for its rightful ownership of the Chagos Archipelago and supporting its journey towards complete independence. This unity is not merely symbolic but is reflected in concrete actions, such as the efforts of the African Union Commission (AUC)—the Secretariat of the AU[7]—

[3] Kwame Nkrumah, 'Our Capital Flows Out in Streams to Irrigate the Whole System of Western Economy' (inaugural ceremony of the OAU Conference, 24 May 1953) <https://speakola.com/political/kwame-nkrumah-inaugural-ceremony-of-the-oau-conference-1953> accessed 17 May 2024.

[4] AU 'Decision on the Decolonization of Africa' (34th Ordinary Session of the Assembly of the AU Addis Ababa 2021) Assembly/AU/Dec.812 <https://au.int/sites/default/files/decisions/40231-assembly_au_dec_796_-_812_xxxiv_e.pdf> accessed on 17 May 2024.

[5] For instance, Question of Mauritius, UNGA Res 2066 (XX) (16 December 1965), which stated that detaching part of a colonial territory was against customary international law; International Covenant on Civil and Political Rights UNGA Res 2200A(XXI) (16 December 1966) on the right of self-determination (together with the Study of the Special Rapporteur Gross Espiell: UN (Sub-Commission on Prevention of Discrimination and Protection of Minorities), 'The Right to Self-Determination: Implementation of United Nations Resolutions (1980) E/CN.4/Sub.2/405/Rev.1); Declaration on the Granting of Independence to Colonial Countries and Peoples UNGA Res 1514(VX) (14 December 1960) (adopted by 89 votes to none; 9 absentations): 'Any attempt aimed at the partial or total disruption of the national unity and the territorial integrity of a country is incompatible with the purposes and principles of the Charter of the United Nations.'

[6] PCA, *In the Matter of the Chagos Marine Protected Area Arbitration (Mauritius v. United Kingdom)* Final Award, ICGJ 486 (PCA 2015) 18 March 2015.

[7] For an overview of the AUC's structure, see 'AU Commission' (*African Union*) <https://au.int/en/commission> accessed 24 September 2024. The AUC is constituted by a chairperson, deputy chairperson, eight commissioners, and staff. The chairperson and deputy chairperson are elected by the Assembly of the AU and the commissioners by the Executive Council.

which assert its stance on the legal consequences of the separation of the Chagos Archipelago from Mauritius in 1965. This chapter delves into the process by which the AU, and more specifically the AUC, participated in the advisory proceedings before the International Court of Justice (ICJ) leading up to the ICJ's 2019 Advisory Opinion on the Legal Consequences of the Separation of the Chagos Archipelago from Mauritius in 1965. This chapter reflects on how the AUC took the initiative[8] to submit memorials in the advisory proceedings before the ICJ, which was subsequently supported by the policy organs of the AU.

II. Historical Overview of the Pursuit of the Return of the Chagos Archipelago to Mauritius

Mauritius is an African Island State in the Indian Ocean. It has been subjected to French and British ruling. The UK colonized Mauritius from 1810 until 1968 and Chagos from 1814 until today.[9] Mauritius was part of the British Indian Ocean Territories (BIOT). In 1965, in a conference held in London prior to Mauritian independence, the British Government negotiated with the then Mauritian Government the status of Mauritius, including the Chagos Archipelago. During the conference, the British Government offered the representatives of Mauritius independence on one condition: that they would sign an agreement to separate Chagos from Mauritius. This Agreement was signed in 1965.[10]

After gaining independence, Mauritius started to call on the UK to return the Chagos Archipelago to its sovereignty. Ever since then, the response of the UK has constantly been the same: Chagos will be returned to Mauritius once it is no longer needed for military purposes.[11]

As of 1980, Mauritius started to move within international organizations to resolve the situation of the Archipelago. This included the United Nations (UN)[12] and

[8] Here we understand initiatives as defined in the Preface of this book:

> action(s) of IO secretariats and/or their heads, which (1) aims to meet a need of the IO, its membership, its secretariat, or other internal or external stakeholders, (2) is novel, or previously unfamiliar to the IO in question, and (3) pushes the boundaries of the IO beyond its founding or prior operational activities, thus resulting in IO change.

[9] 'Definitive Treaty of Peace and Amity Between His Britannic Majesty and His Most Christian Majesty of France' (concluded at Paris on 30 May 1814) 1 British and Foreign State Papers 151 (UN Dossier No 445). The treaty was concluded in French.

[10] British Indian Ocean Territory Order 1965 (SI 1965 No 1920), amended by the British Indian Ocean Territory (Amendment) Order 1968 (SI 1968 No 111), at Annex 1. The new colony consisted of the Chagos Archipelago (detached from Mauritius) as well as the Aldabra, Farquhar, and Desroches islands (detached from Seychelles).

[11] Christian Nauvel, 'A Return from Exile in Sight? The Chagossians and Their Struggle' (2007) 5 Northwestern Journal of International Human Rights 1, 6 <http://www.law.northwestern.edu/journals/jihr/v5/n1/4/Nauvel.pdf> accessed on 17 July 2014.

[12] UNGA Verbatim Record (9 October 1980) 35th Session A/35/PV.30, UN Dossier No 269.

the OAU, which were at the heart of this action. There were numerous decisions adopted by the OAU in support of the Mauritian cause and calling upon the UK to return Chagos to Mauritius.[13]

It has been the wish of the AU that the Chagossian question be settled in all its aspects through a comprehensive, just, and lasting resolution in accordance with international law.[14] The AU has continuously deplored the continued unlawful occupation by the UK of the Chagos Archipelago. The AU has also deplored the British refusal to let the Republic of Mauritius exercise sovereignty over the Archipelago, which has resulted in the decolonization of Africa remaining incomplete.[15]

However, there were very limited means left for Mauritius to assert and prove its legal rights concerning Chagos. One of these remaining means was to bring the issue before the ICJ. Mauritius raised the question of the illegality of its incomplete independence in a draft resolution put forward by the African Group in New York to the UN General Assembly (UNGA) for consideration and adoption.

On 22 June 2017, the UNGA, at the 88th Meeting of its 71st Session, after a heated debate between the different positions of the member states and by a vote of 94 in favour to 15 against, adopted Resolution 71/292, by which it decided, pursuant to Article 65 of the Statute of the Court, to request the ICJ to render an advisory opinion on the legal consequences of the continued administration of the Chagos Archipelago by the UK.[16]

[13] Organisation of African Unity. Assembly of Heads of State and Government seventeenth ordinary session 1980 AHG/RES. 99 (xvii) resolution on the Diego Garcia in which it 'demands' that Diego Garcia be 'unconditionally returned to Mauritius'.

[14] AU Assembly Decl 3 (XXI) (2013) Assembly/AU/Decl.3(XXI). See also Assembly of Heads of State and Government of African Unity, AHG/Res 99 (XVII) (1–4 July 1980).

[15] On 30 January 2017, the AU Assembly adopted resolution AU/Res.1 (XXVIII) on the Chagos Archipelago, which resolved to support Mauritius with a view to ensuring 'the completion of the decolonization of the Republic of Mauritius', AU Res 1(XXVIII) (30 January 2017). See also Assembly of Heads of State and Government African Economic Community, Res AHG/Dec.159 (XXXVI) (10–12 July 2000); AU Assembly Res 1(XVI) (30–31 January 2011) Assembly/AU/Res.1(XVI); AU Assembly Dec 331(XV) (27 July 2010) Assembly/AU/Dec.331(XV); AU Assembly Dec 684(XXX) (28–29 January 2018) Assembly/AU/Dec.684(XXX).

[16] The precise questions raised were as follows:

(a) Was the process of decolonization of Mauritius lawfully completed when Mauritius was granted independence in 1968, following the separation of the Chagos Archipelago from Mauritius and having regard to international law, including obligations reflected in General Assembly resolutions 1514(XV) of 14 December 1960, 2066 (XX) of 16 December 1965, 2232 (XXI) of 20 December 1966 and 2357 (XXII) of 19 December 1967?

III. The AUC's Role in Initiating the AU's Participation in the ICJ's Advisory Opinion Proceedings

Based on the request of the UNGA, the Court called upon member states of the UN to submit their written statements to express their views on the question. As the then AU Legal Counsel, I was invited by the Mauritian Government to attend a meeting they were organizing in The Hague to encourage states and possibly the AU to take part in the advisory proceedings in early December 2017. After the meeting, I requested the initial approval of HE Mr Moussa Faki Mahamat, the Chairperson of the AUC, to go ahead and support the Mauritian cause via a submission by the AUC before the ICJ.

It is crucial to highlight that this initiative constituted a precedent, as it was the first time that the AU made a submission in advisory proceedings before the ICJ. It is important to recall that the AUC's decision to support Mauritius in its quest for complete decolonization stemmed from the fact that one of the primary objectives of the AU is the complete decolonization of the African continent. Initially, Mauritius approached the AUC, inviting it to assist it in supporting its cause and to make the submission to the ICJ. The time we had to do so was very tight as the deadline for submission was approaching[17] and there was no mandate from AU member states. However, we had previous decisions adopted by the AU policy organs (ie the Permanent Representatives Committee, the Executive Council, and the General Assembly) in support of Mauritius' independence, on the basis of which we decided to request the Court. At the end of the day, the case was to support the same cause.

However, another hurdle arose, which was financing. With no direct mandate from the policy organs, there were no financial means to support moving forward to honour the invitation. Yet, due to the importance of decolonization to the African Continent, I decided to move ahead and submit the request to HE Mr Moussa Faki Mahamat, the AUC Chairperson, who recognized the

(b) What are the consequences under international law, including obligations reflected in the above-mentioned resolutions, arising from the continued administration by the United Kingdom of Great Britain and Northern Ireland of the Chagos Archipelago, including with respect to the inability of Mauritius to implement a programme for the resettlement on the Chagos Archipelago of its nationals, in particular those of Chagossian origin?

See 'Request for an Advisory Opinion of the International Court of Justice on the Legal Consequences of the Separation of the Chagos Archipelago from Mauritius in 1965' UNGA Res 71/292 (22 June 2017) UN Doc A/RES/71/292.

[17] The Court fixed 30 January 2018 as the time limit within which written statements on the question may be presented to it and 16 April 2018 as the time limit within which States and organizations having presented written statements submit written comments on the other written statements.

significance of the case and the importance of AU's advocacy for the independence of Mauritius. He was a great supporter, granted us the approval to prepare the submission, and allowed us to use the existing funds which had originally been reserved for legal proceedings to defend the Union (part of the Office of the Legal Counsel's Budget) to move ahead and work on the submission.

IV. The AUC's Journey to Bring the ICJ's Advisory Opinion to Fruition

The journey to making a submission on behalf of the AU regarding an advisory opinion from the ICJ was a multifaceted endeavour that involved strategic planning, legal expertise, and diplomatic coordination. This journey started by looking into African expertise to assemble a team of African lawyers. I requested a few members of my Office to come up with a list of African counsels who had prior experience before the ICJ and have a deep understanding of international law to assist me in working on the AU's submission. At this juncture, I chose from the list Dr Mohammed Gomaa, Head of the Arbitration Department at Zaki Hashem & Partners, and Professor Makane Moïse Mbengue, Professor at the University of Geneva Law School, as both had the required expertise to represent the AU. I submitted a new request for approval to the AUC Chairperson to have both lawyers as counsels in this case, and we received it on time before our first trip to Mauritius. Our small team of three African lawyers and a few assistants included Dr Elise Abonnant and Mr Mohamed Salem Boukhari, who managed to present a robust submission based on solid legal arguments and precedents.

With time running against us, we made the aforementioned strategic decision to request the ICJ to grant the AU a 30-day extension to adequately prepare the pleadings.[18] Citing Article 66 of the ICJ Statute, this request emphasized the importance of thorough preparation and the complexity of the legal issues at hand. As the Legal Counsel of the AU, also taking into account major concerns of several African States, I sent a letter to the Registrar of the Court on 10 January 2018 in order to request authorization for the AU to be permitted to furnish information on the questions submitted to the Court and to be granted an extension of one month for the filing of its written statement.[19] As a result, on 17 January 2018, the Court issued an Order pursuant to Articles 48 and 66, paragraph 2, of its Statute to extend the time limit within which all written statements on the

[18] It was problematic for us as first-timer to intervene and to ask for an extension at the last minute. We did not know how the Court would receive such a late request from an observer organization.

[19] *Legal Consequences of the Separation of the Chagos Archipelago from Mauritius in 1965* (Advisory Opinion) ICJ Rep 2018, 7 <https://www.icj-cij.org/sites/default/files/case-related/169/169-20180117-ORD-01-00-EN.pdf> accessed 24 September 2024.

questions may be filed before the Court. The Court fixed the deadline to 1 March 2018 for the written submissions, and 15 May 2018 as the time limit within which States and Organizations having presented written statements could submit written comments on the other written statements.[20]

Upon receiving approval to intervene as an observer organization, efforts within the AUC were intensified to utilize the additional time in conducting comprehensive research, consulting with stakeholders, and refining legal arguments to strengthen the AU's position. Within the extended time frame, the AU team prepared and submitted the first pleading to the ICJ. This pleading encapsulated the AU's legal arguments, factual analysis, and policy considerations, presenting a cohesive and persuasive case in support of Mauritius' quest for independence. Concurrently, discussions were held with representatives from Mauritius to coordinate efforts and present a unified position at the 30th Ordinary Session of the Assembly of Heads of State and Government of the Union (the AU Assembly), held on 28–29 January 2018 in Addis Ababa, Ethiopia,[21] to adopt a decision on the issue. This included addressing the advisory opinion, advocating for the AU's involvement, and highlighting the importance of decolonization and sovereignty within the African context.

Consequently, the AU Assembly adopted Decision (Assembly/AU/Dec.684(XXX)), entitled Decision on Chagos Archipelago,[22] in which the Assembly acknowledged the new deadline and called upon states to make submissions in the advisory proceedings before the ICJ to support the call of Mauritius for decolonization, as well as commended 'the Chairperson of the Commission for the efforts exerted to make an AU submission and succeeding in bringing in the extension for the deadline' and requested 'him to carry out the necessary campaign to bring more AU and UN States and other Organizations to support the call for the complete decolonization of the Republic of Mauritius as well as to make submissions in accordance with Article 66 of the ICJ Statute'.[23] Thus, the AU Assembly approved the initiative that had been launched by the AUC to participate in the advisory proceedings, and the steps the AUC had swiftly taken towards this goal, within only a few weeks in early 2018.

Six African States[24] and the AU confirmed their participation in the oral proceedings and made pleadings before the Court from 3 to 6 September 2018.

[20] ibid.

[21] 'Decision on Chagos Archipelago, 30th Ordinary Session of the Assembly' AU Res Assembly/AU/Dec.684 (XXX) (28–29 January 2018).

[22] ibid.

[23] ibid para 10.

[24] In order to bring together all African member states, the AU urged all member states to submit their respective written submissions to the ICJ in support of the Republic of Mauritius on or before the deadline of 1 March 2018. These efforts led the AU and six African States to submit their written statements to the Court. After the latter had received the written statements and, subsequently, the written comments filed by different States and the AU, it requested the said States, as well as the AU,

That was a historical moment for the AU, which participated for the first time in its history in advisory proceedings before the ICJ—the UN's principal judicial organ—and voiced its concerns regarding the decolonization process of Chagos.

In its statement, the AU addressed the questions posed by the UNGA to the ICJ. As it is in the AU's profound interest to complete the decolonization process of Mauritius and to see an Africa free from colonization, the written statement incorporated all AU and OAU Decisions on the matter. The Advisory Opinion on the Chagos, rendered on 25 February 2019,[25] was a milestone in international law. The ICJ found that it has jurisdiction despite claims that the matter was of a bilateral nature. The Court pronounced itself on the questions of law by concluding that the independence of Mauritius was unlawfully completed.[26]

V. Conclusion

In conclusion, the AU's involvement in advocating for the complete independence of Mauritius has been a testament to Africa's unwavering commitment to justice, sovereignty, and international law. It also showcases a novel initiative launched by the AUC under significant time constraints and eventually endorsed by the membership of the AU. Through proactive measures, diplomatic engagement, and legal strategies, the AUC demonstrated leadership and solidarity in addressing historical injustices and promoting equitable solutions. This was recognized by the Assembly of Heads of States and Governments of the AU in its 2019 Decision on Decolonisation of Chagos Archipelago[27], in which it commended 'the Commission for the excellent work done on behalf of the African Union in the ICJ legal proceedings in both the written submissions and oral hearings',[28] and requested 'the Chairperson of the Commission, through the Office of the Legal Counsel, to maintain the efforts to follow up on the ICJ

to inform the Court, by 15 June 2018 at the latest, if they intended to take part in the oral proceedings in The Hague. Following the notice made by the Court, the AU once again, on 4 May 2018, reminded all member states to notify the Registry of the Court of their eventual intent to take part in the oral hearings regarding the request for an advisory opinion in support of the Republic of Mauritius.

[25] *Legal Consequences of the Separation of the Chagos Archipelago from Mauritius in 1965* (Advisory Opinion) ICJ Rep 2019, 95 <https://www.icj-cij.org/sites/default/files/case-related/169/169-20190225-ADV-01-00-EN.pdf> accessed on 31 May 2024.

[26] 'Advisory Opinion of the International Court of Justice on the Legal Consequences of the Separation of the Chagos Archipelago from Mauritius in 1965' UNGA Resolution 73/295 (22 May 2019) UN Doc A/RES/73/295. Through this UNGA Resolution, the UNGA took note of the Opinion of the ICJ and made certain recommendations regarding the completion of the decolonization process of Mauritius.

[27] 'Decision on Decolonisation of Chagos Archipelago, adopted at the 32nd Ordinary Session of the Assembly' AU Res Assembly/AU/Dec.747(XXXII) (10–11 February 2019).

[28] ibid para 4.

Advisory Opinion on the "Legal Consequences of the Separation of the Chagos Archipelago from Mauritius in 1965" and to report on the results of these efforts in the next Assembly session in February 2020'.[29] The Assembly repeated the same language in its 33rd Session[30] and further requested from 'the Chairperson of the Commission, through the Office of the Legal Counsel, to maintain the efforts to follow up on the implementation of UNGA Resolution 73/295, and consider participation in any proceedings that will contribute to the decolonization of Mauritius and the safeguard of the right of return of the former inhabitants of the Chagos Archipelago, and to report on the results of these efforts in the next Assembly Session in February 2021'.[31]

The AU's submissions made to the ICJ and its participation in the advisory proceedings represent a significant step forward in the pursuit of fairness and accountability. It underscores Africa's voice on the global stage and reaffirms the continent's stance on upholding fundamental principles of self-determination and territorial integrity. It is also an example of a unique initiative by the Secretariat of the African Union—the AUC—subsequently approved and supported by the AU membership.

Moving forward, it is imperative for the AU to continue its efforts in advocating for the rights of Mauritius and other nations facing similar challenges. By championing legal mechanisms and collaborative initiatives, Africa can contribute to a more just and equitable international order where sovereignty and the rule of law are upheld for the benefit of all nations and peoples. In essence, the AU's engagement in the Chagos Archipelago issue serves as a beacon of hope and resilience, highlighting the organization's role in shaping a better future for Africa and the world at large.

[29] ibid para 7.

[30] 'Decision on Decolonisation of Chagos Archipelago, adopted at the 33rd Ordinary Session of the Assembly of the Union' AU Res Assembly/AU/Dec.788(XXXIII) (9–10 February 2020).

[31] ibid para 9.

12
Concluding Commentary
Secretariats as Innovators

Jacob Katz Cogan

One of the key myths of international organizations (IOs) is that secretariats only implement the decisions and policies of the organization's member states. As the practitioner-authored chapters in this part (and in this book) demonstrate, and as the academic literature has shown as well, secretariats do much more than execute the decisions of states. Indeed, at important moments, secretariats are essential to the IO decision-making process—including by proposing and developing innovative ideas, strategies, and policies that extend the work of the organization and adapt the institution's role and functions to contemporary challenges. Secretariats are thus, in reality, not just clerks diligently following commands; they are change agents themselves, operating with others, including states, to move organizations in innovative directions.

Myths, like the one of the passive secretariats, are attractive and necessary because they reinforce the core beliefs underlying the international system. One such belief is that states, and only states, are international decision makers—either through their own actions or by delegating powers to state-driven international institutions. Only exceptionally (and with limits) do states bestow authority on non-state-controlled bodies, such as an international court. The official stance that secretariats only act as secretaries and only work outside of politics fits the foundational narrative that assumes the singular role of states and their privileged position in the international system. To imagine secretariats as anything else would undercut one of international law's key tenets. As a matter of internal logic, the myth is thereby essential.

The myth effectively obscures the IO initiatives described in this part, but those who work in and with organizations know how things actually work. Secretariats are not just implementers; they are innovators. This shadow world is essential to member states, as it allows them to call upon and benefit from the skills and expertise of the secretariat. Its informal existence allows states to have the best of both worlds. The shadow space also allows secretariats to establish and exert their own authority. Within any IO, an operational code exists that recognizes the contours of the secretariat's discretion and its role as innovator.

Jacob Katz Cogan, *Concluding Commentary* In: *International Organization Initiatives.* Edited by: Gabrielle Marceau and Henner Gött, Oxford University Press. © Oxford University Press 2025. DOI: 10.1093/9780197803325.003.0013

In her contribution, Margherita Melillo explains one reason why secretariats are given space, beyond their formal mandates, to innovate. As she explains, IO secretariats are 'knowledge actors' that utilize their 'technical expertise to de-politicize their actions'[1]. Expertise is a defining feature of secretariats, a function of the technical focus of their work, and a consequence as well of their staff's permanence and longevity, which makes them repositories of knowledge. Melillo is quick to point out that expertise is not inherently non-political, even though equating one with the other is a common strategy of those who wish to describe their preferred policy outcomes in neutral terms. She notes that expertise, in the form of producing, storing, and mobilizing knowledge, can be used by secretariats in a variety of ways: instrumentally (to solve a basic problem), symbolically (to enhance the legitimacy of an outcome), and strategically (to promote a preferred policy or expand powers). Expertise is one (and perhaps a necessary) reason why secretariats can influence policy decisions, but expertise itself is insufficient to effect change. Other factors, including 'the amount, quality, and type of expertise', are relevant.[2] The chapters in Part II demonstrate in practice Melillo's argument.

Huw Llewellyn shows how the 'legal technical expertise' of the United Nations Office of Legal Affairs (OLA) was critical to the establishment of the International Criminal Tribunals for the former Yugoslavia and Rwanda, the Extraordinary Chambers in the Courts of Cambodia, and the Special Tribunal for Lebanon. Navigating complicated diplomatic and legal terrain, OLA identified key issues and, acting both pragmatically and in accordance with established principles of international law, carefully counselled participants in the drafting of the tribunals' founding documents. The form of OLA's contribution varied. Sometimes, OLA would assist by affirmatively avoiding legal hazards; at other times, OLA would negotiate the inclusion of provisions to comply with international standards or overcome a party's concerns. OLA's initiatives, in these examples, manifested through technical solutions in the context of complicated negotiations.

Focusing on the World Bank's growing engagement with environmental matters, Charles Di Leva describes two initiatives: the development of environmental standards and the provision of climate finance. In response to concerns about the impact of the Bank's projects on the environment, the Bank took a series of steps over many years leading to the establishment of the Independent Inspection Panel in 1993 and the Environmental and Social Framework, which went into force in 2018. As Di Leva explains, alongside these moves to mitigate and prevent harms, the Bank has increasingly employed its resources to support

[1] Margherita Melillo, 'IO Secretariats as Knowledge Actors', Chapter 6 in this volume.
[2] ibid.

multilateral climate agreements, most recently committing to ensuring its operations are 'Paris Aligned'. The Bank's initiatives have adapted the organization to contemporary environmental priorities in ways not anticipated by the Bank's founders.

Gian Luca Burci and Ana Balcazar-Moreno describe the actions taken by the Secretariat of the World Health Organization (WHO) in response to the COVID-19 public health emergency. The Secretariat took reactive measures, including publishing a significant amount of information and guidance on the WHO website, 'aggressively' using social media and press briefings, and joining in the creation of the Access to COVID-19 Tools-Accelerator (ACT-A) and COVID-19 Vaccines Global Access (COVAX) in ways that went beyond the scope of its previously asserted authority. It also engaged in longer-term preventative initiatives, including creating global hubs for facilitating the exchange of data, know-how, training methods, technology, and biological materials; working with the G-20 on the creation of a Pandemic Fund; entering into a memorandum of understanding with three other IOs to enhance cooperation in the prevention of the spread of disease; and piloting a Universal Health and Preparedness Review. As Burci and Balcazar-Moreno explain, though the WHO's legal documents, including the WHO Constitution and the International Health Regulations, provide authority to the Secretariat, 'this authority has been exponentially developed during the recent health crises' in the form of these initiatives.[3]

Ronald Steenblik and Helen Mountford explain how the Secretariat of the Organisation for Economic Co-operation and Development (OECD) extended the scope of the organization's work by proposing that it take up the topic of fossil fuel subsidies. Previously, an informal agreement between the OECD and the International Energy Agency (IEA) prevented the OECD from working on energy matters. But in response to the G-20's 2009 request that 'relevant institutions . . . provide an analysis of the scope of energy subsidies' (the reduction of which would reduce greenhouse gases), the Deputy Director of the OECD's Environment Directorate, Ms Mountford, urged the OECD Council to approve work on an inventory of government support to fossil fuels. More than other organizations, including the IEA, the OECD had the relevant expertise in measuring the full range of government subsidies to producers and consumers. The Council's authorization of the inventory moved the organization into a novel area, and the successful compilation of the inventory has had broad influence.

Namira Negm explains how the African Union Commission decided on its own initiative to participate on behalf of the African Union (AU) in the International Court of Justice (ICJ) advisory proceedings on 'Legal

[3] Gian Luca Burci and Ana Balcazar-Moreno, 'WHO's Reactions to COVID-19: Between Politics and Managerialism', Chapter 9 in this volume.

Consequences of the Separation of the Chagos Archipelago from Mauritius in 1965'. Though the Commission's decision to participate in support of Mauritius's decolonization arguments aligned with prior AU decisions, the Commission had no mandate to participate in the proceedings, nor had the AU previously appeared at the Court. Nonetheless, at the request of Ambassador Negm, who was then Legal Counsel, the Commission's chairperson approved the preparation of a submission to the Court. Subsequently, the AU Assembly adopted decisions approving and praising the Commission's actions relating to the ICJ advisory proceedings.

In these case studies, we see clearly the real change that secretariats can make on their own initiative and the variety of ways in which they innovate. Sometimes, secretariats act seemingly entirely on their own. The African Union Commission's decision to submit a written statement in the ICJ Chagos advisory proceedings is quite stunning in the decision's evident assumption of a capacity to act independently of any clear mandate from the AU's member states. Presumably, the Commission's chairperson had good confidence that participating in the proceedings would be endorsed by the AU Assembly (given the AU's prior decisions), and so perhaps the assertion of authority (and its precedential value) is not as significant as it might appear. The WHO Secretariat's response to the COVID-19 emergency provides an additional example of independent action. But, here too, there are circumstances that might explain the extent of the actions taken. The WHO Secretariat's initiatives took place in the context of a global pandemic. The context explains why the Secretariat might have felt it could act with a certain amount of leeway. In both of these examples, the secretariats, to use Melillo's categories, are acting strategically to promote preferred policies.

The initiatives that Huw Llewellyn, Charles Di Leva, and Ronald Steenblik and Helen Mountford recount are more modest in their form, though no less important. Llewellyn's OLA finds innovative solutions to complex problems as they arise in high-stakes negotiations. Di Leva's World Bank officials work within the organizations to adapt it to developments in international environmental law. Steenblik and Mountford's OECD staff encourage member countries to approve work in a novel and sensitive area. In Melillo's framing, these Secretariats were acting instrumentally as problem-solvers and occasionally symbolically to enhance the organization's legitimacy.

The innovative work of secretariats, as exemplified in these chapters, is seldom appreciated or recognized. Both the myth of state control of IOs and the non-political characterization of the international bureaucracy hide what those who work in IOs know well. Melillo argues that 'from the perspective of practitioners and policymakers, understanding the importance, but also the limits, of IO secretariats' role as knowledge actors can also help shed light on their overall role in international governance and demystify some myths'.[4] That is certainly correct. Though experienced professionals are familiar with the creative potential of secretariats, research such as that presented in this volume provides insights that offer greater understanding of the possibilities and constraints of IO initiatives. At the same time, there is some advantage to maintaining the myths that obscure the creative work of secretariats. Myths are constitutive—allowing systems to function in a complicated world, and they are protective—providing secretariats space to provide their expertise. Myths allow IOs room to operate.

[4] Melillo (n 1).

PART III

THE ROLE OF HEADS OF SECRETARIATS IN INITIATING IO CHANGE: FUNCTIONAL FORMALISM AND PLURALISM

13

The Role of Heads of Secretariats in Initiating Change

Functional Formalism and Pluralism

Naphtali Ukamwa[*]

I. Introduction

As international organizations (IOs) have pushed the boundaries of their mandates, their heads of secretariats (HoS) have often spearheaded those initiatives. Although considerable scholarship exists on how IOs are remoulding their objectives,[1] the literature on how HoS initiate changes in these organizations is limited, and the latter remains largely undertheorized.[2] HoS are the public faces of IOs,[3] illustrating the struggle of IOs for autonomy from their member states. The autonomy of HoS, in this context, signifies the actions of HoS that push the limits of their traditional administrative role.[4] Thus, the autonomy of HoS is a construct of their power as capacity to initiate changes.[5] Theorists on the autonomy of IOs, in particular social constructivists in international

* I would like to thank Christiane Ahlborn, Gabrielle Marceau, and Henner Gött for their valuable reviews and comments on the initial drafts of this chapter. All errors remain mine.

[1] See generally Tana Johnson, *Organizational Progeny: Why Governments Are Losing Control over the Proliferating Structures of Global Governance, Transformations in Governance* (online edn, OUP 2014); Christian Kreuder-Sonnen, 'International Authority and the Emergency Problematique: IO Empowerment Through Crises' (2019) 11(2) International Theory 182–210.

[2] The International Court of Justice has acknowledged the independence of the UN from its member states. Thus, the UN can initiate court proceedings against any state. See generally *Reparation for Injuries Suffered in the Service of the United Nations* (Advisory Opinion) ICJ Rep [1949] 174; Darren Hawkins and others (eds), *Delegation and Agency in International Organizations* (CUP 2006); Michael Barnett and Martha Finnemore, *Rules for the World: International Organizations in Global Politics* (Cornell UP 2004).

[3] Bob Reinalda and Kent Kille, 'The Evolvement of International Secretariats, Executive Heads and Leadership in Inter-organizational Relations' in Joachim Koops and Rafael Biermann (eds), *Palgrave Handbook of Inter-Organizational Relations in World Politics* (Palgrave Macmillan 2017) 217–42.

[4] A similar definition can be found in Andrew P Cortell and Susan Peterson, 'Dutiful Agents, Rogue Actors, or Both? Staffing, Voting Rules, and Slack in the WHO and WTO' in Darren Hawkins and others (eds), *Delegation and Agency in International Organizations* (CUP 2006) 400: 'the distinction between autonomous action—international bureaucrats' behaviour that is outside the parameters of their authority—and discretion—the independence that member states grant to bureaucrats to fulfil their delegated mandate.'

[5] See s II on functions and powers.

Naphtali Ukamwa, *The Role of Heads of Secretariats in Initiating Change* In: *International Organization Initiatives*. Edited by: Gabrielle Marceau and Henner Gött, Oxford University Press. © Oxford University Press 2025.
DOI: 10.1093/9780197803325.003.0014

relations, agree that HoS possess significant powers to act autonomously of the member states.[6] There are two sub-strands of this idea of autonomy: negative and positive autonomy.[7] Negative autonomists advocate the general impropriety of state intervention in the exercise of the functions of HoS. Therefore, given the international character of IOs, HoS, obtaining their authority from the internal law of the organization, are rational (ie intentional) actors performing impartially their duties.[8] Positive autonomists emphasize the freedom that HoS retain to pioneer initiatives and strategic vision of the organization in the interests of member states. However, positive autonomists, who are largely principal–agent theorists, add that legitimacy and resource considerations are formal constraints on the capacity of HoS to initiate changes.[9] It is the latter understanding of autonomy that this chapter questions and considers formalistic and will contrast with a pluralist understanding of the role of HoS. Positive autonomy is formalistic because it focuses on a unitary understanding of the role of HoS (ie the role of HoS is only administrative or that HoS are to exercise a set of functions presumed to be strictly administrative, which do not involve initiating changes).

This chapter argues that the principal–agent approach/positive autonomy is contradictory and unrealistic in so far as it links the autonomy of HoS with the formalistic necessity to seek legitimacy from member states. This approach restricts the capacity of HoS to undertake initiatives. As the chapters in this volume illustrate, the extent to which HoS can successfully undertake initiatives depends on a combination of their ability to use their broadly attributed powers in the IO constituent instruments, their leadership expertise and personality, and the circumstances and the attitude of member states. The positive autonomy thesis is contradictory because it cannot be argued that HoS are autonomous, on the one hand, and contend, on the other hand, that they still require member states to legitimate their initiative, even when they have not acted ultra vires. This contradiction does not sit well with the

[6] ibid. See nn 1–4 in this chapter. The role of IO heads is interpreted to include the functions and powers of the IO and what secretariats do under the direction of the IO head. Initiatives are defined as policies and actions of IO heads that exceed the remit of their vested powers. The idea of autonomy, which this chapter denounces, is supported by scholars who believe IO initiatives are illegitimate: see generally Roland Vaubel, 'Principal-Agent Problems in International Organizations' (2006) 12 Review of International Organizations 125; Cortell and Peterson (n 4) 255–80; Johannes Urpelainen, 'Unilateral Influence on International Bureaucrats: An International Delegation Problem' (2012) 56(4) The Journal of Conflict Resolution 704.

[7] ibid.

[8] This idea resonates from rational-legal theory of bureaucracy: see Touko Piiparinen, 'Secretariats' in Jacob Katz Cogan, Ian Hurd and Ian Johnstone (eds), *The Oxford Handbook of International Organizations* (online edn, OUP 2017) 839–58.

[9] The role of the HoS is interpreted to include the functions of the IO and what the secretariat does under the direction of the IO heads. Initiatives are defined as policies and actions of IO heads that exceed the remit of their vested powers. The idea of autonomy, which this chapter denounces, is mostly supported by scholars who believe IO initiative is illegitimate, see the studies in nn 2 and 4.

reality that HoS may perform in-the-first-place or simple interpretations of the constituent instrument where it is necessary for the execution of their day-to-day functions,[10] and in situations of collective crises and existential threats arising from climate change, digital technology/artificial intelligence, and pandemics.[11] According to the International Court of Justice (ICJ) in *Certain Expenses Advisory Opinion*, 'each organ [of IOs] must, in the first place at least, determine its own jurisdiction'.[12] According to Schermers and Blokker, such interpretations generally are not authoritative or binding unless the constituent instrument is amended to embody such interpretations.[13] However, Alvarez, citing Sohn, suggests that such interpretations, when done in lawful pursuit of the constituent instrument and accepted by members, are binding, which may serve as precedent for future actions of the organization.[14] Thus, the extent of the deference of member states to the simple interpretation of HoS may differ among IOs. One example is Article 51.1 of the Association of Southeast Asian Nations (ASEAN) Charter, which provides for the powers of the Secretariat (and by extension the HoS powers) to interpret the ASEAN Charter at the request of a member state in line with the rules of procedure that the ASEAN Coordinating Council may specify. Another example is the International Labour Organization (ILO). Once the ILO Secretariat—the International Labour Office—offers an opinion to the Governing Body and it is published without opposing views, and if the International Labour Conference later incorporates a similar provision in another Convention, it is presumed that the provision should be construed in the same way as the interpretation that the Secretariat has provided.[15]

[10] José Alvarez, '"Constitutional" Interpretation' in *International Organizations as Law-Makers* (online edn, OUP 2010) 79 and the literature cited therein.

[11] Elihu Lauterpacht, 'The Development of the Law of International Organization by the Decisions of International Tribunals' (1976) 152 Collected Courses of the Hague Academy of International Law, 460, states that 'there exists a specific rule of the law of international organization to the effect that recourse to such practice is admissible and that states, on joining international organizations, impliedly accept the permissibility of constitutional development in this manner'.

[12] *Certain Expenses of the United Nations (Article 17, Paragraph 2 of the Charter)* (Advisory Opinion) ICJ Rep [1962] 151, 168.

[13] Henry Schermers and Niels Blokker, *International Institutional Law: Unity Within Diversity* (Vol 5 rev edn, Brill, Nijhoff 2011) 858.

[14] Alvarez (n 10) 79–80, citing Louis B Sohn, 'Interpreting the Law' in Oscar Schachter and Christopher C Joyner (eds), *United Nations Legal Order* (Harvard UP 1995) fn 169, 174.

[15] See, for instance, 'Interpretation Decisions of the International Labour Conference' (1950) 33 ILO Official Bulletin 305 <https://webapps.ilo.org/public/libdoc/ilo/P/09604/09604(1950-33).pdf> accessed 30 September 2024; 'Interpretation of the Decisions of the International Labour Conference' (1938) 23 ILO Official Bulletin 30–33 <https://webapps.ilo.org/public/libdoc/ilo/P/09604/09604(1938-23).pdf> accessed 30 September 2024, cited and referenced in Schermers and Blokker (n 13).

This chapter offers a conceptual analysis of the role of HoS.[16] First, it outlines the functions of HoS, the types of power available to them, and how they may use such powers/functions to initiate change. Second, it conceives the strict administrative approach to the role of executive heads as functionally formalist and argues that this approach does not reflect the intrinsic autonomy that HoS hold to undertake initiatives and respond effectively to emergencies. Third, it proposes a pluralist understanding of the role of executive heads, arguing that often the internal law of IOs is sufficiently flexible to allow the role of the executive heads to develop in ways that justify their expansive and autonomous conduct. By pluralist understanding, it is meant that the functions of HoS are not restricted to only administrative duties but involve the exercise of multiple forms of power, which justifies situations where HoS undertake initiatives based on a simple interpretation of their mandate.

II. Functions and Powers of Heads of Secretariats

The terms 'powers' and 'functions' of HoS are often used interchangeably (which is not wrong).[17] However, the context of this chapter demands a slim distinction inherent in these terms. The Permanent Court of International Justice (PCIJ) states that

> [a]s the European Commission is not a state, but an international institution with a special *purpose*, it only has the *functions* bestowed upon it by the Definitive Statute with a view to the *fulfilment of that purpose*, but it has the *power to exercise these functions* to their full extent, in so far as the Statute does not impose restrictions upon it.[18]

This quote implies a distinction between functions and powers. The functions of HoS are the duties and responsibilities, or the purpose of their office based on the constituent instruments. The powers of HoS entail their authority,

[16] The law of IO is largely practitioner led: see Christiane Ahlborn, 'From Functionalism to Constitutionalism: Translating Theories on IO Powers into Practice', Chapter 3 in this volume. For theoretical analysis on IOs, see Jan Klabbers, 'Theorizing international Organizations' in Anne Orford and Florian Hoffmann (eds), *The Oxford Handbook of the Theory of International Law* (OUP 2016) 618–34. The IO literature on HoS merely devotes a few pages to the analysis of functions of IO heads and are mainly on the administrative functions with little emphasis on the expansive character of these functions/powers.

[17] Dinah Shelton, 'Form, Function, and the Powers of International Courts' (2009) 9 Chicago Journal of International Law 537–71.

[18] *Jurisdiction of the European Commission of the Danube Between Galatz and Braila*, PCIJ Rep Series B No 14 [1927] 64 (italics are the author's).

which includes the legal capacity to 'make change'.[19] While IO constituent instruments often mention the functions, duties and responsibilities of HoS, the term 'power' is hardly used. Chapter XVI of the Charter of the Organization of American States (OAS) appears to recognize the distinct spheres of functions and powers of HoS. While the OAS Charter speaks generally of the functions of the Secretary-General, it uses the term 'authority' in Article 110: '[t]he authority to which the preceding paragraph [on functions] refers shall be exercised in accordance with the present Charter'. Therefore, authority connotes legal power: the ability to effect changes based on the constituent instrument.[20] Some duties of the HoS such as drafting the agenda of meetings or sending invitations to members or non-members of the organization and checking the records of representatives do not create a legal consequence *stricto sensu*; they are merely administrative functions. When HoS undertake initiatives, they not only exercise functions but also exercise legal power because initiatives create legal and relational consequences within and outside their organizations.

A. Functions

The functions of HoS are phrased very broadly in IO constituent instruments in ways that give HoS some degree of autonomy and flexibility when exercising these functions in response to emerging problems confronting the organization.[21] The broad frame of the functions of HoS may have evolutionary reasons: at the time of creating the UN, and the role of the Secretary-General, global governance and regimes had not proliferated as they are today. Nevertheless, the fact that there is no call for an amendment to the UN Charter on functions of HoS may in some ways suggest that functional autonomy is intrinsic in the mandate of the Secretary-General.

HoS have the general obligation to efficiently carry out the 'ordinary businesses' of the organization, including hiring and firing staff, determining

[19] Steven Lukes, *Power: A Radical View* (2nd expanded ed, Palgrave Macmillan 2005) 69, defines power as 'being able to make or to receive any change'.

[20] This assertion proceeds on the idea among socio-political scientists that where law is the basis of power, it is an authority (legal power). See generally Ian Hurd, 'Legitimacy and Authority in International Politics' (1999) 53(3) International Organization 379, 400–03.

[21] An example of a broad frame of HoS' power is Article 97 of Charter of the United Nations (adopted 26 June 1945, entered into force 24 October 1945) 1 UNTS XVI (hereafter UN Charter). See Simon Rushton, 'The UN Secretary-General and Norm Entrepreneurship: Boutros Boutros-Ghali and Democracy Promotion' (2008) 14 Global Governance 95–97; Kent Kille and Roger Scully, 'Executive Heads and the Role of Intergovernmental Organizations: Expansionist Leadership in the United Nations and the European Union' (2003) 24(1) Political Psychology 175–90. For a discussion on how external factors shape policy and decisions in the World Bank, see Bruce Rich, 'The Emperor's New Clothes: The World Bank and Environmental Reform' (1990) 7(2) World Policy Journal 305–29.

staff terms of service, and maintaining the independence of international civil service.[22] In addition, the executive head is in charge of preparing budgets of the organization and ensures that the meetings of relevant organs and committees are running efficiently.[23] Organs and committees of IOs may request the secretariat to prepare reports and studies and the HoS oversee these tasks.[24] Also, the executive head, through staff members, may provide support in legal and technical opinions and resolutions in conferences. Furthermore, HoS are responsible for submitting regular reports on the work of the organization and overseeing the depositary function of IO secretariats in respect of multilateral treaties.[25] These reports offer a summary of the work implemented and are a significant information source. The depositary function of HoS includes sending notice to member states of signatures, accession, and reservations, as well as sending copies of the treaties to member states.[26]

Moreover, HoS may act as legal representatives of their organizations in judicial proceedings (such as advisory proceedings, cases of staff employment, privileges and immunities of IO officials/agents, and the property of the organization) before international courts and have the authority to enter into various international contracts/pacts with states and other actors.[27] It is within the prerogative of the HoS to choose to waive or uphold the immunity of an IO official/agent in judicial proceedings.[28] This duty is an offshoot of the obligation

[22] See the UN Charter (n 21) arts 100–101; the Constitution of the International Labour Organization (adopted 1 April 1919, entered into force 28 June 1919) Pt XIII of the Treaty of Versailles, as amended (hereafter ILO constitution) art 8(1); Articles of Agreement of the International Monetary Fund (adopted 22 July 1944, amended effective 26 January 2016) 2 UNTS 39 (hereafter IMF Articles) art XII, s.4(b); World Trade Organization Agreement: Marrakesh Agreement Establishing the World Trade Organization (15 April 1994) 1867 UNTS 154 (hereafter WTO Agreement) art VI (3). See generally Theodor Meron, 'The Role of the Executive Heads' (1982) 14 New York University Journal of International Law and Politics 861.

[23] Charter of the Organization of American States (30 April 1948, amended by the Protocol of Managua of 6 October 1993, entered into force on 29 January 1996) art 112 (d) (hereafter OAS Charter); Revised Treaty of the Economic Community of West African States (24 July 1993) 2373 UNTS 233 (hereafter ECOWAS Treaty) art 19 (3)(f).

[24] OAS Charter (n 23) art 112(d); ECOWAS Treaty (n 23) art 19(3)(f).

[25] UN Charter (n 21) art 98; Constitution of the United Nations Educational, Scientific and Cultural Organization (4 November 1946) 4 UNTS 275 (hereafter UNESCO Constitution), art VI (3); Convention Establishing the World Intellectual Property Organization (14 July 1967) 828 UNTS 3 (hereafter WIPO Convention) art 9(5); OAS Charter (n 23) art 112(g); ECOWAS Treaty (n 23) art 19(3)(e).

[26] UN Charter (n 21) art 102; ILO Constitution (n 22) art 19(5); OAS Charter (n 23) art 112.

[27] *Applicability of Article VI, Section 22 of the Convention on the Privileges and Immunities of the United Nations* (Advisory Opinion) ICJ Rep [1989] 177. See also *Difference Relating to Immunity from Legal Process of a Special Rapporteur of the Commission on Human Rights* (Advisory Opinion) ICJ Rep [1999] 62. An example of ordinary contractual case against an IO is *Komlan Raymond Koudo v ECOWAS Parliament*, ECW/CCJ/JUD/39/21 (27 October 2021).

[28] See *Difference Relating to Immunity from Legal Process of a Special Rapporteur of the Commission on Human Rights* (n 27) para 46: the ICJ stated in para 60 '[t]he Secretary-General, as the chief administrative officer of the Organization, has the primary responsibility to safeguard the interests of the Organization; to that end, it is up to him to assess whether its agents acted within the scope of their functions and, where he so concludes, to protect these agents, including experts

of the HoS to provide functional protection to staff members and other agents of the IO.[29] HoS can enter into contracts/pacts with states and other actors, for example, for the service and supply of goods or to make arrangements regarding the seat of the organization.[30] These contractual powers of HoS may be considered as justifying the recent initiatives of HoS that foster inter-IO and IO-States partnerships as discussed in this book.

B. Powers

The scope of the powers of HoS may be inferred from the objectives of IOs and the functions of HoS as stated in the constituent instrument and further developed in IO practice of responding to crises.[31] HoS may choose from a range of ways to exercise their powers in line with the constituent instruments. These powers are broadly classified here as express and non-express powers. Express powers are clearly stated in the constituent instruments. Apart from the explicit administrative functions mentioned in the previous section, the role of HoS triggers the domain of non-express powers when they undertake initiatives that are not expressly stated in the constituent instruments.[32] Non-express powers, a term of art, mean the powers of HoS that are the fruits of their express powers in the constituent instrument and such powers include implied, incidental, and discretionary powers. 'Non-express powers' is used instead of 'implied powers' because the latter does not cover other types of power that HoS exert. One example of non-express powers is implied powers such as undertaking initiatives in situations of emergency. Lauterpacht rightly submits that implied powers

on mission, by asserting their immunity'. See also United States, City Court of New Rochelle, Westchester County on *Complaint of Donnely v Ranollo*, 8 November 1946, 67 NYS.2d 31 (City Ct 1946): the UN did not waive the immunity of the driver of Secretary-General Trygve Lie, who was charged for violating traffic laws while driving the SG.

[29] ibid.

[30] United Nations: United States of America 1947 Headquarters Agreement (1947) <https://treaties.un.org/doc/Publication/UNTS/Volume%2011/volume-11-I-147-English.pdf> accessed 23 June 2024.

[31] Robert Cox and Harold Jacobson (eds), *The Anatomy of Influence: Decision Making in International Organization* (Yale UP 1973) 8–11.

[32] Non-express powers have not been used to qualify powers of HoS, which falls outside express power. Express and implied powers have been discussed widely; see, eg, Niels Blokker, 'Constituent Instruments' in Jacob Katz Cogan, Ian Johnstone, and Ian Hurd (eds), *The Oxford Handbook of International Organizations* (1st edn OUP 2016) 943–61; Jan Klabbers, 'The Life and Times of the Law of International Organizations' (2001) 70(3) Nordic Journal of International Law (Acta Scandinavica juris gentium) 287–317. See also Akshaya Venkataraman, 'Taking Initiatives in the WTO: The Role of an Executive Head in Steering Change', Chapter 18 in this volume, discussing 'initiatives linked directly to functions, powers, and express duties' in the WTO Agreement.

'are essential for the performance of the functions in respect of which express powers are conferred'.[33] The ICJ, in the *Use of Nuclear Weapons in Armed Conflict Advisory Opinion*, confirms that IOs, by extension HoS, exercise implied powers.[34] For example, despite the lack of an express mandate in the constitution of the World Health Organization (WHO), the Director-General of the WHO partnered with other national stakeholders to establish two initiatives, the Access to COVID-19 Tools Accelerator (ACT-A) and COVID-19 Technology Access Pool (C-TAP), in response to the COVID-19 pandemic.[35] The World Health Assembly acknowledged and commended the role of the WHO in the ACT-A initiative.[36] This implies that the World Health Assembly either acquiesced to the action of the Director-General or, by its conduct, accepted the authority of the DG to undertake initiatives based on the WHO constitution.[37]

The domain of incidental powers allows executive heads to undertake initiatives necessary and proper in the performance of their express mandate.[38] For example, contrary to the International Health Regulation, the WHO Director-General reported on the cholera outbreak in Guinea without the consent of Guinea. However, the Director-General justified this action as necessary and intrinsic in Article 2 of the WHO Constitution, which stipulates the mandate of the organization given the global scale of the outbreak. He gained the support of WHO Committee on Communicable Diseases and Executive Board for his actions.

However, incidental powers are not implied powers even though they sometime overlap as in the Guinea cholera example. In the *Reparation for Injuries Case*, the ICJ mentions the powers of an IO that are not express in nature but are considered 'by necessary implication as being essential to the performance of its duties'.[39] These powers may be construed as incidental powers, which are exercisable when, based on reasonable necessity, HoS undertake initiatives that are outside their express mandate and justify these initiatives as proper courses of action given the circumstances. For instance, the initiatives of the WHO Director-General that include partnerships with other stakeholders as a response to COVID-19 (as mentioned previously) may be considered as incidental

[33] Lauterpacht (n 11) at 432.

[34] *Legality of the Use by a State of Nuclear Weapons in Armed Conflict* (Advisory Opinion) ICJ Rep [1996] 66, 79.

[35] See Gian Luca Burci and Ana Balcazar-Moreno, 'WHO's Reactions to COVID-19: Between Politics and Managerialism', Chapter 9 in this volume.

[36] ibid.

[37] ibid.

[38] For another example of incidental powers, see WHO, 'WHO Framework of Engagement with Non-State Actor (adopted on 28 May 2016 during the Sixty-ninth session of the World Health Assembly), Res WHA69(10) para 73 <https://apps.who.int/gb/ebwha/pdf_files/wha69/a69_r10-en.pdf> accessed 4 September 2023.

[39] See *Reparation for Injuries* (n 2) 179.

in nature. While the exercise of incidental powers may appear subjective (ie HoS' interpretation as an expert),[40] these powers are often incident-specific and are invoked to deal with serious issues of international public interest such as climate change or the pandemics.[41] Given the high degree of subjectivity in the exercise of incidental powers, the HoS have a serious task of obtaining the support of member states (and this task is not a formal constraint on initiating change). Thus, constitutional legitimacy may pose some limitations on prerogatives of HoS in exercise of incidental powers, and the HoS best strategy in getting support for such initiatives may depend on the technical nature of the mandate of the secretariat. However, the exercise of implied powers by HoS tilts towards the objective and simple interpretation of their express powers and the purpose of the organization as the basis for undertaking initiatives. One way to consider the implied powers of HoS could be to examine the capacities of HoS which arise from 'secretariat powers' such as the authority to enter into contracts, which can be the basis for initiatives that involve inter-IO partnerships to respond to crises.

Discretionary powers may be invoked when the executive heads decide whether or not to undertake a given action. This form of power results from what may be termed 'silence zones' of IO objective, which justifies HoS-initiated changes provided such matters are neither prohibited nor regulated. Thus, the UN Secretary-General under Article 99 of the UN Charter is conferred with the discretion to 'bring to the attention of the Security Council any matter which in his [or her/their] opinion may threaten the maintenance of international peace and security'. For example, Antonio Guterres on 6 December 2023 invoked this discretion to inform the UN Security Council of the possibilities of the breach of global peace and security resulting from the situations of hostilities in Israel and the Occupied Palestinian Territory.[42] Although the Constitution of the WHO is somewhat more conservative on the functions and powers of the Director-General,[43] it confers on the Director-General the discretion to determine what amounts to a public health emergency of global concern.[44]

Nevertheless, the exercise of non-express powers follows from an understanding of the powers of HoS to undertake a simple interpretation of the

[40] The subjective interpretation may be knowledge based. Other terms such as 'epistemic' may be used: see Burci and Balcazar-Moreno (n 35).

[41] The idea of incidental powers flowing from delegated powers has been discussed in domestic administrative law contexts: See *People ex rel. Hubbard v Colorado Title & Trust Co.* (1918) 65 Colo 472, 178 Pac 6 cited in 4th edn, Ray A Brown, 'Administrative Commissions and the Judicial Power' (1935) 19 Minnesota Law Review 261, 292.

[42] UN, 'Letter by the Secretary-General to the President of Security Council invoking Article 99 of the United Nations' (6 December 2023) <un.org/sites/un2.un.org/files/sg_letter_of_6_december_gaza.pdf> accessed 10 February 2025.

[43] Constitution of the World Health Organization (entered into force 7 April 1948) 14 UNTS 185 (hereafter WHO Constitution) ch VII.

[44] ibid, art 12.

constituent instrument. Member states hold the power to render authoritative interpretations.[45] It does not preclude HoS from rendering simple interpretations (which in practice often remain the sole interpretations and therefore, in de facto, become quasi-authoritative interpretations). While the constituent instruments of some IOs provide mechanisms for authoritative-interpretation functions, other IOs do not have such provisions.[46] In some IOs such as the International Monetary Fund (IMF), the executive heads can interpret the scope of their functions in line with the object and purpose of the constituent instruments to deal with emerging necessities.[47] According to Alvarez, 'in the absence of express charter authority conferring the power to interpret, no organ is so entitled and each member can interpret for itself what the charter means'.[48] It follows that where the constituent instrument has no express provision on which person or body has the power of authoritative interpretation, HoS (apart from their simple-interpretation power) may undertake authoritative interpretation to justify their initiatives. This is possible in IOs such as WHO, United Nations Educational, Scientific and Cultural Organization, and International Maritime Organization, which have no provision on authoritative interpretation in their constituent instruments.[49] According to Rushton, even when provisions are made for a formal interpretation, HoS still informally interpret the instrument in justifying their actions.[50] Thus, since the constituent instrument is a living instrument, it is malleable to deal with emerging issues, which then justifies the initiatives of HoS.[51]

[45] The PCIJ stated 'it is an established principle that the right of giving an authoritative interpretation of a legal rule belongs solely to the person or body who has power to modify or suppress it'. In this context, it would mean that the member states of the IO have power of authoritative interpretation. See *Delimitation of the Polish-Czechoslovakian Frontier (Question of Jaworzina)* (Advisory Opinion) PCIJ Rep Series B No 8 [1923] 37. See also *Territorial Dispute (Libyan Arab Jamahiriya/Chad)* ICJ Rep [1994] 6, 31ff.

[46] Alvarez (n 10) 74–79.

[47] See the preamble to Institut de droit international, 'Are Their Limits to the Dynamic Interpretation of the Constitution and Statutes of International Organizations by the Internal Organs of Such Organizations?' Resolution 7th Commission (Online Session: Institut de droit international, 2021), 'refer to the interpretation of constituent instruments in order to achieve perceived needs of an international organization that are consistent with its object, purpose and functions'. IMF Articles (n 22) art XVIII. See generally Frederick Mann, 'The "Interpretation" of the Constitutions of International Financial Organizations' (1968–9) 1 British Yearbook of International Law 43.

[48] Alvarez (n 10).

[49] ibid.

[50] Rushton (n 21) 98.

[51] This view may be inferred from Guy Fiti Sinclair, 'IO Initiatives, Ideology, and the Imaginaries of Liberal Reform', Chapter 2 in this volume.

III. Conceptualizing the Autonomy of HoS

The autonomy of HoS empowers them with the agency to undertake initiatives, which may also be interpreted as agency for transforming their (administrative) functions into powers. Thus, as Foucault once stated, freedom may be both a precondition and condition for the exercise of power.[52] This analysis proceeds on the common ground of existing debate on the autonomy of HoS, which is: the secretariat (including the HoS) possesses some degree of independence from member states. Social constructivists in international relations argue that HoS possess a significant degree of autonomy.[53] This approach on autonomy includes two different sub-strands: negative-autonomy and positive-autonomy strands.[54] The negative-autonomy approach advocates the general impropriety of state intervention in the exercise of the functions of HoS. A positive-autonomy approach emphasizes the freedom that IO heads have to pioneer novel initiatives and express the strategic vision for the interests of member states. Positive autonomists argue that legitimacy and resource considerations are formal constraints to the capacity of HoS to initiate changes.[55] It is the latter understanding of autonomy that this section questions and considers formalistic and will contrast with (a proposal for) a pluralist approach to the role of HoS. The theories of HoS autonomy that will be discussed below are mutually inclusive; IO heads should perform their express functions but where a formal understanding of their functions is unhelpful, a pluralist approach justifies their role to undertake initiatives. As discussed later in this section, the justification for undertaking initiatives offers a theoretical account for their implied, incidental, and discretionary powers arising from the internal law of the IOs.

Historically, the idea of the independence of IO secretariats (including their HoS) has a long pedigree in the debate on the relationship between the Secretariat of the League of Nations and its member states.[56] One possible

[52] Michel Foucault, 'The Subject and Power' (1982) 8(4) Critical Inquiry 777, 790, 'freedom may well appear as the condition for the exercise of power (at the same time its precondition, since freedom must exist for power to be exert)'.

[53] See nn 2–4.

[54] ibid.

[55] The role of the IO head is interpreted to include the functions of the IO and what the secretariat does under the direction of the IO heads. Initiatives are defined as policies and actions of IO heads that exceed the remit of their vested powers. This idea of autonomy, which this chapter denounces, is mostly supported by scholars who believe IO initiative is illegitimate: see generally Vaubel (n 6); Cortell and Peterson (n 4); Urpelainen (n 6).

[56] The Secretary-General as the human face and representative of the organization is exemplified in the UN system (at least in principle). See generally Stephen M Schwebel, 'The International Character of the Secretariat of the United Nations' (1953) 30 British Yearbook of International Law 71; Nigel White, 'The League of Nations, Autonomy and Collective Security' (2020) 8(1) London Review of International Law 99; Klaas Dykmann, 'How International Was the Secretariat of the League of Nations?' (2015) 37(4) The International History Review 721–44; Leland Goodrich, 'From League of Nations to United Nations' (1947) 1(1) International Organization 3–21.

inference from the example of the League of Nations is that the independence of the secretariats and their executive heads is a precondition for the performance of their functions and exercise of powers under the constituent instrument. Thus, guided by the vague list of functions in the internal laws, executive heads have justifications for autonomy to undertake initiatives in the interest of their organizations. Thus, if the legal framework of the organization does not restrict the relevant initiative, and unless the member states of the organization push back post facto, it could be interpreted in favour of the autonomy of the executive head to decide what course of action to follow.[57] Nevertheless, one concedes here that the appointment of executive heads may be one of many practical limitations on their autonomy, and this is evident in IOs such as the North Atlantic Treaty Organization because of the nature of their objectives.[58] While, in principle, member states have equal voting rights in formal procedures to appoint HoS,[59] such formal procedures of appointment reveal less about the intrinsic politics that restrict the degree of power available to HoS.[60]

A. Functional formalism

Functional formalism underpins the view that HoS are not empowered to undertake functions outside the express provisions of their mandates. It may also be considered the rule of attributed powers.[61] Formalists are sceptical of the autonomy of HoS, and they advocate for a clear separation of the role of HoS (mainly administration) from politics and innovation in a way that obliterates the capacity of HoS to undertake initiatives. For example, the UN Secretary-General, if described in a functional formalist sense, is a 'secretary' and not a

[57] *Jurisdiction of the European Commission of the Danube* (n 18) 64, stating that if the constituent instrument does not restrict a given function, then an IO can exercise it.

[58] The rotation of IO leadership is one way states have attempted to address the issue of hegemony. See Ngaire Woods, 'The United States and the International Financial Institutions: Power and Influence Within the World Bank and the IMF', in Rosemary Foot, S Neil MacFarlane, and Michael Mastanduno (eds), *U.S. Hegemony and International Organizations: The United States and Multilateral Institutions* (OUP 2003) 92–114; Simon Chesterman, 'The Appointment of Executive Heads of International Organizations' in Jacob Katz Cogan, Ian Hurd, and Ian Johnstone (eds), *The Oxford Handbook of International Organizations* (OUP 2016) 822–38.

[59] The equal vote rule does not apply practically in IOs such as the World Bank and the IMF. Other IOs such as NATO do not have formal appointment rules for HoS but adopts 'informal diplomatic consultation among the member countries': NATO Secretary General <http://www.nato.int/cps/en/natolive/topics_50094.htm> accessed 11 February 2025; Chesterman (n 58).

[60] Chesterman (n 58).

[61] For a discussion on attributed powers in IO context, see Niels Blokker, 'International Organizations or Institutions, Implied Powers' (*Max Planck Encyclopaedia of Public International Law*, 2021) <https://opil.ouplaw.com/display/10.1093/law:epil/9780199231690/law-9780199231690-e467> accessed 10 February 2025.

'general'.[62] A rule of legislative interpretation may also justify the formalist approach, and it is expressed in the Latin maxim *expressio unius est exclusio alterius*, which means 'the expression of one subject, object, or idea is the exclusion of other subjects, objects, or ideas'.[63] Thus, if the constituent instrument does not mention a function, it should be interpreted as excluding an executive head from undertaking such a function.[64] When HoS exceed their administrative functions, they threaten not only state sovereignty but also the neutrality and impartiality of their mandates. Therefore, control factors such as the political organs, member states, or even the administrative tribunal are necessary to curb the potential excesses of HoS.[65] Functional formalism, in the contemporary world where HoS have to adapt to emergencies, may restrict the range of non-express powers of HoS.[66]

The realist theory of IO underpins the formalist approach to the role of HoS.[67] Realists argue that HoS operate in an arena laden with state power, and it is the member states that dictate what HoS can and should do.[68] One challenge with this viewpoint is that it does not address whether, in reality, the administrative functions of HoS are neatly delineable from politics intrinsic in execution of their mandates and their powers to initiate change.[69] Moreover, generalizations on the nature of the role of IO heads should be made with caution because IOs are diverse. However, most IOs—even in technical sectors—will at some point have to respond to new needs of their institutions or their member states. Realist thought will expect them to admit their limitations and loyally await instructions from their member states. In reality, secretariats tend to become more active and creative, which—from a normative standpoint—also seems to be the preferable option.

[62] For a discussion on the subject of UNSG being a secretary or general, see generally Simon Chesterman (ed), *Secretary or General? The UN Secretary-General in World Politics* (CUP 2007).

[63] This is not an express rule of interpretation under the Vienna Convention on the Law of Treaties; it is mostly invoked in domestic courts. See Clifton Williams, 'Expressio Unius Est Exclusio Alterius' (1931) 15 Marquette Law Review 191.

[64] Lauterpacht (n 11).

[65] Administrative tribunals mostly review the administrative functions of the IO heads such as the dismissal of staff members (this is not controversial in this context). See Judgements of the UN Administrative Tribunal Numbers 29–38 (AT/DEC/29-38).

[66] The non-express powers of HoS have been discussed above.

[67] On arguments for limited functions of IOs based on principal–agent account, see Jan Klabbers, 'The EJIL Foreword: The Transformation of International Organizations Law' (2015) 26 European Journal of International Law 9, 10–11, 18, 21, 24.

[68] ibid 6–8.

[69] See the discussion on incidental and implied powers above.

B. Functional pluralism

The functional-pluralist approach to the role of HoS, which I propose here, extends the discussion on the types of HoS power beyond mere administration.[70] The principal–agent model argues that since legitimacy and resources constrain the autonomy of HoS, HoS are restrained from initiating changes. This practice of seeking legitimacy continues to date.[71] However, the appropriate locus to find justifications for the scope of HoS powers/functions is the constituent instrument.[72] The constituent instruments of many IOs do not limit the functions and powers of HoS in ways that prohibit initiatives of HoS. One implication that can be made here is that executive heads who enjoy the type of broad powers that the UN Secretary-General possesses can undertake initiatives that stretch the limits of their traditional functions. In highly technical IOs, knowledge-based reasons may justify expansive initiatives. What often determines the success or failure of such initiatives is not legitimacy or resource considerations, but the personality and expertise of the relevant executive head.[73] IO practices show how member states have expressly or implicitly accepted the HoS-led initiatives.[74] For example, the duty of the UN Secretary-General to present reports is almost of no significance unless the UN Secretary-General could use it, as they often do, to make some recommendations that may have the effect of initiating changes.[75]

Inherent in functional pluralism is the understanding that considering external factors, such as changes in the global political, economic, and security landscape or emerging issues of climate change and pandemic, the executive heads have opportunities to adapt and expand their role to address these challenges. These changes may involve revising existing norms, developing new policies, or collaborating with other stakeholders to achieve shared objectives.[76]

[70] See nn 2–4 on the principal–agent approaches.

[71] Ian Johnstone, 'The Role of the UN Secretary-General: The Power of Persuasion Based on Law' (2003) 9(4) Global Governance 441–58.

[72] The political nature of the powers of the Secretary-General under Article 99 was fully recognized by the Preparatory Commission. See Report of the Preparatory Commission of the United Nations, Section 2.16. See also Kofi Annan, *Dag Hammarskjöld and the 21st Century* (4th Dag Hammarskjöld Lecture, 6 September 2001).

[73] This argument is rebuttable on several grounds such as where member states exercise protest or adopt voting processes to quash an initiative introduced by IO heads. For how member states can protest against the IO heads initiative, see Dan Sarooshi, *International Organizations and Their Exercise of Sovereign Powers* (OUP 2007) 110.

[74] Vienna Convention on the Law of Treaties (adopted 22 May 1969, entered into force 27 January 1980) 1155 UNTS 331, arts 39–40.

[75] UN Secretary-General Kofi Annan proposed 'the Responsibility to Protect' in his report during the sixtieth anniversary of the United Nations: See Mona Ali Khalil, 'The Evolution of UN Secretary-General Initiatives to Respond to Violent and Non-Violent Threats to International Peace and Security', Chapter 14 in this volume.

[76] See, eg, 'One Health', an inter-IO initiative, discussed in Burci and Balcazar-Moreno (n 35). For discussion on public–private global health partnership, see Jelena Madir, 'IOs Initiatives: Gavi, the Vaccine Alliance', Chapter 28 in this volume; Fady Zeidan and Jean Abboud, 'The Global

For example, the expansion of the role of the World Bank from primarily economic issues to addressing environmental and climate challenges has been made possible by its leadership (such as President Barber Conable) exercising express and non-express powers.[77] In reality, functional pluralism does not give HoS a *carte blanche* to engage in a frolic of lawlessness in the exercise of their functions and powers. Practical matters also require HoS to gain membership support, which is necessary to secure resources to execute their proposals.[78] However, according to Jenks, the Secretary-General, beyond the strength of their personality, should be protected from political pressure.[79] As such a view is difficult to implement in most IOs, the extent to which the HoS can get such support is a matter of individual expertise and leadership skills. The success of Director-General Marcolino Candau in developing the technical assistance programme of the WHO during the 1960s was not attributed to available resources, but rather largely to his full control of the secretariat and his capacity to use his good personal relations with developing states and the United States of America.[80] Still, the circumstances and the context need also to offer opportunities for such initiatives to occur.

IV. Conclusion

This chapter shows that while social constructivists in international relations argue that HoS possess a considerable degree of autonomy from member states, principal–agent theorists contend that legitimacy and resource considerations are formal constraints on the capacity of HoS to initiate changes. It argues that the latter approach, which is a formalist image of the role of HoS, is contradictory and unrealistic. While this formalistic view claims that HoS are independent, it constrains the scope of their functions to a strict administrative duty. This chapter proposes a pluralist understanding of the role of HoS based

Fund to Fight AIDS, Tuberculosis, and Malaria: Partnerships, Collaborations, and Initiatives with International Organizations', Chapter 27 in this volume.

[77] See Rich (n 21).
[78] S M Schwebel, *The Secretary-General of the United Nations: His Political Powers and Practice* (Harvard UP 1952)107.
[79] Clarence Jenks, 'Some Problems of an International Civil Service' (1972) 2 Report of the Special Committee for the Review of the United Nations Salary System, 27 UN Doc A/8728 132, 139–40.
[80] Marcos Cueto and Bob Reinalda, 'Candau, Marcolino Gomes' in Bob Reinalda, Kent J Kille, and Jaci Eisenberg (eds), *IO BIO, Biographical Dictionary of Secretaries-General of International Organizations* (Institute for Management Research) <www.ru.nl/fm/iobio> accessed 26 December 2023. See also Cox and Jacobson (n 31) 200, 383; Bob Reinalda, 'Relations Among Secretaries-General of International Organizations' 10–11 <https://library.ifla.org/id/eprint/898/1/201-reinalda-en.pdf> accessed 30 September 2024, stating that 'success is a matter of both internal and external leadership capacities'.

on the constituent instruments of IOs and the power of simple interpretation that HoS possess. A functional-pluralist view of the autonomy of HoS more accurately emphasizes the imperative to initiate changes in situations of collective crises (such as pandemics and climate change). Constituent instruments and other rules of the organization enable the pluralist functions/powers of executive heads in ways that may not be achieved solely through the exercise of their traditional administrative functions when addressing problems that require urgent solutions. Thus, a pluralist understanding of the functions of HoS brings about the full actualization of the role of HoS as evident from the recent practices of IOs. Therefore, legitimacy and resource concerns are not formal limitations on the powers of HoS to initiate changes. Nevertheless, whether these changes, when initiated, eventually fail or succeed depends on the personalities, leadership, and skills of the HoS. While the skills, leadership, and personalities of HoS are not the exclusive determinative factors of successful or failed initiatives, legitimacy and resource concerns are not formal constraints on the powers of HoS to initiate changes. Rather, these concerns are a test of their expertise and personality, and further steps in implementing their guaranteed expansive and pluralist functions/powers if they manage to make wise use of it.

14

The Evolution of UN Secretary-General Initiatives to Respond to Violent and Non-Violent Threats to International Peace and Security

Mona Ali Khalil

I. Introduction

The Charter of the United Nations (UN) envisions at least three explicit roles for the Secretary-General. Article 97 stipulates that he (or she) shall be the chief administrative officer of the UN; Article 98 provides that he (or she) shall perform the functions entrusted to him (or her) by the General Assembly (UNGA), the Security Council (UNSC), and other principal organs; and Article 99 empowers him (or her) to bring to the attention of the UNSC any matter that in his (or her) opinion may threaten the maintenance of international peace and security.

Deriving from these powers and building on the established practice of the UN, the role of the UN Secretary-General has evolved in ways not explicitly provided for in the UN Charter. Throughout the history of the UN, successive Secretaries-General have launched initiatives that have not only created unforeseen roles for the Secretariat but have also introduced new tools for the maintenance of international peace and security. Notably, Secretary-General Dag Hammarskjöld designed the UN's first peacekeeping force launching one of the most important tools of the UN's peace and security toolbox. Secretary-General Boutros Boutros-Ghali promulgated an Agenda for Peace that laid the foundation for three decades of preventive diplomacy, peacemaking, peacekeeping, and pioneered a new era of peacebuilding. Secretary-General Kofi Annan codified the Responsibility to Protect as a UN doctrine for the protection of civilian populations against genocide, ethnic cleansing, war crimes, and crimes against humanity. Secretary-General Ban Ki-moon established the UN's first health-keeping mission: the UN Mission for Ebola Emergency Response (UNMEER).

Mona Ali Khalil, *The Evolution of UN Secretary-General Initiatives to Respond to Violent and Non-Violent Threats to International Peace and Security* In: *International Organization Initiatives*. Edited by: Gabrielle Marceau and Henner Gött, Oxford University Press. © Oxford University Press 2025. DOI: 10.1093/9780197803325.003.0015

This chapter explores these Secretary-General initiatives[1] and identifies their contribution to the UN's response to violent as well as non-violent threats to international peace and security.

II. The UN's First Peacekeeping Force

Although the UN Charter does not mention the word or the concept of 'peacekeeping', nothing in the text of the UN Charter precludes it.[2] According to Swedish historians, for Secretary-General Dag Hammarskjöld, 'this void was an opportunity rather than a constraint'.[3]

When the Israeli army invaded Egypt on 29 October 1956, with the support of the United Kingdom and France, Secretary-General Dag Hammarskjöld was shocked by the violations of the UN Charter and upheld the view that all member states, including the permanent members of the UNSC, have a binding obligation to respect and ensure respect for the UN Charter.[4] The fact that two permanent members were involved in the aggression did not deter the Secretary-General. He announced to the UNSC that '[a] Secretary-General cannot serve on any other assumption than that . . . all Member nations honour their pledge to observe all Articles of the Charter'[5] including, inter alia, Article 2(4) which obliges all member states to 'refrain in their international relations from the threat or use of force against the territorial integrity or political independence of any state'.[6] With the support of the United States of America (USA) and Canada, he sought to restore peace and preserve territorial integrity in accordance with the Purposes and Principles of the UN Charter.

[1] This volume defines 'initiative' as 'action of IO secretariats and/or their heads, which (1) aims to meet a need of the IO, its membership, its secretariat, or other internal or external stakeholders, (2) is novel, or previously unfamiliar to the IO in question, and (3) pushes the boundaries of the IO beyond its founding or prior operational activities, thus resulting in IO change', see Gabrielle Marceau and Henner Gött, 'Preface' in this volume.

[2] The chapter refers to the UN Emergency Force as the first UN peacekeeping force. This is without prejudice to the United Nations Truce Supervision Organization (UNTSO) as the first group of military observers often referred to as the first UN peacekeeping mission. UNTSO was established pursuant to UNSC Res 50 (29 May 1948) UN Doc S/801, wherein the UNSC called for a cessation of hostilities in Palestine and decided that the implementation of the Israel-Arab Armistice Agreements should be supervised by the UN Mediator, with the assistance of a group of military observers.

[3] Carl Bildt, 'Dag Hammarskjöld and United Nations Peacekeeping' in UN Chronicle, *Pursuing Peace: Commemorating Dag Hammarskjöld* (2011) <https://www.un.org/en/chronicle/article/dag-hammarskjold-and-united-nations-peacekeeping> accessed 1 February 2025.

[4] 'Dag Hammarskjöld' (*UN*, 1956) <https://www.un.org/depts/dhl/dag/time1956.html> accessed 1 February 2025.

[5] UNSC, 'Security Council Official Records' (71st Meeting, 31 October 1956) UN Doc S/PV.751.

[6] Charter of the United Nations (adopted 26 June 1945, entered into force 24 October 1945) <https://www.un.org/en/about-us/un-charter/full-text> accessed 1 February 2025.

Six years earlier, during the crisis in the Korean peninsula in 1950, the UNGA had adopted Resolution 377 (V)[7] also known as the 'Uniting for Peace' Resolution, pursuant to which an emergency special session of the UNGA could be convened by a majority of the members of the UNSC or a majority of the members of the UN in the event of a veto in the UNSC.[8] As explicitly stated in the preamble to UNGA Resolution 377 (V), the failure of the UNSC to discharge its primary responsibility 'does not relieve Member States of their obligations or the United Nations of its responsibility'[9] nor does it 'deprive the General Assembly of its rights or relieve it of its responsibilities under the Charter to maintain international peace and security'.[10]

Thus, when Israel, with Britain and France, invaded Egypt in 1956,[11] the first emergency special session of the UNGA was convened at the request of the UNSC. The UNGA adopted Resolution 997 (ES-I) calling for an immediate ceasefire and the withdrawal of all foreign forces from Egyptian territory.[12] The Secretary-General was requested to observe and report promptly on compliance to the UNSC and the UNGA, for such further action as those bodies might deem appropriate in accordance with the UN Charter.[13]

The Secretary-General went well beyond observing and reporting as requested by the first emergency special session of the UNGA; he devised the concept of a peacekeeping force. Further to discussions with Secretary-General Dag Hammarskjöld, the representative of Canada proposed[14] and the UNGA

[7] UNGA, Resolution 377 A (V): 'Uniting for Peace' (3 November 1950) UN Doc A/RES/377, 10.

[8] ibid: UNGA Res 377 A (V) was adopted by the UNGA in response to the deadlock in the UNSC during the crisis in the Korean peninsula in 1950. The Union of Soviet Socialist Republics (USSR) had exercised its veto against a US draft resolution in the UNSC condemning the Democratic People's Republic of Korea's continued defiance of prior UNSC resolutions imposing measures to protect the Republic of Korea. In response to the Soviet veto, the USA 'succeeded in persuading the General Assembly that it should claim for itself a subsidiary responsibility with regard to international peace and security', as enunciated by Article 14 of the UN Charter (n 6). The result of these efforts was Resolution 377 A (V) also known as the 'Uniting for Peace' resolution. See the Introductory Note by Christian Tomuschat, UN Audiovisual Library of International Law <https://legal.un.org/avl/ha/ufp/ufp.html> accessed 1 February 2025.

[9] UNGA Res 377 (V) (3 November 1950) <https://documents.un.org/doc/resolution/gen/nr0/059/75/pdf/nr005975.pdf> accessed 1 February 2025.

[10] ibid.

[11] In total, as of 1 March 2024, the UNGA has convened a total of 11 emergency special sessions under the 'Uniting for Peace' resolution including the ongoing 10th and the 11th emergency special sessions dealing with the wars in Israel/Palestine and Ukraine respectively. See UN, 'Emergency Special Sessions' <https://www.un.org/en/ga/sessions/emergency.shtml> accessed 1 February 2025.

[12] 'UN Background Paper on the Establishment of UNEF' <https://peacekeeping.un.org/en/mission/past/unef1backgr2.html> accessed1 February 2025.

[13] UNGA Res 997 (ES-I) (30 October 1956) UN Doc A/RES/997(ES-I) (adopted by 64 votes to 5; with 6 abstentions) <https://digitallibrary.un.org/record/208414?ln=en&v=pdf> accessed 1 February 2025. The dissenters were Australia and New Zealand, in addition to France, Israel, and the United Kingdom.

[14] 'UN Background Paper on the Establishment of UNEF' <https://peacekeeping.un.org/en/mission/past/unef1backgr2.html> accessed 1 February 2025.

immediately adopted Resolution 998 (ES-I).[15] In that resolution, the UNGA requested, 'as a matter of priority, the Secretary-General to submit to it within forty-eight hours a plan for the setting up, with the consent of the nations concerned, of an emergency international United Nations Force to secure and supervise the cessation of hostilities'.[16]

On the very same day, the Secretary-General submitted his first report on the plan for an emergency international UN Force, including immediately setting up a UN Command. All of the Secretary-General's recommendations were endorsed by the UNGA and included in Resolution 1000 (ES-I) by which the first-ever UN peacekeeping force—United Nations Emergency Force (UNEF I)—was established to monitor the ceasefire and supervising the withdrawal of foreign troops from Egyptian territory.[17] Having devised the concept of the peacekeeping force within days, Secretary-General Dag Hammarskjöld assembled UNEF I within weeks.[18]

The landmark initiative of the Secretary-General, with the support of the USA and Canada, to introduce the first ever peacekeeping force in the first ever emergency special session was one of Secretary-General Dag Hammarskjöld's most enduring legacies. While the first peacekeeping force was designed by the Secretary-General and authorized by the UNGA, since then, peacekeeping has become one of the UNSC's most prominent tools for the maintenance of international peace and security. Since the UNGA's authorization of UNEF I in 1956, the UNSC has mandated more than 55 UN peacekeeping missions and operations[19] including the 11 that are currently active.[20]

[15] UNGA Res 998 (ES-I) (4 November 1956) UN Doc A/RES/998(ES-I) <https://digitallibrary.un.org/record/208415?ln=en&v=pdf> accessed 1 February 2025.

[16] ibid, the voting was 57 to none, with 19 abstentions: Egypt, France, Israel, the United Kingdom, and the Soviet Union and Eastern European States were among the abstainers.

[17] UNGA Res 1000 (ES-I) (5 November 1956) UN Doc A/RES/1000(ES-I); as with UNGA Res 998 (ES-I), the voting on resolution UNGA Resolution 1000 (ES-I) was 57 votes to none, with 19 abstentions. Egypt, France, Israel, the United Kingdom, the Soviet Union and Eastern European States abstained https://digitallibrary.un.org/record/208417?ln=en&v=pdf> accessed 1 February 2025.

[18] Carl Bildt, 'Pursuing Peace: Commemorating Dag Hammarskjöld' (2011) <https://www.un.org/en/chronicle/article/dag-hammarskjold-and-united-nations-peacekeeping> accessed 1 February 2025.

[19] UN Peacekeeping Operations, 'Special Political Missions and Other Presences' <https://www.unmissions.org/> accessed 1 February 2025.

[20] List of current missions available at UN Peacekeeping Operations, 'Where We Operate' <https://peacekeeping.un.org/en/where-we-operate> accessed 1 February 2025, including the UN Peacekeeping Force in Cyprus (UNFICYP); UN Organization Stabilization Mission in the Democratic Republic of the Congo (MONUSCO), UN Multidimensional Integrated Stabilization Mission in the Central African Republic (MINUSCA), UN Interim Force in Lebanon (UNIFIL), UN Mission in the Republic of South Sudan (UNMISS), UN Disengagement Observer Force (UNDOF) as well as in UN Interim Security Force for Abyei (UNISFA), UN Truce Supervision Organization (UNTSO), UN Military Observer Group in India and Pakistan (UNMOGIP), UN Interim Administration Mission in Kosovo (UNMIK), and UN Mission for the Referendum in Western Sahara (MINURSO).

III. The Agenda for Peace

Thirty-five years after the establishment of the first peacekeeping force in 1956, Secretary-General Boutros Boutros-Ghali issued 'An Agenda for Peace' which had a decisive impact on shaping the UN's response to threats to international peace and security.

In January 1992, the UNSC invited Secretary-General Boutros Boutros-Ghali, who had just assumed office, to prepare an 'analysis and recommendations on ways of strengthening and making more efficient, within the framework and provisions of the Charter, the capacity of the United Nations for preventive diplomacy, for peacemaking and for peace-keeping'.[21] In his report entitled 'An Agenda for Peace',[22] Secretary-General Boutros Boutros-Ghali went above and beyond the UNSC's request by introducing post-conflict peacebuilding as a new concept and a new tool in the UN's toolbox for international peace and security. His initiative heralded several innovations.

Secretary-General Boutros Boutros-Ghali's concept of peacebuilding expanded the concept of peace and security to include 'sustained, cooperative work to deal with underlying economic, social, cultural and humanitarian problems to ensure the durability of an achieved peace on a durable foundation'.[23] As he envisioned it, 'preventive diplomacy is to avoid a crisis; post-conflict peacebuilding is to prevent a recurrence of crisis'.[24]

He also envisioned a novel and unique entity which is uniquely a subsidiary body of three principal organs of the UN. The Peacebuilding Commission (PBC) is one of the main outcomes of the peacebuilding component of the Agenda for Peace[25] and is elected from and reports to the UNGA, the UNSC, and the Economic and Social Council.[26] Initially established in 2005 to support peace efforts in conflict-affected countries with their consent, the PBC was further mandated in 2016 to promote an integrated, strategic, and coherent approach to peacebuilding: to act as a bridge among the principal organs and relevant UN entities and to convene all relevant actors of the UN system.[27]

[21] UNSC, 'Note by the President of the Security Council' (31 January 1992) UN Doc S/23500 <https://www.securitycouncilreport.org/atf/cf/%7B65BFCF9B-6D27-4E9C-8CD3-CF6E4FF96FF9%7D/PKO%20S%2023500.pdf> accessed 1 February 2025.

[22] The Agenda for Peace in A/47/277-S/24111 <https://digitallibrary.un.org/record/145749> accessed 1 February 2025.

[23] ibid para 57.

[24] ibid para 21.

[25] UNGA, 'The Peacebuilding Commission' (20 December 2005) UN Doc A/RES/60/180 and UNSC Res 1645 (20 December 2005) UN Doc S/RES/1645.

[26] United Nations Peacebuilding Commission, 'Peacebuilding Commission Support Branch' <https://www.un.org/peacebuilding/commission> accessed 1 February 2025.

[27] UNGA, 'Review of the United Nations Peacebuilding Architecture' (12 May 2016) UN Doc A/RES/70/262 and UNSC Res 2282 (27 April 2016) UN Doc S/RES/2282.

According to the International Crisis Group, Secretary-General Boutros Boutros-Ghali's Agenda for Peace was 'a foundational statement of the UN's role in stabilising the post-Cold War world. . . . Its vision of an activist, interventionist UN set the terms for policy discussions around the organisation in the ensuing three decades'.[28]

Secretary-General Boutros Boutros-Ghali saw the end of the Cold War as 'a second chance' to create the world as it was envisioned in the UN Charter. He talked of drawing back 'from the brink of a confrontation that threatened the world and, too often, paralysed our Organization'.[29] Almost presciently, he warned that shared interests, 'not the threat of the veto or the power of any group of nations', should govern the work of the UNSC.[30] He cautioned that the Charter principles 'must be applied consistently, not selectively, for if the perception should be of the latter, trust will wane and with it the moral authority which is the greatest and most unique quality of that instrument'.[31]

The current Secretary-General, Antonio Guterres, noted that the Agenda for Peace was adopted at the end of the Cold War when the 'improvement in relations between States' had helped to 'forge consensus in the UNSC and empowered the Organization to address threats to collective security'.[32] He observed that this 'unity of purpose has waned' and that a transition to a new global order is underway, defined by increased multipolarity and fragmentation as well as by greater competition among major powers and a loss of trust between the Global North and South.[33]

Thus, in July 2023, thirty years after Secretary-General Boutros Boutros-Ghali launched the Agenda for Peace, Secretary-General António Guterres announced a 'New Agenda for Peace' presenting his vision for multilateral and collective security based on international law and outlining his recommendations to address the violent and non-violent threats to international peace and security from terrorism and war, including nuclear war, to pandemics and climate change.[34]

[28] Richard Gowen, 'What's New About the UN's New Agenda for Peace?' (*Crisis Group*, 19 July 2023) <https://www.crisisgroup.org/global/whats-new-about-uns-new-agenda-peace>, accessed 1 February 2025.

[29] The Agenda for Peace in A/47/277-S/2411 <https://digitallibrary.un.org/record/145749> accessed 1 February 2025, para 75.

[30] ibid para 78.

[31] ibid para 82.

[32] UN, 'A New Agenda for Peace' 3 <https://www.un.org/sites/un2.un.org/files/our-common-agenda-policy-brief-new-agenda-for-peace-en.pdf> accessed 1 February 2025.

[33] ibid 3–4.

[34] ibid.

IV. The Responsibility to Protect

In light of the failures of the UN to prevent the genocides in Rwanda and Srebrenica in 1994 and 1995, respectively, Secretary-General Kofi Annan led the initiative to introduce and codify the Responsibility to Protect—generally known as R2P—as a UN doctrine. R2P seeks to enshrine the promise that 'Never Again' would the world stand by while mass atrocity crimes are taking place under the UN's watch.

In his report to the Millennium Summit held by the UNGA in 2000, Secretary-General Kofi Annan proposed that 'the international community find better ways to enforce international and human rights laws, including ensuring gross violations are punished, to protect the vulnerable. National sovereignty must not be used as a shield for violations of people's rights, and the Security Council should consider armed intervention in cases of mass murder'.[35] In response to Secretary-General Kofi Annan's challenge, the Government of Canada established the International Commission on Intervention and State Sovereignty (ICISS) which articulated the concept of R2P.[36] Secretary-General Kofi Annan led the initiative to codify R2P as a UN doctrine. On the occasion of the UN's sixtieth anniversary in 2005, he issued a report entitled 'In Larger Freedom: Towards Development, Security and Human Rights for All'.[37] In that report, Secretary-General Kofi Annan noted that the ICISS and the High-Level Panel on Threats, Challenges and Change[38] had endorsed 'an emerging norm that there is a collective responsibility to protect'.[39]

Secretary-General Kofi Annan urged UN member states to embrace R2P as a basis for collective action against genocide, war crimes, ethnic cleansing, and

[35] Kofi A Annan, '"We the Peoples": The Role of the United Nations in the 21st Century' <https://digitallibrary.un.org/record/413745?ln=en> accessed 1 February 2025.

[36] International Development Research Centre, *The Responsibility to Protect: Report of the International Commission on Intervention and State Sovereignty* (IDRC 2001) <https://idrc-crdi.ca/en/book/responsibility-protect-report-international-commission-intervention-and-state-sovereignty> accessed 1 February 2025.

[37] UNGA, 'In Larger Freedom: Towards Development, Security and Human Rights for All' (21 March 2005) UN Doc A/59/2005 <https://digitallibrary.un.org/record/550204?ln=en> accessed 1 February 2025.

[38] The UN High Level Panel on Threats, Challenges and Change was appointed by Secretary-General Kofi Annan in 2003 to analyse threats and challenges to international peace and security. It presented its report in December 2004. It was chaired by former Prime Minister of Thailand, Anand Panyarachun, and its members included several former heads of government and foreign ministers including Yevgeny Primakov (former Prime Minister of the Russian Federation); Qian Qichen (former Vice Premier and Minister for Foreign Affairs of China); David Hannay (former Permanent Representative of the United Kingdom to the United Nations and United Kingdom Special Envoy to Cyprus Brent Scowcroft (former Lt General, US Air Force and US National Security Adviser), UN, 'A More Secure World: Our Shared Responsibility' (2004) <www.un.org/peacebuilding/sites/www.un.org.peacebuilding/files/documents/hlp_more_secure_world.pdf> accessed 1 February 2025.

[39] ibid para 203. UNGA, '2005 World Summit Outcome' (16 September 2005) UN Doc A/RES/60/1 <https://docs.un.org/en/A/Res/60/1/> accessed 1 February 2025.

crimes against humanity, and to agree to act on this responsibility.[40] He laid out the three pillars of R2P stating that:

> This responsibility lies, first and foremost, with each individual State, whose primary raison d'être and duty is to protect its population. But if national authorities are unable or unwilling to protect their citizens, then the responsibility shifts to the international community to use diplomatic, humanitarian and other methods to help protect the human rights and well-being of civilian populations. When such methods appear insufficient, the Security Council may out of necessity decide to take action under the Charter of the United Nations, including enforcement action.[41]

R2P was ultimately adopted unanimously by the Heads of State and Governments of all UN member states at the UN World Summit in 2005. In paragraphs 138 and 139 of the World Summit's Outcome Document,[42] they decided that:

> 138. Each individual State has the responsibility to protect its populations from genocide, war crimes, ethnic cleansing and crimes against humanity. This responsibility entails the prevention of such crimes, including their incitement, through appropriate and necessary means. We accept that responsibility and will act in accordance with it. The international community should, as appropriate, encourage and help States to exercise this responsibility and support the United Nations in establishing an early warning capability.
>
> 139. The international community, through the United Nations, also has the responsibility to use appropriate diplomatic, humanitarian and other peaceful means, in accordance with Chapters VI and VIII of the Charter, to help to protect populations from genocide, war crimes, ethnic cleansing and crimes against humanity. In this context, we are prepared to take collective action, in a timely and decisive manner, through the Security Council, in accordance with the Charter, including Chapter VII, on a case-by-case basis and in cooperation with relevant regional organizations as appropriate, should peaceful means be inadequate and national authorities are manifestly failing to protect their populations from genocide, war crimes, ethnic cleansing and crimes against humanity.[43]

[40] Secretary-General Kofi Annan stated that: 'we must embrace the responsibility to protect, and, when necessary, we must act on it', 'In larger freedom: towards development, security and human rights for all', UNGA, 'In Larger Freedom: Towards Development, Security and Human Rights for All' (Report of the Secretary-General, 23 May 2005) UN Doc A /59/2005/Add.1 <https://digitallibrary.un.org/record/550204?ln=en> accessed 1 February 2025.

[41] ibid.

[42] 2005 World Summit Outcome (n 39).

[43] ibid paras 138 and 139.

In its Resolution 1674 (2006),[44] the UNSC reaffirmed the provisions of paragraphs 138 and 139 of the 2005 World Summit Outcome Document, thereby bringing its own R2P imprimatur.

According to the Global Centre for the Responsibility to Protect,[45] since 2006, the UNSC has invoked R2P in more than 80 UNSC resolutions.[46] While the UNSC has invoked R2P in many situations, it has only exercised the third pillar of R2P in one situation in the Libyan Arab Jamahiriya. Acting under Chapter VII of the UN Charter, the UNSC imposed enforcement measures, including referring the situation in Libya to the International Criminal Court and authorizing States, acting individually or through regional and other arrangements, to use force to protect civilians and civilian-populated areas under threat of attack.[47] As a result of concerns that the authorization to use force to protect civilians was abused to effectuate regime charge, efforts to invoke the third pillar of R2P again have thus far failed.

Secretary-General Kofi Annan's initiative to codify R2P as a UN doctrine was successfully and unanimously adopted by the UNGA and later reaffirmed by the UNSC. While UN member states were ready to accept R2P as a matter of principle, they have yet to accept it as a matter of practice.

V. The UN's First Health-Keeping Mission

While UN peace operations and authorizations of the use of force respond to violent threats to international peace and security, the UN was faced with a non-violent threat in the context of the Ebola crisis in West Africa. In their letter of 29 August 2014,[48] the Presidents of the Republic of Guinea, the Republic of Liberia, and the Republic of Sierra Leone detailed the impact of the Ebola virus disease and its implications for West Africa and beyond. In that letter, the Heads of State

[44] Operative para 4 of UNSC Res 1674 (28 April 2006) UN Doc S/RES/1674 (2006) <https://docs.un.org/en/S/RES/1674(2006)/> accessed 1 February 2025.

[45] Global Center for the Responsibility to Protect, 'What Is R2P' <https://www.globalr2p.org/what-is-r2p/> accessed 1 February 2025.

[46] The UNSC resolutions relating to the crises in Central African Republic, Côte d'Ivoire, Democratic Republic of the Congo, Liberia, Libya, Mali, Somalia, South Sudan, Syria, and Yemen, as well as thematic resolutions concerning the prevention of genocide, prevention of armed conflict, and restricting the trade of small arms, 'UN Security Council Resolutions and Presidential Statements Referencing R2P' (*Global Centre for the Responsibility to Protect*) <https://www.globalr2p.org/resources/un-security-council-resolutions-and-presidential-statements-referencing-r2p/> accessed 1 February 2025.

[47] UNSC Res 1970 (26 February 2011) UN Doc S/RES/1970 (2011) and UNSC Res 1973 (17 March 2011) UN Doc S/RES/1973 (2011).

[48] UNSC, 'Letter Dated 15 September 2014 from the Secretary-General Addressed to the President of the Security Council' (15 September 2014) UN Doc S/2014/669 <https://docs.un.org/en/S/2014/669> accessed 1 February 2025.

requested 'a coordinated international response to end the outbreak and to support the societies and economies of affected countries during the outbreak'.[49]

In identical letters dated 17 September 2014 addressed to the Presidents of the UNGA and UNSC,[50] following consultations with the Director-General of the World Health Organization (WHO), Secretary-General Ban Ki-moon conveyed his decision and confirmed his intention 'to immediately establish a United Nations Mission for Ebola Emergency Response (UNMEER)' and to appoint a Special Representative to head the UN system-wide mission. Secretary-General Ban Ki-moon envisioned that UNMEER would 'harness the capabilities and competencies of all the relevant [UN] actors under a unified operational structure to reinforce unity of purpose, with the "singular strategic objective and purpose" to work with others to prevent the spread to unaffected countries'.[51]

In reaching this unprecedented decision, Secretary-General Ban Ki-moon invoked his intention 'to make maximum use of the authority provided to [him], including in the area of human resources, in order to promote the timely and effective response to the Ebola crisis'.[52] He noted that:

> [n]o one country, no one organization has the resources to stem the tide of the Ebola crisis. Each Government is ultimately responsible for its own people. The Governments and the people of West Africa have asked for our help. We must come together as one United Nations, and we call upon Member States to join us in answering their call.[53]

On 18 September, the UNSC adopted Resolution 2177 (2014),[54] in which it determined that 'the unprecedented extent of the Ebola outbreak in Africa constitutes a threat to international peace and security'; acknowledged the Secretary-General's intention 'to convene a high-level meeting on the margins of the sixty-ninth [regular session of UNGA] to urge an exceptional and vigorous response to the Ebola outbreak' and requested the Secretary-General 'to help to ensure that all relevant UN System entities, including the WHO, accelerate their response to the Ebola outbreak in accordance with their respective mandates and in collaboration with governments of the region and those providing assistance'. In doing so, the UNSC refrained from taking the lead and allowed the

49 ibid.
50 'Identical Letters Dated 17 September 2014 from the Secretary-General Addressed to the President of the General Assembly and the President of the Security Council' (17 September 2014) UN Doc A/69/389–S/2014/679 <https://digitallibrary.un.org/record/779651?ln=en> accessed 1 February 2025.
51 ibid 2.
52 ibid 5.
53 ibid 5.
54 UNSC Res 2177 (18 September 2014) UN Doc S/RES/2177 (2014).

UNGA to be the first to endorse the Secretary-General's decision to establish UNMEER acting on behalf of the entire UN membership.

On 19 September, the UNGA adopted Resolution 69/1,[55] by which it unanimously welcomed the Secretary-General's intention to establish UNMEER and requested that he promptly execute his intention. The UNGA called upon all member states, relevant UN bodies, and the UN system to provide their full support to UNMEER.[56] Secretary-General Ban Ki-moon established UNMEER on the same day.

At his own initiative, with the UNSC's encouragement and the UNGA's endorsement, Secretary-General Ban Ki-moon established the UN's first health-keeping mission. UNMEER was also the first UN system-wide mission and its first mission responding to a non-violent threat to international peace and security.

UNMEER was a new type of UN operation—an embodiment of 'Delivering as One'—led by the UN, guided by the technical expertise of the WHO, supported by the UN Development Programme (UNDP), the UN Children's Fund (UNICEF), and the World Food Programme. It partnered with governmental agencies including the American and Chinese Centers for Disease Control as well as non-governmental organizations including Médecins Sans Frontières. UNMEER closed on 31 July 2015 having achieved its core objective of scaling up the response on the ground and supporting nationally led efforts to stop the spread of Ebola.[57]

VI. Conclusion

The foregoing initiatives by successive UN Secretaries-Generals not only created unforeseen roles for themselves but have also introduced new tools for the maintenance of international peace and security: from the first peacekeeping force to the first health-keeping mission; from the Agenda for Peace to the Responsibility to Protect. Secretary-General Dag Hammarskjöld designed the UN's first peacekeeping force with the support of the USA and Canada and with the authorization of the first emergency special session of the UNGA.

[55] UNGA, 'Measures to Contain and Combat the Recent Ebola Outbreak in West Africa' (19 September 2014) UN Doc A/RES/69/1 of 19 September 2014.

[56] UNGA, 'United Nations Mission for Ebola Emergency Response and the Office of the Special Envoy on Ebola' (Report of the Secretary-General, 24 September 2014) UN Doc A/69/404 <https://docs.un.org/en/A/69/404> accessed 1 February 2025, and UNGA Res 69/3 (9 October 2014) UN Doc A/RES/69/3.

[57] 'UN Mission for Ebola Emergency Response (UNMEER)' (*Global Ebola Response*, 24 November 2014) <https://ebolaresponse.un.org/un-mission-ebola-emergency-response-unmeer> accessed 1 February 2025.

Secretary-General Boutros Boutros-Ghali seized upon an intergovernmental request for a routine report to launch an ambitious Agenda for Peace that laid the foundation for three decades of preventive diplomacy, peacemaking, peacekeeping, and peacebuilding. Secretary-General Kofi Annan responded to the UNSC's failures to prevent genocide in Rwanda and Srebrenica by promulgating the Responsibility to Protect as a UN doctrine. Secretary-General Ban Ki-moon established UNMEER—the UN's first health-keeping mission—to harness the capabilities of the UN system to stop the spread of Ebola.

These four initiatives demonstrated that the UN Secretaries-General were willing and able to take the lead, when necessary, to fulfil the Charter's promise on behalf of 'We The Peoples'. They showed moral courage, found legal basis, forged political consensus, and achieved operational results to respond to violent and non-violent threats to international peace and security. Each, in his own way, responded to the needs of the moment, demonstrating leadership and strategic vision, while showing respect for the ultimate authority of the UNGA and UNSC. Each, in his own way, tapped the full potential of the Secretary-General's powers and prerogatives in fulfilment of the UN's objects and purposes: from reversing aggression to empowering peacebuilders; from enshrining the UN's responsibility to protect civilians; and from mass atrocity crimes to mobilizing the UN system to stop the spread of a deadly disease. Each, in his own way, designed a novel way to save lives and to promote international peace and security.

15

The Financial Action Task Force

Coming of Age: Becoming an International Organization

*David Lewis**

I. Introduction

The Financial Action Task Force (FATF) was established through the Group of Seven (G7) Economic Declaration 1989[1] as a temporary 'ad hoc group'[2] to follow, examine, and develop measures against the laundering of the proceeds of illegal drug trafficking. Over the years, its membership and remit have grown. Today, it is an intergovernmental policy-making body with an 'open-ended Mandate',[3] including the financing of terrorism[4] and the proliferation of weapons of mass destruction.

The FATF comprises 38 countries, the European Commission, and the Gulf Co-operation Council. Countries translate the FATF standards into their domestic frameworks and, through a peer-review mechanism of Mutual Evaluations,[5] assess each other on their technical compliance and effective implementation of such standards, a negative outcome of which can impact trade,

* Disclaimer: To protect the confidentiality of plenary discussions and avoid harming international negotiations or relationships, the author refers only to topics discussed and the considerations given to these topics. No reference is made to the position of individual office holders, national delegations, or individual representatives of FATF members, FSRBs, or Observer organizations.

[1] G7, 'Economic Declaration: Paris Summit' (16 July 1989) para 53 <https://g7.utoronto.ca/summit/1989paris/communique/index.html> accessed 18 September 2024.

[2] FATF, 'Annual Report 1990–1991' (13 May 1991) s III.B 'Institutional Arrangements' <https://www.fatf-gafi.org/content/dam/fatf-gafi/annual-reports/1990%201991%20ENG.pdf> accessed 18 July 2024.

[3] Declaration of the Ministers of the Financial Action Task Force of 12 April 2019 and FATF Mandate, https://www.fatf-gafi.org/content/dam/fatf-gafi/images/brochures-other/FATF-Ministerial-Declaration-Mandate.pdf.coredownload.pdf, accessed 18 July 2024.

[4] In October 2001, following the 11 September terrorist attacks in the United States of America, 'the FATF expanded its mandate to deal with the issue of the financing of terrorism, and took the important step of creating the Eight Special Recommendations on Terrorist Financing.': <https://www.fatf-gafi.org/content/dam/fatf-gafi/recommendations/FATF%20Standards%20-%2040%20Recommendations%20rc.pdf> accessed 18 July 2024.

[5] FATF, 'FATF Issues New Mechanism to Strengthen Money Laundering and Terrorist Financing Compliance' (2013) <https://www.fatf-gafi.org/en/publications/fatfrecommendations/documents/fatfissuesnewmechanismtostrengthenmoneylaunderingandterroristfinancingcompliance.html> accessed 18 July 2024.

David Lewis, *The Financial Action Task Force* In: *International Organization Initiatives.* Edited by: Gabrielle Marceau and Henner Gött, Oxford University Press. © Oxford University Press 2025. DOI: 10.1093/9780197803325.003.0016

investment, and aid prospects. FATF has also established the Global Network composed of 9 FATF-style regional bodies (FSRBs)[6] and over 20 observer organizations, including the Organisation for Economic Co-operation and Development (OECD), United Nations (UN), World Bank Group, International Monetary Fund (IMF), International Criminal Police Organization (Interpol), and European Union Agency for Law Enforcement Cooperation (Europol).[7] Through membership of FSRBs and/or the FATF, more than 200 jurisdictions have committed to fully implementing FATF Standards.

The FATF institutional structure comprises the Plenary, President, Vice-President, Steering Group, Working Group Co-Chairs, and Secretariat. At the Plenary, officials from the Global Network convene three times a year under the chairmanship of the President, a senior official from a member country. Representatives of FSRBs and Observers participate in Plenary meetings and the associated Working Group meetings; as there is no voting, all those attending can inform and influence decision-making, yet only the views of FATF members count towards reaching consensus. The FATF Plenary appoints the President from among its members. Both the 2019 FATF Ministerial Declaration and Mandate, as well as the FATF Internal Governance Principles (IGP), identify the Plenary[8] as the only decision-making body and member-led process. As such, the President and the Secretariat are accountable to the Plenary.[9] The President convenes and chairs the meetings of the Plenary and the Steering Group, and oversees the FATF Secretariat (led by the Executive Secretary and is in charge of supporting the work of the FATF membership and Global Network). The Secretariat is based in Paris and hosted administratively at the OECD while keeping the independence of the FATF's functions and international representation.[10]

The FATF essentially has three core functions: (i) brings together government experts to understand how money is laundered and terrorist organizations are funded, (ii) sets global standards to mitigate these risks, and (iii) assesses these standards' implementation. The assessments are peer reviews, that is, conducted by other jurisdictions, and result in public reports. Countries with strategic

[6] See, FATF, 'High-Level Principles for the Relationship Between the FATF and the FATF-Style Regional Bodies' (2019) <https://www.fatf-gafi.org/content/dam/fatf-gafi/Global-Network/High-Level%20Principles%20and%20Objectives%20for%20FATF%20and%20FSRBs.pdf> accessed 18 July 2024.

[7] FATF, 'FATF Global Network' <https://www.fatf-gafi.org/content/fatf-gafi/en/countries/global-network.html> accessed 18 July 2024.

[8] Ministerial Declaration (n 3) para 16.

[9] FATF Mandate (n 3) paras 44, 50.

[10] ibid paras 3, 33, 46. The FATF Annual Report 1990–1991 indicates that: 'The OECD would limit itself to secretariat functions, collating, co-ordinating and summarizing responses from FATF members and supporting the FATF presidency . . . It would not become involved in any enforcement activity.'

deficiencies related to anti-money laundering (AML) and counterterrorist financing (CFT) are given an opportunity to address them before being publicly listed.

This chapter offers a unique perspective on the evolution of an intergovernmental body through a series of initiatives introduced by the Head of the FATF Secretariat, between 2015 and 2022, to strengthen, professionalize, and transform FATF from an informal ad hoc group to a recognized international organization (IO), furthering its aims responding to the needs of its membership and challenging environments. While the FATF operated under a time-limited mandate agreed upon by the ministers and representatives of its member jurisdictions and had no formal legal basis, the global threats it was set up to tackle were escalating. It was clear that its mission would be perpetual and needed greater support. In response to these pressing challenges, after 30 years of operating on a time-bound basis, FATF ministers agreed on, inter alia, (i) an open-ended mandate, (ii) its role in leading global action to counter money laundering, terrorist financing, and the financing of proliferation of weapons of mass destruction, and (iii) greater ministerial engagement and support through regular ministerial-level meetings, term extension of its Presidency to a two-year term, and a new funding model.[11]

II. Consideration of FATF's Legal Status

In 2016, the Secretariat led an initiative to review and better understand FATF's legal status and options for its future. This process was triggered by various issues, from 'niggles' to more substantial challenges, mainly due to the lack of formal legal status, including questions on FATF's recognition and participation in UN meetings and relationship issues between it and the OECD (eg regarding the operation and independence of FATF Secretariat, which is employed by and subject to the OECD's legal status, and this extended to the protection of the intellectual property of the FATF).

For this review process, the Secretariat sought advice and input from FATF members and received instrumental inputs from the OECD, the European Commission, and the French delegation to the FATF.[12] The Secretariat considered similar entities' legal status and institutional arrangements, for

[11] Ministerial Declaration (n 3).

[12] Inter alia, FATF, 'FATF Report to G20 Leaders' Summit' (6 July 2017), 'Section: Update on FATF's Ongoing Work to Strengthen Its Institutional Basis, Governance and Capacity' <https://www.fatf-gafi.org/content/dam/fatf-gafi/reports/FATF-Report-to-G20-July-2017.pdf.coredownload.pdf≥ accessed 18 July 2024. See also FATF, 'FATF Report to G20 Leaders' Summit' (27 June 2019), 'Strengthening the Institutional Basis, Governance and Capacity of FATF' <https://www.fatf-gafi.org/content/dam/fatf-gafi/reports/G20-June-2019.pdf.coredownload.pdf> accessed 18 July 2024.

example, the Egmont Group of Financial Intelligence Units, the FSRBs, and the Financial Stability Board. The process revealed different options, from a treaty-based organization (where members adopt a formal instrument underpinning it) to national domestic legal arrangements. It was far from clear, and even contested by FATF members, whether the legal status of the OECD extended to the FATF. Complexity was manifested, for example, in diplomatic issues around whether visiting delegates to FATF meetings could enjoy the privileges and access provided for delegates of OECD meetings in Paris or for UN members attending meetings in New York.

The catalyst for reviewing FATF's legal status included its consideration as a 'member-led' rather than a 'secretariat-led' body and the dynamics between individual members and FATF's permanent staff. In some respects, the FATF suffered from the success of the OECD, with individual FATF members not wishing to lose influence. The review led to substantial debate among members. Whilst some saw its legal status as necessary to strengthen governance and accountability, others saw it as unnecessary bureaucracy that would reduce the effectiveness of the body.

There was also a strong case for the FATF already having an independent legal personality under international law based on how it had operated in practice over a long period, for example, regular meetings of officials from member countries, with an agreed mandate and governance framework. After several debates in FATF Plenary, it was agreed to maintain the status quo. Those other entities with various forms of legal status analysed in the review process were arguably not more effective or even less so. Additionally, consideration was given to the fact that FATF was already accountable to its membership, albeit their knowledge of FATF and engagement was mixed.

However, there is ongoing debate outside the Organization and its members about FATF's legitimacy, transparency, and accountability.[13] This is partly due to the 'compliance-industrial complex' it has contributed to create and the subsequent significant costs for the private sector and the public sector in lower-income and developing countries. Therefore, it is likely that the FATF will review its legal status again and its relationship with other IOs, including the OECD and the UN.

[13] Royal United Services Institute, 'The Future of the Financial Action Task Force Improving the Least Bad Option?' (RUSI Conference Report, 4 January 2024) <https://static.rusi.org/Future-of-FATF_web_final.pdf> accessed 18 July 2024. Mark Nance, 'The Regime That FATF Built: An Introduction to the Action Task Force' (2018) 69 Crime, Law and Social Change, 109–30.

III. Strengthening FATF Leadership

Another Secretariat-led initiative to strengthen and professionalize the FATF was to examine the composition of its leadership. Whilst the staff of the FATF Secretariat is recruited by the OECD through fair and open competition, the next President was effectively selected by the currently sitting President, with no agreed and published process or transparency, and with formal approval and appointment by the Plenary being little more than a 'rubber stamp'. This led in 2019 to the term of the President being extended from one year to two years and the position of the Vice-President being strengthened. Previously, the practice had been for the President to serve for one year,[14] with the Vice-President as the next President. The President would typically be a deputy minister from an FATF member, two or three levels up from FATF heads of delegation.

The President appoints a number of individuals or countries to serve as a Steering Group during his/her term. The process involves the President selecting whom he/she wants in this group and then seeking formal approval from the Plenary, often seen as a rubber-stamping exercise. The central role of the Steering Group is to advise the President. It is not a decision-making body and has no formal role in governance or decision-making. This is partly due to members' preference to refrain from delegating authority to any other country or group of countries. Consequently, there is no governing board, a feature commonly found in other, public and private sector, organizations.

Driven by several factors, the Secretariat was prompted to consider the FATF's leadership, including the need to secure senior-level leaders from among the membership who could sit alongside and build relationships with Members' ministers to ensure their support and engagement. This required the incumbent to have greater credibility at ministerial level and to be in post long enough to develop relationships at that level. This became particularly critical after the Secretariat successfully secured a seat for the FATF at the table during meetings of G7 and Group of 20 (G20) Finance Ministers and Central Bank Governors. The model the Secretariat had in mind was provided by the Financial Stability Board (FSB), where the Chair serves a five-year term, he/she does this in addition to her/his day job, rather than a full-time role, and is a subject matter expert, as well as having a ministerial level position.[15] Therefore, Mark Carney (FSB Chair from 2011 to 2018) was seen as the role model.

[14] FATF Annual Report (n 2).

[15] Established in 2009, the Financial Stability Board is based in Basel, Switzerland. On 28 January 2013, the Board was established as a not-for-profit association under Swiss law. See Financial Stability Board, 'Charter of the Financial Stability Board' (restated and amended on 19 June 2012) <https://www.fsb.org/wp-content/uploads/FSB-Charter-with-revised-Annex-FINAL.pdf> accessed 18 July 2024.

This issue was discussed with the President and the Steering Group's members, and different options were considered. Across the membership, there was a general agreement to extend the term of the FATF President, but only up to two years, mainly due to concerns about what would happen if the FATF got stuck with a 'bad' or 'ineffective' President. Other members were concerned that extending the term would reduce the opportunity for all members to be President. Yet, in practice, the power of the President is limited, and few countries propose candidates. However, countries recognize the attractiveness of hosting an annual meeting with several hundred officials from 200 countries and 20 IOs. The question, therefore, became a matter of kudos that members prefer securing.

To address the concerns of smaller-economy members who felt unable to afford to put forward an FATF President, the post of Vice-President was strengthened, becoming a substantial role rather than a President-in-waiting. However, there was no agreement to define the process for selecting these roles or for requirements and qualifications for assuming the role of either the President or Vice-President. Members wished to retain maximum flexibility in this regard.

The outcome of this initiative is that, today, the President and Vice-President are both two-year positions,[16] providing them with an enhanced opportunity to build relationships with and, therefore, influence the ministers of governments worldwide. However, without any agreed qualifications, experience, or other requirements for these roles, their impact remains variable and can be hindered in practice if, inter alia, their day job is as an official more junior than ministerial level, or equivalent, in a regulatory body.

IV. Governance Structure and Transparency

Besides the President and Vice-President, the FATF is effectively led by Co-Chairs of various permanent Working Groups and Temporary Project Teams. Similar to the President and Vice-President, these roles are carried out by members on top of their day jobs. There was no clear or formalized selection process for the Co-Chairs. For practical reasons, these positions were typically filled by those members with the most interest and resources to provide them. They became hereditary positions, with jurisdictions retaining leadership of each working group and passing on the position to another member of their own jurisdiction when the incumbent retired or moved on to another position in government.

[16] FATF Mandate (n 3) paras 31, 35.

It was considered that the absence of open and clear selection processes did not reflect a mature, transparent, and accountable IO and was unfair to other members who were unable to contribute to the FATF's leadership. To be a truly 'member-led' organization, as its members wished it to be, the FATF needed to ensure greater equality of opportunities for all members to contribute. The FATF Internal Governance Principles (IGP) provided for this, but they were not being enforced at a high level. Presidents were often not keen to enforce them as their short tenure meant they relied heavily on the goodwill of those members already occupying these positions. Nevertheless, the Secretariat managed to gradually improve the process, making it more transparent and equitable, including agreements on simple measures such as circulating a document at each Plenary Meeting stating the Co-Chairs' names and jurisdictions, with their terms' start and end dates. It became clear to all members (i) whose delegates often changed and held little organizational memory, (ii) which Co-Chairs had served for long time, and (iii) which countries' Co-Chair had not changed.

The next stage was to seek agreement to communicate formally to all members when the end of the term of a Co-Chair approached and to invite them to propose candidates to replace those Co-Chairs. The President would then be encouraged to consult the Steering Group on the selection of such replacements, taking into account information provided by the Secretariat on the candidates' qualifications and experience, positions held by their jurisdiction in the FATF, and other relevant information to achieve a balance in policy-making, such as whether they came from a common law or civil law jurisdiction.

This process was adopted, became standard practice, and led to more members having the opportunity to participate in FATF's leadership. However, some of those positions are very resource-intensive, and while many countries would like to contribute, they neither have the expertise nor the capacity to do so. Thus, a small group of better-resourced members continue to dominate the leadership of the FATF.

V. International Personality: A Seat at the Table (G7/G20)

Although the FATF was created by the G7, and both the G7 and G20 regularly called upon it, and their members repeatedly expressed commitment to the implementation of its Standards, as of 2015, the FATF was not represented in, or given the opportunity to inform, G7 and G20 meetings. While other IOs, routinely referenced in G7 and G20 communiqués and on which they relied, had a regular seat at the table, the FATF did not, despite being regularly referenced and asked to perform various tasks.[17]

[17] For example, '[a]t the 2015 Antalya Summit, G20 members continued their engagement by calling on the FATF to "report back to our Finance Ministers and Central Bank Governors by their

For the FATF to have a more significant impact, it needed to have a seat at the table alongside other organizations, such as the OECD, UN, IMF, World Bank Group, and FSB. The Secretariat took the initiative to raise this issue with officials of G20 Presidencies and their representatives in the FATF. The Secretariat sought support from the FATF President and the Steering Group, and promoted the FATF to be invited to such meetings. The FATF President and Executive Secretary attended a meeting of G7 Finance Ministers and Central Bank Governors in Japan in 2016,[18] and, subsequently, the Executive Secretary was invited to participate in the Third G20 Finance Ministers and Central Bank Governors Meeting in China.[19] After these initial meetings, where the Executive Secretary represented the FATF as a 'G20 Deputy', the FATF President and Executive Secretary were invited to all subsequent meetings of G20 Finance Ministers and Central Bank Governors and some equivalent G7 meetings.

The benefits of this recognition and participation became clear, including the opportunity to raise the profile and understanding of the FATF at ministerial level. Participating in G20 meetings meant that ministers could see, hear from, and engage with the FATF directly rather than simply receiving a briefing paper on FATF from their officials acting as FATF heads of delegations. It also meant that as the FATF is twice the size of the G20 in terms of members and its Global Network is larger than the United Nations, the FATF could speak on behalf of all its members and a much wider group of jurisdictions when engaging with and advising the G20 as an observer organization. Instead of putting the FATF in thrall to the G20, a fear of some non-G20 members of the FATF, it served to ensure that the G20's views were informed by the FATF as a whole and its broader jurisdictions community.

In addition, there were several other benefits. The process previously described of strengthening the leadership of the FATF was, in part, possible because the Secretariat recognized the importance of building personal relationships and having bilateral meetings at ministerial level at the margins of the meetings. FATF was missing out on this opportunity, and with the FATF President changing annually, there were only one of two opportunities for them

first meeting in 2016 on the steps countries are taking to address the weaknesses identified to cut off terrorism-related financial flows". G20 Research Group, '2022 G20 Bali Summit Final Compliance Report: Bribery' (14 July 2023) <https://www.g20.utoronto.ca/compliance/2022bali-final/05-2022-g20-compliance-final-bribery.pdf> accessed 18 July 2024.

[18] FATF, 'FATF at G7 Meeting in Sendai' <https://www.fatf-gafi.org/content/fatf-gafi/en/publications/Fatfgeneral/Fatf-at-g7-meeting-in-sendai.html> accessed 18 July 2024. G7, 'G7 Action Plan on Combatting the Financing of Terrorism' <http://www.g7.utoronto.ca/finance/g7_action_plan_on_cft_en.pdf> accessed 18 July 2024.

[19] Notably, the G20 issued a Communiqué highlighting the role of the FATF: G20, 'Communiqué G20 Finance Ministers and Central Bank Governors Meeting' (28 July 2016) <http://www.g20chn.org/English/Documents/Current/201607/t20160728_3091.html> accessed 18 July 2024.

to meet ministers before a new person came into the post. Securing a longer Presidency term for the FATF was intended to put the President in a better position to build and benefit from relationships at leader level. The FATF attended its first G20 Leaders Meeting in 2021.

There were also more practical benefits. For instance, there are long meetings of G20 Deputies and Officials required to negotiate communiqué text in the weeks and days before the ministerial meetings. Often, those Deputies would have little or no awareness of their national position on FATF issues or of the consensus of FATF members on issues ranging from the transparency of beneficial ownership to the regulation of virtual assets and the financing of terrorism and proliferation of weapons of mass destruction. Regarding these issues, in G20 meetings, some countries would seek to undermine a consensus achieved in the FATF, including arguing for deferral to the UN Security Council, for example, where they might have a veto. Through the participation of the senior FATF official in their communiqué drafting sessions, the Organization was able to inform the G20 of the commitments already made by those countries in the FATF.

Securing a seat at the table for the FATF at the G20, the G7, and other international fora has been one of the most impactful ways in which the Secretariat supported the development of the FATF and its evolution into a recognized and impactful IO and active delivery partner for the G20. It facilitated the FATF to advocate for greater attention and focus on the harms of money laundering and terrorist financing, and the need to provide better funding and resources for the global response to these threats. While this requires additional resources from the FATF to prepare for and participate in the G20 meetings, the benefits far outweigh the costs, and this practice is now well established and likely to continue.

VI. The FATF Mandate: From a Temporary Task Force to a Permanent Organization

In 2019, the FATF held a rare Ministerial Meeting to review its mandate. These meetings typically happened every four or eight years in the margins of the IMF/World Bank Annual Meetings, as most ministers would be there (albeit it was an extra trip for countries where the Minister of Justice, rather than Finance, would hold the FATF portfolio).

The first FATF Ministerial Meeting was held in 2019 after several years without holding one.[20] Feedback from previous Ministerial Meetings was that

[20] In 2019, this issue was raised by the FATF President Marshall Billingslea. See 'Remarks by FATF President Marshall Billingslea' (*FATF*, 12 April 2019) <https://www.fatf-gafi.org/content/fatf-gafi/en/publications/Fatfgeneral/Speech-fatf-ministerial.html> accessed 18 July 2024.

they could be largely perfunctory. The Chair would go around the table, ministers would stress the importance of fighting money laundering and terrorist financing, and they would agree to extend the mandate of the FATF again. This time, though, the Ministerial Meeting represented an opportunity for change.

The FATF Presidency was held by the United States of America (USA), which has always been the leading player in the FATF. The FATF President was a senior and influential ministerial-level representative of the US Government, and he had led initiatives on pressing global issues, including the regulation of virtual assets on counterterrorist and proliferation financing. He had participated directly in the only ever meeting of Finance Ministers of the UN Security Council, which was focused on the response to the Islamic State of Iraq and Syria (ISIL), al Qaeda (AQ) and Affiliates. The FATF had been attending the G20 for a couple of years already, and the threats FATF was responsible for tackling, from terrorism to cryptocurrencies, were centre stage. This Ministerial Meeting provided the opportunity to recognize the enduring mission of the FATF and, after 25 years, to give it a permanent mandate and get ministers to meet more regularly, every two years, which would attract the resources it needed to have a greater impact.

VII. Conclusion

The initiatives analysed were all led by the Head of the FATF Secretariat and had to be achieved in addition to 'business-as-usual' directed by members. This demonstrated the potential of the Secretariat's leadership, which sits at the heart of any IO. Often, there is no process or structure to enable such initiatives. Developing and delivering them is a complex matter of influencing a large group of senior stakeholders, building an evidence base, and gradually building support from members and external stakeholders.

Other initiatives also played an essential part in helping the FATF evolve as an IO. These included attracting and developing voluntary contributions and using them to create sustainable new capacities, such as training and mentoring officials from non-member countries and a professional media and communications team to provide a better understanding of the FATF and its mission in the public eye. By attracting voluntary contributions, the Secretariat was able to undertake these initiatives and increase its staff and budget threefold in six years.

The pandemic also provided opportunities to strengthen the role, adaptability, and resilience of the Secretariat for the benefit of members, including the introduction of webinars to engage a much wider audience and for the production and distribution of FATF Secretariat staff papers (akin to IMF staff papers), which make more of the considerable knowledge and experience of staff. The Secretariat used these opportunities to produce some of the most impactful papers that have ever come out of the FATF, including on COVID-19-related Money Laundry and Terrorist Financing Risks and Policy Responses[21] and the State of Technical Compliance and Effectiveness of the FATF Standards.[22]

The success of these initiatives lies in getting the FATF as a body of members on board with these initiatives and ultimately agreeing to change things as a result. Member participation in, and their ownership of, IOs is vital, but effective leadership from strong independent Secretariats is also essential, which is often overlooked or undermined to the detriment of members' interests and the mission of the IO. Strong independent secretariats are the only way to ensure and enable truly member-led IOs that are not at the whim of any one personality, member country or group of countries. This is more important than ever as we witness growing threats to multilateralism. Only through robust initiatives, such as those discussed in this chapter, is it possible to build sustainable, democratic, and effective international solutions to common and pressing needs and threats.

[21] FATF, 'COVID-19-Related Money Laundering and Terrorist Financing Risks and Policy Responses' <https://www.fatf-gafi.org/en/publications/Fatfgeneral/Covid-19-ml-tf.html> accessed 18 July 2024.

[22] FATF, 'Report on the State of Effectiveness and Compliance with the FATF Standards' <https://www.fatf-gafi.org/en/publications/Fatfgeneral/Effectiveness-compliance-standards.html> accessed 18 July 2024.

16

UNESCO's Recommendation on the Ethics of Artificial Intelligence (2021)

A Case Study in Intergovernmental Leadership and Consensus Building

Gabriela Ramos

I. Introduction

The global digital transformation is one of the major challenges our societies are facing. The proliferation of artificial intelligence (AI) technology is already affecting every aspect of our lives, economies, and communities. With the advent of generative AI, the speed and breadth of this disruption have increased. AI's potential and promise to boost productivity and well-being are significant, but there are also well-known documented negative impacts and downside risks. Therefore, it is imperative to frame the development and deployment of AI technologies in an ethical manner to respect and promote human rights.

AI is a governance challenge that must be coordinated at the multilateral level, and the United Nations Educational, Scientific and Cultural Organization (UNESCO) has contributed to this effort through its unique mandate for ethics of science and technology. For UNESCO, AI is not a technological issue but a societal one. The Organization's delivery of the first-ever global standard on the ethics of AI and the impact it has achieved can be explained by a very effective combination of several factors: first and foremost, there was strong leadership at the top. Director-General Audrey Azoulay initialized the process by publicly placing the idea of a normative instrument and signalling this as a priority since her arrival at UNESCO.[1] Other important factors were strong analytical content ensured by a world-class group of international experts representing all the

[1] Audrey Azoulay, 'UN Chronicles: Towards an Ethics of Artificial Intelligence' <https://www.un.org/en/chronicle/article/towards-ethics-artificial-intelligence> accessed 8 August 2024. UNESCO's World Commission on the Ethics of Scientific Knowledge and Technology's Preliminary study on the Ethics of Artificial Intelligence, which kick-started the process and laid the foundation for the next steps: World Commission on the Ethics of Scientific Knowledge and Technology, 'Preliminary Study on the Ethics of Artificial Intelligence' (*unesci.org*, 2019) <https://unesdoc.unesco.org/ark:/48223/pf0000367823?posInSet=1&queryId=259b10f3-9d43-4c77-a764-911ae36e926a> accessed 8 August 2024.

Gabriela Ramos, *UNESCO's Recommendation on the Ethics of Artificial Intelligence (2021)* In: *International Organization Initiatives*. Edited by: Gabrielle Marceau and Henner Gött, Oxford University Press.
DOI: 10.1093/9780197803325.003.0017

regions, considerable member state engagement, and a capable secretariat managing the process and ensuring a positive outcome.

In November 2021, 193 countries reached the most comprehensive international consensus on AI by adopting the Recommendation on the Ethics of Artificial Intelligence (the 'Recommendation').[2] This unique global instrument has served as the compass for our work on AI around the world; we have engaged with governments to work in tandem on building the institutional and regulatory frameworks that countries need to deal with this technology. The Recommendation remains the only truly global instrument for AI governance at the time of writing. UNESCO is currently leading the way in turning this commitment into action, assisting countries with its implementation.

The rise of generative AI has validated UNESCO's stance. The long-held belief that regulation will stifle innovation was prevalent at the time of the adoption in November 2021. However, the mindset has shifted it to a more informed and complex one, helped by the subsequent launch of the AI safety summit by the United Kingdom in 2023 followed by the Republic of Korea, the United Nations Secretary General's Global Digital Compact, and the 2025 AI Action Summit in France. Indeed, the public debate has evolved, and stakeholders recognize that the discussion cannot only refer to regulations but to a wider set of policy instruments, including investments and incentives, to help countries be better prepared and benefit from AI, while controlling the downside risks. There is a growing recognition that policies, context, and institutional settings matter. With its practical content and processes, UNESCO's work on the ethics of AI is now seen as a major contributor to this narrative, advancing a set of tools that can address many of the core issues. The Recommendation thus constitutes a useful case study for possible success of intergovernmental initiatives and the importance of good substance, hard political work, and implementation tools to change the situation on the ground.

II. Overview of Events

Beginning in 2018, when UNESCO's World Commission on the Ethics of Scientific Knowledge and Technology started working on a report on the ethical issues of AI, the process of achieving consensus among all of UNESCO's 193 member states was a long and challenging one. A first draft of the Recommendation was prepared by the Ad Hoc Expert Group (AHEG), appointed by the Director-General in March 2020, with revisions based on

[2] UNESCO, 'Recommendation on the Ethics of Artificial Intelligence' (2021) <https://unesdoc.unesco.org/ark:/48223/pf0000381137> accessed 8 August 2024.

consultations conducted amongst regional stakeholders in the latter half of 2020, before being sent to member states in solicitation of their feedback.[3]

From 26 to 30 April 2021 (First Session) and 21 to 25 June 2021 (Second Session), an intergovernmental meeting of the Special Committee of Technical and Legal Experts nominated by the member states was convened by the Director-General in accordance with the Resolution of UNESCO's General Conference adopted at its 40th session (40 C/Resolution 37) and the decision of the Executive Board at its 210th session (210 EX/Decision 35).[4]

Intersessional Consultations (1–11 June 2021) were then held to advance the elaboration of the Recommendation by the 41st session of UNESCO's General Conference in November 2021, as per the Resolution of the General Conference adopted at its 40th session (40 C/Resolution 37).[5] At the conclusion of the sessions, a preliminary text of the Recommendation was finalized and ultimately adopted by consensus.

Of course, the Recommendation is owned by UNESCO's member states. But the Secretariat's role was indispensable in shaping the instrument, securing an able Chair with whom a strong and constructive working relationship could be established, and guiding the outcomes by engaging with capitals to explain the issues. Capable staff can push for more powerful outcomes.

III. Development Stage

A. AHEG Working Group

The Recommendation on the Ethics of Artificial Intelligence is a solid instrument. Its strength is derived from the fact that the text was developed by 24 high-level independent experts who were proposed by member states and appointed by the Director-General. Crucially, these experts came with multidisciplinary expertise and from different regions, cultures, and traditions.

Before joining UNESCO, I spent quite some time among economists at the Organisation for Economic Co-operation and Development (OECD). The difference at UNESCO is that having experts from various and diverse disciplines allowed for a broader scope of the discussion and a greater focus on the human content. The AHEG, which was chaired by Emma Ruttkamp-Bloem from South

[3] UNESCO, 'Final Report by the Rapporteur of the Intergovernmental Meeting Related to a Draft Recommendation on the Ethics of Artificial Intelligence (26–30 April 2021 and 21–25 June 2021)' (25 June 2021) SHS/IGM-AIETHICS/2021/JUN/INF.5 8 <https://unesdoc.unesco.org/ark:/48223/pf0000377572> accessed 8 August 2024.

[4] UNESCO (n 3) 1.

[5] ibid.

Africa, was ambitious, knowledgeable, and keenly focused on protecting and promoting human rights. The text was drafted over six weeks and incorporated the feedback, comments, observations, and proposals we received from 48 member states and 2 observers throughout January and February 2021.[6]

When I took up my functions as UNESCO's Assistant Director-General in charge of the Social and Human Sciences Sector in July 2020, ensuring the elaboration and adoption of the Recommendation became one of the major priorities not only of the Sector but of UNESCO itself, with strong support from the Director-General. The draft document had already been drafted, and it was as solid as it could get, with the alignment of the ethical framework with the enhancement and promotion of human rights and human dignity, with fair, inclusive, and sustainable outcomes. It also included principles of transparency, accountability, privacy, and the rule of law, as well as policy chapters focused on the application of AI (such as education, labour, health, well-being, and the environment).

However, I noticed the absence of a focus on equality of boys and girls, and men and women, and insisted on including a chapter. With the support of the Chair and one of the members, we introduced this missing element. I also insisted on having comprehensive implementation commitments embedded in the text and asked the Chief of the Bioethics Section, Dafna Feinholz, to work with the experts to design an implementation mechanism. The following discussions delivered the Readiness Assessment Methodology (RAM),[7] a tool that supports member states in evaluating their governance capacities and developing tailored policy recommendations for ethical AI governance. My previous experience as Chief of Staff and Sherpa at the OECD taught me that effective implementation and impact of global standards can only be attained if monitoring and follow-up are integrated from the outset.

The draft text contained 4 values, 10 principles, and 11 policy areas. It incorporated very strong commitments, such as banning social scoring, mass surveillance, and granting legal personality to AI developments. It also prohibited abuses of cognitive biases and manipulation derived from human–computer interaction and related to convergent technologies such as neurotechnology. It calls for transparency and liability frameworks, and an outcome-based approach. This turned the conversation from a purely technical one to a societal one. Therefore, by design, the draft was intended to operate in simultaneity: (1) creating a comprehensive, human rights-centred ethical framework applicable to the entire AI lifecycle that would be translated into member states' legal

[6] ibid.

[7] UNESCO, 'Readiness Assessment Methodology: A Tool of the Recommendation on the Ethics of Artificial Intelligence: UNESCO Digital Library' (2023) <https://unesdoc.unesco.org/ark:/48223/pf0000385198> accessed 8 August 2024.

frameworks (2) with practical applications accommodating the context-specific needs and concerns of member states.[8]

B. Intersessional consultations (1–11 June 2021)

Approximately 300 participants represented 102 member states and the 2 then non-member states (The Holy See and the United States of America). The vast majority of member states were very supportive of the draft text during the first session, recognizing that UNESCO had the right mandate and scope to lead this work.

At the negotiation phase, identifying an effective Chair who would help deliver the outcome, who was also ready to interact with the Secretariat (and change the mindset of mistrust that sometimes prevails in the UN institutions), and who could give room to my interventions as Assistant Director-General was critical. We encouraged Ambassador Adam Almulla, the Permanent Delegate of Kuwait, to consider the role. His appointment, approved by our member states, was an excellent outcome; the Chair was respected and trusted by the rest of the delegations.

One strategy employed by the Chairperson and the Secretariat was the proposal of a methodology that served to structure and focus discussions. Amendments were only allowed if they (1) were of high importance for the countries, (2) focused on the substance of the Recommendation, (3) preserved the effectiveness of this non-binding instrument, and (4) avoided issues that were already debated or that might be addressed elsewhere in the text, as well as issues regarding specific language, style, or other details that are not related to the substance of the instrument.[9] By suggesting this methodology, which was then proposed by the Chair, we introduced a conducive framework and thus managed to steer the further work in a productive direction.

These criteria were largely agreed upon by the member states and were used in the subsequent consultations. To pragmatically tighten the timeline and ensure progress after a slow first few days, the Secretariat played a robust balancing and conciliatory role, thus acting in proportion to the urgency of the addressed issues.

The first day of the intersessional consultations proved difficult despite the Chair's positive working methodology. Several member states submitted amendments that slowed the advancement of the text down considerably. On the second day, however, the discussion of the issue of non-discrimination

[8] UNESCO (n 3) 2.
[9] ibid.

between boys and girls, and men and women, saw some countries make concessions in order to achieve a consensus. A similar vein of accelerating advancement occurred on the third day in relation to privacy and data protection. On day 4, a number of member states started to respond to attempts to water down the Recommendation from other member states; at the same time, previously member states with core positions began to be less disruptive through discussions made with other parties at the Consultation, something that was followed on day 5.

Perhaps the most significant breakthrough occurred on day 6, when the Recommendation's primary tools were adopted. The Secretariat was proactive; we kept permanent contact, through our mobile phones, with a large group of members from different regions that wanted to ensure a strong outcome from the negotiations. Before the negotiation sessions, we connected with member states and shared our concerns about amendments intended to weaken the text. The discussions were staged effectively, and the fact that there was a large group of countries at different levels of development pushing for a strong outcome helped. However, for difficult delegates, we spent time negotiating and establishing a relationship of trust. We also established contact at a high level in their capitals to avoid being caught in local dynamics with little room to change. This was particularly important for one member state that was being particularly negative regarding the chapter on implementation. I actually reached out to their Ministers and Sherpa to open the room for convergence.

In the final days, UNESCO continued to stay on the right track, with an absolute majority of states supporting a largely retained text. Member states were particularly on task in withdrawing their amendments following discussions or even proactively.

In addition to a committed Chair and an engaged Secretariat, there were two additional elements. The first was to change the mindset that assumed the need for unanimity in decision-making. Even though the rule is 'consensus', this had, over the years, evolved to a search for 'unanimity'. This meant spending long hours trying to convince the extremes. The other mindset that was not in line with the written rules is the role of the Chair. The gentlemen's understanding among ambassadors is that the Chair is a 'facilitator'. Again, this meant lengthy discussions to give room to all voices, no matter the level of support for certain positions.

Our strategy here was to promote consensus and to abide by the rules that established that the Chairs would manage proceedings to reach an outcome. The Chair is, therefore, not a witness but an actor with a clear role to foster consensus. New to UNESCO, I informed myself about the rules and regulations (which confirmed consensus and the clear leadership of the Chair) and made them available to the Chair.

The negotiations were also conducted in the context of the COVID-19 pandemic, which considerably complicated matters, moving the debate out of the conference room and onto a Zoom call. Envisaging the complications, I reached out to Pascal Saint-Amans, the then director of the OECD's Centre for Tax Policy and Administration and my former colleague. Pascal had been conducting the OECD Base Erosion Profit-Sharing (BEPS) negotiations, securing a global taxation agreement despite the shift to a virtual format, and his advice was very valuable.

In the end, lockdowns were a blessing in this regard. Starting with the Austrian delegate, the online chat function was actively used by member states that wanted to push for more impactful language and who were systematically opposed to amendments that would weaken the instrument. Every time there was an attempt to water down the Recommendation, a group of countries would raise objections in the chat and a cascade would follow, allowing the Chair to quickly reject the proposed changes.

A very close and trusting relationship between the Chair, myself, and the team was instrumental, too. We listened to each other, and although the Chair was ultimately in charge of the process, he trusted us and followed our advice often. He also changed the prevalent practice at UNESCO, which casts the Secretariat aside. On the contrary, he gave ample room for my participation, which many member states appreciated, and helped maintain a high level of ambition.

C. Second phase of the Category II Meeting on the Recommendation on the Ethics of AI (21–25 June 2021)

Two member states challenged the Chair's working method in the Second Phase of the Category II Meeting on the Recommendation. They asked to reopen many of the paragraphs that had already been discussed in the intersessional consultations, reasserting their previously proposed amendments and asking for additional ones. Other member states roundly rejected this push, though the two insisted that their objections be bracketed and addressed at a later stage, notably references to religious traditions, deleting references to the precedence of human rights, and adding references to boys and men whenever girls and women were referenced.

Given that the Chair's working methodology was challenged at the outset, and that the same two member states repeatedly emphasized the non-binding nature of previous discussions, the fact that compromises were found on each of the amendments, including bracketed issues, over the next few days should not be understated. In particular, the Chairperson of the AHEG Bureau was asked to assuage member states' concerns about the relationship between ethics and law, notably, that ethics would not replace law in any way; a compromise was reached through the proactive intervention of the Secretariat to say that ethical values and principles can help develop and implement policy measures.

On the fifth and final day of the Second Phase, the Recommendation was approved by all member states after significant redrafting—a significant outcome given the two member states' pushbacks on days 1–2 of the Second Phase. Ultimately, one member state's withdrawal of their proposals and the other's additional note were the result of the member states' strong responses and the negotiating power of the Chair and the Secretariat.

IV. Key Takeaways

Important lessons can be distilled from the process of achieving such a strong text of the Recommendation with unanimous support. Chief among them is the fact that international leadership must be strong, even non-neutral, in particular instances. The Secretariat had to, and did, assert values that necessarily have political content. A prima facie neutral stance on an issue like equality of boys and girls, and men and women, for instance, would revert to not speaking on circumstances of tremendous inequality and would thus be non-neutral in itself. Worse, it would have stripped the Recommendation of its meaning altogether and defeated the point of formulating such a normative instrument at a global forum like UNESCO's. After all, UNESCO, like every UN organization, is committed to protecting and promoting the universality of human rights. These principles are not up for debate, and the Secretariat must defend them accordingly. I see this as our role.

Second, harnessing strong support from member states is crucial to building consensus. Giving space to certain member states to strongly disagree with amendments allowed for the Secretariat to gain momentum and leverage for the preclusion of said amendments where they would have watered down the Recommendation. Building rapport with member states and keeping a finger on the pulse of discussions was a strength of the Chair and the Secretariat that allowed advancement on the issues rather than remaining stuck at an impasse arising from endless debate and disagreement. Here it paid off that the Chair was ready to interact and cooperate with the Secretariat.

Third, a deep knowledge of the issues and negotiation of appropriate compromise in non-essential areas was as important as keeping a handle on issues of absolute importance. Take a paragraph from the environment and ecosystems policy chapter, for instance, where the disagreements expressed by five members in the intersessional consultations led to the deletion of a sentence but retention of the precautionary principle against environmental degradation. An international organization cannot be seen to operate in the interests of only a particular selection of countries. It must work as far as is practicable to accommodate the interests of all its member states.

The intersessional consultations offer a prime opportunity to observe these three strengths of the UNESCO Secretariat in action. The format of the Working Group, as decided by the Director-General, was instrumental in influencing how proceedings developed: decision-making capacity lay with the plenary, and member states were always in control.[10] At the First Session, less formal settings were used to facilitate the process of accommodating extensive deliberations amongst different member states in consensus building on issues of sensitive content. A triumph for the robust role of the Secretariat was the sensing among countries that the language and the substance of the Recommendation had to be strong and undiluted in order not to be emptied of meaning altogether.

Consider, *arguendo,* the classification of rights. Some countries were more willing than others to apply the terminology to freedoms (at minimum) apropos of privacy, data protection, access to information, and being informed on algorithmic processing. Two countries reflected in the report that should the right to privacy be explicitly termed as such, it would have been preferred to have the right formulated per the Universal Declaration of Human Rights. To achieve consensus, the rights terminology was removed in relation to being made aware that a decision was made by an AI system, and also in relation to a proposed right to information.

Similarly, while some member states were in favour of fleshing out guidance to countries on data protection frameworks that would lean towards a higher degree of detail, others wanted a higher degree of flexibility for countries to formulate their own data protection frameworks. To achieve consensus, international law, data protection principles, and standards were referenced, and certain examples were removed (though it should be noted that important core aspects such as informed consent for data processing and safeguards were retained). This flexibility to safeguard core issues was a vital propulsive force in discussions. Issues were further raised by two member states, and the response from the Secretariat in marshalling support nonetheless is instructive. A brief and non-exhaustive adumbration of the substantive issues raised is as follows: there was opposition to the use of the terminology of evaluation, but this was assuaged by the UNESCO Secretariat clarifying that they would assist member states in implementation but not rank them through minor adjustments in the text to harmonize with other Recommendations. One member state raised their concern on leaving out the term 'minority languages', arguing that it would risk language minorities being less able to access education on the ethics of AI. On the proposal to develop a

[10] UNESCO (n 3) 5.

global readiness methodology (the 'RAM' as mentioned earlier), designed to assess where countries are in their capacities to implement the Recommendation, one country opposed the term 'global', as it seemed to imply that all countries should abide by it. It suggested to replace 'global' with 'UNESCO' and in this sense, the support for the follow-up was clearly assigned to the Secretariat.

V. Implementing the Recommendation

Since the Recommendation was adopted, UNESCO has moved fast based on the mandate we received in the text, ensuring that the Recommendation did not become an act of lip service. Immediately after the adoption of the normative instrument, we convened an open and informal group of supportive 'early adopter' member states in early 2022 (the group was eventually renamed the Group of Friends). Efforts were made to represent every part of the world, and UNESCO used its vast network of Field Offices to undertake an inclusive, democratized regional approach through roundtables and conferences.

Once more, we focused on mobilizing financial and in-kind support to implement the Recommendation. The governments of Japan, Canada, and Quebec, the European Commission, the Patrick J. McGovern Foundation, and the Development Bank of Latin America supported the implementation work. Not wasting any time, we convened a group of top experts to develop the Readiness Assessment Methodology and the Ethical Impact Assessment.[11] We partnered with the likes of the Alan Turing Institute and the Thomson Reuters Foundation and delivered a strong tool, which not only measures access, infrastructure, or skills but also the societal, cultural, and institutional context. After its elaboration, we also launched a programme to implement it. Today, we are overseeing 70 Readiness Assessment Methodology exercises being conducted all around the world.

As AI is a fast-developing technology, we ensured the right modalities for mutual learning and registering of best practices. UNESCO established the Global Forum on the Ethics of Artificial Intelligence,[12] where countries can exchange with top experts, civil society, and the business sector. The second edition of the Global Forum was held in Slovenia in February 2024, which counted the participation of 67 member states. We launched the network of AI Experts without Borders, the Women4Ethical AI platform, and the Observatory on the Ethical

[11] UNESCO, 'Ethical Impact Assessment: A Tool of the Recommendation on the Ethics of Artificial Intelligence' (2023) <https://unesdoc.unesco.org/ark:/48223/pf0000386276> accessed 8 August 2024.

[12] UNESCO, 'Global Forum on the Ethics of AI 2024' <https://www.unesco.org/en/forum-ethics-ai> accessed 8 August 2024.

Governance of AI. All this infrastructure supports countries in advancing the effective implementation of the Recommendation.

There have also been regional platforms for implementation, both in Latin America, with the support of the governments of Chile and Uruguay, and in Africa, with the UNESCO Southern Africa sub-Regional Forum on Artificial Intelligence, in Namibia.[13] In Latin America, a Regional Council was launched with the support of the Latin American Development Bank (CAF). In April 2024, UNESCO's Director-General launched the Chilean Readiness Assessment Methodology.[14] The launch was accompanied by the Minister of Science's announcement of a proposed legislative bill on AI governance that was sent to the Senate. The Minister recognized that the bill was enriched by UNESCO's Readiness Assessment Methodology tool. This is impact on the ground.

In March 2024, the United Nations General Assembly adopted a landmark resolution on AI which included significant reference to not only the Recommendation but also the two tools and UNESCO's Global Forum.[15]

The G7 and G20 digital tracks are also being strongly interwoven, with the Brazilian G20 Presidency and Italian G7 Presidency featuring at the 2024 Global Forum, and the Hiroshima Process coming under UNESCO's ambit. Leading in these spaces helps to make the Recommendation count, amplifying the reach and significance of existent attention to implementation. UNESCO's leading role was highlighted again in consultations on the Interim Report of the Secretary-General's AI Advisory Body, wherein the importance of our work was advocated for by member states. The work that lies ahead remains ever-expanding, but the Recommendation as a foundation for all future work on the ground is insuperable in reach, representation, and force.

VI. Conclusion

The Recommendation was never intended to be a rubber stamp containing more normative content than praxis. Political leadership at the level of diplomatic engagement, negotiation, and resolution was key to reaching a consensus among 193 countries with differing interests. For that consensus to then become something operationalizable is another ball game altogether. It is not just about the participation and cooperation of member states, though it is integral.

[13] UNESCO, 'Southern Africa Sub-Regional Forum on Artificial Intelligence, 7–9 September 2022' <https://sarfai2022.org/#/home> accessed 8 August 2024.

[14] 'Chile: Artificial Intelligence Readiness Assessment Report: UNESCO Digital Library' (2023) <https://unesdoc.unesco.org/ark:/48223/pf0000387216> accessed 8 August 2024.

[15] UNGA 'Seizing the Opportunities of Safe, Secure and Trustworthy Artificial Intelligence Systems for Sustainable Development' UN Doc A/78/L.49 (2024) <https://digitallibrary.un.org/record/4040897?v=pdf&ln=en> accessed 12 September 2024.

For an intergovernmental referent to be achieved and then actually adopted, implemented, and used by member states is often a mammoth task.

Member states own the Recommendation. But a strong push from a unifying body of leadership is crucial: at UNESCO, in achieving the production of the Recommendation, that which lies at the heart of all the work that UNESCO does, a strong Secretariat was absolutely critical to leading with a human rights-centred approach in a changing world. UNESCO's unique mandate to develop and implement ethical frameworks for science and technology has never been more critical. Tracing the intergovernmental process of formulating, passing, and implementing the Recommendation exemplifies UNESCO's leadership in this field and provides a strong roadmap for future use of our mandate and for other organizations to follow in this vein.

17

Is Too Much Vision a Handicap for an Executive Head? Some Thoughts on W Jenks' Curtailed Mandate as ILO Director-General

Francis Maupain

I. Introduction

While the biography of Clarence Wilfred Jenks begs to be written, the contributions he made to the development of the International Labour Organization's (ILO) constitutional development and practice, first as Legal Adviser and then as Principal Deputy Director-General, are abundantly documented. The most significant illustrations of these contributions are his roles in drafting the Declaration of Philadelphia and establishing a procedure for universal protection and promotion of freedom of association based on ILO constitutional principles.

Jenks' election as ILO Director-General could have been the crowning glory of this exceptional career and contributions.

However, this is not what happened. This chapter focuses on two key initiatives Jenks took as the ILO Director-General at the beginning and at the end of his short and uncompleted mandate: the appointment of a Soviet Assistant Director-General and a due process plea made to the International Labour Conference. While Jenks took both initiatives with the deep conviction that they were in the long-term interest of the ILO, they had very negative and even (as far as the second is concerned) fatal consequences for their author.

This is in sharp contrast to the impressive long-term impact of Jenks' previous legacy as a member of ILO Secretariat. His legacy, particularly as regards freedom of association, strikingly manifested itself just a few years after his untimely death with the Solidarność saga.

It therefore seemed of direct relevance to the object of the present exercise to review these episodes and to reflect on the reason for and lessons—if any—to be drawn from such a contrasting record of initiatives taken as a Director-General and contributions as a member of the Secretariat. Further, it serves as a reminder

Francis Maupain, *Is Too Much Vision a Handicap for an Executive Head? Some Thoughts on W Jenks' Curtailed Mandate as ILO Director-General* In: *International Organization Initiatives.* Edited by: Gabrielle Marceau and Henner Gött, Oxford University Press. © Oxford University Press 2025. DOI: 10.1093/9780197803325.003.0018

that initiatives taken in international organizations, while necessary, also involve an element of risk-taking.

II. Clarence Wilfred Jenks: A Brief Background

When he was elected as ILO Director-General, Jenks was a man of two parallel careers, both of which were sufficient to earn him global fame. In one role, he made an immense and visionary contribution to international law by paving the way for the elaboration of space law. From that point of view, the rumour regarding his likely election to the International Court of Justice that circulated in 1973 seemed entirely plausible. In addition to space law, he made history as an ILO official in the most difficult circumstances. Among many contributions as Legal Adviser, he played a decisive role in ILO's move to Montreal when the Second World War broke out.[1] With Edward Phelan, he co-authored the Declaration of Philadelphia in a unique drafting exercise in which the tripartite constituents played little part.[2] Further, he served as the key artisan behind the ILO's separation from the defunct League of Nations and its establishment as the first Specialized Agency of the new United Nations (UN) system.

Indeed, Jenks had reached the highest possible status as an international civil servant. As pointed out by Morgenstern,[3] Jenks was an essential contributor to the law and ethics of international civil service within the UN in general, as well as to the establishment of an extraordinary *esprit de corps* in the ILO, at least among staff lawyers.[4] Interestingly, his first decision when he assumed Office as ILO Director-General in July 1970 was to change his signature from Clarence W Jenks to Wilfred Jenks, as if he wanted to open a completely new chapter in his professional existence. But it did not prove easy to take leave of his old legal self. The question this chapter addresses is the extent to which the difficulties he encountered as Director-General had anything to do with his vision of the role of law in the march towards the 'organized government of mankind'.

Robert Ago, the eminent Italian lawyer and one of his closest friends, indirectly voiced the concern that his extraordinary accomplishments as an international lawyer could become a handicap as a Director-General. As a member of

[1] Antony Evelyn Alcock, *History of the International Labour Organisation* (Palgrave Macmillan 1971) 159–60.

[2] Jean Michael Bonvin, '*L'Organisation international du travail*' (Presses Universitaires de France 1998) 56–60. Bonvin goes as far as to compare the way this text was drafted to Rawls' methodological fiction of the 'veil of ignorance' behind which the principles of justice could be established.

[3] Felice Morgenstern, 'Wilfred Jenks in the ILO' (1975) 46 British Yearbook of International Law xvii.

[4] This fed the legend to which Cox also contributed of the great divide between lawyers and economists within the Office.

the ILO Governing Body (GB), Ago had campaigned for Jenks' election against that of Francis Blanchard, despite French pressure on Italy. As soon as the result was known, Ago is reported to have said '*Maintenant, il va falloir protéger notre ami contre lui-même*'. (Now, we must protect our friend against himself.)

Robert Cox, a well-known theoretician of international relations, expressed this idea more crudely in two articles. Coincidentally, the first of these 'ILO: Limited Monarchy' was published in 1973,[5] the year of Jenks' death; and the second, 'Labor and Hegemony', was published in *International Organization* in 1977,[6] the year when the US notice of withdrawal from ILO membership became effective.

In these two contributions, Cox highlighted the extraordinary complexity of the ILO Director-General's task of reconciling the divergent and changing interests of the ILO's tripartite constituents to produce relevant and dynamic programmes. During the Cold War, this difficulty was exacerbated by the rapid expansion of the ILO's membership and the rivalries between the three groups. The complex task required self-restraint to maintain the fragile balance between the divergent claims of his different 'clients'. In Cox's view, this balance had been superbly kept during David Morse's tenure, although precariously, thanks to the exceptional complementarity between his diplomatic skills and the mastery of the legal and administrative complexities of his principal deputy, Jenks. While not explicit, Cox's articles suggest that this delicate balance was lost when Jenks was left alone in the driving seat[7] due to both personality factors and the functionalist approach that permeated his vision of law and its role in the march towards world government.[8]

According to Cox, Jenks considered that the ILO's 'historical mission' had less to do with its limited role as custodian of the 'branch of universal law that regulates labour conditions' than with the realization of 'ideals which are fundamental, universal and eternal' through the development of fundamental human rights.[9]

Notwithstanding Cox's affectation of 'scientific' objectivity, his analysis was tainted by a personal grudge: his confrontation with Jenks on the degree of autonomy the Institute could enjoy in its research activities and publications led

[5] Robert W Cox, 'ILO: Limited Monarchy' in Robert W Cox and others (eds), *The Anatomy of Influence: Decision Making in International Organization* (Yale UP 1973) 345–48.

[6] Robert W Cox, 'Labour and Hegemony' (1977) 31(3) International Organization 385–424.

[7] For instance, he warns at the end of his first article against the consequences of 'bad judgment' from the Director-General that could lead to the disintegration of the very delicate balance which had been established in the system.

[8] John Mainwaring, '*The International Labour Organization: A Canadian View*' (Canadian Government Publishing Centre 1986) 102–03.

[9] Cox, 'ILO: Limited Monarchy' (n 5) 121–22.

to Cox's resignation from his last post at ILO as Director of the International Institute for Labour Studies in 1972.[10]

With the benefit of some half-century of hindsight, it is interesting and revealing to revisit the final years of Jenks' tenure. Jenks had to face a crisis as soon as he took up the Office of Director-General with two decisions that were made and justified on legal grounds (and for one of them with specific reference to due process). Within both decisions, there were elements of tragedy.

The half-century decades of sea change—which have affected the international system since these tragic events—tell us about the 'immanent force' of legal principles and, more specifically, freedom of association to which Jenks rightly gave central importance in his vision of the ILO's 'historical mission'.

III. The ILO Director-General, Collateral Victim of His Commitment to the Rule of Law?

In this section, let us briefly recall the two 'fatal' legal decisions taken by Jenks, that respectively opened and tragically closed his three-year mandate as Director-General.

A. The Astapenko appointment

Almost immediately after his assumption of Office as Director-General, Jenks had to face a major crisis with the United States of America (USA) as a result of the initiative he took within the framework of his recognized prerogatives, and in accordance with established procedure, to appoint a high-ranking official of the former Union of Soviet Socialist Republics (USSR), a decision that had been in the pipeline long before his election.

Indeed, in his 1973 *Anatomy of Influence*, Cox goes as far as to suggest that Jenks' predecessor, Morse, had stepped down from office precisely because he realized the growing US' distrust towards the ILO. Cox suggests that US' distrust, on account, inter alia, of its alleged 'softness on communism' would prevent two essential moves Morse had in mind to renovate and adapt the ILO to its new environment. One of which was that it would make it impossible to appoint Pavel Astapenko, a citizen of the USSR, to a high-ranking job, which he was under strong pressure to do from the Eastern Bloc.

[10] The Institute had been established at Morse's initiative some years earlier inter alia to create some space for research that would be free from the constraints to which regular programmes were subject.

The exact reasons why Jenks decided to go ahead with this appointment immediately upon his assumption of office remains speculative. It is likely that in his mind (as in Morse's),[11] this decision was not only inevitable but also legitimate, if not overdue, from the viewpoint and logic of ILO universality.

In addition, as Cox recognized in 'Labor and Hegemony', 'this appointment was a "nonsense issue" from a practical viewpoint since the post to which Astapenko was appointed was one of "well paid supernumerary" without real influence on policy decisions'.[12]

However, in a context where the Director-General largely owed his election to active US support (the USSR had supported his French rival Blanchard), the somewhat casual way[13] in which the US Government was informed of the decision was taken by them as a breach of faith and—even more so—by the American Federation of Labor and Congress of Industrial Organizations (AFL-CIO) which had actively been involved in the campaign for his election. Under pressure from the first president of AFL-CIO, William George Meany, the US Congress ultimately decided to suspend the US contribution that represented a quarter of the ILO budget.

The sad paradox of the situation is that while the decision had to do with Jenks' profound commitment to ILO universality, it led to a most severe setback to ILO universality from a practical and symbolic point of view after his tragic death: the withdrawal of the USA. There are reasons to believe, as discussed below, that it was in a desperate bid to stop this imminent US exit that Jenks' took the unprecedented initiative of intervening at the International Labour Conference (ILC) in 1973 to question the legal validity of an ILC draft resolution condemning Israel.

B. The 'fatal' 1973 ILC crisis: Due process, a matter of life and death?

It is intriguing that in 'Labor and Hegemony',[14] Cox makes only a passing reference to the fact that 'Jenks broke under the mounting pressure' in 1973 without mentioning the tragic circumstances which led to it. The circumstances began at the end of its 58th session (1973) when the ILC Plenary had before it for final adoption a draft resolution prepared by the Resolutions Committee concerning

[11] Mainwaring (n 8). Mainwaring, who is a reliable witness of that period, also notes that 'Morse realized the claim of the second largest ILO member country . . . could not be resisted indefinitely'.

[12] Cox, 'Labor and Hegemony' (n 6) 401.

[13] Morse is reported to have told Jenks: 'Wilfred, you did the right thing the wrong way'. For a fairly detailed account of the circumstances, see the PhD thesis of Grégory Théodore Kruglak, *The Politics of United States: Decision-Making in United Nations Specialized Agencies: The Case of the International Labor Organization* (University Press of America 1980) 149–65.

[14] Cox, 'Labor and Hegemony' (n 6) 414–15.

'the policy of Discrimination, Racism and Violations of Trade Union Freedoms practiced by the Israeli Authorities in Palestine and the Occupied Territories'.

The proposed resolution invited the Conference to not only 'condemn' the policy in question but also to request the GB 'to set up a committee to investigate on the spot (*ex post!*) Israel's persistent violations of trade union freedoms and its discriminatory practices against Arab workers'. However, the day before considering this resolution, the Plenary was called upon, under its pre-established agenda, to listen to the Director-General's traditional 'reply' to the Conference deliberations.

This reply is usually a routine exercise. Jenks, however, chose to address the substantive and very delicate due process issue involved in the text head-on. He pointed out that the draft raised some 'special questions' from the viewpoint of the ILO's tradition of due process that he felt his 'impartial duty' led him to raise. He then went as far as to 'implore the Conference to think many, many times before it abandons this tradition [of due process]'. He emphasized in particular that the ILC was not a Tribunal and that 'for the Conference first to condemn and then to call for an inquiry the terms of reference of which would be to confirm such condemnation, would be to offend the principle of due process on which all our work relating to the implementation of conventions rests'.[15]

It is difficult to assess the exact impact this due process plea had on the delegates at the ILC.[16] Whether or not as a result of the Director-General's 'imploration', the resolution failed to be adopted for lack of a quorum. However, immediately after the failure to reach a quorum, the Director-General had to face long hours of chaotic proceedings, with successive waves of virulent personal attacks from Arab countries, supported by the G-77 and socialist countries of Eastern Europe.[17] There are reasons to believe[18] that the Director-General never recovered from these chaotic sittings and personal attacks which he had to face in forced silence and with tight jaws. He suffered a heart attack a few weeks later in Rome and passed away on 9 October 1973, the very day that he was considered to be sufficiently fit to fly back to Geneva.

[15] International Labour Conference (58th Session) Record of Proceedings (Geneva 1973) 707.

[16] The workers and a number of governments did point out that there were specific procedures to establish the extent to which Israel as a party to Convention No. 111 was indeed violating its obligation of non-discrimination in the occupied territories. The question is in fact more complex to the extent that the violation was not taking place within Israel's boundaries but in the occupied territories. On the one hand, the occupying power has a duty to respect national legislation in force, but on the other hand, doubts existed at the time as to whether it could be made accountable for a violation of its own obligations under a ratified Convention outside its recognized territory without in some way legitimizing the occupation.

[17] The gist of these attacks was that as Chief Executive, he had overstepped his constitutional mandate.

[18] As Roberto Ago himself did on 13 November 1973 when he took the floor on behalf of the whole Government group on the occasion of the tribute paid to Jenks by the GB following his death.

The difficult but inescapable question is whether he intervened on this issue in full awareness of the bitter outcome his remarks were likely to provoke. In his personal memoirs, Nicolas Valticos, one of Jenks' closest and most respected collaborators and friends, reported that when he routinely received the draft of the Director-General's reply from Jenks' secretary, he rushed to Jenks' office to try and persuade him to omit or change his comments on the resolution. He pointed out that the adoption of a resolution by the ILC was a political matter, and it was not for the Secretary-General of the ILC (ie the ILO Director-General) to tell delegates what they had to do. Jenks replied that he felt a duty to intervene to safeguard the rule of law and the future of the ILO. He insisted that, in any case, his mandate would soon be coming to a close and that his real concern was to leave to the younger generations a strong organization for the future.

On the face of it, Jenks' decision looks almost like a textbook illustration of the opposition between the ethics of conviction and the ethics of responsibility. There are, however, reasons to believe that his intervention was not moved by the concern for due process alone, but at least as much by an equally respectable attempt to shift the course of ILO-US relations from its separation course.

Indeed, there were reasons for Jenks to believe that the withdrawal of the US' financial contribution to the ILO budget was only the first step towards their withdrawal from the ILO altogether. In his memoirs, Francis Blanchard rightly recalls that the Swiss local press had already explicitly discussed in June 1971.[19]

It seems plausible that this prospect may have inspired Jenks to send signals that the ILO was a unique and irreplaceable bastion of pluralism and due process in the UN and that it was committed to promoting development through institution-building, the rule of law, the autonomy of social actors, and the development of a middle class as an alternative to, and natural barrier against, class struggle. This was reflected in the choice of leaders he invited to address the ILC.[20]

Valticos' memoirs hint that the Director-General had received encouragement from the USA to take the stand he took. In the middle of the chaos that followed the non-adoption of the draft resolution, the US Government delegate, Mr Persons, 'speaking on behalf of a government which had its differences of opinion with the Director-General', took the floor to say with 'more feeling and conviction than many other Government representatives that his stand in his speech of yesterday concerning the necessity to uphold constitutional processes

[19] Francis Blanchard, *L'Organisation Internationale Du Travail: De La Guerre Froide à Un Nouvel Ordre Mondial* (Seuil 2004) 92–94.

[20] Including President Bourguiba of Tunisia a few days before his intervention, and the year before the much more controversial Shah of Iran.

in this Organisation should be commended and supported' and to 'thank him for those statements'.[21]

Whether this stand could have changed the shifting course of US-ILO relations remains a matter of speculation because Jenks passed away three months later.[22] It is part of the implacable logic of this tragedy that this desperate move, like his untimely death, may have contributed to precipitating the very fate that he was trying to spare the ILO, that is, the withdrawal of the USA.

In 1974, a resolution very similar to the 1973 draft was adopted.[23] It invited the GB and the Director-General to use all the means at their disposal inter alia 'to put an immediate end to these violations and discriminatory practices'.[24] This text and its adoption met with inter alia the vehement objections of the AFL-CIO representative, Bert Seidman, who invoked Jenks' memory and explicitly warned 'the implications of these events are very serious for the future of the ILO'.[25] The contrast between Jenks' unprecedented intervention in 1973 and the prudent attitude adopted by his successor, Francis Blanchard, who in 1974 safely chose to deliver his reply to the Conference discussions after the resolution had already been adopted, had not escaped the attention of ILO critiques in the AFL-CIO and in Zionist circles close to it. For many of them, the time had come to inflict on the ILO the terminal punishment it deserved. This feeling was exacerbated when, the following year, the PLO was granted an observer status at the ILC.[26] The punishment came very shortly after that in November 1975 with Henry Kissinger's letter giving notice of the US' withdrawal from the ILO on three main grounds: the erosion of tripartism, double standards in the discharge of its supervisory duties, and politicization, all of which were reflected, in varying degrees, in the 1974 resolution. As we will now consider, the US' prompt return as early as 1980 may be regarded as a stunning tribute to the 'immanent force of freedom of association' to which Jenks contributed more than anyone else.

[21] International Labour Conference (59th Session, Geneva, 1994), *Record of Proceedings* (ILO 1975) 757.

[22] The same applies to the question of how, had he survived, he could have rebuilt bridges with the Arab world. It is noteworthy that the Government delegate of Egypt (where Jenks had made a State visit not so long before) Mr Salama was fairly moderate in his criticism and went as far as (initially) 'not challenging his impartiality or his integrity': ibid 732.

[23] International Labour Conference (59th Session) Record of Proceedings (Geneva 1975) 808.

[24] ibid.

[25] ibid 417.

[26] Kruglak (n 13) 223–26.

IV. The 'Immanent Force' of Freedom of Association as Jenks' Posthumous Vindication and Enduring Legacy

As we have seen, Jenks' unprecedented procedural intervention can be interpreted as a desperate move to safeguard ILO universality against the catastrophic consequences of a possible US withdrawal. From this point of view, he certainly acted in line with the ILO Director-General's specific role, which is recognized under the tradition established by Albert Thomas, ILO's first Director-General.

While Jenks' move was a fairly predictable failure, the prompt return of the USA in 1980 came as a posthumous vindication for his career-long contribution in promoting 'the immanent force' of freedom of association. This immanent force may become of particular relevance again in the emerging new world order. One of the reasons that explains the US' return to the ILO is the key role ILO's complaint procedure was starting to play in connection with the recognition and protection of Solidarność as an independent union rather than as a transmission belt for the Polish Communist party.

More than anyone else, Jenks, as ILO Legal Adviser and subsequently as Principal Deputy Director-General, contributed to establishing the importance and special status of freedom of association. He was, in particular, the main 'inventor' of the universal freedom of association procedure that, as it developed, met with such hostility by the Soviet bloc that Morse was ready to sacrifice it in 1957.[27]

Given this historical context, one might wonder if the universal promotion of freedom of association may not again turn out to be one of the few universally relevant and efficient tools; tools that are available to maintain at least partially the universality of the multilateral system against the risk of its further fragmentation into hostile socio/ideological/economic blocs.

V. Conclusion

As far back as 1964, EB Haas warned against the illusions of a 'unilinear pluralist path' towards the continued expansion of human rights as the necessary way to some sort of world government.[28] This strikingly lucid remark was partly aimed at Jenks and what Haas considered his flamboyant functionalist rhetoric. In today's divided context around values, it may be, on the contrary, read as an

[27] Wilfred Jenks, *The International Protection of Trade Union Freedom* (Stevens & Sons 1957) 196. Jenks also played a key role in the establishment of the McNair fact-finding Committee.

[28] Ernst B Haas, *Beyond the Nation State: Functionalism and International Organization* (ECPR Press 2008).

(involuntary) tribute to Jenks' enduring legacy. The relevance of freedom of association and its promotion is all the more significant now, in different respects and degrees, in the context of two competing hegemons as regards their far-from-exemplary law and practice.[29] They are the two most pro-eminent countries that have not ratified the relevant conventions (no. 87 and 98). Further, despite the claim by the present US administration that it is 'the most pro-workers' in decades, US business continues to fiercely fight workers' attempts to organize, as illustrated recently with Amazon.[30]

This state of affairs would seem to present a positive opportunity for the Director-General and the International Labour Office to emulate the remarkable precedent established in no less difficult circumstances, in the middle of the 'real' Cold War. The Director-General (then David Morse) and Jenks managed to obtain on the same day in 1955 the acceptance of both the USA and the USSR to have an objective assessment of the situation of fact carried in both countries by the independent Committee led by Judge McNair.[31]

This precedent brings us back in conclusion to the specific roles of the ILO Secretariat and Executive Head. These roles seem to be both more necessary and more difficult than ever at a time when their capacity to propose bold actions appears to be kept under closer scrutiny, if not curtailed, by constituents. It requires an unusual combination of negotiating skills that Morse possessed more than anyone, the analytical and practical capacity to build institutional bridges towards the future, and the true sense of purpose that was the mark of Jenks.

[29] Clifford B Donn and Minghua Zhao, 'Freedom of Association: A Comparison of China and US Approaches to International Labour Organization Standards' in Jill Jensen and Nelson Lichtenstein (eds), *The ILO from Geneva to the Pacific Rim: West Meets East* (Palgrave Macmillan 2016) 251–76.

[30] Michael Sainato, '"War of Attrition": Why Union Victories for US Workers at Amazon Have Stalled' *The Guardian* (8 April 2023) <https://www.theguardian.com/technology/2023/apr/08/long-fight-organize-us-workers-amazon> accessed 4 September 2024.

[31] Jean de Givry, *Droits de l'homme, Travail et Syndicats: L'action de l'Organisation Internationale Du Travail Dans Le Domaine de La Liberté Syndicale et Des Relations Professionnelles de 1944 à 1985* (Editions universitaires 1989) 83–91. Such a move would be made easier in present circumstances by the provisions of the 1998 Declaration and its follow-up (including the system of annual reviews for countries that have not ratified).

18

Taking Initiatives in the WTO

The Role of an Executive Head in Steering Change

*Akshaya Venkataraman**

I. Introduction

Since 1995, the Directors-General of the World Trade Organization (WTO) have, as heads of the WTO Secretariat, played a significant role in shaping the work of the organization. Every so often, Directors-General have responded to the needs of WTO's membership by undertaking initiatives.[1] Although these initiatives were previously unfamiliar to the WTO at the time of their undertaking, they have influenced how the organization adapts to a changing world. This chapter provides examples of a few such initiatives, highlighting what considerations allowed them to come into fruition, how the Directors-General drove them forward, and what became of these initiatives after their implementation.

Section II of this chapter provides an overview of three considerations that inform the ability of the WTO Director-General, and the Secretariat, to undertake initiatives. Bearing these considerations in mind, Sections III and IV provide illustrations of initiatives by the Director-General, all of which can be tied to the overarching mandate of the WTO. The chapter places the initiatives in two broad categories. The initiatives discussed in Section III are linked directly to the functions, powers, and duties explicitly identified in the Marrakesh Agreement, while the initiatives in Section IV are not.

* The author thanks Chibole Wakoli for shaping the draft and providing indispensable insights into the initiatives.

[1] Defined in the Preface as:

> (1) an IO action taken that is novel, or previously unfamiliar to the IO in question, aimed at meeting the needs of the IO or its membership and (2) which are actions of IO secretariats and/or their heads that push the boundaries of the mandate of an organization, beyond its founding operational activities (without constituting an 'ultra vires' act), in responding to new needs of their members.

Akshaya Venkataraman, *Taking Initiatives in the WTO* In: *International Organization Initiatives*.
Edited by: Gabrielle Marceau and Henner Gött, Oxford University Press.
DOI: 10.1093/9780197803325.003.0019

II. Considerations That Inform the Ability of the WTO Director-General to Undertake Initiatives

The WTO's mandate, its 'member-driven' ethos, and the absence of prescribed powers and duties for the WTO Director-General influence the Director-General's capacity to undertake initiatives. This section provides an overview of each of these factors.

First, the Director-General and the Secretariat have a responsibility to help ensure that the WTO functions properly, that its role is well understood by the international community, and that it delivers on its mandate.[2] The mandate of the WTO is to provide the common institutional framework for the conduct of trade relations among its members.[3] In delivering on its mandate, the WTO performs several key functions,[4] including providing fora for negotiations and dispute settlement; administering the trade policy review mechanism; and facilitating the implementation, administration, and operation of the WTO Agreements. The examples in this chapter illustrate that several of the initiatives undertaken by the Director-General, while novel, are linked directly to the functions, powers, and duties explicitly identified in the Marrakesh Agreement, whereas others are not.

Second, while the term 'member-driven organization' does not appear anywhere in the WTO Agreements, there is no debate that the WTO, like the General Agreement on Tariffs and Trade (GATT) before it, is a 'member-driven organization'. This term has no official definition but has been understood to imply that decision-making at the WTO, including the processes leading to the decision, is the sole preserve of WTO members. Indeed, some members are of the view that in a member-driven organization, the Secretariat's role 'must be solely one of support, not of initiative'.[5] This view may have limited the scope of activities that could be undertaken by the Director-General and the Secretariat.[6] That said, the initiatives highlighted in this chapter demonstrate that there remains room for the Director-General, aided by the Secretariat, to innovate solutions to novel problems affecting the WTO and its membership. In this regard, the 'member-driven' nature of the WTO has meant that the successful initiatives undertaken by the Director-General have subsequently received the tacit or express approval of the WTO membership.

[2] Peter Sutherland and others, 'The Future of the WTO: Addressing Institutional Challenges in the New Millennium' (Report by the Consultative Board to the Director-General Supachai Panitchpakdi, WTO 2004) 73 <https://www.wto.org/english/thewto_e/10anniv_e/future_wto_e.pdf> accessed 2 August 2023.

[3] Marrakesh Agreement Establishing the World Trade Organization (adopted 15 April 1994, entered into force 1 January 1995) 1867 UNTS 154 (Marrakesh Agreement) art II:1.

[4] Marrakesh Agreement (n 3) art III.

[5] Sutherland and others (n 2) 73.

[6] ibid 69, 73.

Third, Article VI:2 of the Marrakesh Agreement requires the Ministerial Conference to not only appoint the Director-General but also 'adopt regulations setting out the powers, duties, conditions of service, and term of office of the Director-General'.[7] One may argue that in order to categorize an action as an 'initiative', there should be clarity on what the Director-General's prescribed powers and duties are. Nevertheless, while the procedures for the appointment of the Director-General and terms of office are in place,[8] the WTO has yet to prescribe expressly all the powers and duties of the Director-General. Some scholars posit that the lack of an express job description for the Director-General makes the office over-dependent on the prevailing and often transient political mood of members rather than on the long-term interests of the WTO.[9] However, one may also view the absence of an express list of powers and duties as less of a limitation and more of an enhanced opportunity for the Director-General to undertake initiatives in the interests of the WTO and its membership.

Bearing these considerations in mind, Sections III and IV offer illustrations of the WTO Director-General's initiatives, all of which can be tied to the overarching mandate of the WTO and were a response to the evolving needs of the WTO and its membership. The initiatives discussed in Section III can be directly linked to a function, power, or duty explicitly identified in the Marrakesh Agreement. Initiatives in Section III were very often the result of the ambition of a Director-General to transform such existing function, power, or duty in the Marrakesh Agreement to accommodate the circumstances of the time. Initiatives in Section IV are not rooted in or borne out of transformation of functions, duties, or powers of the Director-General identified in the Marrakesh Agreement. They propel the overarching mandate of the WTO to evolve in new directions. The line between these two categories of initiatives is hazy. Some initiatives do not fall cleanly within any one category. For instance, COVID-19 was the first-time a public health crisis was the primary driver for new initiatives: much of the work on COVID-19 was carried out, both, through transformation of existing WTO operations (such as new forms of collaboration with other IOs) and entirely new functions (such as collaboration with private sector vaccine manufacturers).

[7] Such requirements can also be found in the constitutive documents of other organizations such as: IBRD, 'Articles of Association' (27 June 2012) <https://www.worldbank.org/en/about/articles-of-agreement/ibrd-articles-of-agreement> accessed 04 September 2024 (art V: s 3H, s 5). The language of the Marrakesh Agreement, nevertheless, remains interesting given that it leaves open-ended not just the terms of service contracts or remuneration for the executive head (as in the case of IBRD) but also the fundamental 'powers' and 'duties' of the Director-General. This vacuum, as noted above, is both a limitation and an opportunity.

[8] WTO General Council, 'Procedures for the Appointment of Directors-General' (10 December 2002) WT/L/509 <https://docs.wto.org/dol2fe/Pages/SS/directdoc.aspx?filename=Q:/WT/L/509.pdf&Open=True> accessed 4 September 2024.

[9] Sutherland and others (n 2) 74.

Nevertheless, the two categories, set out in Sections III and IV, may provide a useful lens through which one perceives the initiatives of the Director-General.

III. Initiatives Linked Directly to Functions, Powers, and Duties Explicitly Identified in the WTO Agreements

Though the Ministerial Conference has not prescribed expressly the powers and duties of the Director-General, certain duties and responsibilities undertaken by the Director-General can be tied to specific provisions of the WTO Agreements. These include the Director-General's role as the head of the WTO Secretariat,[10] facilitator of negotiations at the WTO,[11] administrator of certain dispute settlement functions,[12] and the focal point for WTO cooperation with the International Monetary Fund (IMF), the World Bank Group, other international organizations (IOs)[13], and non-governmental organizations (NGOs).[14] As discussed below, some of these roles have evolved at the initiative of the Director-General, beyond what is expressly prescribed in the WTO Agreements. This section highlights the Director-General's transformation of the trade monitoring and reporting functions to improve the quality and breadth of trade-related information reported (Subsection A), the enhanced involvement of Directors-General in mediation proceedings (Subsection B), and the innovations aimed at enhancing the WTO's engagement with NGOs and civil society beyond what is expressly prescribed in the WTO Agreements (Subsection C).

[10] Marrakesh Agreement (n 3) arts VI:1, VI:3, VII:1, XIV:3.

[11] ibid art III:2.

[12] Understanding on Rules and Procedures Governing the Settlement of Disputes (15 April 1994) LT/UR/A-2/DS/U/1 (DSU) see arts 5.6, 8.7, 17.9, 21.3(c), 22.6, and 24. See also WTO, 'Establishment of the Appellate Body: Recommendations by the Preparatory Committee for the WTO Approved by the Dispute Settlement Body' (10 February 1995) WT/DSB/1 5; Rules of Conduct for the DSU (11 December 1996) WT/DSB/RC/1, arts VI:4(c), VIII:11.

[13] Marrakesh Agreement (n 3) art III:5. For example, on behalf of the WTO, the Director-General signed cooperation agreements with the IMF and the World Bank Group. See also WTO, 'Minutes of the General Council Meeting' (17 August 1995) WT/GC/M/5 7; WTO Agreements with the International Monetary Fund and the World Bank (18 November 1996) WT/L/194 WT/L/195.

[14] Marrakesh Agreement (n 3) art V. For example, at the General Council meeting of 15 November 1995, the Director-General informed the General Council that the WTO and the United Nations had concluded an arrangement on 29 September 1995 in the form of an exchange of letters between the UN Secretary-General and the Director-General. This was in line with the mandate given to the Secretariat on 3 April 1995. WTO, 'Minutes of the General Council Meeting' (15 November 1995) WT/GC/M/8 18. The texts of the arrangement were circulated to members in document WT/GC/W/10.

A. Trade monitoring and reporting

The objective of the WTO's Trade Policy Review Mechanism (TPRM) 'is to contribute to improved adherence by all members to rules, disciplines and commitments' made under the WTO Agreements.[15] In order to achieve this objective, the Trade Policy Review Body is required to, inter alia, undertake an annual overview of developments in the international trading environment, which are having an impact on the multilateral trading system. This overview is to be assisted by an annual report by the Director-General 'setting out major activities of the WTO and highlighting significant policy issues affecting the trading system'.[16] Between 1995 and 2005, this report, officially titled 'Overview of Developments in International Trade and the Trading System: Annual Report by the Director-General', covered general trends in world trade and provided an overview of WTO activities.[17] However, respective Directors-General transformed the content of this report after 2005, reflecting novel actions taken to meet the evolving needs of the membership, some of which were precipitated by an unforeseen global crisis.

In 2003, Director-General Supachai Panitchpakdi rolled out the first WTO World Trade Report. This annual publication, although not expressly mandated in the WTO Agreements, is intended to contribute to the public debate on trade policy and the multilateral trading system.[18] The World Trade Report had a substantial overlap of information with the TPRM Annual Report by the Director-General.[19] This, together with the fact that the TPRM Annual Report did not draw conclusions on key trends in trade policy-making, caused a discontinuation of the latter between 2006 and 2008.[20]

During the financial crisis in 2008, Director-General Pascal Lamy set up a Task Force on the Financial Crisis within the WTO Secretariat. The Task Force prepared reports on trade-related developments associated with the financial crisis.[21] The initial intention of the Director-General was for the work of the Task

[15] WTO, 'Trade Policy Review Mechanism as Amended by the General Council' (26 July 2017) <https://www.wto.org/english/docs_e/legal_e/29-tprm_e.htm#:~:text=%28i%29%20The%20purpose%20of%20the%20Trade%20Policy%20Review,of%2C%20the%20trade%20policies%20and%20practices%20of%20Members> accessed 23 June 2024 (TPRM).

[16] TPRM (n 15) para G.

[17] WTO, 'Overview of Developments in International Trade and the Trading System: Annual Report by the Director-General' (1 December 1995) WT/TPR/OV/1 <https://docs.wto.org/dol2fe/Pages/SS/directdoc.aspx?filename=Q:/WT/TPR/OV1.pdf&Open=True> accessed 4 September 2024.

[18] WTO, 'New WTO Report Focuses on Questions of Development' (PRESS/348, *WTO* 14 August 2003), <https://www.wto.org/english/news_e/pres03_e/pr348_e.htm≥ accessed 1 September 2024.

[19] Peter Pedersen and others, 'WTO Trade Monitoring Ten Years on Lessons Learned and Challenges Ahead' (15 May 2018) Staff Working Paper ERSD-2018-07 4.

[20] ibid.

[21] Gabrielle Marceau, 'IGOs in Crisis? Or New Opportunities to Demonstrate Responsibility?' (2011) 8 International Organizations Law Review 1, 9.

Force to be internal. However, at a meeting of the heads of delegations (HoDs) and subsequently at a General Council meeting, the Director-General's work received support from WTO members. The Director-General was encouraged to report, in writing, to the WTO membership on the work of the Secretariat Task Force.[22] This led to the resumption of the TPRM's Annual Report by the Director-General[23] in 2009, albeit in an entirely different format and titled 'Overview of Developments in the International Trading Environment: Annual Report by the Director-General'. The 2009 report focused on the trade-related consequences of the global financial crisis.[24] Since 2009, these more comprehensive TPRM Annual Reports by the Director-General have been published annually. The reports not only set out the major activities of the WTO and highlight the significant policy issues affecting the trading system, but they also provide details on the implementation of the WTO Agreements and suggestions on the way ahead for certain issues.[25] The TPRM is considered one of the 'main channels used by the WTO to promote accountability, predictability and transparency' in the multilateral trading system.[26] The Annual Reports of the Director-General are considered a core pillar of this system as they 'strengthen the transparency objective' of the TPRM.[27]

B. Enhanced role in mediation

The WTO's Understanding on Rules and Procedures Governing the Settlement of Disputes (DSU) grants the Director-General the authority to act as a mediator in disputes between members. Specifically, Article 5.6 of the DSU states that 'the Director-General may, acting in an *ex officio* capacity, offer . . . mediation with a view to assisting Members to settle a dispute'. To facilitate his role under Article 5, Director-General Mike Moore proposed procedures to the membership, which made it clear that '[r]equests under Article 5 may only be made after commencement of a formal dispute'.[28] However, on one occasion, the Director-General, at the request of parties, went beyond the express scope articulated in Article 5.6 of

22 Pedersen and others (n 19).

23 TPRM (n 15) para G.

24 WTO, 'Overview of Developments in the International Trading Environment' (18 November 2009) WT/TPR/OV/12 <https://docs.wto.org/dol2fe/Pages/SS/directdoc.aspx?filename=Q:/WT/TPR/OV12-00.pdf&Open=True> accessed 4 September 2024.

25 ibid.

26 WTO, '30 Years of the Trade Policy Review Mechanism' <https://www.wto.org/english/tratop_e/tpr_e/tprm30_e.htm> accessed 1 September 2024.

27 ibid.

28 WTO, 'Article 5 of the WTO Dispute Settlement Understanding: Communication from the Director-General' (17 July 2001) WT/DSB/25 (Article 5 Communication).

the DSU and Article 5 procedures proposed by Director-General Mike Moore, albeit in the same spirit of assisting members to settle their disagreement.

On 4 September 2002, the Philippines, Thailand, and the European Communities (EC) jointly requested mediation by the Director-General, or someone appointed by him. The purpose of the requested mediation was to examine the extent to which the legitimate interests of the Philippines and Thailand were being unduly impaired by the EC's implementation of the preferential tariff treatment for canned tuna originating in the African, Caribbean, and Pacific group of states (ACP). Of significance is that the requesting members did not consider the matter at issue to constitute a 'dispute' within the meaning of Article 5.6 of the DSU.[29] Nevertheless, the requesting members agreed that the mediator could be guided by procedures similar to those envisaged for mediation under Article 5 of the DSU.[30] The Director-General accepted this request and appointed his Deputy Director-General to serve as the mediator.[31] The matter was eventually resolved through this mediation process, the results of which were kept confidential.[32] This situation therefore required the Director-General to offer mediation for a matter that did not fall strictly within the scope of Article 5 of the DSU. In exercising their duties under the DSU, WTO Directors-General have traditionally confined themselves to the tasks prescribed expressly in the DSU. To operate within the interpretative confines of the DSU is also an expectation placed on the members of the WTO.[33] It was, therefore, a strategic innovation on the part of the Director-General to find a solution within the DSU while accommodating the members' hesitance in considering this matter as a dispute.

C. Collaboration with NGOs

Article V:2 of the Marrakesh Agreement permits the General Council to make appropriate arrangements for consultation and cooperation with NGOs concerned with matters related to those of the WTO. The Director-General, as head of the WTO Secretariat, facilitates this consultation and cooperation. In some instances, the Director-General has initiated the contact and cooperation with NGOs.

[29] WTO, 'Request for Mediation by the Philippines, Thailand, and the European Communities: Communication by the Director-General' (16 October 2002) WT/GC/66 (Request for Mediation).

[30] Article 5 Communication (n 28).

[31] Request for Mediation (n 29).

[32] WTO, 'Request for Mediation by the Philippines, Thailand, and the European Communities: Joint Communication' (1 August 2003) WT/GC/71.

[33] DSU (n 12) art 23(1).

Perhaps the most prominent example of the Director-General's initiatives with respect to cooperation with NGOs is the WTO Public Forum. The Public Forum is an annual outreach event during which interested non-governmental stakeholders from around the world meet at the WTO and interact with the Secretariat and the WTO membership. The stakeholders include NGOs, academia, business, other IOs, and the media. The aim of the Public Forum is to discuss 'the latest developments in global trade and to propose ways of enhancing the multilateral trading system'.[34] The Public Forum was originally conceived of in 2001 by Director-General Mike Moore as a 'Public Symposium on Issues Confronting the World Trade System'.[35] The Director-General explained that the Symposium was intended to increase the WTO's transparency, public accountability, and involvement with political and civil society,[36] following the backlash against globalization at the turn of the millennium.[37] Despite pushing for greater involvement of non-governmental stakeholders, the Director-General was careful to emphasize that 'there is a fundamental difference between transparency and participation on the one hand and negotiations on the other—which in the end only Governments can do'.[38]

The new Public Symposium was both novel and controversial. Some members were of the view that the idea of the WTO hosting public symposia pushed the boundaries of the mandate of the WTO beyond its founding operational activities.[39] Several members at the time considered that 'it is not the job of the WTO to embrace NGOs and civil society'. Instead, these members were of the view that engagement with these stakeholders 'should be done at the national level in the formation of national policy positions'.[40] Despite this initial opposition, the Symposium was held successfully[41] and eventually gained the support of WTO members. Its successor, the Public Forum, is considered one of the WTO's flagship events.[42]

[34] WTO, 'Public Forum' <https://www.wto.org/english/forums_e/public_forum_e/public_forum_e.htm> accessed 29 August 2023.

[35] ibid.

[36] Mike Moore, 'Open Societies, Freedom, Development and Trade: Director-General Mike Moore's Speech at the Plenary Opening WTO Symposium on Issues Confronting the World Trading System' (*WTO*, 6 July 2001) <https://www.wto.org/ENGLISH/news_e/spmm_e/spmm67_e.htm> accessed 29 August 2023.

[37] A notable manifestation of the backlash were the protests at the WTO Ministerial Conference held in Seattle in 1999.

[38] Moore (n 36).

[39] ibid.

[40] ibid.

[41] While some WTO members were against the Public Symposium, the following members sponsored its launch: Canada, European Commission, Japan, the Netherlands, Norway, Sweden, Switzerland, the United Kingdom, and the United States. See Moore (n 36).

[42] The Public Forum attracts over 2,000 representatives each year from civil society, academia, business, government, IOs, and the media. See WTO (n 34).

IV. Initiatives Not Linked Directly to Functions, Powers, and Duties Explicitly Identified in the WTO Agreements

This section looks at novel initiatives undertaken by respective Directors-General in response to the COVID-19 crisis (Subsection A) and vis-à-vis development-related activities of the WTO (Subsection B).

A. Initiatives in response to the COVID-19 crisis

In March 2020, Director-General Roberto Azevêdo invited all WTO members to submit information to the Secretariat and notify trade and trade-related measures introduced in response to the COVID-19 pandemic.[43] The Director-General also set up a task force of experts from within the Secretariat to monitor the impact of COVID-19 on trade flows and the overall global economy.[44] On 25 June 2020, in tacit approval of the Director-General's initiatives, the Cairns Group (a group of members) called on the Secretariat to continue its monitoring of COVID-19 trade-related measures.[45]

Director-General Ngozi Okonjo-Iweala led the WTO's cooperation with other IOs to offer a comprehensive approach to dealing with the COVID-19 pandemic. For example, at a meeting on 15 June 2021, the Director-General, on behalf of the WTO, partnered with the Directors-General of the World Health Organization (WHO) and the World Intellectual Property Organization (WIPO) to launch a trilateral collaboration framework. The three organizations committed to working closely together to help overcome the COVID-19 pandemic and its devastating human, social, and economic impacts. This collaboration included the joint launch, with the WHO and the WIPO, of the Trilateral COVID-19 Technical Assistance Platform on 11 April 2022.[46] As discussed in

[43] WTO News, 'DG Azevêdo Requests WTO Members to Share Information on Trade Measures Related to COVID-19' (25 March 2020) <https://www.wto.org/english/news_e/news20_e/dgra_24mar20_e.htm≥ accessed 30 June 2023. As of 21 March 2023, WTO members had submitted a total of 538 notifications related to COVID-19. WTO, 'WTO Members' Notifications on COVID-19' <https://www.wto.org/english/tratop_e/covid19_e/notifications_e.htm≥ accessed 20 August 2023.

[44] WTO News (n 43).

[45] The Cairns Group members, on whose behalf the communication was sent, are Argentina, Australia, Brazil, Canada, Chile, Costa Rica, Indonesia, Malaysia, New Zealand, Paraguay, Peru, and Uruguay.

[46] WIPO, 'WHO, WIPO, and WTO Launch Trilateral COVID-19 Technical Assistance Platform' (*WIPO*, 11 April 2022) <https://www.wipo.int/policy/en/news/global_health/2022/news_0003.html#:~:text=WTO%20Director%2DGeneral%20Okonjo%2DIweala,access%20to%20COVID%2D19%20vaccines%2C≥ accessed 20 August 2023. In addition, on 14 July 2023, WTO, WIPO, and WHO launched the second update of the publication titled 'Integrated Health, Trade and IP Approach to Respond to the COVID-19 Pandemic'; WTO, 'WTO, WHO, and WIPO, An Integrated Health, Trade and IP Approach to Respond to the COVID-19 Pandemic' (Second update, May

Section III, Article V of the Marrakesh Agreement provides very generally for cooperation with IOs. However, the Director-General's actions leading to the launch of the trilateral collaboration framework with WHO and WIPO fall within this book's definition of an initiative in two ways. First, the unprecedented close nature of the cooperation among the three IOs was aimed at meeting the unforeseen public health needs of the WTO membership occasioned by the COVID-19 crisis. Second, in responding to the new COVID-related needs of WTO members, the trilateral collaboration's focus on 'public health' as the key driver and priority, as opposed to trade, pushed the boundaries of the mandate of the WTO beyond its founding operational activities which are trade-centred.[47]

B. WTO Chairs Programme

In the preamble to the Marrakesh Agreement, WTO members recognize 'that there is need for positive efforts designed to ensure that developing countries, and especially the least developed among them, secure a share in the growth of international trade commensurate with the needs of their economic development'. However, the WTO Agreements do not include binding obligations detailing what the 'positive efforts' should be. That said, since its inception, the WTO has continued the GATT tradition of offering training, technical cooperation, and other development-related activities. These activities are aimed at building human and institutional capacity in developing and least-developed economies 'so that they can benefit to the maximum from their trading opportunities'.[48] Many of these activities are member-driven but some, such as the WTO Chairs programme, have resulted from initiatives by the Director-General.

Director-General Pascal Lamy launched the WTO Chairs Programme to foster research, training, and outreach activities of relevance to governmental policymakers and other stakeholders at universities in developing countries and least developed countries. Academic institutions that are awarded 'WTO Chairs' receive support in the areas of research, curriculum development, and outreach activities. The chair-holders are selected through a competitive process. Fourteen institutions were originally selected as WTO Chairs for a four-year term in 2009. Seven institutions were added to the Programme in May 2014. In

2023) <https://www.wto.org/english/res_e/booksp_e/who_wipo_wto_2023_e.pdf> accessed 4 September 2024.

[47] For more details, see Gabrielle Marceau and Mishael Wambua, 'The (New) Role of the WTO in Vaccine Distribution and Equity' (2022) 45 Houston Journal of International Law 1, 1.

[48] WTO, 'The State of World Trade, Trade Policy and the WTO' (28 November 1996) WT/TPR/OV/2, 6.

December 2021, following the selection process for Phase 3 of the Programme, 17 more institutions were chosen to join the network of WTO Chairs, with 5 more expected to join in 2025.[49]

V. Conclusion

The Director-General, as head of the WTO Secretariat, plays a significant role in shaping the work of the organization. The Director-General's role is circumscribed by the mandate of the WTO, the 'member-driven' nature of the organization, and the functions, powers, and duties that can be discerned from the WTO Agreements. Despite these limits, respective Directors-General of the WTO have displayed creativity and innovation in undertaking initiatives. The positive impact of initiatives by the Directors-General has been especially evident in moments of crises, such as during the financial crisis and the COVID-19 pandemic. While some of the initiatives are linked directly to the functions, powers, and duties explicitly identified in the Marrakesh Agreement, others are not. Despite this distinction, ultimately, all the examples in this chapter of Director-General initiatives can be tied to the overarching mandate of the WTO and were motivated by a desire to respond to the evolving needs of the WTO and its membership.

[49] WTO, 'Chairs Programme' <https://wtochairs.org/about-us> accessed on 20 August 2023.

19

The International Energy Agency at 50

The Astounding Environmental Shift from an Organization Focused on Fossil Energy Supply to a Clean Energy Authority

André-Philippe Ouellet

I. Introduction

Among international organizations (IOs), technical organizations remain in the shadows and are relatively unknown to the public, including international lawyers. Despite this relative anonymity, technical organizations such as the International Energy Agency (IEA) have been providing cash value to their members, with highs and lows, for a few decades. The IEA now counts 31 members, which are all Organisation for Economic Co-operation and Development (OECD) members. The situation is changing, however, as IEA ministers agreed to initiate India's accession process, despite India not being an OECD member, and seem keen to include developing countries in the future.[1]

The IEA's work has historically been crucial, given the importance of energy input for industrialized countries. The organization was born in 1974, in the direct aftermath of an oil shock following the 1973 Yom Kippur War. As per its constituent instrument, the *Agreement on an International Energy Programme* (IEP), the IEA's main mission is to 'promote secure oil supplies on reasonable and equitable terms' between members while reducing the dependence on 'imported oil', including by conserving energy, developing alternative energy sources, and enriching uranium.[2] Although the IEA was set up within the OECD's greater framework, it is an autonomous agency.

[1] IEA, 'IEA to Start Membership Talks with India in Major Step Forward for Global Energy Governance' <https://www.iea.org/news/iea-to-start-membership-talks-with-india-in-major-step-forward-for-global-energy-governance> accessed 22 May 2024. In addition, developing countries such as Indonesia are also seeking OECD membership. Although the IEA is avant-garde about including non-developed members, the broader OECD membership is following a similar path.

[2] Agreement on an International Energy Program (adopted 18 November 1974, entered into force 19 January 1976) 1040 UNTS 271, Preambular paras 1 and 6 (IEA's Agreement).

André-Philippe Ouellet, *The International Energy Agency at 50* In: *International Organization Initiatives.* Edited by: Gabrielle Marceau and Henner Gött, Oxford University Press.
DOI: 10.1093/9780197803325.003.0020

During the 1990s, the global energy context changed as oil production diversified and risks of oil embargoes decreased significantly.[3] From the early 2000s, the IEA started diversifying its activities and adopted a much more active posture on the environment and renewable energy. It, nevertheless, continued to maintain its traditional role of monitoring energy supplies and ensuring members kept sufficient oil reserves.

The IEA turned 50 in 2024. Following this anniversary, this chapter aims to tell the story of its transformation from an oil and gas *obsédé* to an environmental paragon. This transformation was progressive and owed much to the initiatives taken by its successive Executive Directors, that is, IEA's heads. This transformation accelerated in 2015 with the appointment of Dr Fatih Birol as Executive Director.

In a way, the IEA had no choice but to evolve as the energy market's volatility significantly decreased while members began to be preoccupied with climate change.[4] The IEA's progressive shift towards renewable energy and the environment was thus strategic.[5]

Section II of this chapter outlines the context of the IEA's creation, architecture, aims, and action. Section III then fleshes out the environmental initiatives and incremental shift towards renewable energy. Section IV analyses the current IEA situation, the acceleration of environmental initiatives since the mid-2010s. Finally, Section V discusses the challenges ahead for the IEA.

II. Understanding the IEA: Constituent Instrument and Early Days

In 1973, following the Yom Kippur War, or the fourth Arab–Israeli War, oil prices quadrupled worldwide as many Arab countries imposed an embargo on oil exports to many Western countries, in particular the United States.[6] In reaction, 17 OECD members decided to establish the IEA to predict energy crises, prepare for scarcity scenarios, and ensure they would dispose of data to act swiftly in case of need.[7]

[3] Thijs Van de Graaf and Dries Lesage, 'The International Energy Agency After 35 Years: Reform Needs and Institutional Adaptability' (2009) 4 The Review of International Organizations 293, 294.

[4] Henry Kissinger, 'The Future Role of the IEA', Speech on the Occasion of the 2009 Meeting of the IEA's Governing Board at the Ministerial Level, Paris (14 October 2009) <https://www.henryakissinger.com/speeches/the-future-role-of-the-iea/> accessed 4 September 2024; Thijs Van de Graaf, 'Obsolete or Resurgent? The International Energy Agency in a Changing Global Landscape' (2012) 48 Energy Policy 233, 234.

[5] Van de Graaf and Lesage (n 3) 313–15. Another element was the 'cartel powers' of the Organization of the Petroleum Exporting Countries, which started to unilaterally set price targets at the end of the 1960s.

[6] Richard Scott, *The International Energy Agency: Beyond the First 20 Years, Origins and Structure*, vol I (International Energy Agency 1994) 19, 28, and 32.

[7] ibid 32, 33.

As noted above, the IEA's constituent instrument, the IEP, results from a common desire of its members to 'secure oil supplies on reasonable and equitable terms'. The vast majority of provisions in the IEA's constituent instrument relate to oil production, management, and sharing in times of crisis, for example, by constituting national reserves supposed to last at least 90 days and sharing the oil between members.[8] The allocation mechanism has seldom been activated, that is, in 1991, 2005, 2011, and 2022 following the Gulf War, Katrina Hurricane, Libya's 2011 crisis, and the war of aggression waged by Russia against Ukraine, respectively.[9]

Beyond oil management, which was a short-term imperative in 1974, members agreed on a 'long-term co-operation on energy' (Chapter VII), which aimed to foster energy research and development in domestic oil production, coal, hydroelectricity, gas, nuclear, solar, and other energies (eg waste, hydrogen, etc), without specific sustainability implications.

To understand how remote environmental considerations were within the IEA at first, one has to know that in 1979, Ulf Lantzke, IEA's first Executive Director, proposed in the *Foreign Affairs* magazine to triple coal production to face lower Organization of the Petroleum Exporting Countries oil production. At the time, Lantzke's coal bet was based on the facts that IEA members already had the 'tools at hand to achieve such expansion' and that '[c]oal is widely available; the technology for coal production, transport, use and conversion into synthetics is known and is constantly improving'.[10]

Therefore, although renewable energies are mentioned in passing in the IEP, the focus was not put on renewable energies for the sake of them being renewable. The fundamental aim of the IEA, as per its constituent instrument, is to secure energy regardless of environmental considerations—the word 'renewable' appears nowhere, and the word 'environment' appears only once[11]—which is likely attributable to the fact that the IEP was drafted in a context of crisis. Yet, the idea of developing alternative energy left the door open for the organization to expand the scope of its activities beyond oil.

Still, IOs' constituent instruments, including the IEP, do not suffice to explain their current actions, as IOs' operations and functioning are often far off from

[8] IEA's Agreement (n 2), see 'Self-Sufficiency' (Chapter I), 'Demand Restraint' (Chapter II), 'Allocation' (Chapter III), 'Information System' (Chapter V), 'Consultation with Oil Companies' (Chapter VI), and 'Emergency Reserves' (Annex).

[9] IEA, 'History' <https://www.iea.org/about/history> accessed 22 May 2024.

[10] Ulf Lantzke, 'Expanding World Use of Coal' <https://www.foreignaffairs.com/articles/1979-12-01/expanding-world-use-coal> accessed 31 July 2021.

[11] IEA's Agreement (n 2); Article 42 mentions the development of 'criteria, quality objectives and standards for environmental protection', yet such considerations are ancillary as being part of a subprovision on 'alternative sources of energy'.

what appears in their founding documents.[12] The next section thus explores developments that fashioned the current IEA.

III. Incremental Initiatives Towards an Environment Shift

As seen above, under Executive Director Lantzke during the 1980s, the IEA was still an organization centred around oil and replacement energies without a specific interest in renewables. Regardless, the IEA's environmental action—as well as development in general—was shaped by its successive Executive Directors despite their functions not being explicitly spelled out in the IEP.[13] Within the IEA, the Executive Director plays an important role as he or she is 'directly and personally involved [. . .] in developing energy policy initiatives'.[14] In the case of the IEA, according to Richard Scott, the IEA's first General Counsel, the Executive Directors' initiatives 'have encompassed most of the major developments in the Agency over the years', including concerning energy and the environment.[15]

The IEA had to wait for Helga Steeg to become Executive Director in 1984 for more environmental considerations to be factored in by the organization. In 1985, the IEA published its first 'recommendation on energy and the environment' to advance 'both energy and environmental policy', and in 1989, IEA ministers adopted a 'Pledge on the Environment' noting for the first time the threat posed by global warming.[16] However, there was still no paradigm change as the IEA still emphasized the importance of increasing 'indigenous fuel production' in 1987.[17] In 1992, Steeg noted that among factors shaping the energy market, there was a 'growing focus on the relationship between energy and environmental policies'.[18] She thus initiated an ad hoc industry group on energy and environment.[19]

During the 1990s, according to Craig Bamberger, a former IEA's General Counsel, members eventually tasked the Secretariat with 'finding long-term

[12] Nicola Bonucci and others, 'IGO's Initiatives as a Response to Crises and Unforeseen Needs' (2022) 20 International Organizations Law Review 1, 431–32.

[13] Scott (n 6) 255. According to Scott, the Executive Directors' functions are to provide 'leadership and direction on energy policy' and include 'political as well as operational and administrative responsibilities'.

[14] ibid 256.

[15] ibid.

[16] ibid 163. See also IEA '1985 Conclusions on Conservation' (1985) IEA/GB(85)46, Annex I, ch III.

[17] Richard Scott, *The International Energy Agency: Beyond the First 20 Years, Principal Documents*, vol III (International Energy Agency 1994) 204.

[18] Scott (n 6) 149. See also IEA '1992 General Policy Guidance and Specific Guidelines for Areas of Co-operation with Non-Member Countries' (1992) IEA/GB(92)25, Annex.

[19] Richard Scott, *The International Energy Agency: Beyond the First 20 Years, Major Policies and Actions*, vol II (International Energy Agency 1994) 214; Scott (n 17) 29.

solutions to [the environmental sustainability] challenge'.[20] However, it is the Secretariat that 'from the outset played an active role' in environment, for example, by making proposals to the Governing Board, including in relation to the 1992 Rio Principles implementation.[21] Part of the Secretariat had long been arguing that the IEA 'should play an active role in the Climate Convention' in internal notes.[22] In 1997, under Executive Director Robert Priddle, the Secretariat took the initiative to prepare a keynote address to be delivered at the third United Nations Climate Change Conference of the Parties (COP), which included reports estimating the CO_2 emissions for fuel production in 140 countries[23] and later aimed at 'influencing the outcome' of COP-4.[24]

One of the main tools of the Secretariat to shape environmental considerations and influence the membership is through publications,[25] such as the World Energy Outlook (WEO). The Secretariat independently publishes reports under the authority of the Executive Director. In turn, the 'intention' to publish reports was sometimes 'noted' or 'shared' by the Governing Board, resulting in the board issuing a formal recommendation.[26] For instance, in 1993, Executive Director Steeg took the initiative to spearhead a Secretariat 'strategic paper' titled 'Policy Review: The IEA in a Changing World', which 'gave a new direction to the Agency'. This initiative led to the IEA 'Shared Goals' adoption by IEA Ministers in June 1993, which fostered the three 'Es': Economic Security, Economic Development, and Environmental Protection.[27]

During the late 1990s, the IEA 'moved strongly into environmental work generally and expanded the scope of its overall work'[28] as environmental concerns became one of the 'core elements of IEA policy and operations'.[29] Before the G8 Gleneagles 2005 Summit, the IEA Secretariat spearheaded environmental activities while gathering increasing support from the membership.[30] Indeed, initially, IEA's member states 'were not keen on paying for' environmental tasks but

[20] Craig Bamberger, *The International Energy Agency: The First 30 Years: Supplement to Volumes I, II & III*, vol IV (International Energy Agency 2004) 208, 228.
[21] ibid 219, 225, and 228.
[22] ibid 220, 221.
[23] ibid 225.
[24] ibid 226.
[25] Bonucci and others (n 12) 438–39.
[26] Scott (n 17) 210, 289.
[27] Harald Heubaum and Frank Biermann, 'Integrating Global Energy and Climate Governance: The Changing Role of the International Energy Agency' (2015) 87 Energy Policy 229, 232; Van de Graaf and Lesage (n 3) 303–04. See IEA Ministers, 'Shared Goals' (4 June 1993) <https://iea.blob.core.windows.net/assets/b01dc266-6b76-4cb6-846b-b236cb50af93/IEASharedGoals-1993.pdf> accessed 04 September 2024.
[28] Scott (n 19) 19.
[29] ibid 24.
[30] Van de Graaf and Lesage (n 3) 314.

eventually came to support the Secretariat's work on environmental issues,[31] especially after the G8 tasked the IEA with drafting a climate change action plan.[32]

Another (external) reason that prompted environmental work within the IEA was the setting up of a global competitor agency, the International Renewable Energy Agency (IRENA), in 2009.[33] According to Heubaum and Biermann, the IEA's new role changed under new circumstances[34] as it faced increased internal and external pressure.

During the late 2000s, keeping the chain going, Nobuo Tanaka, then Executive Director, held that energy consumption was 'patently unsustainable—environmentally, economically, and socially' and that action had to be taken.[35] Under Executive Director Tanaka, the IEA proposed a clean energy new deal following the 2008 financial crisis.[36] Then, the turn towards the environment became more apparent when Maria van der Hoeven became Executive Director in 2011.[37] For instance, in 2013, she affirmed that 'radical action is needed to curb greenhouse-gas emissions, yet that radical action is disappointingly absent' while additional climate-sensitizing reports were published under her authority.[38]

IV. The IEA as a Flag Bearer of the Green Transition and New Leadership

Although the climate issue has been a growing parameter within the IEA since the 1990s, a real change in the institutional paradigm occurred during a subsequent phase as about 10 years ago, the IEA was still considered a fossil fuel institution.

Yet, over the past decade, it has become evident that the IEA's image has radically changed. One of the key factors for this is the appointment in 2015 of Fatih Birol as the still-incumbent IEA's Executive Director. From the start of his term as Executive Director, Birol took the initiative to present a modernization strategy that consisted of three pillars: energy security beyond oil, work with emerging economies, and a greater focus on clean energy technology.[39] In his previous role as IEA's chief economist, Executive Director Birol was already described as a 'vocal advocate of acting on climate change', which explains the

[31] ibid.
[32] For further details on the G8 implication, see Bonucci and others (n 12) 470.
[33] Van de Graaf and Lesage (n 3) 309; Bonucci and others (n 12) 470–71.
[34] Heubaum and Biermann (n 27) 230.
[35] Van de Graaf and Lesage (n 3) 314.
[36] Van de Graaf (n 4) 240.
[37] Heubaum and Biermann (n 27) 234–35.
[38] IEA, 'Redrawing the Energy Climate Map' (IEA 2013).
[39] IEA (n 9).

IO's shift observable through its publications, for example, the WEO.[40] Those publications afford the Secretariat some leeway to push new topics forward, as the reports are not subject to members' review.[41] Thanks to the IEA's flexibility, including through publications, the Secretariat has 'a chance to pursue more independent agendas', including climate change, which, although present, was not a core IEA issue in 2015.[42]

Indeed, the IEA was still seen by climate activists as being 'too cozy with the oil and gas industry' during the first years of Birol's mandate.[43] However, he has made considerable efforts since he entered the agency to 'change the organization's agenda and reputation' through a new clean energy focus.[44] One of his landmark projects was the launch in 2021 of the 'Net Zero by 2050' report by the IEA, which was the 'culmination of the IEA's pioneering work on energy data modelling'.[45] According to Birol, the report came as a tool to help bridge 'the gap between rhetoric and actions'; on its publication date, it received the political support of 22 IEA members (about 70% of members).[46] The report posits no new fossil fuel investments are needed to ensure the world's energy needs. It advocates refraining from investing in new fossil fuel exploitation projects while existing projects satisfy the world's energy demand during the transition. The report was labelled as a 'rallying cry for climate advocates' and a turn in Birol's push to transform the IEA 'into a clean energy authority'.[47] Another of Birol's initiatives was to convene the IEA 'Clean Energy Labour Council' in 2022[48] to factor in the perspective of the labour sector in climate discussions. In addition, in the 2023 WEO, the IEA predicted the demand for oil and gas would peak around 2030,[49] which sparked further controversy.[50] This led the *Time* magazine to list Executive Director Birol as one of the 2023 Most Influential Climate Leaders in Business.

The IEA, under Birol's leadership, also sought to use the 2022 gas crisis as a springboard for its platform, calling for more investment in clean

40 Heubaum and Biermann (n 27) 233.
41 Van de Graaf and Lesage (n 3) 304; Heubaum and Biermann (n 27) 232, 236.
42 Heubaum and Biermann (n 27) 233.
43 Justin Worland, 'Inside Fatih Birol's Push to Transform the IEA into a Clean Energy Authority' (*Time*, 23 February 2024) <https://time.com/6768028/fatih-birol-transform-iea-clean-energy/> accessed 22 May 2024.
44 ibid.
45 IEA, 'Net Zero by 2050: A Roadmap for the Global Energy Sector' (IEA 2021) 3.
46 ibid.
47 Worland (n 43).
48 IEA, 'Clean Energy Labour Council Fostering Dialogue Between the IEA, Stakeholders and the Labour Sector' <https://www.iea.org/about/structure/clean-energy-labour-council> accessed 9 September 2024.
49 IEA, 'World Energy Outlook 2023' 26 <https://iea.blob.core.windows.net/assets/86ede39e-4436-42d7-ba2a-edf61467e070/WorldEnergyOutlook2023.pdf> accessed 9 September 2024.
50 Worland (n 43).

energy technology and showing that reliance on fossil fuels can have dire consequences.[51] Indeed, the IEA showed its relevance after Russia's invasion of Ukraine by proposing a 10-point plan to reduce the EU's reliance on Russian gas—this, not only to diversify the range of Europe's gas providers but also to decarbonize energy sources.[52] The President of the European Union (EU) Commission, Ursula von der Leyen, even affirmed that if the EU had managed to get through this energy crisis, it was 'first and foremost, thanks to [. . .] Fatih Birol and the [IEA]'.[53] This relationship is not always idle as Birol has addressed the EU with acerbic criticism, for example, insisting that the EU made 'two historic monumental mistakes' in terms of energy policy, that is, its negative stance on nuclear energy and past reliance on Russian gas.[54]

Following this success, the IEA increased its cooperation with the EU Commission.[55] In turn, this enabled IEA leadership to adventure in other provinces, for example, organizing a 'Summit on Clean Cooking in Africa' and asking the EU to finance a 'Clean Cooking Initiative for Africa'[56] to reduce pollution otherwise released by cooking stoves. The IEA is not directly concerned or responsible for such issues, as no African country is a member. Still, this action has been justified for the sake of reducing CO_2 emissions alongside addressing human rights concerns.[57] This project comes from an idea Birol launched in 2005 when he was the IEA's chief economist.[58]

[51] Fatih Birol, 'The Global Energy Crisis Highlights the Need for a Massive Surge in Clean Energy Investment' (*Finance & Development*, December 2022) <https://www.imf.org/en/Publications/fandd/issues/2022/12/a-call-to-clean-energy-fatih-birol> accessed 22 May 2024.

[52] IEA, 'A 10-Point Plan to Reduce the European Union's Reliance on Russian Natural Gas' <https://www.iea.org/reports/a-10-point-plan-to-reduce-the-european-unions-reliance-on-russian-natural-gas> accessed 22 May 2024.

[53] Ursula von der Leyen, 'Speech by President von der Leyen at the Plenary Session on the Occasion of the 50th Anniversary of the International Energy Agency' <https://ec.europa.eu/commission/presscorner/detail/en/speech_24_786> accessed 22 May 2024.

[54] Alice Hancock, 'Europe Trails China and US After "Monumental" Energy Mistakes, IEA Chief Says' (*Financial Times*, 14 April 2024) <https://www.ft.com/content/5009e314-fc27-4d7f-8e42-9dbede842991> accessed 22 May 2024.

[55] IEA, 'IEA Executive Director Addresses EU College of Commissioners in Brussels' (*IEA*, 23 February 2022) <https://www.iea.org/news/iea-executive-director-addresses-eu-college-of-commissioners-in-brussels> accessed 22 May 2024.

[56] IEA, 'Summit on Clean Cooking in Africa: Event' (*IEA*, 14 May 2024) <https://www.iea.org/events/summit-on-clean-cooking-in-africa> accessed 22 May 2024.

[57] Frédéric Simon, 'Clean Cooking Stoves for Africa: The IEA's Pitch to EU for COP28' (*Euractiv*, 13 October 2023) <https://www.euractiv.com/section/energy-environment/news/clean-cooking-stoves-for-africa-the-ieas-pitch-to-eu-for-cop28/> accessed 22 May 2024.

[58] IEA, 'A Vision for Clean Cooking Access for All' (IEA 2023) 3–4.

V. Turbulence Ahead in the IEA's Sky

Despite this proliferation of initiatives and projects, or perhaps on account of it, there might be turbulence on the IEA's horizon. First, despite the call for zero new oil and gas projects by the IEA, their number should, in fact, quadruple by 2030.[59] Although many IEA members do support this initiative, others consider that the IEA's environmental shift and the 'Net Zero' report, in particular, are not accurate but rather militant. The report has been opposed by countries such as Australia, an important energy producer, and Japan, a consumer, whose governments openly disagreed with the report's findings.[60] For instance, Australia said that to be a reliable energy partner, it will keep approving new coal[61] and gas projects.[62] Norway, another energy producer, also expressed scepticism.[63]

Likewise, Donald Trump, the new president of the United States of America (USA), might defund the IEA—the USA under Trump as well as under other presidents has defunded or left other organizations in the past—or try to remove its Executive Director through cooperation with other countries like Japan and Australia.[64] For instance, Robert McNally, an influential US Republican and former George W Bush Energy adviser, called the new IEA environmental stance an unfortunate 'politicization' that led the organization to have 'strayed from its mission'.[65] Indeed, its new environmental vocation transformed the IEA from an IO operating in technical shadow to one in the forefront, where it started experiencing criticism from the broader public.[66] Most critics underline the fact

[59] Amanda Chu, 'New Oil and Gas Projects Expected to Grow Despite IEA Warning' (*Financial Times*, 28 March 2024) <https://www.ft.com/content/7b840e9e-a159-446e-872f-6d3d34127e1d> accessed 22 May 2024.

[60] FT Reporters, 'Member Countries Push Back Against IEA's Net Zero Road Map' (*Financial Times*, 23 May 2021) <https://www.ft.com/content/4bbae4a3-cf1f-4a09-9fe5-bf2dc2ee2c9c> accessed 22 May 2024.

[61] Australia Institute, 'Coal Mine Tracker' <https://australiainstitute.org.au/initiative/coal-mine-tracker/> accessed 22 May 2024.

[62] Hannah Ritchie, 'Australia Commits to Gas Beyond 2050 Despite Climate Warnings' (*BBC News*, 9 May 2024) <https://www.bbc.com/news/articles/cjq5gky4e5no> accessed 22 May 2024.

[63] FT Reporters (n 60).

[64] Valerie Volcovici, 'A Second Trump Presidency Would Target IEA's Green Focus, Advisers Say' (*Reuters*, 16 May 2024) <https://www.reuters.com/business/energy/second-trump-presidency-would-target-ieas-green-focus-advisers-say-2024-05-16/> accessed 22 May 2024; FT Reporters (n 60).

[65] Robert McNally, 'Climate Politics Neuters an Energy Watchdog' (*Wall Street Journal*, 12 February 2024) <https://www.wsj.com/articles/activists-neuter-a-global-watchdog-energy-policy-international-energy-agency-1ac4f81b> accessed 22 May 2024.

[66] David Blackmon, 'The International Energy Agency Is Now Just Another Green Activist Campaign' (*The Telegraph*, 3 April 2024) <https://www.telegraph.co.uk/news/2024/04/03/international-energy-agency-iea-green-un-activist-political/> accessed 22 May 2024.

that IEA data appear to be under-estimating the levels of oil consumption, even in the short run, for example, for 2024.[67]

Second, although there is enough hook to support initiatives on the greening of energy supply, one wonders how development initiatives, for instance, the clean energy cooking initiative in Africa—however commendable they are—fit within the IEA's mandate, when other institutions, such as the World Bank, are directly tasked with international development and would be able to implement such programmes. In one sense, it appears paradoxical that the IEA tried to push back IRENA as long as it could for fear that it would overlap with itself while encroaching on the World Bank's mandate. The same could be said regarding the new labour initiatives, which although relevant, seem to omit an important stakeholder: the International Labour Organization.

VI. Conclusion

In conclusion, the IEA's progression from an oil and gas champion to a paragon of green energy has been exponential, with the sustainability movement taking up more space with each new Executive Director. This major change from a focus on fossil fuels to a focus on renewable energy is likely the 'most important and yet often overlooked change the IEA has undergone in the last few years'.[68] From the era of Executive Director Lantzke, where developed countries were looking up for energy alternatives at all costs, for example, coal, to Executive Director Steeg, who timidly but decisively launched new ideas on sustainability, and her successors until the incumbent Executive Director, Birol, there has been a strong paradigm shift within the IEA following the 'Net Zero' 2021 report. This major shift has largely been the deed of the IEA Secretariat. Although there has been sufficient support from members to ensure the IEA's shift towards the environment, this change has mainly been steered by staff, who 'used their high-profile positions to advocate change'.[69]

This shift helped the agency to adapt to new circumstances. In 2021, in contradistinction to 1974, climate change became a major concern while fuel supply became an increasingly minor concern.[70] The IEA thus 'diversified away from its original *raison d'être*' as it shifted away from oil and included environmental issues within its mandate[71] through 'various small steps'.[72] Thus, the climate crisis

[67] David Blackmon, 'Oil Boom 2021: Waiting for the IEA to Make Up Its Mind' (*Forbes*, 12 June 2021) <https://www.forbes.com/sites/davidblackmon/2021/06/12/oil-boom-2021-waiting-for-the-iea-to-make-up-its-mind/> accessed 22 May 2024.

[68] Heubaum and Biermann (n 27) 232.

[69] ibid 232, 235; Van de Graaf and Lesage (n 3) 314.

[70] Heubaum and Biermann (n 27) 236.

[71] Van de Graaf and Lesage (n 3) 311.

[72] ibid 315; Scott (n 19) 40.

allowed the IEA to maintain its relevance. As outlined in other chapters, this aligns with general IO practice, as many initiatives appear to stem from crises that IOs aim to tackle.[73]

According to De Graaf and Lesage, the IEA Secretariat has been a 'driving factor behind the change', although members stopped some initiatives when they felt there was a 'mission creep'.[74] The question here is how far the Secretariat will be able to push to keep making the IEA a green paragon. So far, with more than 20 members supporting the 'Net Zero' initiative, state consent appears solid. However, the US election's outcome, combined with the fact that other governments, for example, Australia and Japan, are dissatisfied, could halt developments. The fact that the EU countries now have a majority voting power within the agency might also play a role as European countries seem keener than the USA to support the IEA in its new green role.[75]

Indeed, under Executive Director Birol, small steps have turned into a revolution as an institution mainly dealing with fossil fuels now calls for a stop to their development. Nevertheless, the IEA is harshly criticized by environmental groups, for example, for branding natural gas as a transition energy—for example, replacing coal with gas—while some groups have labelled gas as the 'new coal'.[76] According to Climate Analytics, the 'Net Zero' plan is insufficient and would not be Paris-Agreement compatible, partly because of an overreliance on natural gas.[77]

All in all, although the IEA's evolution has been remarkable, it will be important to pay attention to the direction it will take. International society appears as polarized as national ones, and the IEA is facing contrary winds, some pushing it to return to its historical role as a 'neutral' data collector, while others consider that the IEA remains too much tainted by its oil and gas past. Depending on the new balance of power within the agency, this trajectory might also be halted or lead to a partial rollback of environmental considerations. In any event, the IEA's evolution is an informative case study as it shows how far an IO can go from its constituent instrument through successive staff initiatives and membership assent, at least implicitly. It will likewise be interesting to see whether the current management will secure enough support to keep operating in provinces that were until recently unknown to the IEA, for example, international development.

[73] Bonucci and others (n 12).
[74] Van de Graaf and Lesage (n 3) 315.
[75] Alex Wilson, 'International Energy Agency: Origins and Developments' (2016) European Parliamentary Research Service 9.
[76] Report criticizing the IEA *passim*; Bill Hare and others, 'Why Gas Is the New Coal' (2021) Climate Analytics.
[77] ibid 12–13.

20

The Driving Role of the Heads of International Organizations

A Case Study Around the Organisation for Economic Co-operation and Development

*Nicola Bonucci**

I. Introduction

The Convention reconstituting the Organisation for European Economic Co-operation as the Organisation for Economic Co-operation and Development (OECD) (hereafter, the Convention on the OECD) is neither particularly long nor particularly detailed. Notably, with respect to the role and responsibilities of the Secretary-General, it is—as many other constitutive acts of international organizations (IOs)—quite laconic, if not lacunar.

The role of the Secretary-General is explicitly addressed in only three articles of the Convention on the OECD, which basically say that Secretaries-General:

i. are 'responsible to Council', 'shall serve as Chairman of the Council meeting at sessions of Permanent Representatives, and assist the Council in all appropriate ways and may submit proposals to the Council or to any other body of the Organisation' (article 10),
ii. appoint staff, and they (as well as all the staff of the Organisation) shall be independent from national pressure (article 11)
iii. prepare and propose the budget to the Council for approval (article 20)[1]

However, this institutional basic text, as complemented by a number of more specific documents, does not provide furtherance of the matter.

As the former Secretary-General of the United Nations (UN), Dag Hammarskjöld, pointed out in a famous lecture he delivered in Oxford in 1961: 'is

* Based on an interview with the former OECD Secretary-General Angel Gurría.

[1] Convention on the Organisation for Economic Co-operation and Development (30 September 1961) 888 UNTS 179 <https://www.oecd.org/about/document/oecd-convention.htm≥ accessed 30 September 2024.

Nicola Bonucci, *The Driving Role of the Heads of International Organizations* In: *International Organization Initiatives*.
Edited by: Gabrielle Marceau and Henner Gött, Oxford University Press. © Oxford University Press 2025.
DOI: 10.1093/9780197803325.003.0021

it possible for the Secretary-General to resolve controversial questions on a truly international basis without obtaining the formal decision of the organ? In my opinion and on the basis of my experience, the answer is affirmative; it is possible for the Secretary-General to carry out in controversial political situations with full regard to his exclusive international obligation under the Charter and without subservience to a particular national or ideological attitude'.[2]

In my experience, the statement made by the UN Secretary-General equally applies to the OECD Secretary-General, and I would like to offer a few illustrations of this based on my own experience as Director for Legal Affairs under the stewardship of then Secretary-General Angel Gurría who led the OECD between 2006 and 2021. For the purpose of this contribution, I have had the pleasure of interviewing Mr Gurría on initiatives he launched or strengthened, and I use several extracts from this interview.

The first two initiatives stem from the financial crisis of 2007–2008 and were initiated by then Secretary-General Gurría. These are:

i. The New Approaches to Economic Challenges (NAEC)[3]
ii. The OECD work on transparency and exchange of information for tax purposes[4]

The other two initiatives were not formally launched by Secretary-General Gurría, but they were strengthened and reinvigorated by him. These are:

i. The Programme for International Student Assessment (PISA)[5]
ii. The Convention on Combating Bribery of Foreign Public Officials in International Business Transactions (hereafter the Anti-Bribery Convention)[6]

Before discussing the role and responsibilities of the OECD Secretary-General (Section II) and the substance of the aforesaid initiatives (see Sections III and

2 Dag Hammarskjöld, 'The international Civil Servant in Law and in Fact' (lecture delivered in Oxford, May 1961) <https://www.daghammarskjold.se/wp-content/uploads/2019/10/ics_100_no_4_oxfordspeech.pdf> accessed 30 September 2024.

3 OECD, 'New Approaches to Economic Challenges' <https://www.oecd.org/naec/> accessed 30 September 2024.

4 OECD, 'Tax Transparency and International Co-operation' <https://www.oecd.org/tax/exchange-of-tax-information/> accessed 30 September 2024.

5 OECD, 'Programme for International Student Assessment (PISA)' <https://www.oecd.org/en/about/programmes/pisa.html#:~:text=PISA%20> accessed 30 September 2024.

6 OECD Convention on Combating Bribery of Foreign Public Officials in International Business Transactions (17 December 1997), S Treaty Doc No 105-43 (hereafter OECD Anti-Corruption Convention) <https://www.oecd.org/content/dam/oecd/en/topics/policy-sub-issues/fighting-foreign-bribery/Convention%20and%20commentaries%20booklet%202024.pdf> accessed 30 September 2024.

IV), I would like to note that the OECD presents several characteristics which make the organization rather unique, including with respect to its working methods.

The OECD works via a bottom-up approach through its more than 200 technical bodies and sub-bodies. The final decision-making body, the Council composed of representatives of all the member countries, validates the work through consensus but typically refrains from intervening in the work carried out at the level of the technical bodies.[7] In addition, the OECD Secretariat has quite a unique role that is best described in a speech of the Japanese Minister of Foreign Affairs on the occasion of the fiftieth anniversary of the OECD in 2011:

> Every year, a number of ministers, policy makers and specialists visit the OECD for various kinds of meetings. They express their views, listen to statements by other participants, and use these as reference for their own policies. *Talented OECD Secretariat members make analyses and policy advice based on such discussions.* (italics by the author)[8]

In this context, and before discussing in detail the initiatives mentioned above, it is important to provide a brief overview of the role and responsibilities of the OECD Secretary-General.

II. The Role and Responsibilities of the OECD Secretary-General

As indicated, the role and responsibilities of the OECD Secretary-General cannot be seen in the sole light of the Convention on the OECD. In addition to delegated powers and the theory of implied powers, practice has enshrined the Secretary-General with a key role in the OECD architecture.

This is reflected in the qualifications set out in Resolution C(2016)70/FINAL of the Council on the selection of the Secretary-General adopted by the OECD Council in 2016 and in particular the paragraph providing that the

[7] For those interested in OECD committees, the Permanent Representation of Poland to the OECD issued a fascinating document entitled 'Inside the OECD: Committees and Their Chairs' (2022) <https://www.google.com/url?sa=t&rct=j&q=&esrc=s&source=web&cd=&cad=rja&uact=8&ved=2ahUKEwjjwo66g62CAxUOTaQEHWiTDngQFnoECCgQAQ&url=https%3A%2F%2Fwww.gov.pl%2Fattachment%2F92887b50-e74b-43bf-a1cd-570b5724db69&usg=AOvVaw2hhoM3w_V2G_FPYEQPJL76&opi=89978449> accessed 30 September 2024.

[8] 'On 50th Anniversary of the OECD' (*Ministry of Foreign Affairs Japan*) <https://www.mofa.go.jp/announce/pm/kan/pdfs/kan_oecd1101e.pdf> accessed 30 September 2024.

Secretary-General has the 'capacity to provide strategic direction to the OECD and to enhance the competence and global influence of the Organisation'.[9]

It is therefore accepted by the OECD members that the Secretary-General shall play a strategic role in their own capacity. This strategic role should be appreciated in conjunction with a specific Secretary-General's power to publish any material prepared under his authority as recognized in paragraphs 13 and 14 of the Annex 'Guidelines for Implementation' to the 2008 'Council Resolution on the Classification and Declassification of Information'.

> 13. As now, main Committees retain the option to ask the Secretary-General to declassify material prepared for them, in those circumstances where Member countries do not wish formally to endorse the content as reflecting their views, but agree that it should be declassified, and thus allow it, if appropriate, to be made publicly available.
>
> 14. The Secretary-General retains the authority to declassify material prepared and remaining under his authority.[10]

These combined features provide a framework around which the Secretary-General can push forward initiatives as we will see by the examples that follow.

III. Initiatives Launched and Promoted by the OECD Secretary-General

A. A pure Secretary-General initiative: The NAEC

The NAEC was an initiative launched in 2012 in the aftermath of the financial crisis of 2007–2008. The OECD indicates that the initiative was set up in order 'to better understand the interconnectedness and complexity of the global economy'.[11] In particular, its purpose:

> was to understand the shortcomings of the analytical frameworks the Organisation had relied upon before the financial crisis of 2007–2008, and

[9] OECD, 'Resolution of the Council on the Procedure for Appointing Future Secretaries-General' (adopted on 23 May 2016) Res C(2016)70/FINAL <https://one.oecd.org/document/C(2016)70/FINAL/en/pdf> accessed 30 September 2024.

[10] OECD, 'Council Resolution on the Classification and Declassification of Information' (10 July 1997, as amended 12 April 2007) Res C/M(97)17 <https://one.oecd.org/document/C(97)64/REV1/FINAL/en/pdf> accessed 30 September 2024.

[11] OECD, 'New Approaches to Economic Challenges (NAEC)' (2012) <https://www.oecd.org/naec/resources/Briefing-Note_New-Approaches-to-Economic-Challenges.pdf> accessed 30 September 2024.

to establish the basis of a better way of producing policy advice based on new frameworks. This involves upgrading models, tools and techniques for analysis and refining the narratives we use to convey policy to decision-makers and the public.[12]

The NAEC was located in the Office of the Secretary-General. This quite unusual administrative arrangement is due the fact that NAEC was initiated by then Secretary-General Angel Gurría. As illustrated by the document titled *NAEC—A Framework Paper*, at the Meeting of the OECD Council at Ministerial Level in May 2012:

> The global crisis was a 'wake-up call' to policymakers around the world. Market and governance failures have led to the most pressing financial, economic and employment crisis of our lifetimes. [. . .] Thus, returning to business-as-usual is not an option. It [was] time to reflect, to revisit and to rethink. In line with the 50th Anniversary Vision Statement, the Secretary-General proposes to develop a reflection process on 'New Approaches to Economic Challenges' at the OECD. The aim [was] to respond to the call by several countries for such a reflection, to learn the lessons from the crisis and derive its policy implications, and to build a more solid path for economic growth and well-being.

The Secretary-General had strongly advocated for the NAEC, overcoming the reservations of some member countries that were concerned that the initiative (as it was premised on the context of the 2007–2008 financial crisis, complexity, and fragility of the global economy) would be used to criticize their domestic policies.

Interestingly enough, the idea was first conceived at the Council of Europe in the context of the annual meeting that the Secretary-General of the OECD holds with the Parliamentary Assembly of the Council of Europe. As noted by the Secretary-General in 2013, when he addressed again the Council of Europe:

> it was in this session of 2011, during our 50th Anniversary, that you [the Council of Europe] asked us [the OECD] to take a hard look at the sources of the [financial] crisis, at the lessons learned, how to avoid such accidents and how to set the stage for stronger, more balanced and more sustainable and inclusive growth.[13]

[12] ibid.

[13] OECD, 'Debate at the Parliamentary Assembly of the Council of Europe: Remarks by Angel Gurría' (1st October 2013) <https://web-archive.oecd.org/2014-01-27/251109-oecd-debate-at-the-parliamentary-assembly-of-the-council-of-europe.htm> accessed 30 September 2024.

Here we have therefore quite a rare, if not unique, example of an initiative generated by the dialogue between the OECD Secretary-General and another IO.[14]

NAEC was initiated by the Secretary-General in spite of the reluctance and lack of enthusiasm of some OECD members (and even of some OECD staff members). The initiative was then vetted one year later by OECD members and was subsequently well enshrined in the OECD framework.

In 2020, the journalist Martin Wolf highlighted in the *Financial Times* that:

> the big question is now whether the essential systems that keep our societies running are adequately resilient. The answer is no. This is the sort of question the OECD's NAEC Unit has dared to address. Inevitably, it has created much controversy. Yet it is admirable that an international organization is daring to do so at all.[15]

Following the designation of a new Secretary-General and the post-2022 geopolitical context, it is not clear if the NAEC initiative is still active.

B. A hybrid initiative: The OECD's work on exchange of information for tax purposes

While the NAEC was pushed by the Secretary-General mostly on his own, the new stream of the OECD's work on exchange of information for tax purposes is a 'hybrid' initiative, that is, an initiative developed by the Secretary-General with the support of some OECD members but opposed by others.

Like NAEC, the Global Forum on Transparency and Exchange of Information for Tax Purposes (GFTEI) is a child of the financial crisis. As of January 2024, the GFTEI brings together 171 countries and jurisdictions. The GFTEI is the leading international body working on the 'implementation of global transparency and exchange of information standards around the world'.[16]

The historical context is accurately described in a book recently published by the former Director of the Centre for Tax Policy and Administration of the OECD, Pascal Saint-Amans.[17] Notably, the issue of tax information exchange

[14] Henner Gött, 'Interactions with the Outside World as a Factor of IO Initiatives', Chapter 22 in this volume.

[15] OECD, 'New Approaches to Economic Challenges (NAEC): Update July 2020' <https://one.oecd.org/document/SG/NAEC(2020)2/en/pdf> accessed 30 September 2024.

[16] OECD, 'Putting an End to Offshore Tax Evasion' <https://www.oecd.org/tax/transparency/> accessed 30 September 2024.

[17] Pascal Saint-Amans, *Paradis fiscaux: comment on a changé le cours de l'histoire* (Seuil 2023) 41–53.

was suddenly brought to the international agenda during the first G20 summit in 2008. According to the summit's final Declaration on 'Promoting Integrity in Financial Markets':

> Tax authorities, drawing upon the work of relevant bodies such as the Organization [sic] for Economic Cooperation and Development (OECD), should continue efforts to promote tax information exchange. Lack of transparency and a failure to exchange tax information should be vigorously addressed.[18]

However, it should be noted that the OECD had not been invited to this first summit.

At the next G20 summit that took place in early April 2009 in London, through their Declaration on 'Strengthening Financial Supervision and Regulation', the G20 Leaders committed:

> to take action against non-cooperative jurisdictions, including tax havens. We stand ready to deploy sanctions to protect our public finances and financial systems. The era of banking secrecy is over. We note that the OECD has published today a list of countries assessed by the Global Forum against the international standard for exchange of information.[19]

This last sentence gave rise to a lot of tensions both within the G20 and at the OECD. The debate in the G20, mainly between France and China, was largely covered at that time by the media. That the G20 took note of the OECD list, rather than endorsing it, reflected a compromise.[20]

In a 2020 podcast, Gordon Brown, the United Kingdom's (UK) Prime Minister at the time of the G20 summit, made clear that tax transparency was '[t]he most controversial issue' and that 'the compromise was that we would not take action as

[18] G20 Research Group, 'Declaration of the Summit on Financial Markets and the World Economy' (15 November 2008) <http://www.g20.utoronto.ca/2008/2008declaration1115.html> accessed 30 September 2024.

[19] 'London Summit: Leaders' Statement' (*G7G20*, 2 April 2009) <https://g7g20-documents.org/database/document/2009-g20-united-kingdom-leaders-leaders-language-london-summit-leaders-statement#section-> accessed 30 September 2024. The list refers to: OECD, 'A Progress Report on the Jurisdictions Surveyed by the OECD Global Forum in Implementing the Internationally Agreed Tax Standard' (2 April 2009) <https://web-archive.oecd.org/2012-06-14/119127-42497950.pdf> accessed 30 September 2024.

[20] 'G20 leaders hail crisis fightback' (*Financial Times*, 2 April 2009) <https://www.ft.com/content/082652de-1fb0-11de-a1df-00144feabdc0> accessed 30 September 2024.

the G20, but ask the OECD to take action' and working, in particular, on the categorization of countries.[21]

However, very little attention was devoted to how the list came about. As Pascal Saint-Amans makes clear, the list, which included several OECD members, had been prepared by the OECD Secretariat based on its analytical work. While circulated to the OECD members, however, it had not been submitted for adoption to the competent OECD body, the Committee on Fiscal Affairs (CFA). Indeed, formal adoption by the members would have required consensus in a context where, as former Secretary-General Gurría indicated in his interview, several members 'were deadly against' this initiative.

This explains the following extract from Mr Saint-Amans' book describing a very tense lunch at the Secretary-General's residence:

> Angel Gurria is facing the wrath of OECD member states who have just learned from the press that they are to find themselves blacklisted by the very organization to which they belong. Ambassadors are laying siege to his office, and finance ministers are calling from their respective capitals. They complain bitterly, and their attacks come in all shapes and sizes. The first argument is that the secretariat is not competent to prepare a list for the G20, a group outside the OECD, eight of whose members do not belong to the organization. A lover of combat and jousting, and a fierce defender of his prerogatives, the Secretary-General asserts that it is within his remit to make public reports on the subjects dealt with by the organization. This dispute over the scope of the secretariat's powers will continue until Gurria leaves the OECD in 2021. States demanded validation of reports made to the G20, which would have required a paralyzing consensus, while the Secretary-General insisted on his right, almost his duty, of freedom of speech, in the interests of the organization.[22]

Following the G20 London summit, the relations between the OECD Secretary-General and the representatives of the OECD members mentioned in the list were sour for months, if not years. However, the political momentum created on that occasion led the OECD to revamp and significantly change[23] the

[21] OECD, 'Gordon Brown shares how far we have come on the fight against tax evasion' <https://www.oecd-ilibrary.org/fr/taxation/gordon-brown-shares-how-far-we-have-come-on-the-fight-against-tax-evasion_286f5df7-en> accessed 30 September 2024.

[22] Saint-Amans (n 17) 45, translated by the author.

[23] OECD, 'Global Forum on Transparency and Exchange of Information for Tax Purposes: Who We Are' <https://www.oecd.org/tax/transparency/who-we-are/history/> accessed 30 September 2024. Also: OECD, 'Recommendation of the Council on Implementing the Proposals Contained in

GFTEI.[24] Indeed, in light of what had effectively become a partnership with the G20, the OECD had to change the nature and purpose of the GFTEI originally established as a simple platform for dialogue between OECD members and selected non-OECD members on tax matters. The new GFTEI has a self-standing and autonomous Secretariat hosted at the OECD[25] and has been granted extensive powers, including the power of evaluating the degree of implementation of OECD tax standards by all GFTEI members. In addition, the GFTEI has been open to all countries on equal footing and is no longer limited to OECD countries only as it originally was.[26]

Today, the international community has achieved great success in the fight against offshore tax evasion and bank secrecy. Working through the GFTEI, countries have implemented robust standards that have prompted an unprecedented level of transparency in tax matters.

Moreover, since then, and in large part thanks to the work on tax, the OECD has been given a seat in the G20 and plays an important role in the shaping of the G20 agenda.

IV. Initiatives Strengthened and Reinvigorated by the OECD Secretary-General's Actions

PISA and the fight against transnational bribery were two initiatives launched by Mr Gurría's predecessor, Mr Donald Johnston (Secretary-General between 1996 and 2006), but these initiatives were pursued and expanded with the appointment of Mr Gurría as the OECD Secretary-General in 2006.

A. Programme for International Student Assessment

The PISA measures 15-year-old students' reading, mathematics, and science literacy every three years. First conducted in 2000, the major domain of study rotates between reading, mathematics, and science in each cycle. PISA also includes measures of general or cross-curricular competencies, such as collaborative

the 1998 Report on Harmful Tax Competition' (16 June 2000) OECD/LEGAL/0305 <https://legalinstruments.oecd.org/en/instruments/OECD-LEGAL-0305> accessed 30 September 2024.

[24] OECD Tax Forum (n 23).

[25] ibid.

[26] OECD, 'Summary of Outcomes of the Meeting of the Global Forum on Transparency and Exchange of Information for Tax Purposes Held in Mexico on 1–2 September 2009' <https://web-archive.oecd.org/2012-06-14/114830-43610626.pdf> accessed 30 September 2024.

problem-solving. By design, PISA emphasizes functional skills that students have acquired as they are near the completion of their compulsory schooling.[27]

The first round of evaluation pushed by Mr Johnston attracted some attention, but also criticisms by certain countries like France, who decided not to participate because it did not agree with the methodology.

When Mr Gurria took the lead of the OECD, he quickly recognized the potential of PISA and put a lot of personal weight into pushing for a strong expansion both in terms of substance and in terms of participation. In terms of substance, the PISA evaluation covers today much more than what had been originally foreseen. In terms of participation, it moved from 43 countries and economies in its first assessment to 81 participants, also including non-OECD members (which currently even represent the majority of the participants).[28]

Interestingly, this expansion was not welcomed by the then United States Administration under Trump, which, not being particularly keen on OECD in general and PISA in particular, identified 'yet another emerging problem: OECD's global ambitions for PISA.'[29] However, this did not stop PISA, which regained support by the Biden Administration.

The lesson to be learned from this case is that successful initiatives are also the product of circumstances. One can indeed legitimately argue that it was much more difficult for a governmental administration like the Trump Administration to stop an ongoing initiative than it would have been to block it at its inception.

B. The fight against transnational bribery

Like PISA, this initiative started before Mr Gurría's appointment as Secretary-General. The fight against transnational bribery was first put on the table in 1989, during the term of Secretary-General Jean-Claude Paye. The work was then pursued by Donald Johnston who played an important role in the entry into force of the Anti-Bribery Convention in 1999.

This Convention, signed in Paris on 17 December 1997 under the auspices of the OECD, establishes obligations on parties to criminalize the bribery of foreign public officials for the purpose of obtaining or retaining business. It covers corruption of public officials of any State, not just of the States Parties to the Convention.[30]

[27] OECD (n 5).

[28] OECD, 'PISA 2022 Results: The State of Learning and Equity in Education' (vol I, 2023) 38–39 <https://www.oecd-ilibrary.org/deliver/53f23881-en.pdf> accessed 30 September 2024.

[29] Mark Schneider, 'PISA Is a Unique Resource for Testing Educational Attainment of 15-Year-Olds in 78 Countries. Adding 40 More Would Be a Mistake' (*Institute of Education Sciences*, 25 February 2019) <https://ies.ed.gov/director/remarks/pisa-2019.asp> accessed 30 September 2024.

[30] OECD Anti-Corruption Convention (n 6).

Countries' implementation and enforcement of the OECD Anti-Bribery Convention[31] are monitored by the OECD Working Group on Bribery[32] through a rigorous peer-review monitoring system. The Parties to the Convention are subject to review by their peers, with experts from different Working Groups on Bribery, and countries serving as examiners of each evaluated country. According to the OECD: 'Transparency International has identified this monitoring mechanism as the "gold standard" of monitoring'.[33]

A few months after the arrival of Mr Gurría as the head of the OECD, the decision of the UK authorities to stop a major investigation on alleged bribery for a huge contract in Saudi Arabia led to acute tension between the UK and the OECD Working Group on Bribery.[34]

The Secretary-General publicly supported the views of the OECD Working Group on Bribery, and this led to a major crisis with the UK government.[35] The matter took a very nasty spin with a personal attack through the public media[36] that led the Secretary-General to issue a public reply.[37] Secretary-General Gurría stated that:

> As Secretary General of the OECD since June 2006, I have spoken out vigorously in favour of international efforts to fight the scourge of corruption in the global economy. I am equally determined to root out any hint of favouritism or corruption within the OECD Secretariat.
>
> We are indeed in dangerous waters. Not only multilateral organisations but businesses and national governments all have a role to play in fighting corruption wherever it rears its head. The OECD's prime role in this respect is to assist the 36 countries that are parties to the OECD Anti-Bribery Convention in ensuring that each one of them fulfils their commitments. In recent months, a number of significant cases have been exposed to the public gaze and discussed

[31] ibid.

[32] OECD, 'Working Group on Bribery in International Business Transactions' <https://www.oecd.org/daf/anti-bribery/oecdworkinggrouponbriberyininternationalbusinesstransactions.htm> accessed 30 September 2024.

[33] Country monitoring of the OECD Anti-Bribery Convention <https://www.oecd.org/daf/anti-bribery/countrymonitoringoftheoecdanti-briberyconvention.htm> accessed 30 September 2024.

[34] Gary Duncan, 'Blair Faces New OECD Pressure on Halted BAE Enquiry' (*The Times*, 18 January 2007) <https://www.thetimes.co.uk/article/blair-faces-new-oecd-pressure-on-halted-bae-inquiry-0mvfrq9zjwc> accessed 30 September 2024.

[35] 'OECD Secretary-General Stresses Governments' Role in Anti-Corruption Drive' (*Defense-Aerospace*, 18 January 2007) <https://www.defense-aerospace.com/oecd-has-serious-concerns-over-bae-saudi-probe/> accessed 30 September 2024.

[36] 'An Angel Flies into Some Flak' (*Economist*, 19 April 2007) <https://www.economist.com/international/2007/04/19/an-angel-flies-into-some-flak> accessed 30 September 2024.

[37] OECD, 'Statement by the Secretary-General, Angel Gurría, in reply to an article in *The Economist* of 20 April 2007' (20 April 2007) <https://one.oecd.org/document/PAC/COM/NEWS(2007)7/en/pdf> accessed 30 September 2024.

by the OECD's Working Group on Bribery. It is no surprise that this attack occurs at this time.[38]

Eventually the matter was disposed of through the enactment of a new and more modern domestic legislation, the UK Bribery Act 2010.[39]

To be noted here was the fact that the Head of the OECD was defending the credibility of an OECD instrument and had the support of an OECD body against an OECD member (or, more precisely, its then government). Observers do indeed recognize that this was a major turning point for the sustainability of the Convention.

What brings together these two precedent examples is the fact that the head of the IO not only has a role in launching new initiatives but also in preserving and strengthening existing ones.

V. Conclusion

We have seen how a head of an IO can push an initiative in such a way that makes it almost impossible for its members to resist, or how they can use the balance of powers between members to promote such an initiative.

Former OECD Secretary-General Gurría in his interview highlighted three crucial factors for initiatives to succeed:

i. a good idea;
ii. whose time has come; and
iii. that is perceived as going in the direction of fairness and justice.

According to Mr Gurría, the idea then becomes so compelling that it generates its own dynamics.

Trying to conceptualize the power of initiative of the head of an IO, one can distinguish three possible operating modes, which are not mutually exclusive:

i. undertaking a unilateral action in the belief/hope that members would follow;
ii. opportunistic use of other fora and/or divergences of views amongst members to promote a particular initiative; and

[38] ibid.

[39] Bribery Act, United Kingdom, 2010 <https://www.legislation.gov.uk/ukpga/2010/23/contents> accessed 30 September 2024.

iii. promoting the initiative in their capacity of guarantor of the Organisation's independence and influence.

In the delicate exercise of leadership of an IO, there can be short-term gains leading to long-term losses, true breakthroughs, and prima facie victories with little effect.

As Mr Gurría indicated in his interview: 'in multilateral organisations, you cannot get any traction if you do not have the large countries on your side', and any initiative requires a 'few believers who are activists' (both in the members and in the staff) to support it.

However, what described above is not a hard science; the interview with Mr Gurría also highlighted the importance of subjective and psychological elements and two are worth mentioning. First, the instinct (in his interview, Mr Gurría used terms like 'nose' and 'smell') that allows the head of an IO to understand that 'the time has come'. Second, the importance of establishing personal links with leaders or other decision makers. As indicated in the interview, 'personal bonds with leaders is crucial because if you do not have them, it does not happen'.

The balance between the head of the IO and the members of the IO is a delicate one, as members are always keen to note that an organization must be member-driven.

Thus, while the head of an IO has an undisputable latitude, they need to use such latitude with care and with a strategic mind.

21
Concluding Commentary
Reflections on IO Leaders' Approaches

Jane Aeberhard-Hodges

I. Introduction

Part III of this book covers crucial questions related to the role of heads of secretariats in initiating international organization (IO) change, addressing the queries put by Birkenkötter in her chapter on change in IOs, namely, what is change in these IOs, how does it occur, and who are the actors that jump-start such change under what conditions? We have a rich gamut of examples of change initiatives, covering seven different IOs: the United Nations (UN, in Chapter 14), the Financial Action Task Force (FATF, in Chapter 15), the United Nations Educational, Scientific and Cultural Organization (UNESCO, in Chapter 16), the International Labour Organization (ILO, in Chapter 17), the World Trade Organization (WTO, in Chapter 18), the International Energy Agency (IEA, in Chapter 19), and the Organisation for Economic Co-operation and Development (OECD, in Chapter 20). There is also one contribution on the role of chief executive heads (in Chapter 13), which finds resonance in the IO-specific chapters.

II. 'Winning' Approaches

Within the framework of this book's reasoning for the success (or not) of change by IOs (generally worded founding documents, strong leaders, strong public support? Other factors?), this Part's IO-specific chapters highlight the importance of leadership in the UN, FATF, UNESCO, ILO, WTO, IEA, and OECD. The examples reveal a variety of 'winning' approaches while also demonstrating that modalities can be widely different.

Ukamwa's chapter unpacks the strict administrative approach to the role of IO executive heads, criticizing its functional formalism, which does not reflect the autonomy that the heads of secretariats have to undertake initiatives and respond effectively to crises. Rather, he proposes a pluralistic understanding of the role of executive heads from the point of view that the internal law of IOs is sufficiently

Jane Aeberhard-Hodges, *Concluding Commentary* In: *International Organization Initiatives.* Edited by: Gabrielle Marceau and Henner Gött, Oxford University Press. © Oxford University Press 2025. DOI: 10.1093/9780197803325.003.0022

flexible to allow their role to grow in ways that can justify expansive and autonomous actions. Ukamwa posits that where the constituent instrument is silent on a particular issue relating to the objective of the organization, IO heads may exercise their power to interpret from the viewpoint that 'the constituent instrument is a living instrument malleable to deal with emerging issues' that may justify expansive actions. The IO-specific chapters also appearing in Part III seem to vindicate this position. Yet, Ukamwa warns that IO executives interpreting the relevant constituent instrument does not give them 'a carte blanche to engage in a frolic of lawlessness in the exercise of their function. Also, practical matters require them to gain membership support, which is necessary to secure resources to execute their proposals'. The IO-specific chapters in Part III likewise raise the post facto seeking of members' agreement (or acquiescence) as one step towards a successful outcome of initiating change.

One message that arises clearly in the examples of this Part is the role of the personal convictions/vision, ethics, and personality traits of the chief executive leaders when it comes to pushing for change initiatives. Here, I agree with Ukamwa's conclusion: 'whether the changes, when initiated, eventually fail or succeed depends on the personality and skills of the Executive Head'.

Let us take first the UN example. For Khalil, the role and functions of the Secretary-General and, with him, the Secretariat at large have evolved and expanded over time. Throughout the history of the UN, successive Secretaries-General have shown independent initiative, which has not only created unforeseen roles for the Secretariat but also introduced new tools for the maintenance of international peace and security. Her chapter explores four initiatives: from the first peacekeeping force to the first health-keeping mission; from the Agenda for Peace to the Responsibility to Protect.

Lewis recalls an exceptional story about the creation of an international governmental organization: the FATF. The FATF was created by the Group of Seven (G7) through the Economic Declaration 1989[1] as a temporary 'ad hoc group'[2] focused on the laundering of the proceeds of drug trafficking. Over the years, however, its membership and remit have grown. Through a series of initiatives, Lewis, as Head of the FATF Secretariat between 2015 and 2022, transformed FATF from an informal ad hoc group to an independent intergovernmental standard-setting body as the global threats to be tackled by FATF were increasing.

Ramos, Assistant Director-General for Social and Human Sciences at UNESCO, details the crucial role that the UNESCO Secretariat played in proposing and developing the first normative instrument on artificial intelligence

[1] G7, 'Economic Declaration' (16 July 1989) <https://g7g20-documents.org/database/document/1989-g7-france-leaders-leaders-language-economic-declaration> accessed 6 July 2024.

[2] FATF, 'Annual Report 1990–1991', s III.B (on Institutional Arrangements) <https://www.fatf-gafi.org/content/dam/fatf-gafi/annual-reports/1990%201991%20ENG.pdf> accessed 6 July 2024.

(AI): the 2021 Recommendation on the Ethics of AI. By working closely with member states, experts, and negotiators, UNESCO leveraged its unique mandate for the ethics of science and technology and successfully delivered an impactful global standard based on promoting human rights, transparency, and human oversight for AI systems. Thanks to the implementation mechanisms embedded in the Recommendation, UNESCO continues to work with governments to steer ethical AI governance around the world.

The personality and leadership skills of successive Directors-General also had a lasting impact on the ILO. Maupin's analysis of two events in C Wilfred Jenks' stewardship throws light on that the Director-General's vision anchored in the rule of law and refers to another commentator[3] contrasting it with the preceding Director-General David Morse's (1948–1970) personal diplomatic skills to show that many skills are needed in the complex context of the ILO and its tripartite structure. The institutional crises at a time of change seem to have motivated Jenks' choices. Desperate times deserve desperate measures? Maupin concludes that there is a need for 'an unusual (impossible?) combination of negotiating skills that Morse possessed more than anyone, and the analytical and practical capacity to build institutional bridges towards the future as well as the true sense of purpose that was the mark of Jenks'.

Moving to Venkataraman's description of secretariat-led innovations in the WTO, the Director-Generals' actions beyond the limits of the WTO mandate are described as having 'displayed creativity'. The point is made that innovations initiated or suggested by the Secretariat, such as the development of procedures for improving the efficiency of the dispute settlement panel process, outreach to non-governmental organizations, the private sector, academia (through the WTO Chairs Programme), and the general public, were especially evident in crises and often a direct response to them. The conclusion that all these Director-General initiatives can be tied generally to the WTO trade increase mandate, and 'were motivated by a desire to respond to the evolving needs of the WTO and its membership', in my opinion, aligns with the ILO Director-Generals' actions that were taken during major institutional crises, and were rooted in a desire to preserve the essence of the Organization's mandate.

The IEA was also the subject of initiatives taken by its Secretariat and its successive Executive Directors since Helga Steeg in the 1990s to shift the activities and goal of this IO away from fossil fuel towards becoming a clean renewable energy authority. Through these initiatives, argues Ouellet, the Secretariat provided its members with cash value in a changing world. The incumbent Executive Director, Fatih Birol, pushed the boundaries even further, making the

[3] Robert W Cox, 'ILO: Limited Monarchy' in Robert W Cox and others, *The Anatomy of Influence: Decision Making in International Organization* (Yale UP 1973) 345–48.

IEA the spearhead of the energy transition despite opposition from fossil fuel producers.

Regarding OECD leadership innovation, according to Bonucci, one particular Secretary-General has used the general wording of Secretary-General duties and powers in constitutive documents as a framework around which to 'push forward initiatives'. One example given, the New Approaches to Economic Challenges Unit (NAEC) launched by the Secretary-General in 2012 and located in his Office, was a response to the financial crisis of 2007–2008. As such, it represented new action in the face of a major challenge, as do the examples of ILO and WTO Secretariat initiatives in Part III. Unpopular at first, the NAEC, following an evaluation one year later, 'is now well enshrined in the OECD framework', hence, receiving membership support. Another of Bonucci's examples, this one being an initiative that commenced before Secretary-General Gurria's term in the form of the 1999 Convention on Combating Bribery of Foreign Public Officials in International Business Transactions (the Antibribery Convention), shows how the Secretary-General's tenacity won out in 'a very nasty spin with a personal attack through the media' by an OECD member state facing allegations of government bribery around 2007. Readers will recognize in Bonucci's excerpt from the Secretary-General's public reply: 'We are indeed in dangerous waters.' ILO Director-General Somavia's strong words and open frustration voiced in his 2012 International Labour Conference *Reply*: 'the consequences of this deadlock were *unfortunate, disproportionate and potentially harmful*' (emphasis added).[4] Moreover, Bonucci notes that these examples show IO heads having a role not only in launching new initiatives but also in preserving and strengthening existing ones. Again, this echoes the Somavia defence of ILO's supervisory system and the Secretariat that serves it.

III. The Additional Aspect of 'Instant Initiatives': Juan Somavia's Innovative Response to the CAS Deadlock at the 2012 International Labour Conference

Another winning approach, that I personally witnessed, is the courageous position taken by ILO's Director-General Somavia regarding the International Labour Conference meltdown over whether the right to strike is covered by the Freedom of Association and Protection of the Right to Organise Convention,

[4] International Labour Conference (Provisional Record 29, 101st Session), Reply by the Director-General to the Discussions of His Reports (Geneva, May–June 2012) para 40.

1948 (No 87, referred to here as Convention 87[5]). On its face, the episode concerns the interpretation of Convention 87's scope to protect the right to strike. At the same time, it affects the fragile balance of power among the ILO's constituents, as well as the Organization's fundamental working method: tripartite social dialogue, building on expertise, mutual trust, and persuasion.

The centrepiece of this story is Somavia's *Reply* at the close of the 2012 International Labour Conference, coincidentally his last year as Director-General (1999–2012) and last time serving as the Conference Secretary-General.[6] In his reply, Somavia launched what might be called an 'instant initiative', an initiative taken essentially on the spot in an unprecedented situation and with little time to prepare and ponder. As will be seen, such an initiative requires both expertise and creativity and thus mirrors the findings of Maupain and others mentioned above. My take from this example is that the innovation and 'initiatives' do not have to be a tidal wave of change; rather, even a targeted intervention, taking advantage of a one-off, public opportunity can assist in defusing the crisis.

The immediate crisis was that the 2012 Conference Committee on the Application of Standards (CAS), whose tripartite membership consists of representatives of governments, employers, and workers, being a standing committee of the International Labour Conference tasked with advancing the implementation of international labour standards using a report prepared by an independent Committee of Experts on the Application of Conventions and Recommendations (CEACR) could not fulfil its mandate because the CAS Employers' members walked out! And when they returned to the room, the Employer members' disagreement on the content of Convention 87 (that it does not cover the right to strike and that the CEACR has no authority to question ratifying States on strikes under this treaty) continued to deeply affect negotiations with their Worker member counterparts, for example no List of Individual Cases was adopted, and CAS could meet to discuss only a few technical cases (related to reporting under the ILO Constitution). Never in the 85-year history of CAS had this happened. To grasp the immediate naming of this procedural issue as a 'crisis', one has to remember the absolutely firm underpinning of the very existence of the ILO and

[5] C087 – Freedom of Association and Protection of the Right to Organise Convention (adopted 9 July 1948, entered into force 4 July 1950) 1520 UNTS 352<https://www.ilo.org/dyn/normlex/en/f?p=NORMLEXPUB:12100:0::NO::P12100_INSTRUMENT_ID:312232> accessed 6 July 2024.

[6] As outgoing Director-General, Somavia had nothing to lose by speaking stridently; echoing his mastery of strategic interventions, his text relied on knowledge of the issue and procedures of social dialogue that could lead to a resolution, hence secretariat expertise, as noted by Margherita Melillo, 'IO Secretariats as Knowledge Actors', Chapter 6 in this volume.

all its work: tripartism and the deep belief in the working together of the three stakeholders in the world of work.[7]

The longer-term crisis was the Employers' arguments that not only did Convention 87 not include the right to strike (hence the CEACR should not present individual observations on the issue in its annual report), but also the CEACR had no authority to interpret Convention 87 in the manner it had done, especially in its comments on the fundamental Convention 87 produced in the 2012 *General Survey on the Fundamental Conventions Concerning Rights at Work*, which was before CAS and which—as usual—had been prepared in draft by the Secretariat under the Director-General. An unstated concern at the time was that if the Employers could reduce the scope of Convention 87, then which treaty might they challenge next, for example the Indigenous and Tribal Peoples Convention, 1989 (No 169) articles on consultation were questioned by the International Organisation of Employers (IOE).[8] This broader attack on the authority of the long-standing supervisory machinery (CEACR established in 1926) was at the back of many International Labour Conference attendees' minds in 2012.

The CAS report[9] faithfully records the discord, including the Friday night 1 June session without Employers, the weekend's informal talks to try to get the stakeholders to compromise, and the Employer members' return with complaints about lack of consultations, poor communications, and Secretariat

[7] Anchored in the International Labour Conference (26th Session), ILO Declaration of Philadelphia (Geneva 10 May 1944), tripartism involves representatives of workers and employers enjoying equal status with those of governments, so that all three stakeholders join in free discussion and democratic decision with a view to the promotion of the common welfare and decent work.

[8] International Labour Conference (110th Session), 'Report of the Committee of Experts on the Application of Conventions and Recommendations: General Report and Observations Concerning Particular Countries' (Geneva 9 February 2022) Report III (Part 1A) ILC.102/III(1A)) 819–41, where implementation by Argentina, Bolivia, Brazil, Chile, Colombia, Guatemala, Honduras, Paraguay, Peru, and the Bolivarian Republic of Venezuela gave rise to IOE comments:

> that the erroneous application and interpretation of the requirement of prior consultation can be a legal obstacle and lead to business difficulties, harm the reputation of enterprises and result in financial costs. The IOE also states that the difficulties to comply with the obligation of consultation may have an impact on the projects that enterprises may wish to carry out with a view to creating a conducive environment for economic and social development, the creation of decent and productive work and the sustainable development of society as a whole.

Could one of the tripartite partners argue that economic inconvenience outweighs the right to free, prior and informed consent, and hence reduce the scope of Convention 169?

[9] International Labour Conference (101st Session) Report of the Committee on the Application of Standards. Part One: General Report (Geneva May–June 2012) Provisional Record 19 (Rev.). For clarity, it should be noted that the List of Individual Cases is negotiated between the Employers and Workers without governments. For a description of the regular supervisory system for verifying the implementation of international labour standards, particularly the annual technical examination by the CEACR and the use of its findings by the tripartite CAS at the International Labour Conference in public debate, see ILO, *Rules of the Game: An Introduction to the Standards-Related Work of the International Labour Organization* (International Labour Office, Geneva 2019) 106–07.

misbehaviour. What was the innovative response to this crisis by the Secretariat under Somavia, and by the Director-General himself? Were his possible reactions limited by the Organization's constitutional provisions regarding the Director-General and Secretariat?[10]

Faced with the Employer/Worker members' deadlock paralysing the CAS, high-level Secretariat staffers tried to defuse the tension. But statements from the representative of the Secretary-General in the CAS and the Legal Adviser failed to end the dispute. At the last hour, the tripartite CAS membership agreed simply to request the governments included in the preliminary list to send a report to the Committee of Experts to be examined at its next session.

So, the CAS closed its (unfulfilled) work, but the Secretariat now intervened at the highest level. Director-General Somavia decided to address the crisis immediately, head-on, in the International Labour Conference plenary when it was his turn to respond to delegates' comments on that International Labour Conference session's proceedings. Somavia did not mince his words:

> I sincerely regret the deadlock that occurred during this year's deliberations of the [CAS], which meant that it was unable to carry out its work. Many delegates expressed their frustration at the fact that the Committee was prevented from fulfilling its role, and I fully support the call of delegates for a rapid resolution to this situation.... the consequences of this deadlock were *unfortunate, disproportionate and potentially harmful* for the ILO.

He carefully cloaked these strong words with supporting statements from a selection of the tripartite membership in order to engage all parties and pave the way for post-2012 dialogue between the constituents. Without expressing a position on the legal issue, he went on to praise the quality of the staff he had managed during the CAS crisis:

[10] Article 8.1 of the ILO Constitution reads: 'There shall be a Director-General of the International Labour Office, who shall be appointed by the Governing Body, and, subject to the instructions of the Governing Body, shall be responsible for the efficient conduct of the International Labour Office and for such other duties as may be assigned to him.' Article 10 lists the functions of the Secretariat under the Director-General to include, inter alia, reports for International Labour Conference agenda items and carrying out duties in connection with the effective observance of Conventions. Article 15 merely requires the Director-General to act as the Secretary-General of the International Labour Conference and to transmit the agenda to the Members and, through them, to the non-Government delegates in a prescribed time delay in advance of the meeting of the Conference. As for the Secretariat's role during the International Labour Conference sessions themselves, the Standing Orders bestow clerical, rather than political 'smooth functioning', duties on the International Labour Conference Secretariat headed by the Director-General. ILO, Standing Orders of the International Labour Conference (Geneva 2021) art 6.

> I also regret the lack of respect towards the CEACR and ILO staff that transpired in the [CAS] discussions. The Committee of Experts are a group of distinguished jurists appointed by the Governing Body. Their calibre, status and dedication honour us. [. . .] I fully support the work of staff who serve [CAS], who are dedicated, competent and high-quality professionals, and whose impartiality, neutrality and balance are unquestionable.[11]

Somavia's deviation from classic, 'uncontroversial' closing remarks, to rebuff any attack on the role of ILO's supervisory mechanism and on the Office staff who serve the mechanism, fits well with the chapters of this book: it demonstrates that brave Secretariat leadership and expert knowledge, combined with efforts to draw in members' *post facto* support, can defuse crises. Academics have since analysed the challenge by the Employers' group that stymied the functioning of a standing committee of the International Labour Conference.[12] However, the impact of Director-General Somavia's innovative approach is seen in that the CAS's functioning has not been so disrupted, since 2012. All parties agree to resolve the opposing views by submitting the issue to the International Court of Justice for an advisory opinion on the question 'Is the right to strike of workers and their organizations protected under [Convention 87]'.[13]

IV. Synthesis

What do these chapters and the ILO Director-General's intervention tell us regarding the role of IOs' secretariats in influencing change? What steps and criteria have worked so that the expansive act succeeds and remains, even being formally absorbed, into the entity's programme and budget? Bonucci's interview with Secretary-General Gurria concludes with three, not mutually exclusive, elements for the success of a secretariat initiative in the absence of clear constitutional authority: taking a unilateral action hoping that members will follow; opportunistically using other fora or members' divergence of views to promote the action; and placing the initiative under the cloak of the leader's capacity as guarantor of the entity's independence and influence. In addition, Gurria mentions

[11] ibid para 41.

[12] Janice Bellace, 'The ILO and the Right to Strike' (2014) 153 International Labour Review 1, 29–70, in particular 56–59; Jeffrey Vogt, 'The Right to Strike and the International Labour Organization (ILO)' (2016) 27 King's Law Journal 1, 110–31.

[13] ILO Governing Body (349th *bis* Session), Record of decisions (Geneva 10 November 2023) GB.349*bis*/INS/1/1/Decision. On 14 December 2023, the Office transmitted to ICJ's Registry a dossier—as required under the Statute of the Court—containing all relevant documents. ILO Governing Body (350th Session), Report of the Director-General: Regular Report (Geneva 4–14 March 2024) GB.350/INS/17 paras 2–5.

the need for having a sense that the timing is ripe and the need for establishing personal bonds with other leaders who could be crucial deciders for the initiative's ultimate success. All IO-specific chapters here point to the existence of a crisis or a pressing need (institutional or global). Hence, timing is a basic criterion. Most of the examples describe the executive heads' strong commitment/vision/personality when faced with the crisis, as well as their recognition that harnessing member nation support (getting allies) early on, even indirectly, was a winning manoeuvre. Most chapters also bring out the fact that the secretariats having specific, related expertise and knowledge made the initiative workable, even change-making. While covering vastly different areas, the chapters in Part III ultimately start to outline common criteria that will be useful for secretariat leaders to ponder and could be useful to track in further IO scholarly research.

PART IV

INTERACTION WITH THE OUTSIDE WORLD AND IO CHANGE

22

Interactions with the Outside World as a Factor for IO Initiatives

Henner Gött[*]

I. Introduction

International organizations (IOs) never walk alone. They exist and operate in constant exchange with the world around them. In virtually every policy field, there are numerous governmental and private actors, each bringing in their different approaches, perspectives, governance models, and agendas. Interactions between IOs and these outside actors play an important role in IOs' initiatives, be it as avenues for an IO to promote its initiatives[1] or as external impulses causing their adaptation.

This chapter studies the impact that interactions with the outside world have on IOs' initiatives.[2] My main argument is that interactions are an important but also elusive factor for IO initiatives, which is why there is a need to enhance their predictability. I propose that apart from policy formulation and implementation, predictability can also be enhanced by articulating and developing legal norms governing IOs' interactions with the outside world.

After some preliminary conceptual remarks in Section II, I sketch the manifold ways in which interactions become relevant for IOs' initiatives in Section III. Subsequently, I address interactions' elusiveness and the need to enhance their predictability in Section IV. Often, the principal focus is on sound policy, coordination, and programming, which, however, face major challenges and could benefit from a common normative framework (Section V). Legal norms can, in principle, provide such a framework. However, a significant part of currently existing legal norms is underdeveloped. I therefore propose further exploration,

* This chapter exclusively reflects the author's personal opinion, was not commissioned by or written on behalf of the Federal Chancellery, and does not represent a statement by the Federal Chancellery.

[1] I use the term 'initiative' as defined in this volume's Preface.

[2] The chapter partly draws on concepts and ideas taken from Henner Gött, *The Law of Interactions Between International Organizations: A Framework for Multi-Institutional Labour Governance* (Springer 2021).

Henner Gött, *Interactions with the Outside World as a Factor for IO Initiatives* In: *International Organization Initiatives*.
Edited by: Gabrielle Marceau and Henner Gött, Oxford University Press. © Oxford University Press 2025.
DOI: 10.1093/9780197803325.003.0023

clarification, and refinement of the law of interactions in order to get a better hold on interactions as a factor for IO initiatives in Section VI.

II. Conceptualizing Interactions with the Outside World: Some Preliminary Remarks

The 'outside world' is a vast and diverse analytical category. It comprises every actor other than the IO itself and its members, hereinafter referred to as 'outside actors'. Among them are non-member states (also referred to as 'third states'), other IOs, and private actors, such as enterprises, trade unions, civil society organizations, and individuals. For greater certainty, I do not count IOs' members as belonging to the 'outside world' here, as they are firmly embedded into IOs' governance models and, therefore, require separate analysis. Consequently, the proposal to develop a law of interactions does not extend to relations between IOs and their members.

For present purposes, interactions are relevant insofar as they influence IOs' evolutionary trajectories, notably their initiatives. Therefore, the term 'interaction' is understood here as an actor's conduct directed at having, or actually having, an effect on the conduct of another actor.[3] Accordingly, an IO's interaction with the outside world is tantamount to an outside actor's conduct either directed at having, or actually having, an effect on the conduct of the IO or vice versa. This definition deliberately focuses on actors as the relevant protagonists of interaction, instead of 'regimes' or other 'non-personal' reference points.

Interactions between IOs and outside actors occur frequently and in great variety. To assess the relevance of interactions for IO evolution, it is crucial to consider their whole spectrum and to avoid limiting the analysis ab initio to, say, instances of open conflict or of direct communication. Similarly, it is important not to limit the analysis to conduct specifically having an effect on IOs' secretariats: while the focus of this volume is on secretariat initiatives, interactions primarily affecting other IO organs or bodies may have indirect or reflexive implications for secretariat initiatives. The following tentative taxonomy groups interactions along four different axes:

1. Interactions' character, ranging from conflict over coexistence, coordination, and cooperation, to alignment and—occasionally—integration.

[3] Gött (n 2) 57, drawing on Jeffrey L Dunoff, 'Mapping a Hidden World of International Regulatory Cooperation' (2015) 78 Law and Contemporary Problems 267, 268; Michael Nunner, *Kooperation Internationaler Gerichte: Lösung Zwischengerichtlicher Konflikte Durch Herrschaftsfreien Diskurs* (Mohr Siebeck 2009) 110–11.

2. Interactions' immediacy, ranging from direct influence through intentional and in-person exchange, to more indirect, coincidental, or reflexive forms of influence.
3. Interactions' formality, ranging from formalized exchange to informally exerted influence.
4. The stage of an IO's work on which, respectively, it exerts influence or on which external influence has an impact on an IO. Such stages may include policy-making, law-making, implementation, or other activity, depending on the respective IO's agenda, competences, and activities.[4]

This taxonomy aims at providing a terminological reference frame to navigate the vast variety of interactions and to help analyse interactive conduct. It is, however, not meant as a strict categorization.[5] Moreover, it should be noted that in reality, interactions often occur in clusters or sequences comprising different kinds of conduct, for example direct and indirect interactions, or formal and informal encounters. In addition, interactions often comprise a wider range of actors, which makes it possible to classify the same pattern of conduct as, say, both a case of interaction between two IOs and between one IO and a non-governmental organization (NGO).[6]

III. Sketching the Relevance of Interactions for IO Initiatives

Interactions with outside actors have influenced IOs' evolutionary paths on numerous occasions. For IO initiatives, this has mainly become relevant in two ways. First, initiatives have themselves involved, or given rise to, interactions with outside actors. Secretariats have chosen to interact with outside actors to enable or enhance their initiatives. Second, interactions have had repercussions on ongoing initiatives, or have induced an IO to launch a new initiative. While a detailed discussion of examples would exceed the scope of this chapter, the following paragraphs briefly sketch some constellations in which interactions with different outside actors became relevant in either of the described ways.

Interactions with third states have been an obvious source of influence on IO initiatives. For a recent example, rising geopolitical tensions and the increasing use of sanctions and other forms of economic coercion have induced the

[4] Gött (n 2) 60ff, building on Sebastian Oberthür and Thomas Gehring, 'Conceptual Foundations of Institutional Interaction' in Sebastian Oberthür and Thomas Gehring (eds), *Institutional Interaction in Global Environmental Governance: Synergy and Conflict Among International and EU Policies* (CUP 2016) 52, 58, 74.

[5] Margaret Young, *Trading Fish, Saving Fish: The Interaction Between Regimes in International Law* (CUP 2011) 86.

[6] Gött (n 2) 59, fn71.

European Commission to propose legislative measures[7] and to launch its 2023 European Economic Security Strategy.[8] But also major political reorientations, changes, and ruptures in third states, such as decolonization, or the end of the Cold War, have led to significant adaptations within both universal and regional IOs.[9] At times, non-member states have actively tried to obstruct and thwart IOs' work.[10] On the other hand, interactions with third states can also be a normal part of an IO's work and have sometimes been formalized, for example through bilateral agreements or by granting a consultative, observer, or associate status, creating 'official' paths for third states to influence an IO's initiatives.[11] Occasionally, events caused by or within third states have even given rise to the 'reactive' establishment of entirely new IOs and have shaped their trajectories from the start, including their secretariats' initiatives.[12]

Likewise, IOs' initiatives have been shaped by interactions with other IOs. Often, this has happened when IOs began to cooperate. Working together meant not only to pursue a common goal but also to revise and adjust one's own internal approaches and processes. For instance, as Yan Liu and Kyung Kwak discuss in this volume (Chapter 25), the International Monetary Fund (IMF) created its Food Shock Window and its Resilience and Sustainability Trust as a result of its cooperation with other IOs in order to respond, in a coordinated manner, to the global food crisis and to climate change.[13] In other cases, one IO provided assistance to another in order to address new topics or create new instruments. An example is the International Labour Office's continuous support to the Council of Europe in developing and revising the European Social Charter, which inter alia

[7] Such as the Commission's proposal for a so-called Anti-Coercion Instrument, which resulted in Regulation (EU) 2023/2675 of the European Parliament and the Council on the Protection of the Union and its Member States from Economic Coercion by Third Countries [2023] OJ L 2023/2675. Already in 1996, the Commission proposed a legislative response against the extraterritorial application of the US embargo against Cuba, resulting in the so-called Blocking Regulation, ie, Council Regulation (EC) No 2271/96 of 22 November 1996 Protecting Against the Effects of the Extraterritorial Application of Legislation Adopted by a Third Country, and Actions Based Thereon or Resulting Therefrom [1996] OJ L309/1.

[8] European Commission, 'Joint Communication to the European Parliament, the European Council and the Council on "European Economic Security Strategy"', JOIN(2023) 20 final.

[9] Matthias Ruffert and Christian Walter, *Institutionalisiertes Völkerrecht* (2nd edn, C H Beck 2015) 18–19; James Sperling and Emil Kirchner, 'The Security Architectures and Institutional Futures of post-1989 Europe' (1997) 4 Journal of European Public Policy 155.

[10] Martijn Groenleer, 'The United States, the European Union, and the International Criminal Court: Similar Values, Different Interests?' (2015) 13 International Journal of Constitutional Law 923, 929–30.

[11] Ruffert and Walter (n 9) 100–01.

[12] eg the ILO, Abdul-Karim Tikriti, *Tripartism and the International Labour Organization* (Almqvist & Wiksell International 1982) 155.

[13] Yan Liu and Kyung Kwak, 'IMF's Responses to New Challenges in the Global Economy: Recent Reforms of Its Financing Toolkit', Chapter 25 in this volume. Other examples are the creation of external relations units or including inter-IO exchange in internal rules, eg International Labour Conference (109th Session) Standing Orders of the International Labour Conference (as amended) (Geneva 18 June 2021) arts 2(3) lit. b), 14(6) and (9), 17bis(1), 56(7) (ILO's Standing Orders).

resulted in a standing working relationship between the Office and the European Committee of Social Rights and its Secretariat.[14] There are also cases in which IOs have set up joint bodies or machinery, which in itself is an evolutionary step forward.[15] Finally, there are cases in which IOs have facilitated the inception of a new IO. For example, as Fady Zeidan and Jean Abboud describe in this volume (Chapter 27), the World Health Organization (WHO) and the World Bank provided initial assistance to the Global Fund to Fight AIDS, Tuberculosis and Malaria, without which the latter would have needed much longer to begin its operations.[16]

Change also occurred through indirect interactions when IOs did not cooperate with each other but simply coexisted. More than once, actions of one IO have induced other IOs to change course, to redefine their positions, and to redistribute their resources. A case in point are the UN World Summit's, the Organisation for Economic Co-operation and Development's (OECD), and the World Trade Organization's (WTO) respective positions taken on the concept of fundamental labour rights in 1995–1996, which gave important momentum to International Labour Organization (ILO) Director-General Hansenne's initiative ultimately resulting in the 1998 ILO Declaration on Fundamental Principles and Rights at Work.[17]

And then, there have been cases of conflictual interactions: IOs coming from different starting points have openly quarrelled over the right way to address an issue and have—sometimes even intentionally—jeopardized each other's work. A *locus classicus* is the World Bank's continuous support for apartheid South Africa and colonial Portugal in the 1960s, defying the UN's explicit demands to cease that support.[18] Another case in point are the IMF's and the OECD's competing initiatives to tackle the 1973 oil price shock. Inter alia, the

[14] Stein Evju, 'The European Social Charter and the International Labour Organisation: Interlinks Past and Present' in Wolfgang Däubler and Reingard Zimmer (eds), *Arbeitsvölkerrecht - Festschrift für Klaus Lörcher* (Nomos 2013) 148, 153. See art 26 of the European Social Charter and art 12 of the European Committee of Social Rights' Rules of Procedure.

[15] For example, the FAO-WHO Codex Alimentarius Commission or the joint ILO-IMO bodies on maritime labour issues, José E Alvarez, *International Organizations as Law-Makers* (OUP 2006) 222; Henner Gött, 'Interactions Between International Organizations: Approaching a Neglected Governance Dimension' (2020) 17 International Organizations Law Review 75, 85 ff.

[16] Fady Zeidan and Jean Abboud, 'The Global Fund to Fight AIDS, Tuberculosis, and Malaria: Partnerships, Collaborations, and Initiatives with International Organizations', Chapter 27 in this volume.

[17] Francis Maupain, *The Future of the International Labour Organization in the Global Economy* (Hart Publishing 2013) 141–42; Virginia A Leary, 'The WTO and the Social Clause: Post-Singapore' (1997) 8 European Journal of International Law 118.

[18] Samuel Bleicher, 'UN v IBRD: A Dilemma of Functionalism' (1970) 24 International Organization 31.

IMF lobbied its members not to support the OECD initiative, which reportedly contributed to the latter's failure.[19]

Finally, many IOs interact with private actors. IOs and outside actors can provide each other with advice, expert knowledge, resources, or financial means. One example, discussed further by Janelle M Diller in this volume (Chapter 23) is the ILO's 'orchestration' of (ie the provision of coordination and assistance to) multi-stakeholder initiatives aiming at improving labour standards along global supply chains.[20] On the other hand, private actors (often NGOs) can also be a considerable source of protest, disagreement, and conflict, putting pressure on IOs to reform and develop their approaches.[21] Many IOs have formalized their interactions with (selected) private actors, for example through consultative mechanisms or the granting of observer status, again creating 'official' ways of influence.[22] Some IOs have significantly developed their approach towards the inclusion of NGOs over time. For example, as early as 1950, the World Bank stopped convening its Advisory Council, foreseen in its Articles of Agreement[23] as a body representing banking, commercial, industrial, labour, and agricultural interests[24], but later initialized topic-specific, less-formalized advisory mechanisms including NGO representatives.[25] Occasionally, private actors are part of an IO's constituency, as notably is the case with trade unions and employers' associations within the ILO.[26] Still, even there, the changing landscape of non-governmental actors in the world of work has repeatedly given rise to demands to develop the ILO's tripartite structure further and provide a greater role to other non-governmental actors[27], which has induced the International

[19] Nicola Bonucci and others, 'IGOs' Initiatives as a Response to Crises and Unforeseen Needs' (2022) 19 International Organizations Law Review 423, 449–50.

[20] Janelle M Diller, 'International Organization Interactions with Multi-stakeholder Initiatives: The International Labour Organization Experience', Chapter 23 in this volume.

[21] Occasionally including even physical interference, see Tony Clarke, 'Taking on the WTO: Lessons from the Battle of Seattle' (2000) 62 Studies in Political Economy 7.

[22] Stephan Hobe, 'Article 71' in Bruno Simma and others (eds), *The Charter of the United Nations: A Commentary* Vol II (3rd edn, OUP 2012) paras 16ff.

[23] Articles of Agreement of the International Bank for Reconstruction and Development (adopted 22 July 1944, entered into force 27 December 1945, as amended effective 27 June 2012) 2 UNTS 134 art V(6) (IBRD Articles of Agreement).

[24] Molly Ruhlman, 'NGOs in Global Governance' in Thomas Davies (ed), *Routledge Handbook on NGOs in International Relations* (Routledge 2019) 51. Ibrahim FI Shihata, *The World Bank Legal Papers* (Martinus Nijhoff 2000) iv.

[25] Advisory Council on Gender and Development, see World Bank, 'Advisory Council on Gender and Development' (*World Bank*, 18 October 2022) <http://www.worldbank.org/en/topic/gender/publication/world-bank-advisory-council-on-gender-and-development> accessed 31 August 2024.

[26] For a brief and concise introduction to the ILO's constitutional functioning, see Diller (n 20). Another IO featuring private actors (and, for that matter, other IOs) in its governance structures is the Global Fund, see Zeidan and Abboud (n 16).

[27] International Labour Conference (102nd Session), Towards the ILO Centenary: Realities, Renewal and Tripartite Commitment, Report of the ILO Director-General (Geneva June 2013) paras 88ff. Faina Milman-Silvan, 'Freedom of Association in Deliberative Spaces: The ILO Credentials Committee' in Adelle Blackett and Anne Trebilcock (eds), *Research Handbook on Transnational Labour Law* (Edward Elgar Publishing 2015) 204, 205ff.

Labour Office to employ a 'tripartism-plus' model of social dialogue in the Rana Plaza Arrangement.[28]

On the whole, it is hardly surprising that interactions and initiatives are intertwined. IOs' membership and fields of work typically overlap with those of other IOs, and they work on matters of interest to third states and private actors. This creates a need for both IOs and outside actors to 'keep an eye on each other', to seize chances to collaborate, but also to adapt their respective activities if necessary.

IV. The Elusiveness of Interactions and the Need to Enhance Predictability

Interactions with the outside world are not only an important consideration, but they are also an elusive factor for IO initiatives.

First of all, the frequency and variety of interactions add a great deal of complexity to IOs' often already complex internal procedures and decision-making processes. Even in cases where environmental parameters are reasonably stable as such, the way whether and how (sometimes competing) outside actors use their respective weight, influence, privileges, and power reservoirs in the context of specific IO initiatives are difficult to anticipate. For an ongoing or envisaged secretariat initiative, this additional layer of complexity can prove challenging.

Moreover, interactions are often inherently ambivalent. On the one hand, there are cogent reasons for IOs to engage with the outside world, as interactions provide significant opportunities to promote their respective causes and to achieve greater coherence with outside actors. In this vein, IOs can increase their initiatives' reach, output, relevance, and legitimacy in the eyes of their constituents.[29] In addition, influence from other IOs, non-member states, and private actors can help to overcome internal gridlock and create momentum for initiatives within the IO.

However, on the other hand, interactions can also lead to tensions. They tend to tease out the differences between the respective IO's governance model, institutional rationalities, and claims to legitimacy, and outside actors' agendas, approaches, and preferences. Furthermore, external influence can become distractive or even interfering.[30] In this vein, interactions can precondition, change, or compromise IOs' initiatives, which again raises complex questions of agency, sound governance, legality, and legitimacy.

[28] Diller (n 20).
[29] Dunoff (n 3) 296.
[30] Maupain (n 17) 111.

Finally, IOs are not necessarily in control of interactions and their effects. Secretariat initiatives can of course be one opportunity to increase and steer back control. Yet, given that virtually all major fields of international policy are densely populated by a range of actors, it would be illusory to believe that any IO could insulate itself against 'unwanted' outside influence or that it could fully control how interactions take place and what impact they have on its own evolution.

From the perspective of IOs, there is, therefore, a need to reduce, if possible, interactions' elusiveness and to make interactions' impact on initiatives more predictable. This is important for practitioners in IO secretariats, who try to find the best way for an IO to deliver its mandate and to formulate, steer, or modify initiatives. At the same time, grappling with elusiveness is also important for policymakers, theorists, and the general public, who might be concerned with questions of initiatives' propriety, legality, or legitimacy.

V. Sound Policy, Coordination, Cooperation, and Programming

Reducing elusiveness and enhancing the predictability of interactions is often seen as a task for coordination, cooperation, and programming.[31] In this logic, interactions must be structured along sound policies to coordinate actors, avoid duplication, foster cooperation, and prevent conflicts between them. There are many mechanisms in place to achieve this, ranging from bilateral contacts between IO officials, intermediate tools like the aforementioned granting of consultative or observer status, to sophisticated and encompassing arrangements like the UN System and its machinery.[32] While these mechanisms have yielded noticeable results, there is an overall impression that they fall short of achieving effective, adequate, and legitimate coordination among actors.[33]

Perhaps most importantly, asking how interactions should (or should not) affect IO initiatives—that is, to tell sound from 'unsound' policy, coordination, and programming—is highly dependent on one's perspective. This perspective is shaped by numerous factors including IOs' constitutional mandates, institutional cultures, rationalities, ideational preconceptions, partisan political interests and demands, resource constraints and needs, the variety of interactions, the aforementioned dilemma of interactions being opportunity and risk at the same time, and many others. These factors—many of which render interactions elusive in

[31] Henry Schermers and Niels Blokker, *International Institutional Law: Unity Within Diversity* (6th edn, Brill 2018) paras 1702ff.

[32] ibid.

[33] Cédric Dupont and Astrid Skjold, 'Coordination Conundrum in the United Nations Development System: Solutions from Self-Managed Organizations' (2022) 3 Global Perspectives 1, 2–3, with further references.

the first place—make it difficult to formulate, consent, and implement coherent policies on interactions and their effects.[34]

It would therefore seem that grappling with interactions requires more than 'just' good policies and cooperation. There is a case for looking for a normative standard—a framework—that surpasses the manifold partisan interests and institutional logics of IOs and outside actors, and provides orientation and mutually acceptable reference points for policy efforts. Such a standard can be implied in notions such as 'sound policy' and 'good governance'. However, it can also derive from social, moral, or legal norms.

VI. A Legal-Normative Perspective on Interactions

The following paragraphs will zoom in on the prospects of law as a normative framework for interactions and their influence on IO initiatives. One of the primary functions of legal norms is to reduce complexity, uncertainty, and unpredictability by structuring and ordering conduct.[35] In the present context, the principal goal of taking a legal-normative perspective is to inquire whether and to what extent there exist legal norms that fulfil this function regarding (aspects of) interactions and their influence on IO initiatives. This in turn requires exploring the scope and content of relevant norms of (positive) law.

A. Domestic and international law

Reconstructing interactions from the perspective of law requires isolating the different legal relationships between IOs and outside actors, and carving out their respective rights and obligations pertaining to interactions and mutual influence.

One principal distinction exists between international and domestic legal relationships. IOs typically possess legal personality in the domestic legal orders of their member states, and often in non-member states as well,[36] which means they can hold legal rights and owe obligations towards outside actors under potentially any of these laws. In principle, this opens the door for domestic legal

[34] Schermers and Blokker (n 31) para 1705: 'A concert needs a conductor.'

[35] Malcolm Shaw, *International Law* (8th edn, CUP 2017) 1; in the context of interactions, Luca Pasquet, 'Dialogue or Interaction? A Non-Cosmopolitan Reading of Transjudicial Communication' in Amrei Müller and Hege Elisabeth Kjos (eds), *Judicial Dialogue and Human Rights* (CUP 2017) 467. See also Bernd Rüthers, Christian Fischer, and Axel Birk, *Rechtstheorie* (12th edn, C H Beck 2022) 49ff.

[36] Edward Okeke, *Jurisdictional Immunities of States and International Organizations* (OUP 2018) 279ff. Schermers and Blokker (n 31) para 1598.

orders to frame interactions in many ways: for example, domestic rules can provide the framework for an IO procuring resources or external expertise from outside actors in the context of an initiative.[37] In cases of undue interference, domestic tort law can entitle IOs to seek injunctions or damages. There are, however, major caveats: for many of their activities, IOs enjoy privileges and immunities.[38] Moreover, the application of domestic law may be overlayered by the IO's own law or general principles.[39] And, finally, larger IOs sometimes actively seek to avoid subjugation to domestic law,[40] which might be considered favourable for an initiative from the perspective of the IO itself, but might still impede the effectiveness and legitimacy of an initiative. These factors create a certain 'lopsidedness' of the pertinent domestic legal norms, and diminish the overall relevance of domestic law as a means of normatively structuring IOs' interactive conduct.

B. IOs' constituent instruments

The situation is no less diffuse when it comes to international legal relationships, that is, rights and obligations IOs and outside actors have towards each other under international law.

A frequently chosen starting point for examining these rights and obligations are IOs' constituent instruments, which in many cases contain provisions on an IO's external relations.[41] For instance, Article 12 ILO Constitution reads:

> 1. The International Labour Organization shall cooperate within the terms of this Constitution with any general international organization entrusted with the coordination of the activities of public international organizations having specialized responsibilities and with public international organizations having specialized responsibilities in related fields.

[37] Schermers and Blokker (n 31) paras 1599–600.

[38] Ruffert and Walter (n 9) 69.

[39] August Reinisch, 'Accountability of International Organizations According to National Law' (2005) 36 Netherlands Yearbook of International Law 119.

[40] Schermers and Blokker (n 31) para 1603, with further references.

[41] Eg Articles of Agreement of the International Monetary Fund (adopted 22 July 1944, entered into force 27 December 1945) 2 UNTS 39 art X; IBRD Articles of Agreement (n 23) art V:8; Constitution of the ILO, Part XIII of the Treaty of Versailles (1919 as amended since) art 12 <https://www.ilo.org/publications/ilo-constitution-0> accessed 19 September 2024; Constitution of the World Health Organization (adopted 22 July 1946, entered into force 7 April 1948) 14 UNTS 185 arts 60–71; Convention establishing the World Intellectual Property Organization (adopted 14 July 1967, entered into force 26 April 1970) 828 UNTS 5, art 13; Marrakesh Agreement establishing the World Trade Organization (adopted 15 April 1994, entered into force 1 January 1995) 1867 UNTS 4, art V.

2. The International Labour Organization may make appropriate arrangements for the representatives of public international organizations to participate without vote in its deliberations.
3. The International Labour Organization may make suitable arrangements for such consultation as it may think desirable with recognized non-governmental international organizations, including international organizations of employers, workers, agriculturists and cooperators.

Such provisions are important because they set the IO's internal legal parameters for interactions and, at the same time, define the role and relevance of outside actors within the IO's internal legal order[42] (often relativizing the former in favour of the IO's own governance model).[43] Sometimes, rules on interactions can also be found in IOs' secondary laws, for example in the accountability mechanisms created by a range of multilateral development banks.[44] A secretariat contemplating to launch an initiative or assessing the impact of external influence on ongoing initiatives will find (some) legal-normative guidance in these primary or secondary rules.

However, it is crucial to recall that both IOs' constituent instruments and secondary law, including any provisions concerning interactions with outside actors, only create rights and obligations among the respective IO and its members. For non-member states and other IOs, constituent instruments and secondary rules are *pacta tertiis* and do not create international rights or obligations, unless there is consent (Article 34 Vienna Convention on the Law of Treaties) or a norm of general international law 'externalizing' the constituent instrument's legal effects vis-à-vis non-members.[45] Regarding non-state actors, IOs' constituent instruments typically entitle IOs to interact (eg by entitling the IO to invite observers).[46] Such competences, however, are again legally distinct from

[42] See the provisions cited above in n 13 and No 1.9.1 of the ILO's Standing Orders (n 13). Sometimes, IO's laws explicitly reference the law and practice of other IOs, eg the WTO Agreement on the Application of Sanitary and Phytosanitary Measures (adopted 15 April 1994, entered into force 1 January 1995) 1867 UNTS 493, preambular clause 5 and Annex A No 3 lit. a.

[43] For examples, taken from the internal laws of the ILO, the World Bank, and the Council of Europe, see Gött (n 2) 181, 211, 222.

[44] Richard Bissell and Suresh Nanwani, 'Multilateral Development Bank Accountability Mechanisms: Developments and Challenges' (2009) 3 Central European Journal of International and Security Studies 154, 161.

[45] Notably 'rules of the organization clauses' like Vienna Convention on the Law of Treaties (adopted 22 May 1969, entered into force 27 January 1980) 1155 UNTS 331 art 5; Kirsten Schmalenbach, 'Article 5' in Oliver Dörr and Kirsten Schmalenbach (eds), *Vienna Convention on the Law of Treaties: A Commentary* (2nd edn, Springer 2018) paras 15–16. See also Vienna Convention on the Law of Treaties Between States and International Organizations or Between International Organizations (adopted 21 March 1986) UN Doc A/CONF.129/15 arts 5, 6, and ILC, 'Draft Articles on the Responsibility of International Organizations' (30 May 2011) UN Doc A/CN.4/L.778 (DARIO) art 64.

[46] Few constituent instruments confer direct rights and obligations on non-state actors, eg the EU treaties, Case 6-64 *Flaminio Costa v E.N.E.L.* [1964] ECLI:EU:C:1964:66.

any outbound external action (eg an invitation to, or an agreement with, an entity to become an observer).[47] Consequently, secretariats may have recourse to the aforesaid rules in the constituent instrument to assure themselves of their competencies and autonomy vis-á-vis their own IO's constituents in the context of an initiative, but not to ascertain external rights or obligations vis-à-vis outside actors.

From a practical perspective, this internal–external dichotomy is somewhat alleviated by the fact that outside actors typically recognize the existence of IOs.[48] Moreover, there has been a long-standing conceptual debate about whether IOs possess 'objective' personality, which is conceived to endow them with rights and obligations vis-à-vis non-members.[49] However, outside actors' recognition of an IO's 'existence' does not automatically amount to a legally relevant acceptance of specific rights or obligations in their mutual relations. Neither does recognizing an IO's legal personality, as legal personality only means that the IO is in principle capable of possessing international rights and obligations in its external relations, but it does not indicate which ones it actually possesses.[50]

C. 'External' international law

It is therefore necessary to also look at 'external' international rules[51]—treaties, customary law, and general principles of law—that are binding on both IOs and their outside counterparts.

Many IOs have concluded treaties with third states and other IOs. Some of these treaties are quite encompassing and elaborate. For example, the European Union has concluded an ever-growing number of trade, partnership, association, and neighbourhood agreements with third states and other regional organizations.[52] These agreements cover a wide array of topics and regulate interactions

[47] Such agreements do not always exist as separate written documents, Schermers and Blokker (n 31) para 176.

[48] Chittharanjan Amerasinghe, *Principles of the Institutional Law of International Organizations* (2nd edn, OUP 2005) 87.

[49] Fernando Lusa Bordin, *The Analogy Between States and International Organizations* (CUP 2019) 5.

[50] Philippe Gautier, 'The Reparation for Injuries Case Revisited: The Personality of the European Union' (2000) 4 Max Planck Yearbook of United Nations Las 331, 336–37; Schermers and Blokker (n 31) para 1570.

[51] External law also includes the internal (domestic) law of states and of other IOs. The following analysis is limited to norms of international law binding both the IO and the outside actor it interacts with.

[52] EU-Ukraine Association Agreement, OJ L 161 (29 May 2014) 3–2137; the EU-SADC Economic Partnership Agreement OJ L 250 (16 September 2016) 3–2120; the EU-Canada Comprehensive Economic and Trade Agreement (hereinafter 'CETA') OJ L 11 (14 January 2017) 23–1079; or the (post-Brexit) EU-UK Trade and Cooperation Agreement, OJ L 149 (30 April 2021) 10–2539.

in several ways: first, they define common goals, which set normative anchors pulling towards convergence of evolutionary trajectories. Second, their substantive provisions provide mutually shared standards each party is bound to observe in the course of interactions.[53] Third, their institutional, administrative, and dispute settlement provisions provide machinery through which both cooperative and conflictual interactions can be (and, sometimes, must be) dealt with.[54] All of these provisions provide reference points and mechanisms that make it easier to structure and to predict interactions' influence on initiatives.

Such comprehensive agreements, however, are rather the exception than the rule. While there are also other types of specific treaties, for example host state agreements, a substantive portion of agreements concluded by IOs are decisively shorter and use broad and general language. A staggering example are the myriad relationship agreements concluded between IOs, including the inter-IO relationship agreements forming the legal backbone of the UN System. These agreements typically provide machinery to facilitate direct communication, mutual support, and cooperation. In doing so, they focus on regulating direct and cooperative interactions, as they presuppose that the contracting IOs are willing to make use of the provided machinery. They can be used by secretariats in relation to initiatives vis-à-vis contracting outside actors that are willing to cooperate. However, they typically do not provide rules governing, say, accidental or conflictual interactions. Thus, a secretariat could not, for instance, invoke an agreement to demand from another IO that the latter not interfere with its initiative. In practice, relationship agreements have been filled with subsequent inter-institutional practice to varying extents, which, however, is much more a consequence of conscious policy decisions than of positive rights and obligations under the respective agreements. Finally, there are many agreements that are deliberately informal and leave the question of their legally binding force open[55] (or, in some cases, explicitly exclude it).[56]

In areas not (or not exclusively) regulated by treaties, there is, in principle, room for customary international law or general principles of law to provide

[53] Eg CETA (n 52) chs 1–25, 27, 28: mutually agreed rules on the parties' trade and economic policies limit their scope for permissible indirect interaction. Some rules also require entering into direct interactions or determine to conduct direct interactions in a certain manner, eg in CETA (n 52) ch 25.

[54] Eg CETA (n 52) chs 26 and 29.

[55] Laurence Boisson de Chazournes and André Nollkaemper, 'Partnerships between International Institutions and Issues of (Shared) Responsibility' (2016) 13 International Organizations Law Review 1, 7.

[56] For example, between the World Bank and regional development banks, Boisson de Chazournes and Nollkaemper (n 55) 7–8. See also 'Memorandum of Understanding Between the European Investment Bank and the International Labour Organization (16 July 2015)' para 6.1 <https://www.ilo.org/wcmsp5/groups/public/---dgreports/---jur/documents/genericdocument/wcms_440265.pdf> accessed 31 August 2024.

a normative framework for IOs' interactions with the outside world. As the International Court of Justice held in its *WHO/Egypt* opinion, IOs 'are subjects of international law and, as such, are bound by any obligations incumbent upon them under general rules of international law'.[57] That being said, the crucial question is not whether IOs can in principle be bound or entitled by customary law and general principles. Rather, the question is which specific unwritten norms, if any, are actually 'incumbent upon them' and must be observed during concrete instances of interaction.[58]

The answer to this question is less than clear. In some areas, there are comparatively developed bodies of customary norms, for example regarding the law of treaties concluded between IOs and states or other IOs[59] or—to a lesser extent—the law of IOs' international responsibility.[60] However, these bodies of norms typically only concern specific subject-matters and types of interactions, while remaining silent on others.[61] Overall, the unwritten law of IOs' interactions with the outside world remains piecemeal.

Scholarly proposals on how to fill these gaps, for example with analogies to legal norms governing inter-state interactions[62] or with principles of Global Administrative Law[63] (GAL), make important contributions to approaching

[57] *Interpretation of the Agreement of 25 March 1951 Between the WHO and Egypt* (Advisory Opinion) [1980] ICJ Rep 73, 89–90.

[58] Gött (n 2) 350; Kristina Daugirdas and Sachi Schuricht, 'Breaking the Silence: Why International Organizations Should Acknowledge Customary International Law Obligations to Provide Effective Remedies' in Peter Quayle (ed), *The Role of International Administrative Law at International Organizations* (Brill Nijhoff 2020) 58–59.

[59] As depicted in the substantive provisions of the Vienna Convention on the Law of Treaties between States and International Organizations or between International Organizations (adopted 21 March 1986) A/CONF.1 (VCLT-IO); James Crawford, *Brownlie's Principles of Public International Law* (8th edn, OUP 2012) 179.

[60] DARIO (n 45); Laurence Boisson de Chazournes, *Interactions Between Regional and Universal Organizations: A Legal Perspective* (Brill Nijhoff 2016) 330–31.

[61] Thilo Rensmann, 'International Organizations or Institutions, External Relations and Co-Operation', *Max Planck Encyclopedia of Public International Law* (OUP 2009) paras 11ff, with further references.

[62] Matthias Ruffert, 'Zuständigkeitsgrenzen Internationaler Organisationen im institutionellen Rahmen der internationalen Gemeinschaft' (2000) 38 Archiv des Völkerrechts 129; Niels M Blokker, 'Proliferation of International Organizations: An Exploratory Introduction' in Niels M Blokker and Henry G Schermers (eds), *Proliferation of International Organizations* (Brill Nijhoff 2000) 28; Christian Tietje, 'Global Governance and Inter-Agency Co-Operation in International Economic Law' (2002) 36 Journal of World Trade 501, 513; Jan Wouters and Jed Odermatt, 'Are All International Organizations Created Equal?' (2012) 9 International Organizations Law Review 7, 13; Bordin (n 49) 326ff.

[63] Nico Krisch and Benedict Kingsbury, 'Introduction: Global Governance and Global Administrative Law in the International Legal Order' (2006) 17 European Journal of International Law 1, 17; Benedict Kingsbury and Lorenzo Casini, 'Global Administrative Law Dimensions of International Organizations Law' (2009) 6 International Organizations Law Review 319 (324). On interactions with outside actors, see Laurence de Chazournes, 'Changing Roles of International Organizations: Global Administrative Law and the Interplay of Legitimacies' (2009) 6 International Organizations Law Review 655; Richard B Stewart and Michelle Ratton Sanchez Badin, 'The World Trade Organization and Global Administrative Law' (2009) IILJ Working Paper 2009/7 (Global

uncertainties in the law. However, to explore a legal-normative framework, it is important to achieve sufficient clarity as to both the analytical method and the content of the norms proposed. For example, GAL creatively oscillates between factual, theoretical, and positive-legal considerations, which is fruitful for crafting normative theory and improving IOs' policies, but ultimately avoids taking a clear stance on which elements of its premises and 'principles' are part of positive international law (and why).[64] Moreover, a common legal-normative framework will arguably have to go beyond principles to be operable and give structure in the light of interactions' complexities.[65]

As far as inter-state analogies are concerned, such analogies require that the inter-state constellation is structurally comparable to IOs' interactions with outside actors. This may be generally true regarding topics such as treaties, diplomatic representation, or—to a lesser extent —responsibility. As to other areas, however, there are important and unresolved structural questions, which, for lack of space, I can only briefly mention here. Are the mission and the agenda of an IO a 'sovereign' sphere of jurisdiction, protected by law against outside interference? Do IOs have a right not to be disturbed by other actors? Do IOs and outside actors encounter each other as equals before the law or does the law acknowledge qualitative differences between them? And finally, insofar as there are no specific norms: what is the legal default rule on interactions? Is there a presumption of legality, an 'interactional *Lotus* rule',[66] or is there instead a presumption of illegality, considering that IOs must remain within their conferred powers? The answers to these questions predetermine the viability of analogies: inter-state norms, which rest upon the default position of sovereign equality, can only be transposed to IOs' interactions with outside actors if differences are duly taken into account and the aforementioned questions are addressed.[67]

Open questions also exist regarding IOs' external legal relationships with private actors. It is, in principle, possible that IOs conclude formal and legally binding international treaties with non-state actors, with the latter being either

Administrative Law Series) <https://www.iilj.org/publications/the-world-trade-organization-and-global-administrative-law/> accessed 31 August 2024.

[64] Critical Jan Klabbers, 'Setting the Scene' in Jan Klabbers, Anne Peters, and Geir Ulfstein (eds), *The Constitutionalization of International Law* (OUP 2009) 28.

[65] Gött (n 2) 421ff.

[66] In the *Lotus* case, the Permanent Court of International Justice held that legal restrictions on states' behaviour cannot be presumed, because international obligations require states' consent in order to be binding upon them: *The Case of the S.S. Lotus (France v Turkey)* PCIJ Rep Series A No 10, 18. See also *Military and Paramilitary Activities in and against Nicaragua (Nicaragua v United States of America)* (Merits) [1986] ICJ Rep 14, 135.

[67] I make this argument in more depth in Gött (n 2) 380.

parties or beneficiaries.[68] The conclusion and implementation of agreements has been a part of secretariat initiatives involving interactions with outside non-state actors. That being said, practice tends to focus on other forms of agreements than legally binding treaties.[69] As to customary law and general principles, one (but certainly not the only) principal question for IOs' initiatives is whether and to what extent IOs are legally bound to respect and promote non-state actors' human rights, and if so, on which legal basis, given that IOs are typically not themselves parties to human rights instruments.[70]

Obviously, the questions posed in this section do not come up in every case. However, they lie at the core of both cooperative and non-cooperative interactions. Therefore, without addressing them, the 'external' international law will keep its blank spaces and will be of lesser use in dealing with the impact of interactions on IO initiatives.

D. A more developed international law of interactions

This leaves open the question of whether the international law of IOs' interactions should be developed further at all. One could argue that even in the absence of sufficiently developed legal norms, IO initiatives involving interactions with outside actors by and large appear to 'work'. Yet, a description of how IOs and outside actors interact in reality says nothing about how they ought to interact. One can certainly take the position that interactions have 'worked well enough'. However, such a statement necessarily presupposes a normative standard that defines when interactions can be deemed to work 'well' or 'well enough'. This again leads back to the question of what this standard is, and how it is set, that is, whether by law, institutional rationalities, political preference, moral convictions, or another norm system.[71]

To be sure, quantitatively speaking, most interactions have not been openly conflictual. However, it would be short-sighted to conclude that—for the sole reason that conflict is not ubiquitous—it would be unnecessary to further explore the legal parameters of interaction. The avoidance of conflict is only the

[68] Examples for existing treaties include the Energy Charter Treaty (adopted 17 December 1994, entered into force 16 April 1998) 2080 UNTS 95 chs III and V (of which contain investors' rights) and Convention on the Rights of Persons with Disabilities (adopted 13 December 2006, entered into force 3 May 2008) 2515 UNTS 3, both acceded to by the EU.

[69] Boisson de Chazournes and Nollkaemper (n 55) 9. Other examples are agreements regarding observer status, Schermers and Blokker (n 31) para 176.

[70] Willem van Genugten, *The World Bank Group, the IMF and Human Rights: A Contextualised Way Forward* (Intersentia 2015) 9ff; Cornelia Janik, *Die Bindung Internationaler Organisationen an internationale Menschenrechtsstandards* (Mohr Siebeck 2012) *passim*.

[71] Gött (n 2) 426.

lowest common denominator. As mentioned before, the social functions and potential real-world effects of law go way beyond.

A more developed law of interactions would of course not be a panacea. There will still be a need to understand interactions better and to formulate sound policies to address their impact on initiatives. The role of law is complementary and is not meant to replace, but rather to support and reinforce such efforts, which in turn may benefit from a supra-partisan, common normative foundation. In this vein, a more developed law of interactions might help to enhance the predictability of interactions and the overall effectiveness, propriety, and legitimacy of IO initiatives.

Ultimately, the impact of interactions on IO initiatives should be addressed through the interconnected use of three approaches, following three leading questions:

1) A factual-empirical approach, asking how interactions influence IOs' initiatives in reality. Its primary method is fact finding through observation, interviews, archival work, and similar activity. There is a growing number of case studies, not least in this volume, contributing to this end.
2) A policy approach, seeking sound policies to steer the way in which interactions influence IOs' initiatives and, ultimately, IO evolution. Its primary method is theorizing, formulating, promoting, and evaluating policies and administrative approaches, both within and outside IOs. Such policies can be adopted in support of IO initiatives, but they can also themselves be (part of) a new initiative.
3) A legal-normative approach, as proposed in this chapter, asking how interactions ought to influence IOs' initiatives according to norms of positive law. Its primary methods are interpretation, legal construction, and refinement, with the overall goal of expounding the normative framework of a law of interactions, which again provides structure, orientation, common ground, and maybe inspiration, for future policies, including future initiatives.

VII. Conclusion

To conclude, interactions with the outside world are an important but also an elusive factor for IO initiatives. Complementing existing efforts to make the impact of interactions by an (international) law of interactions could in principle provide a supra-partisan normative framework to deal with interactions' elusiveness. Yet, such a law is currently underdeveloped. As I have argued in this chapter, its further exploration and refinement could help to deal with the impact of IOs' interactions with the outside world on their initiatives and, ultimately, their own evolution.

23

International Organization Interactions with Multi-stakeholder Initiatives

The International Labour Organization Experience

Janelle M Diller[*]

I. Introduction

In today's evolving regulatory landscape, public international organizations (IOs) established in formal state-based international orders face challenges from transnational economic activity that operates through private contracts in global supply chains (supply chains). Diverse stakeholders across private and public sectors form multi-stakeholder initiatives (MSIs) in efforts to address this transnational regulatory gap, acting in parallel with national and international governance orders and industry standards.[1] Facing their limited influence on transnational relations, secretariats and executive heads of IOs increasingly interact with such MSIs to pursue mutual governance aims that are in line with the IO's goals. However, the IO's international cooperation with its members differs markedly from the plurality and methods of MSI actors and interests outside the IO's constituent order.[2] In such contexts, the IO typically interacts with MSIs using soft non-hierarchical forms of governance known as collaboration and orchestration.[3]

[*] The views are solely those of the author.

[1] There is no single definition of MSIs. MSIs are ad hoc collaborative efforts among various stakeholders who seek a common aim that involves influencing conduct or other governance impact. Different MSIs bring together different combinations of stakeholders, such as multinational and local enterprises, international and local non-governmental organizations (NGOs), governments and IOs, and global and local unions and business associations. Some MSIs develop standards and related certification schemes, while others focus on single issues or 'general human rights, environmental and social issues relevant to a particular industry (or) policy engagement or learning amongst stakeholders to improve business systems'. MSIntegrity, 'About MSIs' <https://www.msi-integrity.org/about/about-msis/> accessed 8 September 2024.

[2] Actors within the IO's constituent order are typically defined in the constituent instrument on which the IO is founded, as further articulated by subsequent agreement or practice agreed by its members. See eg Henry G Schermers and Niels M Blokker, *International Institutional Law* (5th edn, Nijhoff 2011) 722–25.

[3] In 'collaboration', an IO joins the MSI directly as a participant; in 'orchestration', the IO plays an indirect role as a non-participant. Orchestration by IOs has been defined as 'an indirect mode

Janelle M Diller, *International Organization Interactions with Multi-stakeholder Initiatives* In: *International Organization Initiatives*. Edited by: Gabrielle Marceau and Henner Gött, Oxford University Press. © Oxford University Press 2025.
DOI: 10.1093/9780197803325.003.0024

This chapter focuses on the International Labour Organization (ILO)[4] and the initiatives of its International Labour Office (Office) and Director-General[5] to interact through MSIs together with ILO constituents to achieve decent work[6] in transnational supply chains. In a novel use of its constitutional functions,[7] the Office recently invented a method for ILO orchestration of MSIs that responds to its mandate to strengthen its constituents' capacity to influence supply chain working conditions in their countries. The chapter explores the Office's path-breaking design and orchestration of the Rana Plaza Arrangement,[8] or 'RPA', as an MSI to address the deficit of remediation for violations of decent work in the garment supply chain sector in Bangladesh. The chapter analyses the context and launch of the RPA after the worst industrial accident on record and its effects of providing benefits for the victims' needs and stimulating the start-up of a pilot employment injury system in the country. It further traces the influence of the RPA model on the design of the ILO supply chain strategy and action programme approved by the ILO Governing Body in 2023[9] and on transnational actors' decent work practices. The chapter concludes with observations on the extent to which such initiatives point to effective avenues for responsible and joined-up modes of international and transnational governance.

of governance that relies on inducements and incentives rather than mandatory controls'. Kenneth Abbott and others, 'Orchestrating Global Governance' in Kenneth Abbott and others (eds), *International Organizations as Orchestrators* (CUP 2015) 349.

[4] The ILO was established in 1919 under Pt XIII of the Treaty of Peace of Versailles (arts 387–427), reprinted in ILO Official Bulletin I (1919–1920) 332. In 1946, the ILO became a United Nations (UN) specialized agency operating under an agreement between the United Nations and the International Labour Organization, entered into force 14 December 1946, reprinted in ILO Official Bulletin XXIX:6 (1946) 383 (UN-ILO Agreement).

[5] The term 'Secretariat', used in other chapters in this volume, is not used in the ILO context. The ILO Constitution refers to the International Labour Office (referred to as 'Office') and to the Director-General who is responsible for the 'efficient conduct' of the Office. Constitution of the ILO, Part XIII of the Treaty of Versailles (1919 as amended since) arts 8–10 <https://www.ilo.org/publications/ilo-constitution-0> accessed 19 September 2024 (ILO Const). The responsibilities of the Director-General and staff of the Office are 'exclusively international in character' and should be exercised independently of the interest of any member or 'authority external to the Organization': ibid, art 9 paras 4–5.

[6] 'Decent work' combines four constitutional ILO aims: promoting jobs and enterprise, guaranteeing rights at work, extending social protection, and promoting social dialogue. International Labour Conference (97th Session), ILO Declaration on Social Justice for a Fair Globalization (Geneva 13 June 2000) (ILO Social Justice Declaration).

[7] Functions include research and information dissemination and expert advisory services and technical assistance on implementing international labour standards including through social dialogue. See eg ILO Const (n 5) art 10 and Annex pt III (Philadelphia Declaration); ILO Social Justice Declaration (n 6) pt II.A.

[8] 'The Rana Plaza Arrangement' <https://ranaplaza-arrangement.org/> accessed 13 May 2023.

[9] The Governing Body of the International Labour Office ('Governing Body') oversees the work of the Office and is made up of 56 persons: 28 Governments, 14 employers, and 14 workers. ILO Const (n 5) art 7 para 1.

II. ILO Context

As the primary UN agency competent to set and apply global standards for decent work, the ILO has faced increasing demands by its constituents[10] to find relevant and effective ways to prevent and remedy worker abuses linked to onerous terms of production in transnational supply chains.[11] Confronted with a lack of tripartite consensus among constituents at global level on direct ILO action to address such deficits, the Office took the initiative to build collaborative arrangements at country level between national tripartite constituents and local and transnational supply chain counterparts in countries facing decent work deficits in supply chains. This novel application of the Office's constitutional means of action received further impetus from the 2013 collapse of the five-factory Rana Plaza building in Bangladesh, which left 3,200 supply chain workers dead or injured in the worst industrial accident on record.

In the aftermath of uncoordinated efforts by public and private actors to help, the ILO faced calls to act from its constituents and transnational companies and sectoral union federations. As the global agency responsible for social protection standards in case of employment injury, the ILO designed and orchestrated a collaborative arrangement between ILO national constituents and their in-country supply chain counterparts. The core innovation of the Office was to include transnational supply chain actors in the use of its constitutional functions[12] to aid member state governments and social partners to build conditions of decent work in supply chain operations in the country. As with similar Office orchestration initiatives,[13] the Office indirectly provided its influence and expertise to

[10] The ILO constituents are governments, employers, and workers of each member state. Representatives from the tripartite partners form national delegations at the International Labour Conference where the state and non-state delegates share equal power in standard-setting, policy-making, and governance functions (except budget issues). ILO Const (n 5) art 3. International Labour Conference delegates elect their respective state and non-state members of the Governing Body who also share equal tripartite voting power on most matters.

[11] Eg ILO, 'Purchasing Practices and Working Conditions in Global Supply Chains: Results from Field Work in Bangladesh, China, India, South Africa and Turkey' (2021) <https://www.ilo.org/publications/purchasing-practices-and-working-conditions-global-supply-chains-results> accessed 9 September 2024 (supply chain purchasing practices set below production costs had negative impacts on wages, working hours, occupational safety, and health).

[12] ILO Const (n 5) art 10 (duties involving observance of international labour standards, advisory services, technical assistance, information dissemination).

[13] Since 2013, the ILO has served as a non-party neutral chair to the governance committees of the bipartite: 'Accord on Fire and Building Safety for Bangladesh' (signed 13 May 2013) <https://bangladesh.wpengine.com/wp-content/uploads/2018/08/2013-Accord.pdf> accessed 23 September 2024; 'Accord on Fire and Building Safety for Bangladesh: May 2018' (signed 21 June 2017, effective May 2018) <https://bangladesh.wpengine.com/wp-content/uploads/2020/11/2018-Accord.pdf> accessed 23 September 2024 (collectively, Bangladesh Fire Accords); and the sequel 'International Accord for Health and Safety in the Textile and Garment Industry' (1 November 2023) <https://internationalaccord.org/wp-content/uploads/2023/11/International-Accord-for-Health-and-Safety-in-the-Textile-and-Garment-Industry-1-November-2023_Public-Version.pdf> accessed 23

MSI actors, many of whom voluntarily cooperated with the initiative because ILO's aims and methods were perceived as mitigating the risk inherent in operating in the country. Among other innovations, the Office convened a new mode of 'tripartite-plus'[14] social dialogue bringing national tripartite constituents together with transnational supply chain stakeholders in the export sector to identify shared objectives and how to achieve them collaboratively. It also lent its technical expertise to help apply relevant international labour standards in the specific context.

The Office's orchestration of MSIs such as the RPA to advance decent work in supply chains at local level influenced tripartite consensus at global level for ILO action. The method of leveraging Office expertise to build multi-stakeholder cooperation between constituents at country level and transnational supply chain actors influenced the Office design of a comprehensive strategy for decent work in supply chains.[15] In 2023, the Governing Body approved the supply chain strategy and action programme in a decision that implicitly endorsed the Office's novel use of ILO means of action in MSIs to promote decent work in transnational networks of production and distribution.

III. The Practical Arrangement on Payments to the Rana Plaza Victims (RPA)

The RPA served two primary aims: processing and payment of financial benefit awards for the losses of hundreds of injured workers and of the families of 1,135 workers who died in the collapse of the Rana Plaza Building factories, and provision of ongoing necessary medical and allied services for workers' injuries. The Office orchestrated the multi-year initiative in response to requests of various stakeholders, including the national constituents concerned (the Bangladesh

September 2024, under which two global unions operate country-specific safety programmes with global brands.

[14] 'Tripartite-plus' decision-making dialogue involved national tripartite constituents and industry actors, brands, and global union federations in the supply chain and several global and local NGOs concerned.

[15] ILO Governing Body (347th Session), 'ILO Strategy on Decent Work in Supply Chains' (Geneva 27 February 2023) GB.347/INS/8 <https://www.ilo.org/resource/gb/347/ilo-strategy-decent-work-supply-chains> accessed 23 September 2024. The strategy is based on building blocks adopted by the Tripartite Working Group on Options to Ensure Decent Work in Supply Chains (June–July 2022). Previous steps taken to evolve tripartite consensus included the Technical Meeting on Achieving Decent Work in Global Supply Chains (February 2022) and International Law Conference (105th Session) Resolution concerning decent work in supply chains (Geneva 8 July 2016); and the Governing Body follow-up to it, ILO Governing Body (328th Session) 'Decision on the fifth item on the agenda: Follow-up to the resolution concerning decent work in global supply chains ILO programme of action 2017–21' (Geneva 10 November 2016) GB.328/INS/5 (add.).

government and employer and worker organizations), the global union federation (GUF) IndustriALL and its sectoral affiliates in Bangladesh, and brands and retailers sourcing in the country.

The initiative commenced in late 2013 following a high-level Office mission to Dhaka and was overseen by the ILO Director-General and his senior management team until its satisfactory conclusion in 2018. In consultation with the stakeholders, the Office drafted the text of a multi-stakeholder Understanding[16] in which the stakeholder signatories agreed to common aims, guiding principles for implementation (Practical Guidelines), and a multi-stakeholder governance structure (Rana Plaza Coordination Committee or 'RPCC') composed of representatives of signatories. The agreement authorized the RPCC to oversee the scheme, set funding levels, establish administrative mechanisms to process victims' claims following specified procedures, and authorize the payment of awards. The text appointed the ILO as a non-party to serve, through the Office, as the neutral and independent chair of the RPCC and to provide technical information on employment injury standards and actuarial procedures.

A guiding 'single approach' to how benefits would be determined was agreed by the parties to the Understanding based on a Bangladeshi policy adopted prior to the accident. That tripartite-agreed policy had incorporated the unratified ILO Employment Injury Benefits Convention, 1964 (No. 121) as a standard of conduct for remediation of occupational supply chain accidents. With the orchestrated guidance of the Office, the RPCC took decisions that safeguarded the substantive, procedural, and governance aims of the scheme and aligned the claims process with Convention No. 121, local law, and general principles of law.[17]

The RPCC held debates and took decisions subject to a quota of members which required the presence of tripartite national constituents. In consultation with the Government of Bangladesh, the Office as ILO chair submitted agendas and documents in advance to all RPCC members. The minutes of meetings and decisions were prepared for review and approval at subsequent Committee

[16] For the final agreed text of the Understanding signed by the participating stakeholders, see 'Understanding for a Practical Arrangement on Payments to the Victims of the Rana Plaza Accident and Their Families and Dependents for Their Losses' (20 November 2013, as amended) <https://ranaplaza-arrangement.org/MOU_Practical_Arrangement_FINAL-RanaPlaza-c34d165e591e40d43a603e95ac2b38e9.pdf> accessed 23 September 2024. Signatories consisted of the Bangladesh Government; national export industry, employers and workers organizations; global brands and retailers; the transnational sectoral GUF in the industry (IndustriALL); and a global and local NGO.

[17] See Janelle M Diller, 'The Role of the State in the Exercise of Transnational Public and Private Authority over Labour Standards' (2020) 17 International Organizations Law Review 41, 59–65; Rebecca Prentice, 'Workers' Right to Compensation After Garment Factory Disasters: Making Rights a Reality' (*University of Sussex*, 2018) 7 <https://sussex.figshare.com/articles/report/Workers_right_to_compensation_after_garment_factory_disasters_making_rights_a_reality/23455172?file=41164034> accessed 23 September 2024.

sessions. As the work progressed, complex issues of how to apply the principles of Convention No. 121 in line with Bangladeshi law required consultation of local legal experts, including on the definition of 'dependent' and the apportionment of benefits among surviving dependents. Early in its work, the RPCC created an independent website in English and Bangla to inform claimants and the public of the MSI's progress.[18] Recommendations to authorize payment of awards were submitted to the RPCC by the Rana Plaza Claims Administration (RPCA), an independent expert body created by the RPCC to process claimants' data subject to due process and data privacy protocols and to individual claimants' informed consent after meeting with independent public interest counsel. Three high-level jurists serving as Commissioners[19] certified the draft awards before their submission to the RPCC.

The level of financing to pay the claim awards was fixed by the RPCC with the advice and calculations of ILO technical experts. Donations were deposited into the Rana Plaza Donors Trust Fund set up by the Office acting for the ILO as an independent Trustee at the RPCC's request and subject to ILO financial regulations that permitted the holding of third-party funds in trust for purposes consistent with the ILO's mandate. Under the terms and conditions of the Trust Fund, donors could choose to remain anonymous or to be credited as a voluntary contributor on the Arrangement's website. Within two years, by October 2015, the initiative had raised USD 30 million, largely from brands and retailers, to cover the unemployment injury benefits and injury-related medical care of all claimants.[20] After all immediate benefits and medical care were allotted, the remaining funds were transferred for ongoing administration of victims' lifetime benefits and medical care needs by local institutional arrangements approved by the RPCC. By 2018, the RPCC evaluated the work of the scheme through an independent audit and ended the Arrangement after certification that it had been satisfactorily implemented.

Separately, a pilot fund to cover employment injury benefits to garment workers in the export sector was established in 2022 by Government directive and financed by employers with brands and retailers.[21] The aim is to evaluate the

[18] The archived English version of the RPA website at http://ranaplaza-arrangement.org, accessed 23 September 2024, contains the texts of the Understanding and the Terms and Conditions of the Trust Fund, a history of who created the scheme and how it was run, its activities, timelines, and published donors, and the methodology, calculations, and benefit levels used for claims and payment of awards. For full records, see the Office Archives at ILO Geneva.

[19] The Commissioners included two national jurists and the former UN chief of the Iraq-Kuwait Claims Commission who also headed the RPCA. See RPA, 'Commissioners' <https://ranaplaza-arrangement.org/commissioners/> accessed 23 September 2024.

[20] RPA, 'Trust Fund and Full Donor List' <https://ranaplaza-arrangement.org/activities/> accessed 23 September 2024.

[21] ILO Press Release, 'Bangladesh Government Launches First Employment Injury Scheme Pilot in the Garment Sector' (*ILO*, 21 June 2022) <https://www.ilo.org/global/topics/geip/news/WCMS_849244/lang--en/index.htm≥ accessed 23 September 2024.

capacity of the government and stakeholders to sustain such protection after several years and potentially expand its coverage.

IV. Observations and Conclusions

The RPA highlights several elements that can affect the development of similar Office initiatives and their acceptance by the Organization and its members for needed reforms as well as their potential long-term impact on joined-up modes of international and transnational governance.

First, the convergence of certain conditions triggered the interests of the Office and other actors to collaborate in the MSI. For the Office, a shortfall in capacity to achieve compliance with decent work in supply chains through its own state-based tripartite constituents encouraged innovative governance modes that included outside actors.[22] In turn, the constituents and outside actors each had benefits to gain in relying on the authority and know-how of the Office through a defined collaboration.[23] Finally, the member state concerned accepted the novel governance model of technical cooperation that involved multi-stakeholder power sharing—indeed it may have preferred it to direct intervention.[24]

Second, the degree to which the Office initiative meets the needs of the stakeholders affects the ability to resolve the immediate situation as well as the capacity of the Organization to deal with similar challenges in the future. In this case, the Office's novel use of Convention No. 121 (although unratified by Bangladesh) and innovative inclusion of transnational supply chain actors through an MSI served the stakeholders' needs for remediation and desire to minimize the supply chain's reputational risk. It also strengthened the capacity of Bangladeshi law and institutions to address future accidents in supply chains by spawning a pilot fund seen as a 'transformative approach towards an employment injury scheme for all'.[25] The initiative enhanced ILO influence and credibility among transnational supply chain actors that created impetus to improve

[22] In theory, IOs are more likely to orchestrate when they lack certain capabilities needed to achieve their goals through other governance modes, see Abbott and others (n 3). Unlike global sectoral actors such as GUFs and MNEs, the ILO constituents do not detect non-compliance in global value chains. Xinyuan Dai, 'Orchestrating Monitoring: The Optimal Adaptation of International Organizations' in Kenneth Abbott and others (eds), *International Organizations as Orchestrators* (CUP 2015) 139.

[23] Correlated goals encourage orchestration, see Abbott and others (n 3). In the Rana Plaza and Accord cases, the outside GUFs and MNEs sought ILO guidance in a 'bottom up' direction. ibid.

[24] Abbott and others (n 3). The multi-stakeholder approach may help the state to build networks and local capacity without the need for treaty ratification. In the RPA, the Government gave effect to the provisions of Convention No 121 on employment injury benefits without being legally bound to do so. See text of the Understanding (n 16).

[25] See ILO Press Release (n 21) and accompanying text.

practices toward fuller alignment with ILO standards. On the supply chain level, the RPA and similar initiatives demonstrated the efficacy of 'tripartite-plus' social dialogue involving transnational industry and union actors, which influenced the design and adoption of the ILO strategy for decent work in supply chains approved by the Governing Body.[26]

Third, the RPA and similar Office initiatives build sustainable results within the Organization in many cases by growing the practical capacity of the Office and its constituents to connect with outside forces in supply chains that affect decent work. For the Office, MSI interactions offer greater access to compliance information about obstacles to decent work in supply chains, which in turn informs ILO standard-setting, policy-making, and research to tackle such challenges. For national constituents, the opportunity to participate in such MSIs boosts their influence and capacity to work with transnational industry and union federations. In the future, such alliances may enrich sectoral expertise in ILO standard-setting and policy-making to address transnational decent work challenges in supply chains.[27]

Finally, an Office initiative like the RPA demonstrates a potential for hybrid governance that blends the formal authority of governments and IOs with the reflexive and market authority of outside supply chain actors. As long as the Office acts for the Organization within its own legal order in orchestrating an MSI as a non-party, it 'remains within conferred powers'[28] and exercises only indirect influence.[29] The grounding of the secretariat initiative in the IO's legal order is crucial to the eventual acceptance of the initiative or reform by the members through the IO's oversight organs. In the RPA, the IO's constitutional and regulatory authority served as a built-in steering mechanism to define the IO interactions with

[26] See ILO Strategy for Decent Work in Supply Chains (n 15) and accompanying text.

[27] Output 5 of the ILO Strategy on Decent Work in Supply Chains (n 15) aims to develop options for initiatives that complement existing international labour standards to take into account the challenges of cross-border supply chains which may include sectoral approaches. See ILO Governing Body (349th Session), 'Agenda of the Future Sessions of the International Labour Conference' (Geneva 12 October 2023) GB.349/INS/2 paras 24, 42–44 <https://www.ilo.org/resource/gb/349/agenda-future-sessions-international-labour-conference> accessed 23 September 2024. Sectoral expertise among ILO constituents has proven essential to developing and implementing the Maritime Labour Convention. See Maritime Labour Convention (adopted 23 February 2006, entered into force 20 August 2013) 2952 UNTS 3 <https://www.ilo.org/international-labour-standards/maritime-labour-convention-2006> accessed 23 September 2024.

[28] See Henner Gött, 'Interactions with the Outside World as a Factor for IO Initiatives', Chapter 22 in this volume, n 66 and accompanying text. The IO orchestration of an MSI can be considered within its legal authority so long as it is consistent with its own constitutional and regulatory order and with applicable provisions and principles of international law.

[29] Office action as a direct participant in collaboration with private sector actors is governed by constitutional and internal policies and rules, including in public–private partnerships (PPPs) and so-called multi-stakeholder partnerships which must comply with pre-set qualifying criteria before the IO lends its formal authority to the exercise of market-based authority. ILO, 'ILO Policy and Procedure Relating to Public–Private Partnership' <https://www.ilo.org/pardev/public-private-partnerships/WCMS_190854/lang--en/index.htm≥ accessed 3 January 2024.

the MSI without compromise to prioritizing the ILO mandate and coordination with and for its tripartite constituents.

The way in which the secretariat initiatives relate to their IO legal orders not only affects the initiative's impact within the IO but also determines the basis of legal responsibility of the IO to the MSI actors and third parties affected by the MSI's action. In the case of the RPA, the benefit awards had legal consequences on third-party victims' rights under national law as authorized by the state of Bangladesh.[30] In most situations involving allegations of third-party harm suffered from MSI action, the MSI itself has no legal personality to respond to such allegations[31] and legal responsibility falls to the MSI members. While an IO's legal responsibility to non-state and non-IO persons or entities is left open in international law,[32] the ILO's responsibility as a non-party orchestrating the RPA would depend on the compliance of the Office with the rules of the ILO legal order and its control or influence over the alleged harmful conduct. In contrast, the legal responsibility of the individual MSI actors for their separate or collective impacts would align with the legal order(s) in which they operate and, in some cases, with the duty to adhere to responsible governance practices recognized under the evolving law governing MSIs.[33]

In practice, Office orchestration of MSIs like the RPA can contribute to the capacity of state and non-state actors to exercise responsible MSI governance that respects internationally recognized principles such as those that guided the RPA Understanding.[34] By so doing, IO orchestration of MSIs may eventually help innovate effective modes of governance at the nexus of international cooperation and transnational governance.

[30] See Understanding (n 16) Practice Guideline 5.

[31] The MSI has legal personality if it is registered under national law. See Janelle M Diller, 'Multistakeholder Initiatives' in Guy Davidov and others (eds), *Oxford Handbook on the Law of Work* (OUP 2024).

[32] See International Law Commission (ILC), 'Report of the International Law Commission on the Work of Its 63rd Session' (26 April–3 June and 4 July–12 August 2011) UN Doc A/66/10, s V pt E, 'Text of the Draft Articles on the Responsibility of International Organizations'. explicitly limiting international responsibility of IOs to other IOs and to States (see draft arts 33(2) and 50).

[33] OECD, 'Engagement with Trade Unions in Due Diligence Processes Conducted by Industry-led or Multi-Stakeholder Initiatives: Clarification by the OECD Investment Committee' (2021) <https://mneguidelines.oecd.org/engagement-with-trade-unions-in-due-diligence-processes-conducted-by-industry-led-or-multi-stakeholder-initiatives.pdf> accessed 10 February 2025, at n 25, citing 2016 Dutch National Contact Point specific instance (engaging collectively in an MSI does not relieve a company from its own due diligence responsibilities where challenges require it to do so).

[34] See Understanding (n 16) (transparency, equity, rule of law, due process, fair coverage of losses of all victims).

24

How Do External Factors Shape Institutional, Legal, Strategic, or Policy Change in International Organizations

Review of Selected Examples in World Bank Practice

Hassane Cissé[*]

I. Introduction

As a leading international financial institution, the World Bank (Bank) undergoes continual transformation.[1] These transformations often stem from an intricate process of external pressure exerted on the Bank's strategies, policies, operational practices, legal interpretations, and financing modalities.

Since this book is about international organization (IO) initiatives taken by their secretariats or executive heads that push the boundaries of the mandate of an organization beyond its founding operational activities to respond to new needs of their membership, it is important to clarify an issue of terminology in respect of the executive organ of the World Bank. Unlike many IOs, the Bank does not use the term 'Secretariat' to refer to its President (including the management and staff they appoint), who is responsible for the day-to-day operations and activities of the institution. The 'term of art' that is used in the Bank is Management. The Articles of Agreement of the Bank do not use

* The views expressed in this chapter do not reflect the opinions of any institution to which I have been or am presently affiliated. I would like to express my sincere gratitude to Vikram Raghavan, Lead Counsel at the World Bank, and Sean O'Connell, Harvard Law School Class of 2025, for their thorough review, comments, and improvements to the chapter. All opinions and any errors or omissions are my own.

[1] While this chapter is focused on change at the World Bank, it is part of the broader issue of global legal, political, and economic governance which is at present hotly debated around the world. I offered my views on the subject in remarks at the 2020 American Society of International Law (ASIL) annual meeting, 'The Promise of International Law'; Hassane Cisse, 'Remarks by Hassane Cisse' (2020) 114 Proceedings of the ASIL Annual Meeting 43 <https://www.cambridge.org/core/journals/proceedings-of-the-asil-annual-meeting/article/abs/remarks-by-hassanecisse/56434085BC6DEAD064945A70A22BA8C7?utm_campaign=shareaholic&utm_medium=email_this&utm_source=email> accessed 4 September 2024. See also the views of Joseph Stiglitz, Nobel Prize in Economics Laureate and former chief economist of the World Bank: Joseph Stiglitz, *Globalization and Its Discontents* (W.W. Norton 2003).

Hassane Cissé, *How Do External Factors Shape Institutional, Legal, Strategic, or Policy Change in International Organizations*
In: *International Organization Initiatives*. Edited by: Gabrielle Marceau and Henner Gött, Oxford University Press.
 DOI: 10.1093/9780197803325.003.0025

such term but state in Article 5 (on Organization and Management) that '[t]he President of the Bank shall be the chief of the operating staff of the Bank and shall conduct, under the direction of Executive Directors, the ordinary business of the Bank'. Early memoranda of the Executive Directors of the Bank (also referred to as the Board) have used the term 'Management' to refer to the President and his management team, and this term has continued to be used throughout the history of the Bank. The division of labour between the two organs, namely the President and the Executive Directors, is set out in the aforementioned Article 5. For purposes of this chapter, it is important to note that Management is responsible for preparing and proposing to the Board, for its review and approval, new loans as well as new policy, strategic, operational, or institutional initiatives or changes. It is safe to say that at the Bank, initiatives come from the Management, on its own or following a request by Executive Directors. Management carries out all the executive functions of what is traditionally called a secretariat of an IO, but these functions include some that are not present in many IO secretariats because they stem from the nature of the Bank as a lending institution (eg preparation of loans to be submitted to the Board for its approval).[2] For the purposes of this chapter, references to the Bank's initiatives should be understood as initiatives by Management, which are later submitted to the Board for its review and approval or endorsement. The examples discussed in this chapter have typically been conceptualized in proposals by the Management. Once approved or endorsed, the final version reflecting the consensus of the Board becomes part of the operating framework of the Bank and is implemented by Management and staff. The 'initiatives' on sanctions reform and anti-corruption policy (III. A), post-conflict reconstruction (III. B), and adjustment lending (III. C) were conceptualized in Board Papers and implemented through policies or strategies drafted by staff for Management. In circumstances where the request for certain new areas of work originates from one or more Executive Directors—such as the developments in relation to human rights (III. D)—the Management, through its staff, is central to ultimately designing the initiative and also its final implementation.

This chapter examines the ways in which external factors shape institutional change at the World Bank, including Management initiatives and Executive Directors' responses. Section II sketches out a general theory of externally induced change based on my observation and experience at the Bank working

[2] The Bank's set-up is loosely based on the model of a private sector corporation. This has influenced the terminology and concepts it uses as compared to those used by traditional IOs (eg Management instead of Secretariat, Board instead of Council, Conference, Committee, or Assembly; shareholders; weighted voting, etc).

on the issues discussed in this chapter, in various capacities, including as chief counsel for Operations Policy, deputy general counsel, or global practice director. These observations are drawn from having reviewed, commented, co-drafted, and/or signed off on most of the Board papers (ie the management proposal or 'initiative') discussed in this chapter and also having worked on the new or revised policy or strategy implemented as a consequence of these initiatives. Section III reviews four specific instances of externally influenced change at the Bank and their impact on institutional evolution and direction. These instances are first-hand reflections on how these initiatives have developed in the Bank and how they have subsequently shaped the Bank's operations.

II. A Theory of Externally Induced Change

A. Triggers of transformation

At the Bank, the trigger for institutional transformation often occurs following a build-up of external economic and/or socio-political pressures. Just as the factors contributing to these pressures are multifaceted, so too is the ultimate trigger for change. Key among these triggers are (1) developments in global, regional, or national political environments; (2) challenges posed by reforms and opinions adopted by national or international legal institutions; (3) perspectives and critiques from civil society; and (4) the sociological influence of the United States (US) President traditionally selecting the nominee to the position of Bank President, which selection is reviewed by the Executive Directors who alone have the power to appoint the President but have never rejected a US nominee.

Change at the Bank can be catalysed by the actions of other actors, multilateral organizations, as well as of governments. Policy revisions at other international financial institutions, like the International Monetary Fund (IMF) or regional development banks, can function to redirect the Bank's focus. At the country level, the subtler influences of political preference and national mood have similar force. The spillover effects of domestic politics on international policy often magnify individual state concerns into regional, or even global, calls for policy reform. The Bank is not insulated from these pressures. Its Board of Governors is represented by individual member states holding voting shares based on their economic contributions to the organization.

Legislative developments and judicial decisions are a concrete manifestation of these political shifts that sometimes trigger Bank reform. Domestic and international courts have challenged the actions of the Bank throughout its history and triggered institutional realignments.[3] Similarly, the implementation of multilateral treaties, like the Paris Agreement, or international standards, like the United Nations (UN) Sustainable Development Goals, can lead to transformations in the Bank.

The Bank also responds to a variety of civil society pressures. Non-governmental organizations (NGOs) push for reform, academics develop new critiques, media outlets voice criticisms, and public opinion calls for priority shifts. Similarly, the private sector can be an instigator of institutional change. The growing influence of multinational firms and the private sector's role in goods production, service provisioning, and global supply chain maintenance often bring it in contact with the Bank's development mandate. In recent years, the growing presence of NGOs and think-tanks pursuing private–public partnerships and innovative policy has also been influential.

One of the primary sources of change at the Bank is its President: an originally external actor regularly cast as an internal change-maker that leads the Presidency of the Bank and its staff. The Bank's Presidents are traditionally recommended by the United States and have, to date, come from outside the Bank. Most Presidents come from a corporate finance or government background, with fewer from academic or non-profit careers. All have been US citizens.

The sociological impact of this external appointment system is a way to turn views 'from the outside' into Bank initiatives. Presidents arrive with views on development issues and the role of the World Bank that are influenced by their backgrounds and career paths. The symbolic and operational authority wielded by Presidents often helps promote these perspectives and can move the institution in new directions.[4]

B. From internal change process to substantive outcomes

When the external pressure reaches a particular threshold, and in some cases benefits from a catalysing trigger that overcomes any potential or actual internal resistance, be it from within Management, staff, or some Executive Directors, the Bank President initiates an internal review process, on his own or at the request of Executive Directors. The methods of internal review at the World Bank

[3] A recent example is the U.S. Supreme Court's 2019 decision in *Jam v. Int'l Fin. Corp., 139 S. Ct. 759 (2019)*. There, the Court determined that the Bank could not use its mandated privileges and immunities to avoid attachment in cases relating to Bank-funded projects.

[4] Koldo Echebarria, 'Unveiling the True Power of the President of the World Bank' (*Center for Global Development*, 27 June 2023) <https://www.cgdev.org/blog/unveiling-true-power-president-world-bank> accessed 4 September 2024. Echebarria explores the role of the President as an agent for external change in greater detail.

are manifold and intricate. A deep exploration of the specifics of the Bank's internal assessment and review processes is outside the scope of this chapter.

These processes can be—and typically are on major topics—accompanied by a degree of external stakeholder involvement. In some cases, the Bank (usually the President with the Executive Directors' endorsement) creates a panel of non-Bank experts to issue a report and recommendations for action. In other instances, the Bank holds several rounds of external consultations involving governments, civil society groups, and other stakeholders.

For example, when revising its environmental and social safeguard policies, the Bank's conduct of external consultations with NGOs, member governments, civil society, and academia helped to create the Environmental and Social Framework.[5] The Framework implemented many far-reaching reforms and changes in the Bank's operations and had a significant impact on development financing practices.[6]

The outcomes of these internal change processes can be as varied as their causes. In different cases, the Bank has decided to reform its legal, strategic, policy, financial, or even operational modus operandi to adapt to external demands. However, as will be explored further below, when external pressures are deemed less powerful than the perceived institutional or legal risks associated with the desired change, the Bank sometimes attempts a 'compromise' position that falls short of a full transformation.

III. Selected Examples of Externally Induced Legal, Policy, Institutional, or Strategic Change at the World Bank

Having set out a framework for how external pressures become internalized policy change at the Bank, this section explores four important historical applications of this framework. The goal is to contextualize an understanding of the Bank's transformation process, the role of its Management in initiating a change process, the role of its Executive Directors as the authorizing environment, and the complex way in which various institutional, sociological, and operational forces can affect the outcome.

[5] World Bank Group, 'Environmental and Social Framework' <https://www.worldbank.org/en/projects-operations/environmental-and-social-framework> accessed 4 September 2024.

[6] Charles Di Leva, 'The World Bank's Evolution Towards Environmental and Social Responsibilities', Chapter 8 in this volume.

A. Anti-corruption strategy and sanctions reform

Through much of the twentieth century, most economists and development practitioners did not treat corruption as a serious impediment to development. Corruption was regularly viewed and referred to as a necessary 'grease' that smoothed the wheels of some of the Bank's work. In fact, bribery was tax deductible in several Organisation for Economic Co-operation and Development (OECD) countries.[7] However, in the 1990s, there was a gradual change in perspective on corruption amongst IOs, governments, and civil society groups. As Dubois and others explain, 'the 1990s saw a more open recognition and discussion of corruption's harm to development outcomes: in economic literature and beyond'.[8]

For example, in 1993, Transparency International was founded with a mission to 'stop corruption and promote transparency, accountability, and integrity at all levels and across all sectors of society'.[9] This coincided with increased demand for good governance in countries and IOs, and in 1997, the OECD adopted the Convention Against Bribery. Existing anti-corruption laws were more rigorously enforced, such as the 1977 US Foreign Corruption Practices Act,[10] while court decisions in Europe targeted corruption in international business. The UN unveiled its Convention Against Corruption (UNCAC) in 2003. UNCAC is the 'only legally binding universal anti-corruption instrument' and included 140 signatories on ratification.[11]

With external pressure building, the trigger and catalyst for institutional reform came from President James Wolfensohn in his famous 1996 speech decrying what he called the 'cancer of corruption'.[12] The Bank shortly thereafter began openly discussing corruption as a development problem. Dealing with corruption soon featured in several Bank flagship reports, including the 1997 *World Development Report* and the 1997 *Helping Countries Combat Corruption: The Role of the World Bank*.

[7] Martine Milliet-Einbinder, 'Writing Off Tax Deductibility' (2000) The OECD Observer 38.

[8] Pascale Hélène Dubois and others, 'The World Bank's Sanctions System: Using the Debarment to Combat Fraud and Corruption in International Development' in Peter Quayle and Xuan Gao (eds), *Good Governance and Modern International Financial Institutions: AIIB Yearbook of International Law* (Brill 2019).

[9] Transparency International, 'Our Story' <https://www.transparency.org/en/our-story> accessed 4 September 2024.

[10] Dubois and others (n 8).

[11] ibid.

[12] James Wolfensohn, 'People and Development' (Address to the Board of Governors at the Annual Meetings of the World Bank and the International Monetary Fund, 1 October 1996) <https://documents.worldbank.org/en/publication/documents-reports/documentdetail/243871468141893629/People-and-development-address-to-the-Board-of-Governors-Washington-DC-October-1-1996> accessed 4 September 2024.

The outcomes from Wolfensohn's drive for change were significant. In 1996, Bank Management put in place an internal sanctions system to ensure transparency in its projects, and in 1997, the Executive Directors adopted a Bank-wide anti-corruption strategy. Wolfensohn found further successes by establishing a Bank integrity unit (now the Integrity Vice Presidency, INT) with a mandate to combat fraud and corruption.

By the time of Paul Wolfowitz's 2005–2007 presidency, the themes of governance and anti-corruption had emerged as key development priorities for the Bank. Under Wolfowitz, a second burst of institutional transformation on anti-corruption and sanctions issues occurred. As part of this reform process, the Bank 'held consultations with representatives from governments, donor agencies, parliaments, civil society organizations, private sector, media, and other stakeholders' over a three-month period from 2006 to 2007.[13]

The result was the Board's adoption of the 2007 Governance and Anti-Corruption Strategy (the 'GAC Strategy'). The GAC Strategy affected a total change in the Bank's strategic focus on corruption issues, and it was developed with extensive involvement from the Bank's shareholders as well as feedback from external stakeholders. The GAC Strategy had a cascading impact on institutional policies and procedures. The Bank adopted specific guidelines to address fraud and corruption in its projects, made enforceable through legal agreements.

The Bank also overhauled its sanctions system with the assistance of external advice. Wolfowitz appointed former US Federal Reserve Chair Paul Volcker to lead an independent panel to review and strengthen activities within INT and the sanctions system. A 2001 review of the sanctions system by former US Attorney General Richard Thornburg had already begun the reform process.

Among the 2007 Volcker Panel's recommendations was the creation of an independent advisory board with international anti-corruption expertise.[14] This paved the way for the creation of the modern Bank Sanctions Board, which now comprises eminent jurists and practitioners that exercise de novo review authority over the Bank's internal sanctions and governance processes.

[13] Joint Ministerial Committee of the Board of Governors of the Bank and the Fund on the Transfer of Real Resources to Developing Countries, 'Report of the Executive Directors: Strengthening World Bank Group Engagement on Governance and Anti-Corruption' (*World Bank*, 28 March 2007) https://documents.worldbank.org/en/publication/documents-reports/documentdetail/426381468340863478/main-report> accessed 12 September 2024.

[14] Paul Volcker and others, 'Independent Panel Review of the World Bank Group Department of Institutional Integrity' (*World Bank*, 13 September 2007) <http://documents.worldbank.org/curated/en/764111468779100351/Independent-panel-review-of-the-World-Bank-Group-Department-of-Institutional-Integrity> accessed 4 September 2024.

B. New focus on situations of conflict and fragility

In the 1990s, the Bank was increasingly called upon by civil society, shareholders, and UN agencies to assist countries emerging from civil wars and conflict. The Bank's support was particularly sought to bolster nascent peace processes, including in sub-Saharan Africa and Southeast Asia. Pressure built from multiple sources throughout the 1990s, during which the Rwandan and Bosnian genocides and conflicts stand out.[15]

The Bank was initially unable to respond to growing external pressures to combat fragility and conflict. This was in part due to an interpretation of the Articles of Agreement that prohibited using Bank financing for country peacekeeping operations or peacemaking negotiations. However, persistent external pressure encouraged the Bank to identify key entry points through which to support peace and reconstruction efforts while remaining within its development mandate. New Bank policy threaded this fine line by focusing on reintegration after conflict rather than demobilization, which was considered a domestic security matter beyond the institution's legal mandate.[16] In so doing, the Bank drew upon its development expertise and financial resources and worked in close collaboration with partners.

The result was a number of Bank-financed projects approved by Executive Directors upon Management Proposal, for demining, demobilization, and reintegration of ex-combatants in Rwanda and Cambodia. These efforts culminated in the 2002–2009 Multi-Country Demobilization and Reintegration Program (MDRP) for Africa's Great Lakes Region and the Democratic Republic of Congo. The MDRP assisted five countries in reintegrating over 240,000 former combatants and reuniting 53,000 children with their families after conflict.[17] The Bank's acceptance of engagement in these areas encouraged further work in conflict contexts.

In 1997, as part of its institutional response to conflict and fragility, the Bank Executive Directors adopted a Management-initiated and proposed framework for reconstruction activities, which was later codified as Operational Policy (OP) 2.30 (*Development Cooperation and Conflict*).[18] OP 2.30 guided the Bank's

[15] The number of armed conflicts was significantly higher in the first half of the 1990s than over the following decade. Lotta Harbom and Peter Wallensteen, 'Appendix 2A: Patterns of Major Armed Conflicts, 1990–2005' [2006] SIPRI Yearbook 2006 108.

[16] World Bank Group, 'Multi-Country Demobilization and Reintegration Program Final Report: Overview of Program Achievements' (July 2010) <https://documents.worldbank.org/en/publication/documents-reports/documentdetail/481721468149096857/the-multi-country-demobilization-and-reintegration-program-final-report-overview-of-program-achievements> accessed 4 September 2024.

[17] ibid.

[18] World Bank Group, 'Framework for World Bank Involvement in Post-Conflict Reconstruction' (February 1997) OP 2.30.

interventions in critical contexts from Afghanistan to Iraq, Somalia, South Sudan, and Yemen. In 2021, the Bank Executive Directors, upon Management proposal, further revised and updated this policy framework to deepen the Bank's commitment to tackling fragility, conflict, and violence (FCV). The Bank's new FCV Policy provides an authorizing framework for engagements in fragile or conflict-affected countries, clarifies the institution's mandate in areas including peacekeeping and humanitarian disasters, and authorizes Bank support for refugees and host communities.

C. From adjustment policy lending to development policy lending

The transformation of Bank lending from structural adjustment to development policy financing was the culmination of decades of policy pressure. Following global oil shocks in the 1970s that damaged many countries' macroeconomic indicators, the Bank began lending for structural adjustment reforms. The 1980s and early 1990s were the heyday for these adjustment policy loans. The loans encouraged trade liberalization and privatization policies in line with the neoliberal 'Washington Consensus' school of economic thought.

These loans gradually began attracting criticism for their failure to consider the human and social impact of economic reforms. The Bank's conditionality requirements and austerity measures were also increasingly contested, not only by activists but also by economists and borrowing countries. Austerity measures too often led to social strife, political instability, and economic woes.

The Bank persisted in operationalizing some forms of adjustment lending into the 2000s. This reliance was in part due to a belief promoted by the 'Washington Consensus' that long-term macroeconomic stability from structural adjustments would be the reward for short-term socio-economic distress. However, academic theory and on-the-ground evidence showed that these detrimental 'short-term' outcomes were not counterweighted by the mixed macroeconomic and development results of adjustment lending. Triggered to action by this reality, the Bank initiated a process to revise its policy framework for adjustment lending.

In August 2004, the Bank adopted a new operational policy on 'Development Policy Financing'.[19] The new lending framework emphasized strong country ownership of Bank-supported policies and institutional programmes, attention to social and environmental impacts, and stakeholder consultations and participation. In 2005, the Bank undertook a further review exercise to reduce remaining programme conditionality and fine-tune its development policy

[19] World Bank Group, 'Development Policy Financing: Bank Policy' (August 2004) Formerly OP 8.60.

loans. There was afterwards a greater emphasis on supporting operations and programmes that helped countries achieve their Millennium Development Goals (now Sustainable Development Goals), like poverty reduction and human development goals. This transformation ensured the Bank incorporated lessons on development effectiveness for future lending operations.

D. A modest change to human rights considerations in the Bank's operations

Like the issue of corruption, the Bank did not consider human rights to be within its mandate for a considerable portion of its institutional existence. In the 1960s, for instance, the Bank rejected calls from the UN to stop lending to apartheid South Africa. In subsequent decades, the Bank sometimes did not speak out or curtail operations because of human rights violations. Within the Bank, it was felt that adopting a more vocal perspective on human rights—whether in the context of specific projects or as a development objective—would be in breach of the Bank's Articles prohibiting interference in member countries' political affairs, referred to as the 'political prohibition'.[20]

Over the past two decades following 2000, changing public opinion, rising NGO pressures, and growing scholarship and activism have influenced the Bank to reconsider this orthodoxy on human rights. The Bank has had to confront several challenging questions. Should it stop lending to a country with a government that systematically violates human rights? Was it advisable for the Bank to adopt a human rights-based approach to lending? How should human rights be addressed when dealing with the environmental and social impacts of a project? These issues remain hotly contested, especially as there is no shareholder consensus among member countries that make up the Bank's Board.

Despite growing questions about human rights in Bank activities, the catalysing forces of external pressures have been unable to compel transformative change. In 2006, a departing General Counsel, Roberto Danino, issued a nuanced legal opinion potentially opening the door for greater Bank engagement with human rights issues while remaining faithful to the 'political prohibition'. However, this opinion was not ultimately discussed by the Board and thus has not been subsequently fully embraced.

[20] Articles of Agreement of the International Bank for Reconstruction and Development (adopted 22 July 1944, entered into force 27 December 1945, as amended effective 27 June 2012) 2 UNTS 134 art IV s 10 (IBRD Articles of Agreement). See also my article on political prohibition, Hassane Cissé, 'Should the Political Prohibition in Charters of International Financial Institutions Be Revisited? The Case of the World Bank' in Hassane Cissé, Daniel D Bradlow, and Benedict Kingsbury (eds), *The World Bank Legal Review: International Financial Institutions and Global Legal Governance*, vol 3 (World Bank Publications 2012).

More recently, the Bank's Executive Directors adopted a non-binding and aspirational 'vision statement' to accompany The *Environmental and Social Framework*. The vision statement makes certain references to human rights but does not impose any mandatory obligations on the Bank or its operations. The adoption of this 'vision statement', while not the major change advocated by some external stakeholders, remains significant as it is the first time the Bank formally includes such a statement in a major policy document, which could arguably be used later to interpret mandatory policy statements in such documents.

In practice, the Bank sometimes appears to diverge from this 'line in the sand' position regarding political considerations or human rights. For instance, a March 2022 announcement stated: 'Following the Russian invasion of Ukraine and hostilities against the people of Ukraine, the World Bank Group has stopped all its programs in Russia and Belarus with immediate effect.'[21] Other restrictive lending decisions in response to certain conflicts, human rights violations, or even anti-terrorism concerns have occurred in respect of other countries (eg Iran). However, in the recent case of the genocide in Myanmar, the Bank did not stop its programmes in the country.

Much of this divergence between theory and practice results from an inherent tension within the Articles of Agreement. While the Articles outline the 'political prohibition', they also leave the suspension of operations in a given country up to a vote by the Executive Directors.[22] It is hard to see how governments with significant shareholder power on the Board would not consider certain political considerations when determining whether to stop operations in a given country.

IV. Conclusion

Change at the World Bank, as in the case of any large IO, is complex. It is shaped by multifaceted pressures, institutional cross winds, shareholder demands, and the sentiments of global civil society. The Bank has undergone significant evolution in some important respects by responding to these external pressures. This adaptation has involved legal and policy framework reforms, strategic redirections, financial innovations, and operational adjustments.

In some cases, however, the perceived risks or issues associated with a desired change in Bank policy or practice may outweigh the external pressure. As a result, multilateral institutions like the Bank sometimes opt for a compromise rather than a complete overhaul.

[21] World Bank Group, 'World Bank Group Statement on Russia and Belarus' (*World Bank*, 2 March 2022) <https://www.worldbank.org/en/news/statement/2022/03/02/world-bank-group-statement-on-russia-and-belarus> accessed 4 September 2024.

[22] IBRD Articles of Agreement (n 20) art VI s 5.

The Bank's approach to addressing human rights in its operations is a good example of this 'middle way' methodology. Despite strong pressure from NGOs and shifts in public opinion, progress in this area has been slow and fraught with resistance. The Bank continues to grapple with these issues today, and some shareholders remain wary of potentially greater transformations.

In other spaces, such as policy-based lending or anti-corruption practices, the Bank has adopted significant changes as a result of external triggers. The institution today seeks, in some areas, to model new developments on these successful integrations of external demands and internal reforms.

For example, the Bank's 2023 Evolution Roadmap proposes optimizing Bank practices and scaling up Multilateral Development Bank financing. Many of these recommendations doubtless come from growing external calls for the Bank to increase flexibility in the wake of the COVID-19 pandemic and to make more funding available in FCV and climate-affected countries.

The Bank has 'made a public commitment to an inclusive and open consultative process' in producing the roadmap.[23] As the 'Evolution Roadmap' shows, understanding the dynamic interplay between external pressure and internal change remains crucial for those aiming to help influence the Bank's future direction.

[23] Development Committee: Joint Ministerial Committee of the Boards of Governors of the Bank and the Fund, 'Evolution of the World Bank Group: A Report to Governors' (*MDB Reform Accelerator*, 12 April 2023) <https://mdbreformaccelerator.cgdev.org/evolution-of-the-world-bank-group-a-report-to-governors-3/> accessed 12 September 2024.

25

IMF's Responses to New Challenges in the Global Economy

Recent Reforms of Its Financing Toolkit

*Yan Liu and Kyung Kwak**

I. Introduction

Since its establishment in 1944,[1] the International Monetary Fund (the 'IMF' or the 'Fund') has evolved with developments in the global economy. While its overall objective remains the promotion of international monetary and financial stability, the Fund has adapted its roles and policies to respond to the evolution of the international monetary and financial systems and the changing needs of the IMF membership over the years.

The Fund is an international organization established by an international treaty, the Articles of Agreement (IMF Articles).[2] As the charter of the organization, the IMF Articles lay out the powers granted to the Fund and the purposes for which such powers have been granted (IMF mandate).[3] Article I of the IMF Articles provides for an exhaustive list of the IMF's purposes, which includes promoting international monetary cooperation, facilitating the expansion and balanced growth of international trade, promoting exchange stability, assisting the establishment of a multilateral system of payments, and making IMF financing temporarily available to members under adequate safeguards, thus providing them with opportunity to correct maladjustments in their balance of payments without resorting to measures destructive of national or international prosperity.

* The authors are grateful to Wolfgang Bergthaler for his review and comments. The views expressed herein are those of the authors and should not be attributed to the IMF, its Executive Board, or its management.

[1] See 'About the IMF' <https://www.imf.org/en/About> accessed 24 March 2024.

[2] Articles of Agreement of the International Monetary Fund (adopted 22 July 1994, entered into force 27 December 1945) 29 UNTS 2 <https://www.imf.org/external/pubs/ft/aa/index.htm≥ accessed 24 March 2024 (IMF Articles).

[3] IMF, 'The Fund's Mandate: The Legal Framework' (22 January 2010) <https://www.imf.org/en/Publications/Policy-Papers/Issues/2016/12/31/The-Fund-s-Mandate-The-Legal-Framework-PP4421> accessed 24 March 2024.

Yan Liu and Kyung Kwak, *IMF's Responses to New Challenges in the Global Economy* In: *International Organization Initiatives*. Edited by: Gabrielle Marceau and Henner Gött, Oxford University Press. © Oxford University Press 2025.
DOI: 10.1093/9780197803325.003.0026

The IMF's purposes have not changed since the adoption of the Articles in 1944. However, the substantive issues on which the IMF engages with its member countries in carrying out its mandate have evolved.[4] The IMF Articles have generally proved to be sufficiently flexible to respond to changes in the global economy; but when it was not possible to adopt major policy reforms based on the interpretation of the Articles, the IMF has adopted targeted amendments to uphold the rule of law, which is key to the legitimacy, credibility, effectiveness, and transparency of the Fund as an institution.[5] The IMF Articles have been amended seven times to implement major policy reforms, with the latest amendment adopted on 15 December 2010 (effective 26 January 2016).[6] One of the major amendments is the Second Amendment in 1978, which responded to the end to the Bretton Woods System replacing the system of fixed exchange rate with the system of flexible exchange rate.[7]

The IMF has three key functions: surveillance of the international monetary system and the monitoring of members' economic and financial policies, the provision of Fund financing to help member countries address balance of payments (BoP) problems subject to adequate safeguards, and the delivery of technical assistance and financial services. The provision of Fund financing is one of the IMF's purposes set out in Article I(v) of the IMF Articles: '[t]o give confidence to members by making the general resources of the Fund temporarily available to them under adequate safeguards, thus providing them with opportunity to correct maladjustments in their balance of payments without resorting to measures destructive of national or international prosperity.'

The IMF financing (commonly referred to as lending)[8] mandate articulated in the IMF Articles has remained the same since 1944. Over the past 80 years, there have been several notable financial crises engulfing the global economy such as the Latin American debt crisis (1982), the Asian financial crisis (1997), the global financial crisis (2008), and more recently, the devastating impact of the COVID-19 pandemic (2020) and the war in Ukraine (2022). The Fund responded to these

[4] Kristalina Georgieva and Rhoda Weeks-Brown, 'The IMF's Evolving Role Within a Constant Mandate' (2023) 26 Journal of International Economic Law 1, 17–29.

[5] Yan Liu, 'The Rule of Law in the International Monetary Fund: Past, Present and Future' (2018) AIIB Yearbook of International Law <https://www.aiib.org/en/about-aiib/who-we-are/yearbook/_download/rule-law-international.pdf> accessed 24 March 2024.

[6] IMF Articles (n 2).

[7] When the IMF was established at the Bretton Woods conference, it was tasked to oversee the system of stable exchange rates where members' currencies were linked at fixed rates to the US dollar and ultimately to the value of gold. This system of fixed exchange rates collapsed and was replaced in the late 1970s with the system of flexible exchange rate, embedded in the Second Amendment of the IMF Articles, which took effect in April 1978. See Joseph Gold, *The Second Amendment of the Fund's Articles of Agreement* (Pamphlet Series No 25, IMF 1978).

[8] IMF financing in the General Resources Account is not in the form of loans but of swap of currencies or reserve assets. IMF financing in the Poverty Reduction and Growth Trust and the Resilience and Sustainability Trust takes the form of loans.

global and regional financial crises by providing a large amount of financing to members facing BoP difficulties and reforming its policies to better prevent and resolve crises. As the Fund adapted its financing policies in response to changing economic circumstances, it undertook a careful and rigorous assessment of the consistency of such reforms with the Fund's mandate. The Fund's nimble and swift responses while staying within its mandate have enabled the institution to effectively handle global and regional financial crises and economic challenges, while upholding the rule of law, which is key to its legitimacy, credibility, effectiveness, and transparency.

The IMF governance structure consists of the Board of Governors, the Executive Board, and the Managing Director. There is a division of responsibilities amongst these organs by way of delegation, so a reference to the Fund may have different meanings in different contexts, although the term 'Fund' typically refers to the Executive Board. The Board of Governors, the highest decision-making organ of the IMF, can delegate to the Executive Board most of its powers[9] and has made such delegations to the Executive Board. As such, the Executive Board, which is responsible for conducting the business of the Fund,[10] is the primary decision-making organ of the Fund. In turn, the Managing Director conducts the ordinary business of the Fund under the direction of the Executive Board.[11] Given this structure, typically, it is IMF management (ie the Managing Director and Deputy Managing Directors) that initiates and champions new initiatives, and it is IMF staff that act upon such initiatives and develop concrete policy proposals under the direction of IMF management. IMF management engages the Executive Board to consult and explain such policy proposals to seek their feedback and garner their support, presents such proposals for consideration and adoption by the Executive Board, and implements the proposals endorsed by the Executive Board.

This chapter discusses IMF management's pivotal role in initiating nimble and innovative responses to recent challenges facing the IMF membership in discharging the institution's financing mandate. The chapter provides an overview of the key features of the legal and policy framework governing IMF financing. It then discusses how IMF management instituted policy reforms to address recent global challenges such as climate change and pandemic preparedness (II.(A.)) and the global food crisis (II.(B.)) by proposing to establish new financing tools such as the Resilience and Sustainability Trust (RST) and the Food Shock Window (FSW). The chapter concludes that IMF management's

[9] IMF Articles (n 2). Art XII, s 2(b) authorizes the Board of Governors to 'delegate to the Executive Board authority to exercise any powers of the Board of Governors, except the powers conferred directly by this Agreement on the Board of Governors'.

[10] ibid art XII s 3(a).

[11] ibid art XII s 4(b).

(and ultimately the IMF's) ability to develop nimble and swift responses to new challenges in the global economy within the remit of the Fund's mandate is key to the Fund's continued success in meeting the needs of its membership and assisting them in tackling such challenges.

II. IMF Financing: Key Features

In line with its mandate, the IMF may only provide financing to help members address BoP problems subject to adequate safeguards. The IMF can do so (i) from the Fund's pool of general resources, that is, the General Resources Account (GRA) to assist members in addressing their BoP problems, or (ii) from IMF trusts, such as the Poverty Reduction and Growth Trust (PRGT) to address members' BoP problems and assist members' efforts towards solving a protracted BoP need, and the RST to help strengthen members' prospective BoP stability.

Under Article V, Section 3(a) of the IMF Articles, the Fund can provide financial assistance to members if two requirements are met. First, a member should use Fund resources to resolve its BoP problems. Fund resources cannot be provided for any other purposes. Second, a member must use Fund resources to address the underlying BoP problem in a manner that provides adequate safeguards for the temporary use of Fund resources. Thus, Fund financing may only be used to help the member resolve its BoP problems with a view to ensuring its capacity to repay the Fund. This requires an assessment that the member is implementing policies that will address—rather than simply delay—the resolution of its external difficulties and restore medium-term external viability.[12]

Pursuant to Article V, Section 3(a), which authorizes the Fund to adopt policies on the use of its general resources,[13] the IMF has established policies governing GRA financing including conditionality and programme review,[14] phasing,[15]

[12] IMF, 'Changes to the Fund's Financing Assurances Policy in the Context of Fund Upper Credit Tranche Financing Under Exceptionally High Uncertainty' (17 March 2023) <https://www.imf.org/en/Publications/Policy-Papers/Issues/2023/03/17/Changes-to-the-Funds-Financing-Assurances-Policy-in-the-Context-Of-Fund-Upper-Credit-531091> accessed 24 March 2024.

[13] Art V, s 3(a) provides that:

> [T]he Fund shall adopt policies on the use of its general resources, including policies on stand-by or similar arrangements, and may adopt special policies for special balance of payments problems, that will assist members to solve their balance of payments problems in a manner consistent with the provisions of this Agreement and that will establish adequate safeguards for the temporary use of the general resources of the Fund.

[14] IMF, 'Guidelines on Conditionality' (as amended, 25 September 2002) Decision No 12864-(02/102) <https://www.imf.org/External/np/pdr/cond/2002/eng/guid/092302.htm> accessed 24 March 2024.

[15] IMF financing is disbursed in instalments linked to conditions. IMF, 'Relationship Between Performance Criteria and Phasing of Purchases Under Fund Arrangements—Operational

access limits,[16] and debt sustainability, arrears, and financing assurances,[17] with the aim of helping the member to address its BoP problems and to be able to repay the IMF in full and on time. Conditionality (ex -ante and ex -post) is a key feature of Fund financing. [18] Under the IMF Guidelines on Conditionality, the IMF's conditions on a member country's programme of economic, financial, and structural reforms (Fund-supported programme) would need to be established on the basis of variables or measures that are reasonably within the direct or indirect control of the member country and that are generally either of critical importance for achieving the goals of the member's programme, or for the monitoring of the implementation of that programme, or are necessary for the implementation of specific provisions of the IMF Articles or policies adopted under them.[19] The Fund can also provide emergency financing through outright purchases without ex post conditionality and without the need for the member to have in place a Fund-supported programme if certain conditions are met.

In addition to GRA financing, the IMF also provides financing to its members through its trusts whose resources mostly or all come from contributions by IMF members. As noted above, one of the IMF's key functions is to perform technical and financial services. Pursuant to Article V, Section 2(b) of the IMF Articles, the IMF can provide 'technical and financial services' upon request from its members so long as they are consistent with the purposes of the Fund and are financially separate from the IMF's own resources.

The IMF's financial services consist of establishing and administering trusts and other accounts for the benefit of IMF members, including the PRGT and the RST. The PRGT is a trust established under Article V, Section 2(b) of the IMF Articles, consisting of IMF contributions of its gold sale profits and donor resources. PRGT financing is provided on concessional terms to eligible members.

Guidelines' (as amended, 8 March 1985) Decision No 7925-(85/38) in International Monetary Fund Legal Dept, *Selected Decisions and Selected Documents of the International Monetary Fund: Forty-Third Issue* (IMF 2023) <https://www.imf.org/en/Publications/Selected-Decisions/selected-decisions-list> accessed 24 March 2024.

[16] IMF, 'Access Policy and Limits in the Credit Tranches and Under the Extended Fund Facility and on Overall Access to the Fund's General Resources, and Exceptional Access Policy' (as amended, 22 February 2008) Decision No 14064-(08/18) in International Monetary Fund Legal Dept, *Selected Decisions and Selected Documents of the International Monetary Fund: Forty-Third Issue* (IMF 2023) <https://www.imf.org/en/Publications/Selected-Decisions/selected-decisions-list> accessed 24 March 2024.

[17] IMF, 'Reviews of the Fund's Sovereign Arrears Policies and Perimeter' (23 May 2022) <https://www.imf.org/en/Publications/Policy-Papers/Issues/2022/05/18/Reviews-of-the-Fund-s-Sovereign-ARREARS-Policies-and-Perimeter-517997> accessed 24 March 2024.

[18] The legal basis for Fund conditionality is art V, s 3(a). Conditionality is intended to ensure that Fund resources are provided to members to assist them in resolving their BoP problems in a manner that is consistent with the Fund's Articles and that establishes adequate safeguards for the temporary use of the Fund's resources: IMF, 'Guidelines on Conditionality' (n 14).

[19] IMF, 'Guidelines on Conditionality' (n 14).

PRGT financing instruments and its financing policies are largely aligned with those under the GRA. RST financing aims to help members strengthen their prospective BoP stability, which relates to one of the Fund's purposes under Article I(iii). The RST is discussed in more detail below.

III. IMF Management's Initiatives to Respond to Recent Global Challenges

Throughout its history, the IMF has been faced with the call from the international community to respond to new challenges and has responded effectively and swiftly. IMF management has played a central role in developing often innovative policy responses to meet such challenges and membership's needs while making sure that its reform proposals are fully consistent with the Fund's mandate. Two recent examples, the establishment of the RST and the FSW, illustrate IMF management's proactive initiative to come up with an effective response to help member countries address climate change, pandemic preparedness, and food shock.

A. Supporting reforms in climate change and pandemic preparedness through the RST

The lack of affordable financing to assist countries in implementing their climate adaptation, transition, and mitigation strategies has been identified as a key obstacle for the achievement of global climate change goals.[20] The challenges from the COVID-19 pandemic also pose a huge impediment to BoP stability, and resilient and sustainable growth.[21] The Fund has worked on climate issues and pandemic preparedness in cooperation with other organizations, such as the World Bank, the World Trade Organization, and the World Health Organization, among other public and private sector stakeholders, to promote the development and implementation of common policies and strategies. Following the IMF's landmark allocation of approximately SDR 456 billion[22] (about USD 650 billion) to the IMF membership in August 2021,[23] the international community

[20] Georgieva and Weeks-Brown (n 4).

[21] IMF, 'Proposal to Establish a Resilience and Sustainability Trust' (18 April 2022) <https://www.imf.org/en/Publications/Policy-Papers/Issues/2022/04/15/Proposal-To-Establish-A-Resilience-and-Sustainability-Trust-516692> accessed 24 March 2024.

[22] The Special Drawing Rights (SDR) is an international reserve asset created by the IMF to supplement the official reserves of its member countries.

[23] IMF, 'IMF Governors Approve a Historic US$650 Billion SDR Allocation of Special Drawing Rights', Press Release No 21/235 (*IMF*, 2 August 2021) <https://www.imf.org/en/News/Articles/

called for the SDRs issued to IMF member countries with strong reserve balances to be voluntarily channelled to where they are most needed. In response to this call, IMF management came up with the proposal to create the RST, which is financed exclusively by member countries' voluntary contributions, particularly through channelling of these members' SDR holdings to the RST. The RST is the Fund's first financing instrument that does not have any IMF resources.

A key innovative feature of the RST is its legal basis for provision of financing. Financing to support longer-term structural reforms to address challenges relating to climate change and pandemic preparedness would not have been possible under traditional GRA/PRGT financing instruments as it does not fit the parameters of BoP needs (present, prospective, and potential)[24] under the IMF's financing mandate. Under the direction of IMF management, IMF staff conducted a rigorous assessment to make sure that financing under the RST remains consistent with the Fund's BoP focus while addressing longer-term challenges. After thorough research and careful consideration, the RST was designed as a Fund-administered trust to provide financing to help countries implement policies designed to strengthen prospective BoP stability, relating to one of the Fund's purposes under Article I(iii), namely to 'promote exchange stability [and] to maintain orderly exchange arrangements'.

The Fund's purpose under Article I(iii) to 'promote exchange stability' has informed, in the surveillance context, the concept of '*balance of payments stability*', which is defined as a member's BoP position that does not, and is not likely to, give rise to disruptive exchange rate movements.[25] The IMF, in carrying out its surveillance mandate, focuses on those policies of members that can significantly influence present or *prospective* BoP and domestic stability, recognizing that systemic stability (a stable system of exchange rates) is best served by each member promoting its own BoP and domestic stability.[26] The RST would complement the IMF's policy advice in the context of surveillance by providing financial assistance to eligible members to help them implement policies designed to strengthen prospective BoP stability.[27] The RST marks the first time that IMF-administered financing is provided to help members address threats to prospective BoP stability,[28] which speaks to IMF management's ability and willingness to think outside the box to find innovative yet legally sound solutions.

2021/07/30/pr21235-imf-governors-approve-a-historic-us-650-billion-sdr-allocation-of-special-drawing-rights> accessed 24 March 2024.

[24] In addition, PRGT financing has been available to eligible low-income members to help them address their protracted BoP needs.

[25] IMF, 'Proposal to Establish a Resilience and Sustainability Trust' (n 21).

[26] ibid.

[27] ibid.

[28] Georgieva and Weeks-Brown (n 4).

The RST was established as an IMF-administered trust fund, which was authorized under Article V, Section 2(b), consistent with the purposes of the Fund. IMF management and staff designed it to complement the Fund's existing financing toolkit by providing affordable longer-term financing to support low-income and vulnerable middle-income member countries' structural reforms to address longer-term structural challenges relating to climate change and pandemic preparedness, and to bring stakeholders together in the joint effort to tackle climate and pandemic challenges.[29] The focus of the RST is initially on longer-term challenges relating to climate change and pandemic preparedness, and may later expand to other challenges if they are supported by contributors to the RST. It is expected that these reforms will help to catalyse official and private financing, further strengthening countries' efforts to implement reform measures and address risks arising from longer-term challenges.

RST financing may not be approved on a stand-alone basis, and such approval may be granted when the member has a GRA or PRGT financing arrangement or a Fund-supported programme under its non-financing instrument at the same time.[30] An accompanying Fund-supported programme under a GRA/PRGT financing arrangement would focus on existing or potential BoP problems under such a GRA/PRGT financing arrangement.

Financial support from the RST to 143 eligible members takes the form of loans made under a Resilience and Sustainability Facility arrangement. Given the RST's purpose to help members tackle longer-term challenges, RST loans have a 20-year maturity with a grace period of 10.5 years.[31] Relative to the maximum 10 years of loan maturities under other IMF financing instruments, the longer maturity reflects the longer-term nature of the challenges to be addressed by RST financing. RST loans are subject to the SDR interest rate with a modest margin depending on the borrowing country's income level and access to market financing.[32] The RST became effective on 1 May 2022 and operational in October 2022, and total credit outstanding under the RST was SDR 3,224 million as of 31 January 2025.[33]

[29] IMF, 'Proposal to Establish a Resilience and Sustainability Trust' (n 21).

[30] The IMF's non-financing instrument is the Policy Coordination Instrument which involves a Fund-supported programme and is subject to most IMF policies but entails no IMF financing.

[31] IMF, 'Proposal to Establish a Resilience and Sustainability Trust' (n 21).

[32] ibid.

[33] IMF, 'Weekly Report on Key Financial Statistics as of January 31, 2025', <https://www.imf.org/external/np/tre/activity/2025/013125.pdf> accessed 6 February 2025.

B. Creation of the FSW to address the global food crisis

After the war in Ukraine, record food and fertilizer prices led to food price inflation, increasing costs for fertilizers and shortages in food supplies triggering hardship across the global economy. About 50 countries were assessed at that time to be severely affected by the global food crisis.[34] The Fund has been working closely with other stakeholders including the World Bank, the World Food Program (WFP), and the Food and Agriculture Organization (FAO) to provide a coordinated international response to the global food shock, and has provided policy advice, capacity development, and financial support to help those countries affected by the global food crisis.[35]

While IMF financing has been available to countries affected by the global food crisis through Fund-supported programmes and emergency financing instruments, IMF management decided that the IMF lending toolkit needs to be calibrated to better help members address BoP pressures relating to the global food shock. It directed Fund staff to conceptualize and design an additional financing window under the existing emergency financing instruments to make Fund financing more focused and agile in addressing members' urgent BoP needs due to the global food shock.[36]

Since food security is not an issue typically within the Fund's remit, IMF management addressed this issue by focusing on urgent BoP needs arising from the global food shock associated with acute food insecurity, the rising costs of food and fertilizer imports, or substantial cereal export shortfalls, which is the critical requirement for Fund financing. By conceptualizing the FSW as a window under the existing emergency financing instruments,[37] financing under the FSW is narrowly focused on meeting urgent BoP needs of countries, thus staying firmly within the Fund's financing mandate. Also, given that food security is not within the Fund's expertise, the design of the FSW reflected the work of other international organizations such as the United Nations, the FAO, and the WFP by taking into account their assessment of acute food security in the qualification criteria

[34] IMF, 'Global Food Crisis and Food Shock Window: Frequently Asked Questions' <https://www.imf.org/en/About/FAQ/global-food-crisis-and-food-shock-window≥ accessed 24 March 2024.

[35] ibid.

[36] IMF, 'Proposal for a Food Shock Window Under the Rapid Financing Instrument and the Rapid Credit Facility' (5 October 2022) <https://www.imf.org/en/Publications/Policy-Papers/Issues/2022/09/30/Proposal-for-a-Food-Shock-Window-Under-the-Rapid-Financing-Instrument-and-Rapid-Credit-524079> accessed 24 March 2024.

[37] The Fund has two emergency financing instruments, the Rapid Financing Instrument (RFI) and the Rapid Credit Facility (RCF), which provide low access emergency financing outside of a Fund-supported programme and without ex post conditionality to help members address urgent BoP problems arising from a wide range of events and shocks. The RFI is one of the financing instruments under the Fund's GRA that provides rapid, low-access financial assistance to countries facing urgent BoP needs that, if not addressed, would result in an immediate and severe economic disruption. The RCF is the equivalent of the RFI under the PRGT.

for the FSW. All of these are a testament to IMF management's ability to rise to difficult and new challenges through a swift and nimble response appropriate for such challenges, including through collaboration with other international organizations, while making sure of its consistency with the Fund's mandate.

The FSW was established by the Executive Board on 30 September 2022 for 12 months and was later extended until 31 March 2024.[38] During its existence, emergency financing under the FSW was provided to six countries totalling USD 1.8 billion.[39]

IV. Conclusion

Throughout its existence since 1944, the Fund has evolved considerably to adapt to changes in the global economy. While the areas in which the IMF engages have expanded beyond the monetary, exchange rate, fiscal, and financial sector policies typically associated with it, the Fund's involvement in all the areas has been guided by its mandate. The Fund has responded to new challenges in the global economy by quickly adapting its policies but at the same time applying rigorous scrutiny to ensure the consistency of policy reforms with the IMF Articles, thereby upholding the rule of law and safeguarding the Fund's legitimacy, credibility, effectiveness, and transparency.

IMF management has played an instrumental role in the IMF's success in adapting and responding to new challenges. The creation of the RST and the FSW in 2022 in response to climate change and pandemics, as well as the global food crisis, are recent examples of the Fund's agile and swift responses to global challenges while adhering to its mandate. They illustrate the critical role of IMF management in initiating and developing innovative proposals in response to new challenges while ensuring robust legal basis and sound policy objectives in line with the IMF's mandate.

[38] IMF, 'Review of Experience with the Food Shock Window Under the Rapid Financing Instrument and the Rapid Credit Facility' (30 June 2023) <https://www.imf.org/en/Publications/Policy-Papers/Issues/2023/06/30/Review-of-Experience-with-The-Food-Shock-Window-Under-The-Rapid-Financing-Instrument-and-535478> accessed 24 March 2024.

[39] IMF, 'IMF Executive Board Approves an Extension of the Temporarily Higher Cumulative Access Limits Under the Fund's Emergency Financing Instruments and an Extension of the Food Shock Window' (30 June 2023) Press Release No 23/252 <https://www.imf.org/en/News/Articles/2023/06/30/pr23252-food-shock-imf-exec-board-approves-ext-temp-higher-cum-access-limits-emerg-fin-inst-ext> accessed 24 March 2024.

26

Interactions with the 'Outside World' and the Work of the World Health Organization in Revising the Global Health Architecture for Pandemic Prevention, Preparedness, and Response

Steven A Solomon and Kenneth Piercy

I. Introduction

The goal of the World Health Organization (WHO), a specialized agency of the United Nations (UN) system, is, per Article 1 of its Constitution, 'the attainment by all peoples of the highest possible level of health.' 'Health' is defined in the Constitution as 'a state of complete physical, mental and social well-being and not merely the absence of disease or infirmity'.[1]

Taking this capacious definition in mind, this chapter provides a practitioner's views on interactions between WHO and what has been called the 'outside world', including through methods initiated by the WHO Secretariat. Reference is made to a category of entities often referred to as 'relevant stakeholders', it being understood that the authors use this term here in its broadest sense, meaning all those for whom public health is a concern, including, inter alia, not only those entities or actors referred to as having 'effective' or 'official' relations with WHO but also the global public. In this connection, we focus on the activities of WHO's governing bodies (the World Health Assembly, the Executive Board, and subsidiary bodies) and consider how these interactions have influenced, and perhaps could further influence, the WHO's 'evolutionary trajectories', in the words of Henner Gött's chapter in this volume (Chapter 22).

Based on development for the effective implementation of WHO constitutional principle that '[i]nformed opinion and active cooperation on the part

[1] Constitution of the World Health Organization (adopted 22 July 1946, entered into force 7 April 1948) 14 UNTS 185 preambular para 1 (WHO Constitution).

Steven A Solomon and Kenneth Piercy, *Interactions with the 'Outside World' and the Work of the World Health Organization in Revising the Global Health Architecture for Pandemic Prevention, Preparedness, and Response* In: *International Organization Initiatives.* Edited by: Gabrielle Marceau and Henner Gött, Oxford University Press.
DOI: 10.1093/9780197803325.003.0027

of the public are of the utmost importance in the improvement of the health of the people'[2], we pay special attention to the WHO Secretariat's role regarding novel implementation mechanisms of the WHO Framework of Engagement with Non-State Actors. We also discuss recent developments following the onset COVID-19 pandemic and engagement with the 'outside world' via two critical intergovernmental processes established by the World Health Assembly: the Intergovernmental Negotiating Body (INB) to draft and negotiate a WHO convention, agreement, or other international instrument on pandemic prevention, preparedness, and response, and the Working Group on Amendments to the International Health Regulations (2005) (WGIHR), with a special focus on their modalities of engagement for relevant stakeholders, including participating in electronic consultations and holding open public hearings where stakeholders are invited to provide inputs.

II. Participation of the 'Relevant Stakeholders' in WHO's Governing Bodies Activities and Processes: Key Principles

The WHO's main constitutional organs are the World Health Assembly, constituted by delegates representing all of WHO's member states (194 as of the date of this writing), the Executive Board, composed of 34 persons elected by member states, and the WHO Secretariat, led by the Director-General, who is elected by member states.[3] Given its composition, WHO is an intergovernmental organization.

Regarding participation of the 'outside world' in the work of the WHO, Article 71 of the WHO Constitution authorizes the WHO '[to] make suitable arrangements for consultation and co-operation with non-governmental international organizations and, with the consent of the Government concerned, with national organizations, governmental or non-governmental'. In addition, Article 18(h) of the WHO Constitution empowers the Health Assembly to:

> to invite any organization, international or national, governmental or non-governmental, which has responsibilities related to those of the WHO, to appoint representatives to participate, without right of vote, in its meetings or in those of the committees and conferences convened under its authority, on conditions prescribed by the Health Assembly; but in the case of national organizations, invitations shall be issued only with the consent of the Government concerned.

[2] ibid preambular para 8.
[3] ibid art 9.

A critical development in this regard has been the adoption by the World Health Assembly in 2016 of the *Framework of Engagement with Non-State Actors*,[4] commonly referred to as 'FENSA'. This Framework, adopted by the World Health Assembly under Article 23 of the WHO Constitution, and thus of a recommendatory nature, establishes, inter alia, standards for participation of non-governmental organizations, private sector entities, philanthropic foundations, and academic institutions in WHO's activities.

FENSA identifies the benefits and risks of engagement with non-State actors as well as five specific types of interaction with WHO: (i) participation in governing body meetings as well as technical and other meetings; (ii) provision of in-kind and financial resources; (iii) provision of evidence; (iv) advocacy; and (v) technical collaboration.

To manage conflicts of interest and other potential risks, FENSA puts in place a due diligence, risk assessment, and risk management process to be performed by the WHO Secretariat for each proposed engagement. Importantly, when responding to acute public health events within the meaning of the International Health Regulations (IHR) (2005) or other emergencies with health consequences, FENSA provides the WHO Director-General with flexibility to act immediately 'as might be needed in the application of the procedures of this framework in those responses, when he/she deems necessary, in accordance with WHO's responsibilities as health cluster lead, and the need to engage quickly and broadly with non-State actors for coordination, scale up and service delivery'.[5]

With respect to participation in WHO's governing bodies, FENSA regulates the conditions to be met and the procedure to be followed to grant official relations to non-governmental organizations, international business associations, and philanthropic foundations. Specifically, the WHO Executive Board can grant the status of 'being in official relations'; this status is reviewed every three years. In practice, entities in 'official relations' have the right to be represented at sessions of the governing bodies, without the right to vote; they may be invited by the presiding officers to deliver statements on relevant agenda items during the debate; and they may submit such statements in writing for posting on the WHO website.

[4] WHO (Resolution of the World Health Assembly) 'Framework of Engagement with Non-State Actors' (28 May 2016) WHA69.10.

[5] ibid para 73.

III. Engagement of 'Relevant Stakeholders', Including the General Public, in the Development of the Pandemic Accord and Amendments to the IHR (2005)

A. Background on the INB and WGIHR

In December 2021, in response to the consequences of the COVID-19 pandemic, the Health Assembly decided to hold its second-ever special session to discuss the establishment of an international instrument on pandemic preparedness and response. Following therefrom, at that second special session, the World Health Assembly established an INB open to all member states and associate members[6] to draft and negotiate a WHO convention, agreement, or other international instrument on pandemic prevention, preparedness, and response, with a view to adoption under Article 19, or under other provisions of the WHO Constitution as may be deemed appropriate by the INB.[7]

The initial motivator for this action was, in part, impetus from the outside world, including from academics, civil society, and government leaders, many of whom emphasized the need for a new international instrument on pandemics. The adopted decision establishing the INB acknowledged the need to address gaps in preventing, preparing for, and responding to health emergencies, including in the development and distribution of, and unhindered, timely and equitable access to, medical countermeasures such as vaccines, therapeutics, and diagnostics. It also emphasized the need for a comprehensive and coherent approach to strengthen the global health architecture, and recognizing the commitment of member states to develop a new instrument for pandemic prevention, preparedness, and response with a whole-of-government and whole-of-society approach, prioritizing the need for equity.[8] The INB was mandated to deliver its work to the 77th Health Assembly in May 2024; this mandate was further extended at the 77th Health Assembly, with the INB to finish its work as soon as possible and submit its outcome for consideration by the 78th World Health Assembly in 2025, or earlier by a special session of the World Health Assembly if possible in 2024.[9]

In parallel, with respect to the process of amendments to the IHR (2005), the Health Assembly decided at its 75th session to establish the WGIHR and

[6] And regional economic integration organizations, as appropriate.

[7] WHO (Decision of the World Health Assembly) 'The World Together: Establishment of an Intergovernmental Negotiating Body to Strengthen Pandemic Prevention, Preparedness and Response' (1 December 2021) WHASS2(5).

[8] ibid.

[9] WHO (Decision of the World Health Assembly) 'Intergovernmental Negotiating Body to Draft and Negotiate a WHO Convention, Agreement or Other International Instrument on Pandemic Prevention, Preparedness and Response' (1 June 2024) WHA77(20).

to propose a package of 'targeted amendments' to the regulations.[10] As with the INB, the amendments to the IHR (2005) were to be submitted to the 77th Health Assembly in 2024, and the WGIHR concluded its work at that meeting.[11]

Procedurally, both the WGIHR and INB are subdivisions of the Health Assembly and thereby follow applicable Rules of Procedure, resolutions and decisions of the Health Assembly, including those related to the engagement with and participation of non-State actors per FENSA, described above. Further information on the work of the INB and WGIHR is available on the website of WHO's governing bodies.[12]

B. Public hearings to inform the work of the INB

In the decision establishing the INB, the World Health Assembly requested the Director-General to support the work of the INB, by, inter alia, holding public hearings in line with standard WHO practice, prior to the second meeting of the INB, to inform its deliberations.

To encourage participation in these public hearings, the WHO Secretariat used various channels of communication to raise the awareness of stakeholders and the general public about the process. The first round of public hearings was held over four sessions on 12–13 April 2022. The hearings were composed of two components: (i) a spoken component held via a virtual platform and supported by interpretation in all WHO official languages; and (ii) a written component via a dedicated web portal.

Considering that the WHO Constitution provides in its Preamble that '[i]nformed opinion and active co-operation on the part of the public are of the utmost importance in the improvement of the health of the people', when conducting the public hearings, the WHO Secretariat took the initiative to design innovative techniques and methods, including opening the written component of the public hearings to the general public. The authors are not aware of any other UN entity conducting this style of broad public outreach.

The Secretariat also designed a dedicated webpage for the public hearings,[13] where detailed information about the sessions was uploaded, including the

[10] WHO (Decision of the Executive Board) 'Strengthening the International Health Regulations (2005): A Process for Their Revision Through Potential Amendment' EB150(3) (2022); WHO (Decision of the World Health Assembly) 'Strengthening WHO Preparedness for and Response to Health Emergencies' (27 May 2022) WHA75(9) (2022).

[11] See WHO (Decision of the World Health Assembly) 'Strengthening Preparedness for and Response to Public Health Emergencies Through Targeted Amendments to the International Health Regulations (2005)' (1 June 2024) WHA77.17.

[12] WHO, 'Governance' <https://apps.who.int/gb/gov/> accessed 13 August 2024.

[13] WHO, 'Intergovernmental Negotiating Body' <https://inb.who.int/> accessed 13 August 2024.

terms of participation. All submissions received were made available on that website. The public hearings were opened by the Director-General and a Co-Chair of the INB and were moderated by a panel of senior WHO staff. These sessions focused on the guiding question of: 'What substantive elements do you think should be included in a new international instrument on pandemic preparedness and response?'

For the second round of public hearings, held 29–30 September 2022, interested stakeholders were invited to submit a video statement in response to the following guiding question: 'Based on your experience with the COVID-19 pandemic, what do you believe should be addressed at the international level to better protect against future pandemics?'

The overarching aim of the methodology initiated by WHO Secretariat to conduct the public hearings was to approximate, on the global level, a 'town hall' approach, where individuals, speaking on their own behalf or on behalf of their organization, expressed their uncensored views, mindful only of propriety, relevance, and decorum. Such an exceptional approach represents, to the authors' knowledge, the first of its kind in the international organizations arena. Notably, WHO received 448 video submissions for the second round of public hearings, from a broad range of civil society entities and the general public.

From the authors' perspective, these broad-based, inclusive public hearings were a novel step for WHO, taken at a critical time for the WHO when it was, arguably, receiving the highest-ever level of public attention as during the COVID-19 pandemic. The input from these public hearings organized by the Secretariat directly informed both the direction of work and substantive inputs and views of member states in the discussions regarding the pandemic accord, including in the work of the INB.

C. Modalities for engagement of relevant stakeholders in the INB and WGIHR

From its first meeting, following the WHO Secretariat's innovative mechanisms to involve wider and multiform interactions with 'outside' actors through multiple channels, the INB has adopted modalities for the engagement of relevant stakeholders, with these modalities being agreed as a 'living document' to be updated, in order to support broad engagement. These modalities were applied in subsequent meetings and intersessional work of the INB, thereby facilitating participation by relevant stakeholders in the INB's work.[14] In that regard, except

[14] Mindful that this is a 'living document', the most recent version as of the date of this writing is available at WHO, 'Modalities of Engagement for Relevant Stakeholders' <https://apps.who.int/gb/inb/pdf_files/inb9/A_inb9_6-en.pdf> accessed 13 August 2024.

as otherwise agreed by WHO member states, INB meetings were publicly broadcast on the WHO public website. These modalities have also been applied, *mutatis mutandis*, to the WGIHR.

From the perspective of WHO's rules and procedures, these modalities are significantly inclusive. However, many relevant stakeholders and others have articulated that the process of the INB and WGIHR is still not sufficiently open to the public and relevant stakeholders due to, inter alia, the decision of member states to engage in discussions on textual proposals in a 'closed' modality (ie not open to relevant stakeholders and not broadcast). Member states thus face a delicate balance of ensuring and supporting public engagement, while retaining the necessary candour to negotiate the terms of these legally binding international instruments.

IV. Concluding Remarks

As Gött notes in his chapter of this volume (Chapter 22), the concept of the 'outside world' is a vast and diverse analytical category' that includes 'non-member states [. . .], other IOs, and private actors [. . .]'. In the context of the work of the WHO, this diverse group of entities, including the general public, has been active, directly and indirectly, in influencing and supporting the work of the WHO. This is true, in particular, for the ongoing work of WHO's 194 member states to address strengthening the global health architecture for pandemic prevention, preparedness, and response, through the INB and WGIHR.

The engagement and participation of relevant stakeholders has included both formal activities, through the existing governance modalities for the WHO and its constitutional mandate, and informal and indirect activities, through other fora across national and international means. The impacts and effects of this 'outside world' influence, and participation on WHO evolutionary trajectories are yet to be seen. Nevertheless, from experience to date, the authors believe it will be in the benefit of the world's well-being and the goal of achieving the highest possible level of health for all persons.

27

The Global Fund to Fight AIDS, Tuberculosis, and Malaria

Partnerships, Collaborations, and Initiatives with International Organizations

*Fady Zeidan and Jean Abboud**

I. Introduction

It is a truism to note that the notions of collaboration and cooperation constitute the *raison d'être* of international organizations (IOs).[1] Following the emergence of multilateral international institutions at the beginning of the twentieth century, collaboration and cooperation were primarily characterized by their inter-state character with respect to the creation of the IO in question and its governance structures and operational model. With time and globalization, collaboration and cooperation have become imperative in an ever-expanding number of fields. This has resulted in novel forms of IOs as evidenced, for example, by the creation of the Global Fund to Fight AIDS, Tuberculosis and Malaria (the Global Fund).

Since its inception, the concept of partnership has been a core principle of the governance structures and *modus operandi* of the Global Fund. In its essence, the principle provides that to achieve the desired impact, governments, civil society, communities affected by the diseases, technical partners, the private sector, and other stakeholders must all work together and be involved in the decision-making processes. A most recent example of the continued relevance of this principle may be found in the *Global Fund 2023–2028 Strategy, Fighting Pandemics and Building a Healthier and More Equitable World*, which underscores the importance of the delivery of its objectives through the partnership model.

This chapter is divided into three sections. Section II briefly presents the Global Fund's institutional design to contextualize the collaboration initiatives discussed

* The views expressed in this chapter are those of the authors and do not necessarily reflect the views of the Global Fund to Fight AIDS, Tuberculosis and Malaria.

[1] The terms 'collaboration', 'cooperation', and 'partnership' are used interchangeably in this chapter. In their essence, they all refer to the idea of two or more IOs expressing their desire to work (or actually working) together with a view of achieving a commonly shared objective or interest.

Fady Zeidan and Jean Abboud, *The Global Fund to Fight AIDS, Tuberculosis, and Malaria* In: *International Organization Initiatives*. Edited by: Gabrielle Marceau and Henner Gött, Oxford University Press.
DOI: 10.1093/9780197803325.003.0028

in Sections III and IV.[2] Section III focuses on the collaboration and cooperation between the Secretariat and other IOs in the implementation of the Global Fund's standard operating model. Section IV provides examples of the collaboration and cooperation between the Secretariat and other IOs in responding to global challenges and developing novel forms of initiatives in furtherance of the Global Fund's mission.

II. The Global Fund's Institutional Design

The Global Fund was established in January 2002 as a Swiss not-for-profit foundation and has evolved, over time, into an IO.[3] The governing, administrative, and advisory bodies of the Global Fund include the Board and the Secretariat, which were already envisaged under the initial Bylaws of the Global Fund.[4]

The Board is the supreme governing body of the Global Fund, and its composition and decision-making processes reflect the principle of partnership and collaboration. Indeed, the Board currently consists of 20 voting constituencies—ranging from donor and recipient governments to civil society, the private sector, private foundations, and communities affected by the diseases—and 8 non-voting members, which include IOs and technical partners with which the Secretariat works, such as the World Health Organization (WHO), the World Bank, and The Joint United Nations Programme on HIV/AIDS (UNAIDS).[5] In the absence of consensus, the adoption of a decision by the Board requires a qualified majority from the broad range of stakeholders represented on the Board.[6]

The Board exercises all powers required to carry out its purpose, including six core functions pertaining to (i) strategy development, (ii) governance oversight,

[2] The initiatives discussed in this chapter generally refer to the Global Fund's Secretariat-led collaborative arrangements and partnerships with other IOs. These are aimed at carrying out the organization's mandate, especially in a fast-changing global health and development landscape.

[3] For a more in-depth overview of the creation of the Global Fund and the gradual evolution of its status as an IO enjoying privileges and immunities, see Fady Zeidan and Jean Abboud, 'The Global Fund to Fight AIDS, Tuberculosis and Malaria: The Journey of a Public-Private Partnership' in Peter Quayle (ed), *The Role of International Administrative Law at International Organizations, AIIB Yearbook of International Law* (Brill Nijhoff 2020).

[4] The initial Bylaws also referred to the Partnership Forum and the Technical Review Panel, which are still part of the Global Fund bodies. With time, the Committees of the Board, the Coordinating Group, the Office of the Inspector General, and the Independent Evaluation Panel were added to the list of governing, administrative, and advisory bodies of the Global Fund set out in Article 5 of the Global Fund Bylaws: The Global Fund, 'Bylaws' (The Global Fund) <https://www.theglobalfund.org/media/6007/core_globalfund_bylaws_en.pdf> accessed 4 November 2023 (Global Fund Bylaws).

[5] IOs are also represented in the standing committees of the Global Fund Board, in particular the Audit and Finance Committee and the Strategy Committee.

[6] In line with the principle of partnership and to strengthen further the balance between the Board constituencies, if a decision is not adopted through consensus by the Board, it would then require, in order to pass, a two-thirds majority of those present of *both* the group comprising the public

(iii) commitment of financial resources, (iv) assessment of organizational performance, (v) risk management, and (vi) partnership engagement, resource mobilization, and advocacy.[7]

The Secretariat is responsible, among other things, for managing the day-to-day operations of the Global Fund and the overall grant cycle, implementing strategies and policies, supporting fundraising operations and partnerships, and coordinating with relevant agencies and partners.[8] The Secretariat includes around 1,200 staff members who are all based in Geneva, as the Global Fund does not have offices in other countries. It is headed by an Executive Director, appointed by the Board, and is composed of different divisions and departments, including the Grant Management Division, the External Relations and Communications Division, and the Legal and Governance Department.

From its early days, and with a view to swiftly initiate its operations, the Global Fund Board approved important collaboration agreements with other IOs, most notably the WHO and the World Bank.[9] With time, the Board approved a number of decisions conferring, inter alia, signature authority to the Executive Director on behalf of the Global Fund and authorizing her/him to further delegate her/his authority to Secretariat staff, as necessary and appropriate for the day-to-day management of the operations of the Global Fund.[10] The collaboration between the Global Fund and the WHO, the World Bank, and other partner organizations remains a constant feature of the Global Fund's standard operating model, with the Board and the Secretariat playing distinct yet complementary roles to ensure the success of such collaborations and achieve the desired result and impact.

and private donor constituencies (the voting donor group) and the group comprising the recipient countries, civil society and communities' constituencies (the voting implementer group). See Global Fund Bylaws (n 4) art 7.6.

[7] Global Fund Bylaws (n 4) art 7.4.

[8] ibid art 10.2.

[9] To set up its Secretariat, the Global Fund concluded, in May 2002, an Administrative Services Agreement with the WHO that provided for, among other things, the assignment of WHO officials to work on Global Fund projects. This agreement was terminated when the Global Fund became administratively autonomous from the WHO in 2009. Also, in May 2022, the Global Fund and the World Bank entered into a Trustee Agreement—that continues to be operational to this day—for the efficient holding and management of the funds contributed to the Global Fund. Without these initial arrangements, it would have been impossible for the Secretariat to start mobilizing funds and disbursing grants as quickly as it did.

[10] See The Global Fund, 'Board Decisions' (18 October 2018) Board Decision GF/B39/EDP12 <https://www.theglobalfund.org/kb/board-decisions/b39/b39-edp12/> accessed 8 April 2024.

III. Collaboration in the Standard Operating Model

The collaboration of the Global Fund's Secretariat and other IOs can be seen both in the grant-making cycle (A.) and in technical cooperation and additional assistance arrangements that supplement the allocated grants (B.).

A. Grant-making cycle

The Global Fund raises and invests nearly USD 4 billion a year to support programmes to fight HIV, tuberculosis (TB), and malaria and enhance resilient and sustainable systems of health (RSSH) in more than 100 countries.[11] In essence, the contributions to the Global Fund are allocated through grant agreements to principal recipients in implementing countries based on their funding requests for three-year cycles. Funding requests are developed and submitted to the Secretariat by national committees called Country Coordinating Mechanisms (CCMs). These are composed, inter alia, of representatives from the government, civil society, bilateral agencies, and IOs. CCM members offer technical expertise, support resource mobilization, advocacy efforts, and country coordination, and assist with stakeholder management.

The cross-functional country teams managing the overall grant cycle at the Secretariat work in close collaboration with the CCMs to ensure the timely submission of the funding requests and their review by the Secretariat's Grant Approvals Committee (GAC), which recommends the grants to the Board for approval. Technical partners are invited to provide high-level technical advice on the grants' programmatic content to the GAC. Once approved by the Board, the grant confirmations are signed by the Secretariat pursuant to delegated authority, and the grants are disbursed to the designated principal recipient and implemented. The programmes and grants are continuously monitored by local fund agents and subject to the audits and investigations conducted by the Office of the Inspector General.

The principal recipient can be any type of organization, from a government ministry to a community-based organization to a private sector entity. In some cases, IOs—such as the United Nations Development Programme (UNDP), United Nations Office for Project Services, and United Nations International Children's Emergency Fund—are selected by the Secretariat, or in coordination

[11] Funds are raised based on pledges made by governmental and non-governmental donors in replenishment conferences held every three years. The Secretariat plays a crucial role in organizing the replenishment conference along with the authorities of the hosting country. The most recent replenishment, the 7th Replenishment, took place in the United States in 2022 and enabled the Global Fund to raise USD 15.7 billion for the funding period 2023–2025.

with the national stakeholders, to act as the principal recipients of the Global Fund grants.[12] Similar to other principal recipients of Global Fund grants, the role and responsibilities of the IO managing the Global Fund grant in a given country are detailed in high-level agreements and in bespoke confirmations signed between the Global Fund's Secretariat and the specific IO. Throughout the grant cycle, the Secretariat engages with officials in these and other IOs on a variety of issues ranging from the accomplishment of the principal recipient functions to their participation to the CCMs, and, at times, also with respect to the provision of technical cooperation or additional assistance arrangements.

B. Technical cooperation and additional assistance

Multilateral partners (such as the WHO, UNAIDS, STOP TB Partnership, and RBM Partnership to End Malaria) can provide technical assistance to implementing countries in relation to Global Fund grants through, among other things, conducting programme reviews, developing strong national disease and health sector strategies, and providing expert advice in relation to the grant implementation.

In addition to the standard grant model, the Global Fund supports programmes that are linked to the achievement of the wider Global Fund strategy. Following the initial approval of the priority areas by the Board, the Secretariat concludes agreements with a broad range of counterparties and service providers with specific subject-matter or technical expertise including in some cases IOs. This is done to implement, monitor, or report on defined project activities pertaining to one or more strategic initiatives.[13]

Technical cooperation can also be set out in non-financial agreements or memoranda of understanding between the Global Fund's Secretariat and other IOs on mandate-driven collaborations. A recent example is the revised Strategic Framework for Collaboration concluded in June 2023 between the Global Fund's Secretariat and the WHO. The framework builds on the overall strategies of both institutions. It reflects their commitments to accelerate support to countries to achieve the health-related Sustainable Development Goals, including universal health coverage, by covering 35 areas for collaboration pertaining to

[12] Data pertaining to the Global Fund grants, including principal recipients, is available on the following website: The Global Fund, 'Data Explorer' <https://data.theglobalfund.org/> accessed 21 January 2024.

[13] Examples of priority areas for strategic initiatives for the 2023–2025 allocation period pertain, among other things, to community engagement, programmes to remove human rights and gender-related barriers, regional laboratories and national diagnostic networks, effective community systems and equitable access to quality services, equitable access to quality health products, health financing, and emergency funding.

health policies and normative guidance, advocacy and health governance, health products and innovations, and technical support and capacity-building.[14]

IV. Collaboration in Times of Crises and Novel Initiatives

The collaborative relations that are developed and nurtured between the Global Fund's Secretariat and other IOs in the context of the standard operating model can be leveraged to respond swiftly and nimbly to emerging challenges (A.) and to explore novel forms of initiatives to enhance synergies and efficiencies (B.).

A. Responding to emerging challenges

The Global Fund has partnered with other IOs to deliver positive impacts in challenging operating environments, or in non-eligible countries in crisis, where funding could not follow traditional Global Fund implementation arrangements.[15] For example, the Global Fund supported a regional response to the health crisis in Venezuela. Indeed, from 2018 up to December 2021, the Global Fund Board approved three exceptional funding requests for a total of USD 17 million to help mitigate the impact of the public health crisis in Venezuela.[16] The Secretariat worked with the Pan-American Health Organization (PAHO) and UNAIDS to agree on management and implementation arrangements in relation to the funding requests approved by the Board. Through this collaboration, life-saving HIV, TB, and malaria commodities were purchased through PAHO and critical support was provided to civil society through UNAIDS to ensure social monitoring of Global Fund HIV investments and civil society engagement.

[14] The Global Fund, 'Updates: WHO and the Global Fund Announce Commitment for Enhanced Collaboration' (8 June 2023) <https://www.theglobalfund.org/en/updates/2023/2023-06-08-who-and-the-global-fund-announce-commitment-for-enhanced-collaboration/> accessed 1 July 2023.

[15] The Global Fund Eligibility Policy determines which country's disease component may be eligible for a Global Fund allocation. The list of eligible countries is available at: The Global Fund, 'Eligibility List 2023' <https://www.theglobalfund.org/media/12505/core_eligiblecountries2023_list_en.pdf> accessed 11 November 2023. The Global Fund's Challenging Operating Environments Policy aims to improve the effectiveness of activities in insecure and volatile contexts based on principles of flexibility, partnerships, and innovation.

[16] In 2018, Venezuela was not eligible for Global Fund funding. Since then, the Board made funding for malaria and tuberculosis programmes exceptionally eligible for the 2023–2025 allocation period, based on recommendations from technical partners and the Secretariat: The Global Fund 'Eligibility of Venezuela's Malaria and TB Components for the 2023–2025 Allocation Period' (16 August 2022) Board Decision GF/B47/EDP10. Venezuela is also included in the list of challenging operating environment countries.

The Secretariat also played a critical role in the global response to fight the COVID-19 pandemic by establishing and operationalizing a time-bound, Board-approved, mechanism in April 2020—the COVID-19 Response Mechanism (C19RM)—to finance interventions to fight the COVID-19 outbreak and by participating in the foundation and operationalization of the Access to COVID-19 Tools Accelerator (ACT-A) partnership. The emergence of the COVID-19 outbreak threatened the health and community systems of the countries the Global Fund serves, putting supported programmes at critical risk of disruption. Developing a rapid response to fight COVID-19 was, therefore, essential to achieving the Global Fund's core mission and necessary to safeguard its resources for the fight against HIV, tuberculosis, and malaria. Addressing mandate-related considerations when proposing to the Board the creation of the C19RM, the Secretariat highlighted that it did not consider the C19RM to be 'a change in the remit of the Global Fund, rather it is a tactical response to an unprecedented public health emergency that threatens to entirely derail the fight against HIV, TB, and malaria'.[17] The conceptualization, setting up, and operationalization of the C19RM were made possible, thanks to the rapid mobilization of the Global Fund's Secretariat and nimble support from the Board, which led not only the successful response on that front at the country level but also ensured business continuity with respect to all other Secretariat workstreams in a virtual environment.[18]

The collaboration between the Global Fund's Secretariat and UNDP in Afghanistan provides an additional example.[19] In 2021, the Global Fund programmes in Afghanistan faced important challenges, including a liquidity shortage in the banking system, a reduction in the access to healthcare services, and supply chain problems. To bridge the gap in funding from international donors and prevent the country's healthcare system from collapsing, the Global Fund's Secretariat and the UNDP mounted a joint effort to provide interim and emergency funding to support the delivery of essential healthcare services

[17] The Global Fund, 'COVID-19 Response for Business Continuity and Country Support', Board Decision GF/B42/ER09 – Revision 1 <https://www.theglobalfund.org/media/9529/bm42_edp10-11_annex_en.pdf> accessed 11 November 2023.

[18] The initial timeline of the C19RM mechanism was extended in November 2022 and the mechanism broadly operates under the initial underlying principles. In 2021, the C19RM awarded USD 3.5 billion to more than 100 countries to support national COVID-19 responses, mitigate the impact of COVID-19 on HIV, TB, and malaria programmes, and to support the urgent reinforcement of health and community systems. The Global Fund, 'Extension of the COVID-19 Response Mechanism (C19RM)' (15–17 November 2022), Board Decision GF/B48/06 <https://www.theglobalfund.org/media/12477/bm48_06-extension-covid-19-response-mechanism_report_en.pdf> accessed 31 July 2023.

[19] The Global Fund, 'News Releases: Global Fund and UNDP Join Efforts to Maintain Access to Essential Health Services in Afghanistan' <https://www.theglobalfund.org/en/news/2021/2021-10-06-global-fund-and-undp-join-efforts-to-maintain-access-to-essential-health-services-in-afghanistan/> accessed 4 December 2023.

in Afghanistan. The Global Fund's Secretariat and the UNDP were able to leverage their long-standing partnership in Afghanistan to conclude an agreement for the provision of USD 15 million in time-limited emergency funding through the Global Fund's Emergency Fund.[20] The agreement aimed to help ensure that some 2,200 health facilities across the country were maintained at a functional level during a critical interim phase. This collaboration also laid the ground for longer-term initiatives and, following the end of the emergency period, for the funding and implementation of key projects taken over by other IOs.

B. Novel forms of initiatives

In addition to the collaborations and partnerships concluded in the traditional grant cycle model, whether in relation to strategic initiatives or to respond to emerging challenges, the Global Fund's Secretariat has explored novel ways to undertake joint projects and to leverage the efficiencies and synergies with partnering organizations. These novel types of collaborations are generally referred to as 'blended finance', and they combine Global Fund grants with other sources of financing, including investments from development finance institutions.[21]

In the past, the Global Fund has partnered with the World Bank on several occasions to leverage the Bank's comparative strength in relation to innovative financing initiatives. Indeed, both institutions periodically partnered on an ad hoc basis to co-finance investments and complement grant funded programmes, for example, in the Democratic Republic of Congo or in India. These arrangements were challenging and time-consuming as they required an extensive internal consultation process, bespoke negotiation, and, in some cases, even Board approval, as both organizations had to uphold their respective standard policies and requirements.

Building on these past initiatives and with a view to reduce transaction costs, the Global Fund's Secretariat and World Bank teams worked together over several months to explore a new co-financing structure in line with the institutional processes and policies of both organizations. Their efforts led to the signature, in 2019, of a co-financing framework agreement that could be used as a basis for a longer-term and more streamlined approach. The framework

[20] The Emergency Fund is one of the strategic initiatives workstreams approved by the Board, along with corresponding amounts. It aims to respond swiftly and flexibly to emergency situations. The Secretariat has the authority to approve and operationalize the use of funds in the Emergency Fund.

[21] The Global Fund, 'Innovative Finance' <https://www.theglobalfund.org/en/innovative-finance/> accessed 31 July 2023.

agreement provides for a form of co-financing structure between the Global Fund and the World Bank whereby transaction costs are shared and coordination arrangements, in respect of policies and requirements, are established, resulting in the streamlining of financing arrangements vis-à-vis the recipient countries.

Since signing the framework agreement, the Global Fund's Secretariat and the World Bank have signed several co-financing investments. The first was concluded in 2020 and consisted of a USD 36 million joint investment to increase access to quality healthcare, improve the quality of nutrition services, and strengthen health systems in Laos, with the Global Fund contributing USD 10 million. Other examples include recent joint investments in Gambia and Haiti. In the case of Haiti, the Global Fund's Secretariat partnered with the World Bank by leveraging the Global Fund's RSSH grant to Haiti (USD 23.5 million) in a wider programme funded through a World Bank loan that aims at increasing primary healthcare service readiness and strengthening surveillance and response capacity for infectious diseases.

Recognizing the important complementary role of blended finance in respect of the traditional grant investments, the 2019 framework agreement was followed by the approval by the Board in 2023 of a broader framework to guide the development, review, approval, and implementation of blended finance transactions, including with partners beyond the World Bank.[22] The 2019 framework agreement also provided a valuable impetus for extending the cooperation with the World Bank in other novel areas, including climate change. Indeed, the two institutions signed in November 2023 a memorandum of understanding that aims at deepening their collaboration in three areas: (i) climate and health, (ii) health financing, and (iii) regional manufacturing. The overall aim is to support more efficient, effective, and sustainable financing to strengthen health systems in the face of climate change, including through better access to primary healthcare services for the most vulnerable populations, the use of financing modalities (such as joint investments and blended finance), and the strengthening of regional production and procurement of health supplies (eg drugs and medical devices).[23]

The conclusion of this new memorandum of understanding fits within the wider response of the Global Fund to the threat posed by climate change to

[22] The Global Fund, 'Board Decisions' (15 November 2023), Board Decision GF/B50/DP04 <https://www.theglobalfund.org/kb/board-decisions/b50/b50-dp04//> accessed 8 April 2024.

[23] The Global Fund, 'Updates: World Bank and Global Fund: Stronger Collaboration to Tackle the Impact of Climate Change on Health' (22 November 2023) <https://www.theglobalfund.org/en/updates/2023/2023-11-22-world-bank-global-fund-stronger-collaboration-climate-change-health/#:~:text=Specifically%2C%20the%20two%20organizations%20will,for%20the%20most%20vulnerable%20populations./> accessed 4 December 2023.

global health through the use of emergency funding to counter the impact of extreme weather events and via investments to strengthen health systems. In the same vein, the Global Fund announced in December 2023 at the 28th United Nations Climate Change Conference in Dubai its intention to address, together with the Green Climate Fund, the impact of climate change on the health of the most vulnerable communities around the world, by focusing on aligning climate change and health funding, supporting countries to assess needs and access financing, and building evidence of effective interventions.[24]

V. Conclusion

In a resource-constrained environment, collaboration and partnership among IOs are important tools to enhance efficiency and leverage impact. They contribute to strengthening the credibility of IOs and, more generally, the faith that the international community holds in multilateralism.

As shown in this chapter, collaboration and partnership were paramount for the successful setting up of the Global Fund and continue to be a key element of its institutional design and operations. The Global Fund's Secretariat plays an instrumental role in applying these concepts not only in the context of grant cycle implementation, technical cooperation, and additional assistance arrangements but also in responses to emerging challenges and the development of novel synergies and initiatives with peer organizations.

As the world continues to face global challenges, ranging from conflicts to pandemics and climate events, partnership and collaboration will be a continuing topic of attention and interest for national, regional, and multilateral actors. They are crucial to respond to such challenges. The track record of the Global Fund collaborating, not only with other IOs but also with the private sector, civil society, and other national and multilateral partners, positions it in a unique way on the global public health scene and in the quest for a better future and health for all.

[24] The Global Fund, 'Updates: Green Climate Fund and Global Fund Join Forces to Tackle Impact of Climate Crisis on Health' (3 December 2023) <https://www.theglobalfund.org/en/updates/2023/2023-12-03-green-climate-fund-global-fund-join-forces-tackle-impact-climate-crisis-health/#:~:text=The%20two%20largest%20multilateral%20climate,the%20health%20of%20the%20most> accessed 24 September 2024.

28
IOs' Initiatives
Gavi, the Vaccine Alliance

Jelena Madir[*]

I. Introduction

Gavi, the Vaccine Alliance (Gavi) is a public–private global health partnership. Created in 2000, it brought together major stakeholders in immunization with the fundamental goal of improving equitable and sustainable access to vaccines and strengthening immunization systems in the world's poorest countries. Gavi's Board consists of representatives from developing countries, donor countries, the World Health Organization (WHO), the United Nations Children's Fund (UNICEF), the World Bank, the Bill & Melinda Gates Foundation, vaccine manufacturers from both developed and developing countries, civil society, and independent board members.[1]

From a legal perspective, Gavi is a foundation under Swiss law with international institution status. The Headquarters Agreement with the Swiss government gives it privileges and immunities similar to those of traditional international organizations under the Swiss Host State Act.[2] Gavi is thus a *hybrid entity*, as examined in this volume by Hannah Birkenkötter (Chapter 1). This chapter discusses one of the flagship initiatives promoted by the Gavi Secretariat during the COVID-19 pandemic within the multilateral efforts that began in early 2020 to support the equitable development, procurement, and delivery

* The views expressed by the author are made in a personal capacity and do not reflect the views of the European Bank for Reconstruction and Development.

[1] Gavi, 'Board Members' <https://www.gavi.org/governance/gavi-board/members> accessed 14 October 2023.

[2] Swiss Federal Department of Foreign Affairs, 'The Federal Council Concludes a Host Country Agreement with the GAVI Alliance (Global Alliance for Vaccines and Immunization)' (*admin.ch*, 23 June 2009) <https://www.admin.ch/gov/en/start/documentation/media-releases.msg-id-27613.html> accessed 14 October 2023.

For the full text of the Host Country Agreement in French, see Accord entre le Conseil fédéral suisse et GAVI Alliance (Global Alliance for Vaccines and Immunization) en vue de déterminer le statut juridique de GAVI Alliance en Suisse (2009) RO 4567 <https://www.fedlex.admin.ch/eli/cc/2009/541/fr> accessed 14 October 2023.

For further background information on Gavi, Eelco Szabó, 'Gavi, the Vaccine Alliance: A Unique Case Study in Partnership' (2016) 13(1) IOLR 149.

Jelena Madir, *IOs' Initiatives* In: *International Organization Initiatives*. Edited by: Gabrielle Marceau and Henner Gött, Oxford University Press. © Oxford University Press 2025. DOI: 10.1093/9780197803325.003.0029

of COVID-19 vaccines worldwide, in particular, to low- and middle-income countries.

II. Towards the COVAX Facility

At the beginning of the COVID-19 pandemic, Gavi was entrusted with the daunting task of co-leading the only global collaborative mechanism for the Procurement and Delivery of Vaccines Workstream of the COVID-19 Vaccines Global Access Facility (COVAX Facility), the vaccines pillar of the Access to COVID-19 Tools Accelerator (ACT-A) that was set up by the WHO[3] (see also Chapter 9 of this volume, by Gian Luca Burci and Ana Balcazar-Moreno).

The specific question that Gavi was tasked with answering was: How can the world make sure that COVID-19 vaccines, when they become available, are distributed in a fair, rapid, and equitable manner so as to avoid the situation where they are available only to a handful of wealthy countries that have entered into bilateral agreements with vaccine manufacturers?

In response to this challenge, in the summer of 2020, the Gavi Secretariat became the legal administrator of the COVAX Facility,[4] whose purpose was to be a global programme for the development, production, and distribution of COVID-19 vaccines. The COVAX Facility was primarily driven by the Gavi Secretariat, in collaboration with WHO and the Coalition for Epidemic Preparedness Innovations (CEPI). There were different views about how to structure the Facility and who should administer it, but there were no reservations about whether there should be one.

III. Overall Structure and Operations of the COVAX Facility

In structuring the Facility, the Gavi Secretariat was guided by three overarching objectives. First, the Secretariat sought to incentivize manufacturers to expand vaccine production capacity while they were still developing their vaccines. Manufacturers are typically reluctant to risk making the significant investments needed to scale up vaccine manufacturing facilities until they have received approval for a vaccine, which is a lengthy process with uncertain factors. However, if the Secretariat had waited for that, that would have led to significant delays and even greater shortages of vaccines than what the world ended up seeing. To avoid this, and as described in more detail below, Gavi, on behalf of the COVAX Facility, entered into advance purchase commitment agreements with

[3] Gavi, 'What Is COVAX?' <https://www.gavi.org/covax-facility> accessed 14 October 2023.
[4] ibid.

manufacturers, whereby Gavi essentially guaranteed to manufacturers a set demand for their COVID-19 vaccine doses, thereby incentivizing them to scale up their production.

The second objective of COVAX was to guarantee fair and equitable access to COVID-19 vaccines for every country in the world to avoid situations where vaccines were available only to a handful of high-income countries that had entered into bilateral agreements with manufacturers.

The third overarching objective of COVAX was to develop the largest and most diverse actively managed portfolio of COVID-19 vaccine candidates in order to maximize the probability that successful vaccines would be developed and made available.

IV. Structure and Operations of the COVAX Financing Instrument

Broadly speaking, the COVAX innovative financing instrument was structured as follows: high-income and upper-middle-income economies were self-financing participants (SFPs) in the Facility and were required to pay for their vaccine doses. In addition, a group of 92 low-income and lower-middle-income economies could participate in the Facility primarily with support from sovereign donors, who were providing donation funding.[5]

As noted above, Gavi, as an administrator of the Facility, entered into agreements with numerous manufacturers to secure access to vaccine supply on the basis that only 'approved vaccines' would be procured through the Facility. 'Approved vaccine' meant that the vaccine had to be either prequalified by WHO or licensed by one of the so-called Stringent Regulatory Agencies (SRAs).[6]

Structuring a programme that was palatable to the SFPs and, at the same time, did not expose Gavi as an organization to significant financial risks was by far the most challenging aspect of designing the Facility from a legal and risk-management standpoint. In terms of contractual arrangements, there were several key steps in the structure.

First, Gavi entered into a Commitment Agreement with each SFP (typically with the Ministry of Health or its corresponding equivalent) that specified the number of doses of approved vaccines the relevant SFP committed to purchase.

[5] This was possible through the financing instrument called 'COVID-19 Vaccines Advance Market Commitment (COVAX AMC)'. Gavi, 'COVAX AMC' <https://www.gavi.org/gavi-covax-amc> accessed 14 October 2023.

[6] Currently, there is an ongoing transition process to replace the SRAs with the WHO Listed Authorities (WLA) framework, see WHO, 'WHO Listed Authorities' <https://www.who.int/news-room/questions-and-answers/item/who-listed-authorities> accessed 18 February 2025.

Pursuant to this agreement, the SFP made a non-refundable down payment to Gavi. In addition, the SFP provided a financial guarantee 'in form and substance satisfactory to Gavi' within 21 days from the date of the Commitment Agreement.[7]

The commitment amount that each SFP had to pay was calculated based on the product of the so-called Weighted Average Estimated Cost per Dose and the Total Participant Doses. Taking each of these in turn, the Weighted Average Estimated Cost Per Dose was USD 10.55,[8] an amount based on the then-available pricing information from manufacturers in the portfolio of vaccines under consideration by the Office of the COVAX Facility. Importantly, however, SFPs would ultimately purchase approved vaccines at the actual price offered by each manufacturer. Therefore, if it turned out that the estimated cost per dose was higher than the actual price, the SFP would get more doses for its commitment amount and vice versa. The total participant doses equalled 20% of the SFP's population considering that the initial idea was that each SFP would have to enter into a legally binding commitment to purchase, through the COVAX Facility, enough doses to immunize 20% of its population.

Second, Gavi utilized the down payment from the SFPs to enter into advance purchase commitment agreements with vaccine manufacturers. The aim of these agreements was to secure sufficient doses of approved vaccines so that each SFP could receive enough doses commensurate with its commitment.

Third, Gavi allocated an approved vaccine to the relevant SFP. In its notification of allocation, Gavi also directed the SFP to enter a supply agreement with either a procurement agent (UNICEF[9] or the Pan-American Health Organization's Revolving Fund for Access to Vaccines)[10] or the manufacturer directly.[11]

The final step of the structure entailed the SFP complying with its obligation and entering into the supply agreement with the procurement agent or manufacturer, pursuant to which the manufacturer was obliged to deliver the approved vaccine to the SFP.[12]

The SFPs could join the Facility under one of two arrangements: first, under the 'committed purchase arrangement', whereby, broadly speaking, an SFP

[7] WHO, 'COVAX Facility Self-Financing Participants Legal Agreements' <https://www.who.int/docs/default-source/coronaviruse/act-accelerator/covax/covax-self-financing-participants-legal-agreements-and-explanatory-note.pdf?sfvrsn=b5350328_3> accessed 14 October 2023.

[8] WHO, 'Commitment Agreement with the Self-Financing Participants', Sec 1.1, *All-Inclusive Weighted Average Estimated Cost Per Dose* <https://www.who.int/docs/default-source/coronaviruse/act-accelerator/covax/covax-self-financing-participants-legal-agreements-and-explanatory-note.pdf?sfvrsn=b5350328_3> accessed 14 October 2023 (Committed Purchase Arrangement).

[9] UNICEF, 'COVAX: Ensuring Global Equitable Access to COVID-19 Vaccines' <https://www.unicef.org/supply/covax-ensuring-global-equitable-access-covid-19-vaccines> accessed 14 October 2023.

[10] Pan American Health Organization, 'PAHO Revolving Fund' <https://www.paho.org/en/revolving-fund#collapse-accordion-43812-2> accessed 14 October 2023.

[11] Commitment Purchase Agreement (n 8) s 4.

[12] ibid.

would make a relatively small down payment. Further, subject to being allocated the doses of approved vaccines, the SFP would commit to procure the doses, except if the actual price per dose was higher than USD 21.1 per dose (ie twice the Weighted Average Estimated Cost Per Dose).[13] Alternatively, SFPs could join under the 'optional purchase arrangements', whereby, broadly speaking, an SFP could decide whether or not to purchase any approved vaccine candidate allocated to it. In this case, the SFP would have to pay a higher down payment than under the committed purchase arrangements. Thereafter, there were two windows during which the SFP could decide on a particular candidate: before Gavi entered into an advance purchase commitment agreement with the relevant manufacturer[14] or later, in the clinical development process, before Gavi confirmed orders with manufacturers.

V. Risks and Challenges for Gavi

Clearly, the structure of the COVAX Facility for the financialization of global immunization posed numerous risks to Gavi as an intermediary, which the Secretariat tried to mitigate as follows.

First, there was the risk that SFPs would not pay for approved vaccines on time or at all, which would have obliged Gavi to cover any shortfall. As mentioned above, under the commitment agreement, SFPs were required to provide a financial guarantee 'in form and substance satisfactory to Gavi'. This requirement proved quite difficult and time-consuming to obtain for most SFPs, and Gavi eventually obtained a commercial insurance product to mitigate this risk.[15]

Second, yet another risk stemmed from the fact that when the advance purchase commitment agreements were negotiated, no one knew *if* and *when* vaccines would become available. Hence, manufacturers were unable to commit to firm supply schedules, a key provision in standard supply contracts. Further, once vaccines did become available, many manufacturers took a commercial decision to prioritize deliveries to wealthy countries over low-income economies because the former were paying a higher price. In order to try to gain priority for the low-income economies in the delivery queue, Gavi attempted to negotiate

[13] ibid s 2.3.
[14] WHO, 'Commitment Agreement (Optional Purchase Arrangement)', Sec 2.2, 4, <https://www.who.int/docs/default-source/coronaviruse/act-accelerator/covax/covax-self-financing-participants-legal-agreements-and-explanatory-note.pdf?sfvrsn=b5350328_3> accessed 14 October 2023.
[15] Marsh, 'Marsh and Citi Develop Innovative Risk Structure to Help Gavi Speed Delivery of COVAX Vaccines to the World' (*marsh.com*, 17 August 2021) <https://www.marsh.com/us/about/media/marsh-and-citi-develop-innovative-risk-structure-to-help-gavi-speed-delivery-of-covax-vaccines-to-the-world.html> accessed 14 October 2023.

'slot-swapping' with the countries that were ahead in the manufacturer supply queues.[16] In addition, the Secretariat designed a dose donation programme whereby wealthy countries could donate their excess doses to COVAX.[17]

Finally, a third challenge COVAX faced was the fact that manufacturers wanted to be exempt from civil liability for unexpected adverse side effects and conditioned their deliveries on government indemnification for any such claims. For lower-income countries, this kind of financial exposure presented too much risk for already-stretched health budgets, jeopardizing their ability to receive COVID-19 vaccines for their populations. In response, WHO and Gavi set up the first international no-fault compensation scheme available to individuals from the 92 lower-income economies.[18] The benefits of the no-fault compensation scheme include simplified access to compensation, as well as avoiding a lengthy, costly, and complex encounter with the legal system, with no guarantee of success.

Ultimately, the biggest challenge with COVAX was that it entailed putting together something that had not been done before and so, in many ways, was precedent-setting. Despite all the obstacles that it faced, COVAX delivered nearly 2 billion vaccine doses in over 150 countries.

VI. Conclusion

The COVAX Facility, as structured and negotiated by the Gavi secretariat, is likely to be the template for future global risk-sharing agreements and financing instruments in global health governance. It should serve as the basis on which the world prepares for the next pandemic and could also help with other issues the world is grappling with, such as climate change. It is also scalable because it not only tries to find a solution for low-income economies, for which the participation was primarily donor-funded, but also caters to high-income and upper-middle-income economies, which participated on a self-financing basis and were required to pay for their vaccine doses through COVAX. One could envision a similar set-up for a climate change fund, which would require polluters to pay for their greenhouse gas emissions. The above-discussed programme showcases an initiative undertaken by an IO in response to the global pandemic and the creativity it used to respond to a crisis.

[16] Gavi, 'COVAX Slot Swapping: Explained' <https://www.gavi.org/vaccineswork/covax-slot-swapping-explained> accessed 14 October 2023.

[17] Gavi, 'COVAX Dose Donations' <https://www.gavi.org/sites/default/files/covid/covax/COVAX-Dose-Donation-Table.pdf> accessed 14 October 2023.

[18] Gavi, 'The COVAX No Fault Compensation Programme: Explained' <https://www.gavi.org/vaccineswork/covax-no-fault-compensation-programme-explained> accessed 14 October 2023.

29

The Role of Outside Experts in Anchoring Sustainable Development and Climate Protection in ECLAC's Work

Vivian Daniele Rocha Gabriel

I. Introduction

International organizations (IOs) have been going through a process of internal modernization in order to attend to new demands, stay relevant, and maintain legitimacy. In this sense, the assertion of Debre and Dijkstra that 'periods of development may alternate with periods of decline'[1] seems to make sense. It means that IOs may go through a deep crisis but recover, may be 'on standby' to be used when a global problem hits, or states might find new purpose in the IOs[2] and (re)activate them.[3] IOs, in particular their secretariats, have engaged in internal modernization by modifying (and, ideally, improving) their material scope of work.[4] To this end, some organizations have interacted with outside actors in order to benefit from external expertise and perspectives. The presence and involvement of external consultants is a relatively new development.

This brief chapter examines the case of the Economic Commission for Latin America and the Caribbean (ECLAC) Secretariat. It showcases how the ECLAC Secretariat took the initiative of involving outside experts to respond to new challenges in relation to sustainable development, which pushed ECLAC's existing mandate beyond its previous scope.

As highlighted in the Introduction to this volume, 'initiatives' are understood as action of IO secretariats and/or their heads, which aims to meet a need of the IO, its membership, its secretariat, or other internal or external stakeholders, is novel, or previously unfamiliar to the IO in question, and pushes the boundaries of the IO beyond its founding or prior operational activities, thus resulting in IO

[1] Maria Debre and Hylke Dijkstra, 'Are International Organisations in Decline? An Absolute and Relative Perspective on Institutional Change' (2022) Global Policy 1, 21.

[2] In this case, the authors speak of 'zombie IOs'.

[3] Debre and Dijkstra (n 1) 21.

[4] Barbara Koremenos, Charles Lipson, and Duncan Snidal, 'The Rational Design of International Institutions' (2001) 55 International Organization 4, 761–99.

Vivian Daniele Rocha Gabriel, *The Role of Outside Experts in Anchoring Sustainable Development and Climate Protection in ECLAC's Work* In: *International Organization Initiatives*. Edited by: Gabrielle Marceau and Henner Gött, Oxford University Press. © Oxford University Press 2025. DOI: 10.1093/9780197803325.003.0030

change. Initiatives are important because they aim at meeting the needs of the IO or its membership, with actions that are novel or previously unfamiliar to the IO in question.[5]

II. Economic Commission for Latin America and the Caribbean

The United Nations (UN) Economic and Social Council (ECOSOC) is one of the six principal organs of the UN, with the mandate to foster cooperation on economic, social, cultural, educational, and health issues.[6] Its work, inter alia, encompasses coordinating actions for its subsidiary bodies, reviewing policies, and fostering dialogue, as well as providing recommendations, on economic, social, and environmental issues. It has institutionalized ties with specialized agencies and has also formed five regional commissions, one of which is the ECLAC,[7] established by ECOSOC Resolution 106 (VI) of 25 February 1948. ECLAC is not an IO, but a subsidiary organ of ECOSOC with a secretariat led by an Executive Secretary.[8] As ECOSOC's nodal body for Latin America and the Caribbean, ECLAC's primary focus is the socio-economic development of the region. To this end, ECLAC operates as a facilitator and coordinator of actions that reinforce the region's economic relations internally, and with other global partners.[9]

ECLAC's work is two-pronged. On the one hand, it carries out 'thorough and rigorous' research on issues of 'economic, environmental and social development' in the region.[10] On the other hand, ECLAC is not just a research institution but also partners with governments to provide 'technical cooperation and assistance' on cross-cutting concerns.[11] Moreover, ECLAC may make

[5] Nicola Bonucci and others, 'IGO's Initiatives as a Response to Crises and Unforeseen Needs' (2022) 20 International Organizations Law Review 1, 427.

[6] UN, 'ECOSOC at a Glance' <https://ecosoc.un.org/en/about-us> accessed 2 May 2024.

[7] Margarita Fajardo, 'CEPAL, the "International Monetary Fund of the Left"? The Tale of Two Global Institutions' (2023) 128 The American Historical Review 588.

[8] ECLAC's staff forms part of the UN Secretariat and is appointed by the UN Secretary-General: ECOSOC 'Report of the ad hoc Committee on the Proposal for an Economic Commission for Latin America' Res 106 (VI) (25 February 1948) para 14. The Executive Secretary acts in the name of the UN Secretary-General: ECLAC Rules of Procedure of the Commission as adopted by the Commission at its first session and amended at its second, third, fourth, fifth, eighth, and thirteenth sessions, and by the Committee of the Whole at its session in February 1952, Rule 25 UN Doc LC/G.1403/REV.8 (2014).

[9] The 33 countries of Latin America and the Caribbean are member states of ECLAC, together with other nations that have historical, economic, and cultural ties with the region. In total, there are 46 member states and 14 non-independent territories in the Caribbean that are associate members of the Commission. For more details, see ECLAC, 'About' <https://www.cepal.org/en/about#:~:text=The%20Economic%20Commission%20for%20Latin,to%20function%20that%20same%20year> accessed 31 August 2024.

[10] ECLAC, 'History of ECLAC' <https://www.cepal.org/en/about/history-eclac> accessed 31 August 2024.

[11] ibid.

recommendations on any matters within its competence to ECLAC members, associate members, and UN specialized agencies.[12]

III. ECLAC: Sustainable Development and the Role of External Consultants

The original work targets for ECLAC enshrined in Resolution 106 (VI) are markedly different from the contemporary challenges and priorities of the institution. Notably, the respective paragraphs of ECLAC's Terms of Reference only envisage development in the narrower sense of economic and technological development.[13] Throughout the years, however, there has been a gradual and complex transformation resulting in sustainable development taking central priority in the Commission's work. For instance, as recently as October 2022, Executive Secretary José Manuel Salazar-Xirinachs proposed some work targets to ECLAC, highlighting 'promoting sustainability and climate change mitigation' as a priority. This is one of the most prominent examples of a manifestation of the expansion of the material scope of ECLAC through initiatives. This shift towards sustainable development by ECLAC meets the assertion proposed early on in this volume that IOs have been adapting their practices to respond to contemporary challenges (from the most different types of crises, new topics, or urgencies common to the whole society), 'to fill the gaps or silences of their constituent instruments'[14], in this case, regarding sustainable development and mitigating climate change.

But how did the ECLAC Secretariat integrate this topic within its scope? One of the most important initiatives of the ECLAC Secretariat involves the expertise of external consultants, for example, in the integration of sustainable development as one of its new foundations.

[12] ECOSOC 'Report of the ad hoc Committee on the Proposal for an Economic Commission for Latin America' Res 106 (VI) (25 February 1948) para 5.

[13] Ibid, paras 1(a)–(c) envisage that ECLAC would:

> (i) initiate and participate in measures for facilitating concerted action that deal with urgent economic problems arising out of the war, for raising the level of economic activity in Latin America, and for maintaining the strengthening in the economic relations of the Latin-American countries both among themselves and with other countries in the world; (ii) make or sponsor such investigations and studies of economic and technological problems and developments within territories of Latin America as the Commission deems appropriate; and (iii) undertake or sponsor the collection, evaluation, and dissemination of such economic, technological, and statistical information as the Commission deems appropriate.

[14] Bonucci and others (n 5).

UN's 'Regulatory Framework Policy Portal', which provides resources on the administrative regulation of the United Nations Secretariat,[15] defines consultants as 'recognized authorities or specialists in a specific field, engaged by the United Nations under a temporary contract in an advisory or consultative capacity to the Secretariat'.[16] Their assignments typically involve functions close to those of the staff members, and the ECLAC provides a suggestive list of activities typically carried out by such consultants, which include conducting seminars and training courses, preparing technical resources for use in ECLAC meetings, reporting on issues and problems within their brief, and so on.[17] The wider participation of external specialists, who are sometimes more connected to perspectives from the private sector, non-governmental organizations (NGOs), or academia, can bring fresh air, quick responses, and a more practical view to the issues at stake. Moreover, external consultants may raise the overall level of reports and support studies, turning them into one of the main assets of the IO.

In general, the operationalization of the work of experts is done by the ECLAC Secretariat in two ways: (i) contracting individual external experts directly or (ii) engaging external consultants in partnership with state entities. Individual experts may be contracted through direct tenders available on the ECLAC website. A consultant must have special skills or knowledge that the Commission's permanent staff normally does not have and for which there is no permanent need in the Secretariat.

In the context of ECLAC's work, the involvement of external consultants has been important, because it has enabled some capillarity in dealing with specific topics within the general framework of sustainable development and climate change, as some of the instances discussed below indicate.

It is worth noting that ECLAC's 'constituent instrument', the Terms of Reference laid down in ECOSOC Resolution 106 (VI), does not explicitly confer on the Secretariat the power to contract external consultants. Article 1(c) of the Terms of Reference merely provides that ECLAC shall '[u]ndertake or sponsor the collection, evaluation and dissemination of such economic, technological and statistical information as the Commission deems appropriate'. Similarly, para 7(b) of the Terms of Reference and Rules 50 and 51 of the Commission's Rules of Procedure only envisage consultations with NGOs that have been granted observer status by ECOSOC, including the commissioning of specific studies or papers (Rule 51(b)).

[15] UN, 'United Nations Regulatory Framework Policy Portal' <https://policy.un.org/> accessed 2 May 2024.

[16] UN, 'Consultants' <https://docs.un.org/en/ST/AI/2013/4/Rev.1> accessed 13 February 2025. See also UN, 'Employment' <https://www.cepal.org/en/about/employment#consultoria> accessed 2 May 2024.

[17] ibid.

IV. Examples Involving External Consultancies on Sustainable Development and Climate Change

The ECLAC Secretariat has involved external consultants on several occasions. In 2020, the ECLAC Secretariat published the study 'The Outlook for Oceans, Seas and Marine Resources in Latin America and the Caribbean: Conservation, Sustainable Development and Climate Change Mitigation', edited by M Tambutti and JJ Gómez. It aimed to present a regional outlook on UN Sustainable Development Goal 14 (to conserve and to use oceans, seas, and marine resources sustainably) and to identify the main developments, advances, and changes in legal and institutional frameworks, including gaps and barriers. The report provides several recommendations on how governments can re-orient economic activities that are dependent on oceans and marine resources, such that they become progressively more sustainable, and support local communities and indigenous peoples of the region.[18] It recognizes the potential in the region for sustainably repurposing coastal resources, and how 'coastal dwellers and populations' can be integrated into the institutional development of, and governance systems for, the effective management of coastal resources. The report also sets out the research on the basis of which ECLAC aims to continue assisting its member countries in implementing the recommendations.[19]

Given the urgency of global warming, the rising ocean levels, as well as the impact on the population of coastal regions in Latin America and the Caribbean, it is possible to characterize the specific participation of external consultants in producing this report as an initiative because they responded to the need of analysing how to protect and restore ecosystems to achieve healthy and productive oceans of multilateral IOs and individual governments. Despite the authors being ECLAC Secretariat staff, the document is a non-Secretariat paper since it is highlighted that the report does not necessarily reflect the views of the Commission, revealing their participation as autonomous or external researchers.

Besides private consultants, the ECLAC Secretariat has also involved external consultants from other states or state-owned entities. One example of joint partnership of consultants with state entities is the Strategic Alliance between ECLAC and the Federal Ministry for Economic Cooperation and Development (BMZ) of Germany (named Cooperation Programme ECLAC-BMZ/GIZ),

[18] Marcia Tambutti and Jose Gómez (eds), 'The Outlook for Oceans, Seas and Marine Resources in Latin America and the Caribbean: Conservation, Sustainable Development and Climate Change Mitigation' (2011 ECLAC, Project Documents LC/TS.2020/167) 8, 9 <https://repositorio.cepal.org/server/api/core/bitstreams/f7194ce4-f318-47d0-a4a1-b3a1b47673c5/content> accessed 2 May 2024.

[19] ibid.

which has been operational since the 1980s. It aims to contribute to sustainable development and provide a bridge between the regions, mobilizing the knowledge of experts from the most diverse topics. As mentioned above, this kind of project collaborates to deepen knowledge on specific and urgent issues of sustainable development that cannot be covered (or cannot be covered sufficiently) by the ECLAC Secretariat, because of the lack of staff or due to the existence of other priority projects.

One of the projects under the banner of ECLAC-BMZ/GIZ, implemented by teams from ECLAC and the Deutsche Gesellschaft für Internationale Zusammenarbeit (GIZ), a corporation owned by the German state, is the project 'Inclusive, Sustainable and Smart Cities in the Framework of the 2030 Agenda for Sustainable Development in Latin America and the Caribbean'.[20] According to GIZ, this project focuses on advising pilot cities in electromobility and economic development; financing the energy transition and local public transport; promoting digitalization and social integration; improving the circular economy in cities; and integrating gender equality and human rights into decisions and processes.[21]

This cooperation is another example of an initiative because it addresses, through a comparatively new focus, on inclusive, sustainable, and smart cities, and the problems resulting from increasing urbanization, such as pollution and carbon emissions, that require an urgent sustainable solution. Through external specialized consultants, the ECLAC Secretariat is addressing a novel problem and proposing ways to mitigate climate change.

Another project carried out by ECLAC in collaboration with GIZ and the German Federal Institute for Geosciences and Natural Resources (BGR) is the 'Regional Cooperation for the Sustainable Management of Mining Resources in the Andean Countries' (named MinSus). The project was created 'to incorporate social, ecological, and economic standards into mining supply chains with a special focus on the beginning of the chain, i.e. mining'.[22] The MinSus project takes several approaches (such as multi-stakeholder development of good practices, scaling up of successfully piloted new standards, etc) to achieve its goals, and these approaches are adapted to the needs at varying levels of governance and administration.[23] In October 2023, the seminar 'The Future of the Lithium Industry in Chile', attended by representatives of the Government of Chile and Argentina and civil society, in Santiago, Chile, presented advances in the

[20] To see all the projects headed by this cooperation, see ECLAC, 'Cooperation Programme ECLAC-BMZ/GIZ' <https://www.cepal.org/en/cooperation-programme-eclac-bmzgiz/about> accessed 31 August 2024.

[21] GIZ, 'Creating Inclusive and Sustainable Cities' <https://www.giz.de/en/worldwide/92685.html> accessed 2 May 2024.

[22] ECLAC, 'MinSus' <https://www.cepal.org/en/projects/minsus> accessed 2 May 2024.

[23] ibid.

project. The need to improve the societal standing of mining companies in Latin American countries was emphasized, which was identified as one of the highest risks, especially given the low confidence that populations have in the sector.[24]

First, this initiative of the ECLAC Secretariat was the first to deal with problems of mining disasters and questions of sustainable mining. Second, even though the project is specific to Andean countries, the results may have influence on other countries, such as Brazil, which has a major mining sector and experienced serious mining disasters in the past years, such as the rupture of the dams of Mariana and Brumadinho. The ECLAC initiative fosters cooperation towards more responsible business conduct in the entire Latin America and the Caribbean, a real need considering these countries are still major exporters of commodities, particularly mineral resources.

V. Conclusion

In conclusion, it is not always necessary—and, as in the case of ECLAC, not even possible[25]—for organizations to formally amend their constituent instrument. Nor is it necessary to change their bureaucracy in order to adapt to new needs. The ECLAC Secretariat has expanded the scope of its work by integrating components of sustainable development into its fundamental objectives and by counting on the expertise of their external consultants.

It is important to highlight that the collaboration of the Secretariat with external consultants has enhanced the capacity and sophistication of ECLAC's work. Even though using outside experts is not a new tool, it was an innovative way of implementing ECLAC's mandate: it allowed ECLAC to focus on specific issues of the membership and it made use of the most prepared experts to find solutions for the countries of Latin America and the Caribbean. The inputs by these external consultants, covering topics such as the protection of the oceans, the coastal population and economy, urbanization, electric vehicles, and responsible mining, all contributed to successfully integrating sustainable development and climate change into ECLAC's remit as central priorities. The initiative to collaborate with external consultants and the push towards the focus on sustainability as a result of their work serves as an example of the role of initiatives in pushing the mandates of an IO's work.

[24] MinSus, 'El futuro de la industria del litio en Chile' <https://minsus.net/el-futuro-de-la-industria-del-litio-en-chile/> accessed 2 May 2024.

[25] ECOSOC (n 12) para 16, vesting the power to review the resolution in the ECOSOC.

30
Concluding Remarks
Silence

Michael Barnett

I. Introduction

These chapters on the relationship between international organizations (IOs) and their environment provide a grand overview of the many factors that shape IO initiatives and adaptations. Their observations are largely consistent with standard theories of IOs; indeed, the authors often refer to them to guide their observations. Standard theories of IOs are imprinted heavily by rationalism and functionalism. Rationalism, in brief, presumes that actors attempt to maximize their interests under constraints and will choose actions and strategies that will most likely further their interests.[1] Functionalism tends to reduce actors and their actions to their function for maintaining the order or system.[2] In short, a functional theory of IOs explores how their functions, such as information collection, monitoring, and enforcement, advance an IO's mandate and promote cooperation and collaboration between states.

The rationalist and functionalist traditions have been challenged by constructivist and critical theories.[3] Space prevents me from unpacking these theories, but they made inroads into theories of IOs because they identified and explored several blind spots.[4] One, standard IO theories assume a set of fixed interests, often the collective interests of their members or their mandate. Although the

[1] Charles Roger, Duncan Snidal, and Felicity Vabulas, 'The Importance of Rational Institutionalism in the Analysis of Informal International Institutions' [2023] International Politics 1; Duncan Snidal, 'Rationalist Approaches to International Institutions' in Michael Barnett and Duncan Snidal (eds), *Oxford Handbook of International Institutions* (forthcoming OUP 2025).

[2] The classic text is Robert Keohane, *After Hegemony* (Princeton UP 1984). See also Lisa L Martin and Beth A Simmons, 'International Organizations and Institutions' (2013) 2 Handbook of International Relations 326.

[3] My writings tend to follow these alternatives.

[4] Michael Barnett and Martha Finnemore, *Rules for the World: International Organizations in World Politics* (Cornell UP 2004); Leonie Holthaus, 'Practice Theory and the Opening Up of International Organizations' (2021) 1 Global Studies Quarterly 1, 3; Ole Jacob Sending, 'Sociological Approaches to International Institutions' in Michael Barnett and Duncan Snidal (eds), *Oxford Handbook of International Institutions* (forthcoming OUP 2025).

Michael Barnett, *Concluding Remarks* In: *International Organization Initiatives.* Edited by: Gabrielle Marceau and Henner Gött, Oxford University Press. © Oxford University Press 2025. DOI: 10.1093/9780197803325.003.0031

chapters do not specify what IO interests are, my sense is that they follow the standard interpretation.

Constructivists turned interests from an assumption into an empirical inquiry. What other interests might IOs have and where do they come from? What about organizational survival and security? Or the dominant forms of knowledge and ideologies? The chapters by Cissé (Chapter 24) and Liu and Kwak (Chapter 25) point to the 'mandate' as a source of interests, but they can be fairly nebulous, and it is up to the IO to interpret and define what they mean in practice.

Two, standard theories, with the exception of principal-agent approaches, tend to overlook the possibility of IO autonomy, thus reducing their action to the demands by states or the functions they play. Constructivist approaches, on the other hand, theorize various sources of autonomy, including expert and rational-legal authorities. They also refer to organizational culture, recognizing that IOs are more than a bundle of technical rules but rather contain their own ways of making sense of the environment, through routines, scripts, habits, and siloed units, and acting on it. I doubt I have to convince the authors of the importance of these internal features for understanding the initiatives and adaptations of IOs.

Three, standard IO scholarship tends to neglect effectiveness. To some extent, this has less to do with the limits of the theories and more to do with the difficulty of measuring it. But the consequence is that these standard approaches limit themselves to IO design and adaptation, and bracket whether they perform at a high level. But don't we want to know how these initiatives and adaptations turn out?

It is as if the play stopped at Acts I or II and had no Act III. Constructivists have no advantage when it comes to measuring effectiveness, but they do consider effects. There are intended and unintended effects. There is success and failure. There are functional and dysfunctional outcomes.

I organize my commentary around these silences on interests, the internal politics and cultures that shape IO behaviour, and effects. My intent is not to upbraid the chapters or become a missionary for constructivist theories. It is to point out that these things need to be talked about and practitioners are best positioned to do so. These are areas in which they have a clear comparative advantage over scholars because it requires capturing the organizational nuances and idiosyncratic patterns that affect how IOs see and act on the world. Indeed, there are moments when the chapters break the silences. Below, I address these silences and several other issues through the themes of the external environment as a source of interests and initiatives, the politics of adaptation, and the range of results and effects that should get more attention than they do.

II. Environments

The environment—which in my view should include the IO's member states[5]—is the catalyst for initiatives and adaptations. Not always, though. There are countless instances in which IOs initiate action and acquire new tasks because of internal dynamics. For instance, to fulfil their often ambiguous mandates, they must incorporate new variables into their models that force them to expand the scope of their activities.[6] IOs also learn from past experiences.[7] But IOs, just like all organizations, often require a kick in the pants to change their routines, and this kick usually comes from external stimuli, including actors and new problems that must be solved.

The chapters have much to say about the external environment. An interesting point made by several chapters is that they struggle to work within the binary of the IO (inside) and the environment (outside). The difficulty might owe to an environment that is more densely populated, and there are more kinds of partnerships and alliances between IOs and other actors, than ever before; or, relatedly, because IOs are best characterized as simultaneously closed and open systems. I want to flag several points on the environment.

One, there is unanimity across the chapters that IOs now exist in a more densely populated environment, including stakeholders. It might be not that there are more stakeholders but that IOs have moved from a principal-agent to an all-stakeholders view. In other words, IOs are increasingly responsible not just to their principals but also to those who are effected by their actions, as suggested by Solomon and Piercy (Chapter 26). Yet they introduce a subcategory of 'relevant stakeholders', suggesting that while all stakeholders are equal some are more equal than others. Who are they? Are these the affected? The fascinating piece by Diller on the International Labour Organization and the Rana Plaza Arrangement (Chapter 23) implicitly notes that those who were most

[5] I need to flag a critical point of difference between how the volume defines IOs and how the IO literature does, and I follow the latter. In defining the 'outside world', Part IV of this volume treats states as part of IOs. In other words, they are not treated as independent actors. Most standard theories of IOs, however, limit the IO to its secretariat and treat states as part of the environment. This matters for lots of theoretical and empirical reasons. For instance, principal–agent and delegation models of IOs are only possible if we treat states and IOs as separate. Also, international relations scholars often want to know the conditions under which IOs (secretariats) are able to act with agency and even at odds with powerful states, but I am not sure if this question is relevant if states are defined as part of IOs. It would be worth a lengthier conversation between scholars and practitioners about why each operates with a completely different way of conceptualizing IOs.

[6] Barnett and Finnemore (n 4).

[7] Ernst Haas, *When Knowledge Is Power: Three Models of Change in International Organizations* (University of California Press 1990); James March, 'Exploration and Exploitation in Organizational Learning' (1991) 2 Organization Science 1, 71–87.

harmed had relatively little opportunity to register their views.[8] Indeed, the non-governmental organizations that claimed to represent them have been accused of putting their interests before those of the victims.[9] It is not only that there are some actors who assert their right to speak for others; it is also that the voices of the marginalized and vulnerable are silenced or tokenized.[10]

Relatedly, the environment can be a source of IO interests and goals. One last point. As the chapters punctuate, IOs live in a complex world with many different actors that want a piece of them and rivals that want a piece of their action. There often are many different constituencies that must be placated, and sometimes, this can mean adapting in directions that make them uncomfortable or push them to incorporate potentially competing goals. Cissé's chapter on the World Bank illustrates this nicely (Chapter 24). There are lots of different actors, from states to civil society organizations, who expect the Bank to be responsive to their preferences. Sometimes, the IO is able to stand its ground, such as the Bank's ability to rebuff the demand that it more fully integrates human rights into its programmes. But at other times it might attempt to accommodate the many, and at times contradictory, actors' preferences, such as pushing for growth and sustainable development, that introduce organizational 'hypocrisy'.[11] This is not the hypocrisy where an actor intentionally says one thing and does another to bamboozle its audience. Instead, it is a by-product of a world in which IOs must incorporate different kinds of demands from different audiences that want different things, making policy coherence nearly impossible.

The second point comes from Gött's thought-provoking chapter and framework (Chapter 22). First, he argues for a switch in the unit of analysis from initiatives to interactions, a highly valuable observation. In other words, actions are not static reactions to environmental pressures but rather are a product of dynamic interactions between IOs and other actors. Gött further identifies how to best typify these interactions. On the cooperative side, interactions can derive from two or more actors agreeing on what to accomplish and how. On the competitive and conflictful side, interactions can derive from a fight over turf, status and resources, or policy preferences. Importantly, he notes that these

[8] Rebecca Prentice, 'Just Compensation? The Price of Death and Injury After the Rana Plaza Garment Factory Collapse' in Peter Luetchford and Giovanni Orlando (eds), *Research in Economic Anthropology Vol. 39* (Emerald Publishing 2019) 157–78.

[9] Rashedur Chowdhury, 'The Rana Plaza Disaster and the Complicit Behavior of Elite NGOs' (2017) 24(6) Organization 938–49.

[10] Parenthetically, the chapters refer to the collective noun of stakeholders and never names. Are expert communities referring to the McKinseys of the world or expert and professional communities? Why is the Gates Foundation not mentioned in the chapters on the World Health Organization and Gavi (Chapters 26 and 28)? Is this anonymization a case of self-censoring?

[11] Catherine Weaver, *The Hypocrisy Trap: The World Bank and the Poverty of Reform* (Princeton UP 2008).

interactions have become increasingly dense and include more kinds of actors than ever before.

The third point, which also derives from Gött's chapter (Chapter 22), regards the fascinating claim that the external environment is 'elusive'. Gött does not elaborate on what precisely, but my interpretation is that it refers to a worldview in which policymakers see the external environment as almost random and unpredictable. Is this another way of saying it is perceived as high risk and even filled with uncertainty? If so, it runs counter to the tendency of IO scholars to assume a relatively stable and known environment. For instance, the international distribution of state power is fairly stable, and Great, Middle, and Lesser powers stay in their pecking order for lengthy periods. IOs live in a world in which their funding base is largely constant from one year to the next (though there are clear periods in which it is not). The normative and legal constraints also are quite predictable, though Gött sees it otherwise. Chapter 22 advocates for greater legalization because it will enhance predictability.

Fourth, legitimacy is another element of the environment because it is conferred by actors. IOs seek legitimacy that shapes IO interests and initiatives, as highlighted by Rocha Gabriel (Chapter 29) and Liu and Kwak (Chapter 25). Legitimacy has three primary elements. A process that conforms to the societally appropriate ways of making decisions; the contemporary gold standard is a democratic, diverse, and inclusive procedure. Few IOs come close to this standard; indeed, they are often criticized for being illiberal and exclusionary. Another element is whether the actor is viewed as attempting to advance the community's values and interests. Third, IO effectiveness. Organizations that routinely fail will lose legitimacy.

Why care about legitimacy? The classic sociological answer is that the more that actors are conferred legitimacy by critical audiences, the more likely these audiences will comply with their commands. The more primal reason is survival. The first rule of organizational theory is that organizations want to survive, survival is based on resources, and their resource base is provided by actors that give on the basis of their perceived legitimacy. I once asked a high-ranking official at United Nations High Commissioner for Refugees (UNHCR) how he knew it had been a good year. His first and only answer was its financial stability. Relatedly, IO legitimacy is connected to relevance, as discussed in Liu and Kiwak's chapter on the International Monetary Fund (IMF) (Chapter 25). Additional evidence of the priority of organizational survival can be found in the risk models utilized by IOs. Although their models do include risks to their programmes, the emphasis tends to be on risks and threats to the organization's health and well-being. Risk profiles are an MRI of what IOs see as threats.

III. Adaptation

The chapters of Part IV focus on IO initiatives that largely occur in the context of adaptation. Adaptation refers to the fit between the organization and the environment. Specifically, it can be defined as the 'intentional decision-making undertaken by organizational members, leading to observable actions that aim to reduce the distance between an organization and its economic and institutional environments'.[12] This takes us to the choice of initiatives and adaptations. Although IOs often have little choice and will often comply with external demands, there is some autonomy, thus pointing to internal factors such as organizational and bureaucratic processes and the forms of knowledge that are seen as most legitimate and expert. It matters that the IMF and World Bank are populated by highly trained economists and not by anthropologists. Does it not matter that the Gates Foundation and the international financial institutions encourage market-friendly approaches?

Rationalist and functionalist approaches implicitly presume that the selected response is the most efficient. Like the chapters, they omit how the sausage gets made. But there will be an intense process of contestation and arm-twisting laden with power. In other words, not all actors inside and outside the organization matter equally. Sometimes, rival positions will be shaped by a genuine disagreement about which initiative will most likely solve the problem in the most efficient way possible. However, often, their interests imprint their position.

The chapters on United Nations Economic Commission for Latin America and the Caribbean and the International Labour Organization identify the important role of expert and professional transnational communities in the selection process. This variable interests IO scholars, but they have a difficult time assessing its importance without informants. Who are these outside experts and how are they chosen? This is another moment when I wish the authors had abandoned the collective noun for individual names. Who were these outsiders that helped to decide the right model for compensating the survivors of and families of those killed in the Bangladesh factory disaster? Are they insiders/outsiders in the sense that they have temporary staffing in the IO and bring their connections with them? Are these insiders/outsiders part of professional networks? What about the shadowy world of consultancies? The McKinseys of the world are reported to have had an enormous impact on the internal worldviews of IOs. And how are outside experts chosen? Because they are best able to provide objective, impartial knowledge? Or because they will support one faction in an IO debate?

[12] Andew Sarta, Rodolphe Durand, and Jean-Philippe Vergne, 'Organizational Adaptation' 47 Journal of Management 1, 43–75.

IV. Effectiveness and Effects

The standard IO literature is rather thin on effects and effectiveness and the chapters follow suit. There are two stylized ways to think about effectiveness and effects. There are functional outcomes when they adapt in the right ways and deliver more efficient and effective outcomes. Dysfunctional outcomes are those that fail or perhaps make things worse.

There are three primary reasons for dysfunctionality. The first is that organizations are 'designed to fail'. The blueprints for IOs are often not the result of careful cost–benefit calculations and efficiency considerations but rather of vested interests by the most powerful and mobilized. The consequence is that organizational design and adaptation might succeed at protecting the interests of the powerful at the cost of the mandate. The second kind of dysfunction arises from politics. There is often a huge gap between the adaptations that are required to improve efficiency and effectiveness and adaptions that arise from vested interests and politically charged processes. The third kind of dysfunction is what Barnett and Finnemore call a pathology that can be traced to organizational culture.[13] For instance, in a world where most IOs now routinely go through risk exercises, and risk is often defined in terms of risks to the organization, IOs will be more cautious and risk-averse, potentially undermining their effectiveness as measured by the mandate.

There exists the possibility that IO initiatives and adaptations will 'fit' an environment that favours the rich and powerful and not the needs of recipients. The chapter on COVID-19 Vaccines Global Access (COVAX) speaks to the silence on power and outcomes (Chapter 28). In the early days of COVID-19, a couple of veterans from the global vaccine community began to worry about the sort of allocation principles that would guide the distribution of vaccines. If left to power and market considerations, the likelihood was that powerful and resource-rich states would jump to the head of the queue, gobble up the available vaccines, and leave the most vulnerable and marginalized far behind. Triage would occur on the basis of power instead of need. There were two possible ways to mitigate this outcome. One was challenging the World Trade Organization's position on intellectual property rights that gave pharmaceutical companies near-monopoly power over any new vaccine. In other words, the broader international community would need to inject moral considerations into markets. But this option would have unleashed a storm of opposition from Big Pharma and the Gates Foundation, a major player in Gavi and with a strong stake in AstraZeneca. The other way was to work within the market parameters, which COVAX did. COVAX proposed to create a triage system that incorporated fairness principles

[13] Barnett and Finnemore (n 4).

and made the allocation more equitable. But COVAX was doomed to fail because it could not force the biggest states to care more about doses for communities on the far side of the world.

A final point regarding effects and effectiveness concerns accountability. IOs make mistakes of omission and commission, but there are very few ways to hold them accountable for such mistakes. They can harm countless people through their actions and policies and yet escape any costs or consequences. Conversely, those who are most affected often have little ability to hold IOs accountable. As Gött importantly notes, 'IOs enjoy privileges and immunities' that shield them from those who are harmed by their policies. The absence of accountability is a chronic and dismal feature of IO governance.

Academics, policymakers, and practitioners can learn a lot from each other. Academics have built their models based on theory and empirical research that benefit from the experiences and accounts of practitioners. The chapters provide various insights to behold. However, practitioners might learn, as well, from scholarship that explores the silences of mainstream models. All of us in our ivory towers can learn much from each other.

Conclusion: Adaptation, Change, and International Organizations

An Inside–Outside Perspective

Laurence Boisson de Chazournes, Gabrielle Marceau, Henner Gött, Akshaya Venkataraman, and Ana Balcazar-Moreno

I. Introduction

This book has addressed an important gap in the study of international organizations (IOs) and their evolution by pulling back the curtains on the processes behind key initiatives of these institutions. With a wide array of contributors who have experience working with and within IOs, this book is a collection of practitioners' accounts about IO initiatives, the needs underlying these initiatives, and the actors who actualized these needs into action. At the same time, by contextualizing these accounts within the conceptual and analytical frameworks outlined by the academic contributors in this volume, the book offers the opportunity to draw some common lessons and observations on initiatives that lead to adaptation and change in IOs and initiatives that respond to new challenges and needs. In this conclusion, we consider some of these observations and identify important questions raised by the authors in this book.

II. The Relation Between Theory and Practice Regarding IOs' Initiatives

An oft-cited criticism of international law theory pertaining to IOs is its relative lack of use in the actual practice of international lawyers working within these IOs.[1] The rich contributions in Part I of this volume offer two distinct vantage

[1] In the varied contributions in this volume describing the decision-making process that led to the initiatives of these organizations, international law theory appears to have a relatively limited a priori role in the decision-making. See also Christiane Ahlborn 'From Functionalism to Constitutionalism: Translating Theories on IO Powers into Practice', Chapter 3 in this volume.

Laurence Boisson de Chazournes, Gabrielle Marceau, Henner Gött, Akshaya Venkataraman, and Ana Balcazar-Moreno, *Conclusion: Adaptation, Change, and International Organizations* In: *International Organization Initiatives*.
Edited by: Gabrielle Marceau and Henner Gött, Oxford University Press. © Oxford University Press 2025.
DOI: 10.1093/9780197803325.003.0032

points from which theory, despite its relative lack of invocation in everyday IO practice, aids the genesis and implementation of initiatives well.

First, theories offer a legal lexicon to elucidate and explain the operations of an international bureaucracy. Theories present a variety of explanations for what drives initiatives and change, bringing coherence to decision-making in a bid to offer precedent for future decisions.[2] The theoretical frameworks highlighted in this book, for instance, invite the reader to understand the motivations for change by contemplating possible definitions for 'change' in an IO[3]. Similarly, for instance, the metaphor of a 'living constitution' provokes further discussion on how governance models of IOs must balance adaptability and responsiveness with the need for caution and boundaries—a balance between allowing novel action but not that which is ultra vires.[4]

Concomitantly, theories also offer ways to frame and legitimize initiatives taken in times of crises and pressing needs. Many of the initiatives highlighted in this volume were taken in the absence of an explicit mandate and presented uncharted territories for the organization. While these initiatives, more often than not, ultimately found acceptance within the membership of the organizations, early sceptics and critics of such actions did raise worries about the potential for such initiatives to be ultra vires, excessive, or illegitimate.[5] The gamut of theories and concepts presented in the 'academic chapters' then underpin the role of tools such as purposive interpretation[6], the dynamic nature of constituent instruments[7], and recalibrated perspectives on doctrines such as functionalism and constitutionalism.[8] These theories highlight the ability of IOs to remain agile in responding to challenges while ensuring the legitimacy of their initiatives.

At the same time, the practice of IO initiatives may require theory to revisit its own postulates. For instance, the pronounced role of secretariats showcased in the book will further corrode the (already-fragile) basis of simplistic principal–agent models underlying some functionalist strands. Similarly, Global Administrative Law often obviates the secretariats' role and the fact that its impact reaches well beyond mere 'administration' and includes proactive,

[2] ibid.

[3] Hannah Birkenkötter, 'Change in International Organizations', Chapter 1 in this volume.

[4] Guy Fiti Sinclair, 'IOs Initiatives, Ideology, and the Imaginaries of Liberal Reform', Chapter 2 in this volume.

[5] Huw Llewellyn discusses how some countries opposed the setting up of the UN Criminal Tribunals under the aegis of the UNSC, see Huw Llewellyn, 'The Establishment of the UN Criminal Tribunals: The Role of the UN Secretariat', Chapter 7 in this volume.

[6] Fernando Lusa Bordin, 'Interpreting Constituent Instruments to Justify the Evolving Powers of International Organizations', Chapter 5 in this volume.

[7] Niels Blokker, 'The Evolution of IO Powers and Activities: A Legal Framework', Chapter 4 in this volume.

[8] Ahlborn (n 1).

sometimes politically motivated or self-empowering, and often path-altering activities.

III. Understanding Adaptation and Change Within IOs Through Initiatives

The case studies in this book offer a view of the myriad of ways in which change occurs in an IO. Without purporting to review the extent and form of 'mandate expansion' of IOs, the chapters in this volume evince how constantly and fluidly IOs adapt and respond to novel challenges and needs. These case studies portray IOs as a mirror to the ever-changing socio-political world they occupy.

The practitioners' case studies in this book provide some answers (or, more modestly, some possibilities) to two principal questions—what does change in IOs look like in the face of unprecedented needs and crises, and what factors and actors influence this multifaceted process of change.

A. How do IOs adapt?

The case studies in this book tell us that IOs venture into new areas of work, previously unforeseen in the original or previous configuration of their governance model, when crisis prompts or needs so demand. What these new areas of work are depends on different factors. Pressure from activist groups and civil society was key in building the momentum that saw the World Bank take an active role in environmental issues.[9] Personal convictions and prior experience of the Directors-General of the World Trade Organization (WTO) played an important role in pushing the organization to work on COVID-19.[10] But *change* does not only include venturing into an unfamiliar area of work, it can also involve reframing, reinventing, and reconfiguring the IO's activities to address pressing contemporary challenges. For instance, the International Energy Agency (IEA), created with a view to secure oil supplies on equitable terms, now champions clean energy and calls for eliminating reliance on fossil fuels.[11] The United Nations Educational, Scientific and Cultural Organization (UNESCO)

[9] Hassane Cissé, 'How Do External Factors Shape Institutional, Legal, Strategic, or Policy Change in International Organizations: Review of Selected Examples in World Bank Practice', Chapter 24 in this volume.

[10] Akshaya Venkataraman, 'Taking Initiatives in the WTO: The Role of an Executive Head in Steering Change', Chapter 18 in this volume.

[11] André-Philippe Ouellet, 'The International Energy Agency at 50: The Astounding Environmental Shift from an Organization Focused on Fossil Energy Supply to a Clean Energy Authority', Chapter 19 in this volume.

leveraged its experience on ethics to deliver an impactful global standard based on promoting human rights, transparency, and human oversight for artificial intelligence (AI) systems.[12] Some of the initiatives mentioned in this book also illustrate how initiatives shaped the entire trajectory of these organizations. We see how initiatives by its head of secretariat formalized the organizational structure and work mandate of the Financial Action Task Force (FATF),[13] and we learn how initiatives propelled the central mandates of specialized institutions like Gavi, the Vaccine Alliance (Gavi),[14] and the Global Fund to Fight AIDS, Tuberculosis and Malaria (Global Fund).[15]

Importantly, this volume also showcases that change can be witnessed in IOs in not just the outcomes but also in the *processes* by which they operate. Initiatives have led to IOs participating in novel and unprecedented activities—such as the African Union Commission (AUC) making submissions in the International Court of Justice's advisory opinion proceedings. Initiatives have also led these organizations to create new procedural mechanisms to address challenges. We learn how both the International Labour Organization (ILO) and the World Health Organization (WHO) have created stakeholder consultation mechanisms to address unique crises faced by both organizations. The United Nations (UN) Office of Legal Affairs (OLA) drove the expeditious establishment of entirely new institutional structures in the form of criminal tribunals. Organizations like the International Monetary Fund (IMF), the WHO, and the Organisation for Economic Co-operation and Development (OECD) have, over the years, created new tools and responsive mechanisms to address the need for policy reform.

However, the results of these initiatives—the new areas of work and the new processes—offer us little insight into the cohesiveness of models and mechanisms by which such initiatives are introduced and implemented. The case studies presented in these chapters, on the contrary, suggest that initiatives of the secretariat tend to be ad hoc—with actions taken (very often sui generis) at the behest of the individuals in the secretariat spearheading such initiatives, the resources available at their disposal, and the urgency of the needs being addressed. The one common thread linking the chapters in this book on how IOs adapt and change vis-a-vis crises and new needs is, then, the fact that international bureaucracy is at the heart of such change.

[12] Gabriela Ramos, 'UNESCO's Recommendation on the Ethics of Artificial Intelligence (2021): A Case Study in Intergovernmental Leadership and Consensus Building', Chapter 16 in this volume.

[13] David Lewis, 'The Financial Action Task Force: Coming of Age: Becoming an International Organization', Chapter 15 in this volume.

[14] Jelena Madir, 'IOs Initiatives: Gavi, The Vaccine Alliance', Chapter 28 in this volume.

[15] Fady Zeidan and Jean Abboud, 'The Global Fund to Fight AIDS, Tuberculosis and Malaria: Partnerships, Collaborations, and Initiatives with International Organizations', Chapter 27 in this volume.

The chapters in this book suggest that while there may be some common patterns and mechanisms of adaption and change, their specific manifestations and impacts are often contingent upon, inter alia, the unique characteristics of each organization and its environment.

B. Who initiates change and why do IOs adapt?

Change in IOs can follow external or internal pressures; often such pressures or roots of changes are both internal and external. This book paints a complex picture of the drivers of change in an IO. From the outset, this book takes interest principally in initiatives, that is, actions of IO secretariats and/or their heads.[16] Nevertheless, the case studies showcase that factors which drive these initiatives are often a combination of internal and external forces, defying easy categorization. While the secretariats and their heads may have been the ultimate decision makers who created and implemented the initiatives,[17] the impetus is often also provided by external actors and stakeholders[18] or the demands of membership.[19] The opening conceptual chapters of Parts II–IV provide valuable perspectives on understanding the role played by the key actors who have the potential for driving change.

On the one hand, secretariats, portrayed as 'knowledge actors' in Part II of this volume, play a determinative role in shaping the directions in which IOs transform. At the other end of the spectrum, there are external stakeholders, civil society actors, and even other IOs who affect the push–pull of an IO's agenda. One of the important questions that emerges from the case studies analysed in this volume is the extent of influence of each of these actors, and whether any one

[16] Definition of initiatives, outlined in the Preface of this book: The term 'initiative' refers to 'action of IO secretariats and/or their heads, which (1) aims to meet the needs of the IO, its membership, or other stakeholders, (2) is novel, or previously unfamiliar to the IO in question, and (3) pushes the boundaries of the IO beyond its founding operational activities, thus resulting in IO change.'

[17] Part III of this book provides several examples of initiatives where the heads of the organization spearheaded new initiatives. See, for instance, Mona Ali Khalil, 'The Evolution of UN Secretary-General Initiatives to Respond to Violent and Non-Violent Threats to International Peace and Security', Chapter 14 in this volume.

[18] External stakeholders played a key role, for instance, in the ILO's management of the Rana Plaza disaster. On the other hand, a growing environmental conscience globally pushed both the IEA and the World Bank to include climate considerations in their work. See Charles Di Leva, 'The World Bank's Evolution Towards Environmental and Social Responsibilities', Chapter 8 in this volume; Oullet (n 11). Similarly, COVID-19 crisis propelled the WHO to adopt new forms of responses to crises. See Gian Luca Burci and Ana Balcazar-Moreno, 'WHO Reactions to COVID-19: Between Politics and Managerialism', Chapter 9 in this volume.

[19] In the case of AUC's submissions to the advisory opinion on the Chagos Archipelago, the members' goal of a fully decolonized Africa seems to have played an important role in the Commission's decision-making. Namira Negm, 'The African Union Commission's Endeavour with the International Court of Justice for Achieving the Complete Decolonization of Mauritius: The Case of the Chagos Archipelago', Chapter 11 in this volume.

actor has a more determinative impact. The picture that emerges ultimately is that the actions taken to adapt, change, and respond to needs, that is, initiatives as they are conceptualized in this book, are given effect to and implemented by the secretariat with the membership's support. However, the genesis of the initiative can be at the behest of either the secretariat or the so-called outside actors. The extent of influence of either actor is a varying factor, contingent on the individual circumstances of the IO. In the genesis of an initiative, members and constituents of these IOs often have a role to play, just as they always do in legitimizing these initiatives or, as for example in the case of some of Wilfred Jenks' initiatives in the ILO, causing their failure.[20] The hybrid entities discussed in this volume add further nuance to the study of drivers of change in IOs. They raise questions on the interactions between private actors and stakeholders, states, and other IOs when they come together to constitute the membership of an IO (as in the case of Gavi and the Global Fund). It is worth considering how notions of 'external' and 'internal' actors must be reimagined in such organizations.

Conclusions on the actors involved in initiatives and change within IOs are perhaps easier to identify and articulate than the specific motivations and reasons behind why some circumstances, needs, and crises merited the taking of initiatives. Reflections of the various contributors in this volume suggest some possibilities. Personal convictions and priorities of the heads of secretariats are the more evident motivations of some of the initiatives. Some crises had a direct impact on the regular work of IOs like the WHO, ILO, and IMF, potentially prompting new and innovative responses. In some IOs like the IEA, the OECD, the AU, and even the UN, the initiatives of the secretariat were motivated by a need to effectively fulfil pressing goals and needs of the constituent members. It is a question for future research to conceptualize cohesive motivations for such initiatives which apply across IOs.

C. Factors of change: Shared attributes?

While this volume has made significant strides in illuminating the dynamics of change in IOs, it has also raised several important questions that warrant further exploration.

One such question is whether it is possible to generalize a taxonomy of factors for change. The chapters in this book suggest that while there may be some common patterns and mechanisms of change, the specific manifestations and impacts of change are often contingent upon the interplay of a multitude

[20] Francis Maupain, 'Is Too Much Vision a Handicap for an Executive Head? Some Thoughts on W Jenks' Curtailed Mandate as ILO Director-General', Chapter 17 in this volume.

of factors. Arguably, the taxonomies created to divide this volume into different parts—the distinction between secretariats and their heads, as well as internal and external factors—are in and of themselves too coarse-grained and perhaps even artificial. The interactions between the various actors of change inside and outside the IO, the socio-political circumstances surrounding the IO, the novelty of the proposed initiative, resistance or support from the membership or other stakeholders, the expertise and knowledge of the international bureaucracy, and the urgency of the circumstances, all precipitate change, albeit to varying degrees in varying circumstances.

In considering the factors of change in an IO, another question merits further study. What are the factors relevant to the *success* of an IO's initiative? This question is addressed in some capacity in Part III of the book. In examining the role of the heads of secretariats in initiating change, Part III notably offers insights not only into the facets of leadership that contribute to the successful execution of an initiative[21] but also into the political factors that led to the failure of two key initiatives of then ILO Director-General Wilfred Jenks.[22] The concluding commentary succinctly identifies shared attributes in successful initiatives, that is, initiatives that come to be accepted by the IO's membership tacitly or expressly.[23] Ultimately, initiatives appear to require the deliberate confluence of the right set of factors at an appropriate time to meet the respective need as intended.

In addition, whether and to what extent one can conclude that an initiative was successful depends on the relevant benchmark for measuring success. Such a benchmark can emanate (or be deduced) from policy preferences, legal norms, moral convictions, and virtually any other normative reference point. Notwithstanding the fact that in many cases, there might be an overall 'common sense' as to whether a particular initiative succeeded, it must not be forgotten that 'success' is a relative term in need of a benchmark and that conclusions of success may vary depending on which political view, legal interpretation, or moral conviction the observer uses as a benchmark. In deciding whether an initiative was successful, the views and consent of the IO's members will have prominent (if not decisive) weight, although members' positions might again become subject to contestation and disagreement by outside actors, assessing the initiative from different vantage points and invoking different benchmarks.

[21] Naphtali Ukamwa, 'The Role of Heads of Secretariats in Initiating Change: Functional Formalism and Pluralism', Chapter 13 in this volume.

[22] Maupain (n 20).

[23] Jane Aeberhard-Hodges, 'Concluding Commentary: Reflections on IO Leaders' Approaches', Chapter 21 in this volume.

D. Further reflections on the 'need' for IOs to adapt and change

When is there a need for adaption and change to be achieved through initiatives? Many of the initiatives discussed in this book are a clear response to a pressing need created by a *crisis*. Some of these crises are global—the shift away from fossil fuels,[24] pandemic response and preparedness,[25] the global food crisis,[26] and the financial crisis[27]; some are more localized—like the Rana Plaza disaster.[28] But in other instances, the source of the 'need' is less evident. Membership and constituents of the organizations could, on the one hand, have explicitly identified these needs, as in the case of the development of AI standards by UNESCO[29] and the G20's impetus in facilitating the OECD's initiatives on fossil fuel subsidies.[30] In other instances, the need has been articulated within the international bureaucracy—for instance, when the secretariat led an initiative, despite the objections (or silence) of some members, such as the OLA's proactive role in the design of the UN Criminal Tribunals.[31]

What constitutes a 'need for adaption and change' merits further exploration, as does the question of who has the power, capacity, or legitimacy to determine when such a need has arisen.

E. Some remarks on the legality of new initiatives

While this book highlights the novelty and efficacy of actions taken in response to needs, it does not focus on whether these novel activities were already somehow implied in the black letter law of the IO's constituent instrument. This is a conscious outcome for the following reasons. *First*, in many instances, the question of the 'power' of a secretariat to take a particular course of action appears to have not played a very significant role in the taking of these initiatives in times of

[24] Ronald Steenblik and Helen Mountford, 'Fossil Fuel Subsidies at the Organisation for Economic Co-operation and Development', Chapter 10 in this volume; Ouellet (n 11).

[25] Burci and Balcazar-Moreno (n 18); Steven A Solomon and Kenneth Piercy, 'Interactions with the "Outside World" and the Work of the World Health Organization in Revising the Global Health Architecture for Pandemic Prevention, Preparedness, and Response', Chapter 26 in this volume; Madir (n 14).

[26] Yan Liu and Kyung Kwak, 'IMF's Responses to New Challenges in the Global Economy: Recent Reforms of Its Financing Toolkit', Chapter 25 in this volume.

[27] Nicola Bonucci, 'The Driving Role of the Heads of International Organizations: A Case Study Around the Organisation for Economic Co-operation and Development', Chapter 20 in this volume; Marceau and Venkataraman (n 10).

[28] Janelle M Diller, 'International Organization Interactions with Multi-stakeholder Initiatives: The International Labour Organization Experience', Chapter 23 in this volume.

[29] Gabriela Ramos, 'UNESCO's Recommendation on the Ethics of Artificial Intelligence (2021): A Case Study in Intergovernmental Leadership and Consensus Building', Chapter 16 in this volume.

[30] Steenblik and Mountford (n 24).

[31] Llewellyn (n 5).

crises and pressing needs. While in some instances, such as the establishment of the criminal tribunals under the United Nations Security Council (UNSC), such concerns were raised by some members; the legitimization of these initiatives through subsequent acceptance (tacit or explicit) of members has perhaps rendered this question moot in practice for the time being. *Second*, a theoretical conception of the boundaries of an IO's mandate and the consequent determination of whether an initiative is ultra vires would require (i) a case-by-case examination of each of the initiatives and the mandate of the relevant IO, and (ii) an examination of many more 'failed' initiatives—actions attempted with a view to respond to needs, but those which ultimately did not succeed. These are perhaps questions for another volume of research in the future.

IV. Outlook

As IOs continue to adapt, change, and respond to the challenges and opportunities of the twenty-first century, the insights and perspectives offered in this volume will be useful for scholars, practitioners, and policymakers alike. The dynamics of adaptation and change in IOs are not only a subject of academic interest, but they are also of critical importance for understanding the evolving landscape of global governance and the role of these institutions in addressing the pressing challenges facing the international community. Initiatives by the organization's secretariat are, in that sense, a pragmatic effectuation of changes in IOs, keeping in mind that the practice of the IO's membership has been to eventually accept, support, and possibly codify the suggested initiative. In the context of continuous change, both within and around IOs, studies such as this on the interfaces between theory and practice are an important facet of the research agenda on IO adaptation and change.

Index

For the benefit of digital users, indexed terms that span two pages (e.g., 52–53) may, on occasion, appear on only one of those pages.

www.ingramcontent.com/pod-product-compliance
Lightning Source LLC
Chambersburg PA
CBHW061823160926
51621CB00003B/19
9780197803295